Locating Asian Australian Cultures

Locating Asian Australian Cultures is a timely and challenging interdisciplinary compilation that sets a contemporary benchmark for Asian Australian studies and its future directions.

In the dynamic field of diasporic Asian studies, Asian Australian Studies is an emerging and contentious area. Whilst aware of issues and critical developments in North America, Europe, and Asia, Asian Australian studies forges its own specific engagements with questions of identity, racialisation, and nationalisms in a world of globalised cultures and movements. This book deliberately engages with international perspectives on Asian Australian studies that offer contingent connections and address crucial questions for fields that are rapidly 'de-nationalising'.

The volume focuses on Asian Australian cultural production and identity, presenting work that interrogates notions of belonging and citizenship, representational politics, and disciplinarity in the academy. The broad-ranging essays examine the politics of Asian Australian art and literature, as well as the area's significant interventions in disciplinary formations nationally and internationally. Other essays discuss the Vietnamese War memorial in Cabramatta, notions of the 'sacrificial Asian' in contemporary films, and Asian Australian politicians.

This book will be essential reading not only for researchers in Asian Australian studies but also for those with an interest in Asian diaspora and Australian studies.

This book was previously published as a special issue of *The Journal of Intercultural studies*.

Tseen Khoo is a Monash University Research Fellow (2004–2009), based in Sociology at the School of Political and Social Inquiry. She has published on Asian Australian cultural production and politics, multicultural/race issues in Australia, and Asian Canadian literary cultures. She moderates two Asian Australian discussion groups and manages an Asian Australian studies website. Her book *Banana Bending: Asian-Australian and Asian-Canadian Literatures* was published in 2003 (Hong Kong and McGill-Queens University Presses).

Locating Asian Australian Cultures

Edited by
Tseen Khoo

Routledge
Taylor & Francis Group

LONDON AND NEW YORK

First published 2008 by Routledge
2 Park Square, Milton Park, Abingdon, Oxfordshire OX14 4RN

Simultaneously published in the USA and Canada
by Routledge
711 Third Avenue, New York, NY 10017

First issued in paperback 2016

Routledge is an imprint of the Taylor and Francis Group, an informa business

© 2008 Edited by Tseen Khoo

Typeset in Minion by Datapage International Ltd., Dublin, Ireland

All rights reserved. No part of this book may be reprinted or reproduced or utilised in any form or by any electronic, mechanical, or other means, now known or hereafter invented, including photocopying and recording, or in any information storage or retrieval system, without permission in writing from the publishers.

British Library Cataloguing in Publication Data
A catalogue record for this book is available from the British Library

Library of Congress Cataloging in Publication Data
A catalog record for this book has been requested

ISBN 13: 978-1-138-98000-6 (pbk)
ISBN 13: 978-0-415-41148-6 (hbk)

Contents

1. Introduction: Locating Asian Australian Cultures
   TSEEN KHOO 1

2. Disciplining Asian Australian Studies: Projections and Introjections
   JACQUELINE LO 11

3. Re-Configuring the Diasporic and Indigenous in the Art of Zhou Xiaoping
   SOM SENGMANY 29

4. Telling Stories: The Sacrificial Asian in Australian Cinema
   OLIVIA KHOO 45

5. 'The Tyranny of Appearance': Chinese Australian Identities and the Politics of Difference
   CAROLE TAN 65

6. The Aesthetics of Simplicity: Yang's *Sadness* and the Melancholic Community
   GILBERT CALUYA 83

7. Grafton to Guangzhou: The Revolutionary Journey of Tse Tsan Tai
   RODNEY NOONAN 101

8. 'No Place Like Home': The Ambivalent Rhetoric of Hospitality in the Work of Simone Lazaroo, Arlene Chai, and Hsu-Ming Teo
   DEBORAH L. MADSEN 117

9. Touring the Phantom Agent: Recognition, Defacement and the Vietnamese Australian War Memorial
   SCOTT BROOK 133

10. 'Growing up an Australian': Renegotiating Mateship, Masculinity and 'Australianness' in Hsu-Ming Teo's *Behind the Moon*
    ROBYN MORRIS 151

11. Travelling Theory, Reshaping Disciplines? Envisioning Asian Germany through Asian Australian Studies
    MITA BANERJEE 167

12. Asian Australian Citizenship as a Frame of Enactment in the Parliamentary 'First Speech'
   Jen Tsen Kwok   187

13. 'Flexible Citizenship': Strategic Chinese Identities in Asian Australian Literature
   Regina Lee   213

14. Afterword: Other Genealogies of Asian Australian Studies: A Trans-Pacific Perspective
   Evelyn Hu-DeHart   229

15. Conclusion: Locating Asian Australian Cultures
   Tseen Khoo   239

Index   243

Introduction: Locating Asian Australian Cultures

Tseen Khoo

I start this Introduction with an anecdote that I hope conveys the kinds of cross-currents that feed contemporary Asian Australian studies. In October 2005, I was invited to an American Studies conference in Siegen, Germany. The theme of this conference, which was convened by Mita Banerjee and Pia Wiegmink, was 'denationalizing North American studies'. I was approached on the basis of my profile in Asian Australian studies. More relevantly for this conference, my paper addressed the ways in which North American scholarship informed and/or inflected the growing field of Asian Australian studies, and it also examined the consequences of this intellectual traffic in theories of racialisation.

My presentation was very much about the local efficacy of 'importing' theoretical models or scales. Could this Australia-centric work be considered a North American studies paper? The enthusiastic response with which it was met indicates to me that it addressed and complemented other delegates' concerns to a high degree, but the issue of whether a paper that primarily discussed Asian Australian studies could be considered a part of North American studies remains open. The porosity of humanities and social sciences disciplines is an expected feature of contemporary academic environments; what is more interesting here, perhaps, is the breaching and muddying of area studies boundaries. Frayed and challenged by increasingly prevalent considerations of racialisation, institutional and cultural diversity, and reconceptualisations of nation and belonging, I would argue that Australian and North American studies *do* meet, in somewhat fraught terrain, within current understandings of 'Asian Australian studies'. I recount this here to identify a key element of contemporary humanities research that engages with the notion of globalised cultural flows and transnational—or international—deployment of critique and source material: what is at stake in deploying elements of culture out of context? This issue is as much about echoing similar concerns to Sau-ling Wong about the consequences of diasporic Asian literatures leaving 'home' (2002, 2005), as it is my own wariness about imposing North American theoretical models at 'home' in the Australian context.

Wong has astutely discussed the critical ramifications of 'travelling' Asian American literatures, and the processes of recontextualisation that occur. The international context to which she refers most frequently is Chinese-speaking communities outside the US, and her deliberations about the shift in reading strategies—from a 'minoritarian, oppositional critical tradition' (2002: 3) within the US to that of 'Chinese nationalist recuperation' (2002: 10)—offers an instructive counterpoint to the celebration of cultural transnationalism or globalisation. Wong's work further underscores the issue of critical conversations that might be had among 'Western' (for want of a better word) diasporic Asian groups. While considerable work in diasporic Asian cultural studies has occurred around the often contentious Canadian/US dynamic and its archives, scant dialogue takes place between these locations and others such as Australia, New Zealand, or Europe. This is due to the fact that critical and cultural momentum at these sites have been historically much less prominent than that of the US or Canada. That said, activity appears to be waxing in recent years. Several publications in New Zealand, for example, point to a significant increase in the level of interest and research on Chinese New Zealander communities and their histories (Ip 1990, 1996, 2003; Ferrall et al. 2005). These studies are, in the main, concentrated in the disciplines of sociology and history, with little yet in the way of critical cultural research on Asian New Zealander creative works. Aside from Canadian/US studies, Australian/Canadian studies is another area where a handful of projects focused on comparative diasporic Asian literary cultures has taken place (e.g. T. Khoo 2003; Lee 2006; Morris 2006), and this research builds on established intellectual channels between these two countries.

The title of this collection, *Locating Asian Australian Cultures*, flags the emergent state of this critical cultural field while consolidating its momentum. The unique web of circumstances that have given rise to an entity that could be designated 'Asian Australian studies' have manifested relatively recently, even though some of the earliest works about Asian Australian groups and their histories were published many decades ago. As with any emerging 'studies' field, Asian Australian studies' constant features will include deliberations over its own definition, boundaries and purpose. It is useful to bear in mind that Australian studies, with over thirty years of institutional presence, still faces repeated crises in funding and profile (see Carter et al. 2004), with cyclic negotiations about whether the field should concentrate or diffuse (Alomes 2004: 19) and statements that 'the spirit of *internationalisation* [will] provid[e] the richest environment for national studies' (Carter 2004: 109, emphasis in original). As with any nationally-based 'studies', this disciplinary angst over how area studies can rejuvenate their fields by engaging with issues of globalisation and transnationalism is often accompanied by anxieties about the maintenance of contextual specificities. This tense dynamic is a crucial element in the growing momentum of Asian

Australian studies. Jacqueline Lo's essay (p. 11–27) in this volume, 'Disciplining Asian Australian Studies: Projections and Introjections', engages in detail with the formation of Asian Australian studies as a discipline in academe, nationally and internationally, so my Introduction focuses instead on the current Australian sociocultural context, its significance for this field, and the constitution of this collection.

What kind of 'Australia' are we talking about at this point in time? Australia's conservative Coalition government marks a decade at the helm in 2006. In his Australia Day speech this year, Prime Minister John Howard iterated his belief in the 'One People, One Destiny' Federation slogan of 105 years ago. He states that Australia has 'drawn back from being too obsessed with diversity' and that the 'divisive, phoney debate about national identity' is now over (Howard 2006). It is telling that Howard chose to identify Australia's future with a century-old maxim. For Asian Australian communities, this is perhaps even more significant because Federation in 1901 also marked the official introduction of the Immigration Restriction Act, or what has become commonly known as the White Australia Policy. This convergence of the birth of a nation and racialised legislation is not unique; Canada's Chinese Exclusion Act was passed on Dominion (Canada) Day (1 July) in 1923, after decades of Head Tax laws. The relabelling of Canada Day as 'Humiliation Day' by the Chinese Canadian community showcases a very different form of national identification, as does the Australian Aboriginal rebranding of 26 January (Australia Day) each year as 'Invasion Day'. These acts serve as more than mere reminders of each nation's racist history; they render impossible the traditional notions of smooth, desirable national narratives.

This introduction of prohibitive legislation at the same moment of creating nation affects the positioning of Asian Australian groups even now. Commentary about Australian national identity and cultural politics is often discussed by cultural critics through the defining lens of this racially exclusive legislation, and several recent publications testify to the renewed urgency of these investigations into this policy's 'cultural logic', 'legacies and the competing claims of inclusion and exclusion' (Jayasuriya et al. 2003: 4). These studies include *The Long, Slow Death of White Australia* (Tavan 2005) and *Legacies of White Australia: Race, Culture and Nation* (Jayasuriya et al. 2003), both of which make specific reference to the new dynamics of exclusion in contemporary Australia in the wake of the 're-territorialising' of Australian boundaries, *MV Tampa* events,[1] and ongoing global anti-terrorist rhetoric and legislation. In the wake of the race-based violence in Cronulla, New South Wales, at the beginning of December 2005, the violent fissures in Australia's 'national family' (Howard 2006: 1) became even more overt. The aftermath of the riots focused public debate strongly on notions of racialisation, questions of who belongs in the nation, imperatives of cultural assimilation, and the constitution of a 'true' Australian. Treasurer Peter Costello, whom many assume will be the next Australian Prime Minister, has stated that 'anyone not prepared to accept Australian values, and who had citizenship of another country, should not remain an Australian citizen'

('Costello Conducting Wedge Politics' 2006). None of these issues are new, of course, and recent engagements in the public and academic spheres affirm the unfinished (and perhaps undesirable) project of shaping Australia's multicultural—or more to the point, multi-racial—national identity (see Docker and Fischer 2000; Hodge 2006; Markus 2001). The refusal to examine the contested nature of national identity, and Howard's dismissal of these forms of debate as 'phoney', has become a common conservative manoeuvre; in fact, the questioning of what constitutes 'an Australian' has become 'un-Australian'.

Australia is as well known for its avowed policy of multiculturalism (in place since the 1970s) as it is for the White Australia Policy that preceded it. As the plentiful work on multiculturalism and the nation demonstrate, however, having 'multicultural' as a common contemporary defining term for Australia does not mean the spectre of 'Australia Fair'[2] (Kalantzis 2005) is banished. In response to an increasingly conservative government and a fostered culture of suspicion, Ghassan Hage's *Against Paranoid Nationalism* (2003) details the diminishing avenues for hope and the expansion of national worrying for the future in Australia (and Western nation-states in general). Hage focuses his arguments on the relationships between migration, colonisation, and Indigenous dispossession. He states that 'it is only because [he] cares that [he is] shamed by the negative parts of history that have come with the package' (2003: 106). Hage's contributions to contemporary public debates incorporate constant reminders of the 'ongoing colonial features of Australian society' (Stephenson 2005: 124). Discussion about notions of belonging in Australia necessarily invoke questions of dispossession and colonisation. Calls for a dismantling of racially discriminatory structures and institutionalised inequality connect Asian Australian and Indigenous Australian groups as much as it can also divide them (because of their markedly different histories). These ongoing and useful tensions cohere many of the key issues that beset notions of contemporary Australian identity and belonging.

While the idea for this volume was launched by the Locating Asian Australian Cultures symposium I convened in June 2005, this final collection comprises a wider range of papers than were presented at that event. Many of the essays in this volume have been strategically solicited for the purposes of representation from key, active fields within Asian Australian studies. That said, this is by no means an attempt to create an authoritative text for this fast-changing area. The aim is to present a cross-section of ongoing research that will contribute to defining directions for Asian Australian studies in the near future. These directions are open to challenge and conjecture, and invite further engagement with Asian Australian material.

Research about Asian migration and populations in Australia is readily available, from general demographic overviews (e.g. S. Khoo et al. 1993; Jayasuriya and Kee 1999) to specific culture and gender group studies (e.g. Ryan 2003; Thomas 1999). Recent qualitative work in this field, such as Carole Tan's essay (p. 65–82) in this volume and Diana Giese's publications [especially *Astronauts, Lost Souls and Dragons* (1997)], focuses on oral histories and interviews to examine negotiations of societal belonging and the ways in which Asian Australian individuals assert their identities as citizens and members of the broader community. Further, the politicisation of Asian Australian communities and their involvement in representational roles are topics that urgently need interrogation and more primary research to capture the ways in which these groups mobilise their social capital, and exercise modes of cultural citizenship. Jen Tsen Kwok's (p. 187–211) work in this volume focuses specifically on the maiden speeches of Asian Australian parliamentarians and builds on the isolated instances of research on 'ethnic' representation in Australia (see Sawer and Zappala 2001). Stephen Castles and Mark Miller have argued that if migrant communities 'are excluded from political life through non-citizenship, social marginalisation, or racism, they are likely to present a major challenge to existing political structures in the future' (1998: 282), and this only underscores the timeliness and urgency of this research area.

Historical work about Asian communities and individuals in Australia is also a category that is currently enjoying considerable expansion. The most recent Chinese Studies Association of Australia (CSAA) conference that was held in Bendigo in 2005, for example, included the first instance of a 'mainstreamed' Chinese Australian history thread throughout the four days of the event. Note that this does not mean research on Chinese Australian history was absent from previous CSAA conferences. Indeed, panels and foci on Chinese Australian history have been present for some years, many due to the efforts of Henry Chan, a retired academic and founder of the Chinese Australian Historical Society. Recent publications in the field of Asian Australian history testify to its momentum and increasing range (e.g. see Jones' 2002 book on Japanese Australians, *Number Two Home*, and Couchman et al.'s 2004 publication on Chinese Australians, *After the Rush*). More broadly in the area of Asian Australian historiography, the 2004 publication of *Navigating Boundaries: The Asian Diaspora in Torres Strait* brought together scholars whose works shift the status quo. Anna Shnukal, Guy Ramsay and Yuriko Nagata state in the Introduction that 'most scholarship of Torres Strait has focused on Indigenous and colonial histories, relegating the numerically significant Asian presence to the margins' (2004: 3). The collection includes work on the Filipino, Malay, Sri Lankan, Japanese and Chinese groups in Torres Strait and, in the bigger picture, demonstrates the 'polyethnic past' (2004: 1) of many Australian zones. As many have pointed out, the predominance of viewing the nation's history only through Black/White relations and conflicts needs to be eroded in favour of more nuanced studies. Given the publication of *Lost in the Whitewash: Aboriginal-Asian Encounters in Australia, 1901–2001* (Edwards and Shen 2003) and Regina Ganter's forthcoming *Mixed Relations: Histories and Stories of Asian/Aboriginal Contact in North Australia* (2006), these nuanced studies appear to be increasingly prevalent and energetic. This move towards examining alternative links in historical studies has led to focused attention on the diasporic connections between Asian Australians and their 'homeland' groups and political developments. Rodney Noonan's essay (p. 101–115) in this volume about Chinese Australian Tse Tsan Tai's 'revolutionary journey' from Grafton to Guangzhou is one example of research into this kind relationship. As Noonan states, the piece emphasises the 'complex ongoing relationship between diasporic communities in Australia with communities overseas'. Noonan's project complements the expanding body of historical scholarship about political groups, secret societies and clan associations in Australia (e.g. John Fitzgerald's research on transnational histories of Chinese communities in Australia and South China; see Fitzgerald 2004). Thus far, this focus on transnational dynamics has been more commonly found in studies about Asian business networks and entrepreneurs (e.g. Lever-Tracy et al. 2002), but it is an area that is now gaining increased consideration in other disciplines.

Accompanying this momentum in Asian Australian history and sociological activity is the growth of research into the cultural production and politics of Asian Australians. The impetus for Asian Australian studies has been driven in no small part by critical work about the cultural politics of artists of Asian descent in Australia. These diverse artists—working in fields such as literature, film, performance, visual arts, cultural studies, and popular culture—do more than illustrate or convey 'Asian Australian-ness'. Among other things, they also interrogate existing canonical representations and challenge the relative invisibility of Asian Australian interventions into the Australian cultural sphere. Because of this noted energy, it is not surprising then that the majority of the essays in this volume fall within the category of cultural production critique: Deborah Madsen (p. 117–132), Robyn Morris (p. 151–166) and Regina Lee (p. 213–227) focus on literary texts and their representational politics in terms of cultural belonging, and issues of identity and community; Olivia Khoo (p. 45–63) examines the figure of the 'sacrificial Asian' in Australian film; Som Sengmany engages directly with issues of Indigenous/Asian collaborative artwork and its associated political and critical hazards; Scott Brook (p. 133–149) performs an alternative reading of the Vietnamese War memorial in Cabramatta; and Gilbert Caluya (p. 83–100) reads William Yang's photographic production through an aesthetics of simplicity. Lo (p. 11–27) discusses the significance of these cultural productions in more detail in her essay's 'state of play' section. The range of content and variety of approaches in these essays about Asian Australian cultural production testify to the rich state of the field and the numbers of scholars working within it. Because it often takes place across the more established departments and disciplines, it can be difficult to ascertain the momentum of this critical work.

In her essay, Lo also states that '[t]he tension between addressing local issues and the growing popularity of transnational/diasporic studies has been a feature of Asian Australian studies since its inception'. Precisely because of this, and my discussion of issues using Wong's work at the start of this Introduction, I approached Mita Banerjee for her essay (p. 167–185), 'Travelling Theory, Reshaping Disciplines? Envisioning Asian Germany through Asian Australian Studies' and Evelyn Hu-DeHart for her Afterword, titled 'Other Genealogies of Asian Australian Studies: A Trans-Pacific Perspective' (p. 229–237). The broader engagement of Asian Australian studies with cognate, international fields is essential for its viability, expansion and ability to engage more fully with the nature of contemporary diasporic conditions.

Hu-DeHart's Afterword offers crucial insight into the differential formations of Asian American and Asian Australian studies, and gives those who would undertake comparative studies between these areas a perceptive starting point. Her historian's perspective is complemented by her extensive knowledge of the disciplinary development of Asian American studies, and her Afterword is one of the first critical pieces that offers a comparative Asian American and Asian Australian context. Banerjee's essay, on the other hand, focuses on the ways in which a discipline comes into being, and examines possible models for reading these new critical cultural formations. While her discussion of a possible 'Asian German studies' is at an exploratory stage out of necessity, it examines the key issues of cross-contextual applicability and interrogates the utility and limits of more established Asian North American studies frameworks.

Hu-DeHart's presence and participation in the Locating Asian Australian Cultures symposium was a notable and important feature of the event that was very much in this spirit of opening Asian Australian studies to international interest and generating new critical connections. While much work remains to be done in terms of layered localised cultural and political critique and historical recovery work, Asian Australian studies cannot help but benefit from the infusions of diasporic Asian dialogue that are the hallmark of astute contemporary research in these areas. Rather than seeking international recognition to validate its project, Asian Australian studies intervenes in global discussions to ensure that its unique context inflects ongoing critical debates in diasporic Asian studies.

Acknowledgements

The genesis of this collection is the Locating Asian Australian Cultures symposium held in June 2005. It was the first event focused specifically on this field since 1999 (a year that saw both the Alter/Asians and Asian-Australian Identities conferences take place in Sydney and Canberra, respectively). I would like to acknowledge the hosting of this symposium by the National Centre for Australian Studies and the Faculty of Arts at Monash University (Clayton, Victoria), and the support of Sociology (School of Political and Social Inquiry) in the preparation of this publication.

Special thanks to Tom Cho for his superb editing assistance, the anonymous experts for their essay reviews and generous cooperation, and my immediate colleagues for their advice and encouragement.

Notes

[1] In August 2001, the *MV Tampa*, a Norwegian freighter, rescued hundreds of asylum seekers from their sinking Indonesian boat. The Australian government refused to let the freighter land at Christmas Island, and the consequent impasse caused controversy and protests in Australia and the wider international community. These events pushed refugee and asylum seeker issues to the forefront of Australian public debate, leading to intense, ongoing discussions about the composition of Australian society and its 'values'.

[2] The Australian national anthem is titled 'Advance Australia Fair'. The multiple meanings of the word 'fair' exemplify the recurring tensions surrounding notions of national identity, race, and the myth of the 'fair go' in Australian society.

References

'Costello Conducting Wedge Politics'. *The Age*, <http://www.theage.com.au/news/national/costello-using-wedge-politics/2006/02/24/1140670249517.html> (accessed 24 February 2006).

Alomes, S. 'The Beginnings and Futures of Australian Studies.' *Thinking Australian Studies: Teaching across Cultures*. Eds. D. Carter, K. Darian-Smith and G. Worby. St Lucia, Qld: University of Queensland Press, 2004. 7–23, 366–67.

Carter, D. 'Minor Miracle, A Kind of Failure, and Some Small Successes: Australian Studies and Cultural Diplomacy.' *Thinking Australian Studies: Teaching across Cultures*. Eds. D. Carter, K. Darian-Smith and G. Worby. St Lucia, Qld: University of Queensland Press, 2004. 90–109, 370.

Carter, D., Darian-Smith, K. and Worby, G. (Eds.) *Thinking Australian Studies: Teaching Across Cultures*. St Lucia, Qld: University of Queensland Press, 2004.

Castles, S., and M. Miller. *The Age of Migration: International Population Movements in the Modern World*. Hampshire and London: Macmillan, 1998.

Couchman, S., Fitzgerald, J. MacGregor, P. (Eds.) *After the Rush: Regulation, Participation, and Chinese Community in Australia 1860–1940*. Melbourne: Otherland, 2004.

Docker, J. and Fischer, G. (Eds.) *Race, Colour and Identity in Australia and New Zealand*. Sydney: University of New South Wales Press, 2000.

Edwards, P. and Shen, Y. (Eds.) *Lost in the Whitewash: Aboriginal-Asian Encounters in Australia, 1901–2001*. Canberra: Humanities Research Centre, 2003.

Ferrall, C., Millar, P. and Smith, K. (Eds.) *East by South: China and Australasian Orientalism*. Wellington: Victoria University Press, 2005.

Fitzgerald, J. 'The "Australian" in Chinese-Australians of the White Australia Era: A Study of the Australian Kuomintang in the 1920s and 1930s'. *Cultural Pluralism and Civil Society in the Asia Pacific Region in the Era of Globalisation*. Eds. L. Ludi, C. Hong and H. Minyue. Shanghai: Shanghai Shiji Chuban Jituan, 2004. 55–99.

Ganter, R. *Mixed Relations: Histories and Stories of Asian/Aboriginal Contact in North Australia*. Perth: University of Western Australia Press, 2006.

Giese, D. *Astronauts, Lost Souls and Dragons: Conversations with Chinese Australians*. St Lucia, Qld: University of Queensland Press, 1997.

Hage, G. *Against Paranoid Nationalism: Searching for Hope in a Shrinking Society*. Sydney: Pluto, 2003.

Hodge, B. *Borderwork in Multicultural Australia*. Sydney: Allen and Unwin, 2006.

Howard, J. *A Sense of Balance: The Australian Achievement in 2006*. Address to the National Press Club, Parliament House, Canberra, 25 January, <http://www.pm.gov.au/news/speeches/speech1754.html> (accessed 27 January 2006).

Ip, M. *Home Away From Home: Lifestories of Chinese Women in New Zealand*. Auckland: New Women's Press, 1990.

——. *Dragons on the Long White Cloud: The Making of Chinese New Zealanders*. Auckland: Tandem Press, 1996.

—— (Ed.) *Unfolding History, Evolving Identity: The Chinese in New Zealand*. Auckland: Auckland University Press, 2003.

Jayasuriya, L., and P. Kee. *The Asianisation of Australia?* Melbourne: Melbourne University Press, 1999.

Jayasuriya, L., Walker, D. and Gothard, J. (Eds.) *Legacies of White Australia: Race, Culture and Nation*. Perth: University of Western Australia Press, 2003.

Jones, N. *Number Two Home: A Story of Japanese Pioneers in Australia*. Perth: Fremantle Arts Centre Press, 2002
Kalantzis, M. 'Australia Fair.' *Overland* 178 (2005): 5–18.
Khoo, S., Kee, P., Dang, T., and Shu, J. et al. *Asian Immigrant Settlement and Adjustment in Australia*. Carlton: Bureau of Immigration and Population Research, 1993.
Khoo, T. *Banana Bending: Asian-Australian and Asian-Canadian Literatures*. Hong Kong: McGill-Queens University Press and Hong Kong University Press, 2003.
Lee, R. *Theorising the Chinese Diaspora: Canadian and Australian Narratives*. Unpublished PhD thesis. Perth: Murdoch University, 1996.
Lever-Tracy, C, D. Ip, and N. Tracy. 'From a Niche to a World City: Barriers, Opportunities and Resources of Ethnic Chinese Businesses in Australia.' *Chinese Entrepreneurship and Asian Business Networks*. Eds. T. Menkhoff and S. Gerke. London and New York: Routledge-Curzon, 2002. 267–92.
Markus, A. *Race: John Howard and the Remaking of Australia*. Sydney: Allen and Unwin, 2001.
Morris, R. *Looking Through the Twin Lens of Race and Gender: A New Politics of Surveillance in Asian Australian and Asian Canadian Women's Fiction*. Unpublished PhD thesis. Wollongong: University of Wollongong, 2006.
Ryan, J. *Chinese Women and the Global Village: An Australian Site*. St Lucia, Qld: University of Queensland Press, 2003.
Sawer, M., and G. Zappala. *Speaking for the People: Representation in Australian Politics*. Melbourne: Melbourne University Press, 2001.
Shnukal, A., Ramsay, G. and Nagata, Y. (Eds.) *Navigating Boundaries: The Asian Diaspora in Torres Strait*. Canberra: Pandanus, 2004.
Stephenson, P. '"Where are you from?": New Imaginings of Identity in Chinese-Australian Writing.' *Culture, Identity, Commodity: Diasporic Chinese Literatures in English*. Eds. T. Khoo and L. Louie. Hong Kong: Hong Kong University Press, 2005. 107–28.
Tavan, G. *The Long, Slow Death of White Australia*. Melbourne: Scribe, 2005.
Thomas, M. *Dreams in the Shadows: Vietnamese-Australian Lives in Transition*. Sydney: Allen and Unwin, 1999.
Wong, S. *When Asian American Literature Travels: Minority Literature, National Literature, World Literature*. Keynote address presented at the MESEA (Society for Multi-Ethnic Study: Europe and the Americas) conference 'Sites of Ethnicity: Europe and the Americas', Padua, Italy, 2002.
—— 'Maxine Hong Kingston in a Global Frame: Reception, Institutional Mediation, and "World Literature."' *AALA Journal* (Dec 2005): 1–35.

Disciplining Asian Australian Studies: Projections and Introjections

Jacqueline Lo

Preamble

Unlike some areas of academic research that are not so closely caught up with personal identification, research into Asian Australian cultural production tends to be intimately linked with the personal development of the Asian Australian scholar as cultural and political agent. A turning point for me occurred in 1996 when I attended the premiere production of *Burying Mother*, written and performed by Mémé Thorne, an artist of Malaysian–Chinese–Australian descent.[1] The 1996 production was well-received by the reviewers, who were all, incidentally, non-Asians. In particular, critics were impressed by the high production values and by Thorne's skill in drawing together a range of Asian and Western physical-training styles to create dramatic tension.[2] I have written elsewhere about the production's strength in constructing a hybrid speaking position out of the binaries of Self/Other (Lo 1998). There were, however, elements of the mise-én-scene of the production that unsettled me at the time and continued to haunt me for a while. The set design for *Burying Mother* was dominated by huge overhead screen emblazoned with the Chinese character for 'mother'. The set was designed in black, red and white: the overall effect was sleek, minimalist, highly stylised, and stereotypically 'Oriental'. What was most disturbing were the hell banknotes that were left on each seat in the auditorium to directly involve the audience in the staged burial ritual.

In one of the opening scenes of the production, the performer explained through a pre-taped audio-text that the hell banknotes were burnt during one of the many Chinese rites associated with helping the departed soul find its way into the next world. The verbal text with its interruptions of 'ums' and 'ers' put the master-narrative of 'Chineseness' under erasure to signify both the strength of subject identification with Chinese culture, and the awareness that this identification is problematised by a specific bicultural, biracial and diasporic history. The verbal text, however, was only one aspect of the performance. What was I, as an Asian Australian, suppose to make of the Orientalised mise-én-scene? How should I read the presence of the hell banknotes and the staging of burial rites? Were the banknotes simply a part of the hybridity trade in exotica for the West and the Westernised? If so, how was I implicated in this trade?

What I saw in the formal design of the production was an uncertain, ambiguous engagement with Orientalism, manifest mainly through the bricolage of East Asian cultures (Japanese, Chinese and Malaysian), and the fetishising of objects (such as the hell banknotes). My similarly diasporised and hybridised Malaysian–Chinese–Australian background is not particularly attached to traditional rites; like the protagonist, my knowledge of what counts as Chinese tradition is at best shaky, consisting of imperfectly-remembered rituals and family myths. However, as I sat clutching my banknote watching the burial rites on stage, my hands became increasingly clammy. I could almost hear my grandmother telling me that it was *pantang* (bad luck) to play with the dead, and especially to handle those banknotes. I was, however, also entranced by the sheer beauty of the design; the high production quality of the performance drew me in and I surrendered to the pleasure of watching the spectacle unfold. I remember thinking, "This is not good, something's wrong" but it was undeniably gratifying. It was a moment of *frisson*, a kind of unsettling illicit pleasure.

I avoided analysing this experience for some time, but it continued to bother me until I was finally compelled to work through my anxieties in the form of a conference paper. It seemed to me at the time that despite the considerable academic work that has focused on critiquing and disavowing Orientalist tendencies in contemporary cross-cultural interactions, there was little to account for its continuing appeal, much less to explain why Orientalised subjects would choose to identify with and perpetuate this colonialist legacy, even with in the knowledge of its falsity. As Rey Chow points out in her discussion of Orientalist films such as *The Last Emperor*, ethnic spectators occupy an 'impossible space' that almost predetermines its dismissal from theoretical analysis which focuses only on the technicalities of image production (1999: 24). Subjective processes of identification that include desires, fantasies, and sentimentalisms play a crucial role in disciplining the ethnic spectator:

> The identification with an ethnic or 'national' history, and the pain and pleasure that this involves, cannot be understood simply in terms of 'nativism'. The spectator is not simply ethnic but ethnicized: the recognition of her 'Chineseness' is already part of the process of cross-cultural interpellation that is at work in the larger realm of modern history. (Chow 1999: 25)

Thus, it could be said that my unease at the production of *Burying Mother* was not only because I was seduced by the Orientalist images despite knowing that they were 'bad'. On the contrary, it is precisely *because* Orientalism is already a prewritten script in East–West relations that I was able to occupy a dual role as both seduced subject and seducing object of the gaze. Or, to put it another way, there was a double-edged process of simultaneous identification of, and identification with, the spectacle of Orientalism on stage. This is the double-consciousness afforded by a diasporic consciousness; it is the ambivalence of Homi Bhabha's 'Third Space' (1994), and the hybridity of Stuart Hall's 'new ethnicities' (1996). Recognition of my complicated positioning as a racialised spectator, as an Asian Australian critic who is actively implicated in the technology of Orientalism, has since led to a heightened awareness of my own contradictory processes of subjectification and identification in cross-cultural analysis.

Disciplining the Critics

I have chosen to start with this stress on subject formation to underscore the importance of how the disciplining of the critic can impact on the discursive construction of the research object. It is now common practice to consider how specific political and historical trajectories lead to specific forms of scholarship. Tessa Morris-Suzuki (2000), for instance, points at the emergence of multidisciplinary area studies in Asian studies in the United States as part of the Cold War context of intelligence-gathering for the state, and a similar development of Asian studies in Australia after the Pacific War. There is, however, less recognition of the role played by scholars as products and producers of such disciplinary forces. What are the disciplinary forces at work in the emerging field of Asian Australian studies? What kinds of subjectivities are shaping the field?

At the inaugural Asian–Australian Identities conference in Canberra in 1999, there was a palpable sense of history in the making as scholars and cultural producers came together under the rubric of Asian Australia.[3] There was a strong, even euphoric, sense of mutual recognition and affirmation: the majority of the participants were of Asian descent, tertiary educated and comfortably middle-class. Most were first and second generation migrants, in their twenties and thirties, and despite differences in ethnicities and modes of arrival to Australia, there was remarkable similarity in their life experiences as Australians of Asian descent. One conferee ironically referred to the conference participants as his 'yellow posse'. This description was rather telling: it pointed to the elation of finding a community, but it also suggested that, even at this nascent moment of collective identity formation, exclusionary and marginalising practices were already operating, however unconsciously. While there are historical as well as demographic reasons why East and Southeast Asian cultures dominate that particular moment of imagining Asian Australia, it should nonetheless remind us to be more vigilant about the politics of exclusion that come with defining the parameters of Asian Australian identity and culture. In particular, more care needs to be taken to address the relative invisibility of a significant Asian community, namely Australians of South Asian descent, in Asian Australian cultural politics.[4] While this invisibility is largely related to the specifically Australian positioning of the South Asian as 'Indian' rather than 'Asian' (the latter term is generally reserved for so-called 'Orientals' from East and Southeast Asia), it behooves the Asian Australian community to transcend such colonialist categorisations in the interest of building a stronger coalition.

The disciplinary background of Asian Australian scholars is also highly instructive of the kinds of knowledge formations informing the development of Asian Australian studies. A quick scan of research published in the field reveals that while the archive is diverse (incorporating literature, film, theatre, visual art, cultural policy, social anthropology, politics, history, heritage management and so forth), the disciplinary approach is dominated by what I loosely call a cultural studies approach to cultural analysis; that is, the critique of how culture works, how meaning is generated through representation, and the power relations engendered by particular forms of social construction and expression. Current Asian Australian research is characterised by the deployment of European post-structuralist theory crossfertilised with postcolonial, feminist, multicultural and queer theories. This interdisciplinary paradigm points to the historical and institutional backgrounds of the researchers.

Most Asian Australian researchers are the products of the post-Dawkins reform of Australian tertiary education in the late 1980s, a period where Colleges of Advanced Education merged with non-sandstone[5] universities, and which also saw the establishment of new universities such as Murdoch, Deakin and Griffith that were dedicated to interdisciplinary teaching. Openness to interdisciplinarity and the expansion of teaching and research into film, media and communication studies were two positive outcomes of the reform for the humanities. The theoretical orientations and research methodologies of most of the present cohort of Asian Australian scholars can be traced back to this period of structural reform. Their research and teaching are likewise shaped by particular theoretical trends located within Australian universities, by structuralist and post-structuralist theories and feminism that first came into vogue in the 1970s and 1980s, cultural studies in the early 1980s, postcolonialism in the late 1980s and 1990s and, more recently, theories of diaspora, cosmopolitanism and globalisation.

This shared intellectual lineage has led Asian Australian research to focus largely on issues of representation: to analyse the idea of the nation as a process of cultural production, to critique the 'naturalness' of all forms of cultural expressions, and to identify the power relations implicit in cultural formations. It is neither coincidental nor 'natural' that there is this particular theoretical core to Asian Australian studies: the current intellectual apparatus deployed by Asian Australian researchers is directly related to the historical context of their specific disciplining as intellectuals. It is, therefore, crucial to be cognisant that Asian Australian studies in its present incarnation represents only certain kinds of subjects and subject formations, and to remember the limits and partiality of knowledge currently produced by this configuration. Asian Australian scholars need to remain self-reflexive about what they are disciplining, how they are shaping their object of study, and the hierarchies of knowledge that are being set up as part of discipline formations. Asian Australian studies is not an autonomous entity 'out there' waiting to be discovered or revealed, but rather something that is in the process of creating *in situ*.

Locating Asian Australian Studies

It would be foolhardy to attempt to define any area of study that is by its very nature, interrogative, discursive and provisional. However, in order to talk about Asian Australian studies as a field of analysis in any coherent way and to map out a genealogy, I am compelled to represent it as a unified and uncontested category. This is also true of other affiliated fields of research like multicultural studies and Australian studies, which I will be referring to later in this discussion. To talk about fields of studies as categories at all, it is necessary, as Graeme Turner puts it, to "invent them a little—to construct an intellectual formation of greater coherence, homogeneity and stability than actually exists" (1996: 7–8).

At the most basic, Asian Australian studies is the critical analysis of the culture, history and politics of Australians of Asian descent. Race plays a crucial role in the construction of Asian Australian identity but as we stressed in *Diaspora: Negotiating Asian-Australia*, the concept of race is not deployed as biological 'fact' but rather used strategically to unite people of various Asian ethnicities thereby enabling a degree of political solidarity and critical purchase (Gilbert et al. 2000: 2). Thus, race is used in Spivak's sense of 'a strategic use of a positive essentialism in a scrupulously visible political interest' (1988: 205). The concept of strategic essentialism suggests that it is possible to utilise specific signifiers of racialised identity to challenge and destabilise hegemonic discourses that marginalise Australians of Asian descent, while simultaneously acknowledging the internal contradictions and differences within the category of Asian Australian so as to ensure that such essentialisms are not reproduced by the very apparatuses that we are trying to dismantle (Lowe 2003: 151)

In order to fully grasp the deployment of race in Asian Australian cultural politics, it is necessary to take a historical view of the management of cultural and racial difference in Australia. It is widely acknowledged that race has played a foundational role in the establishment of Australia as a (post)colonial nation. The influx of European migrants from places like Greece and Italy after World War II necessitated a redefinition of the White nation (famously imagined as united by 'the crimson thread of kinship' to Britain). With the introduction of official multiculturalism in the 1970s, there was a shift to a new emphasis on the productivity of cultural difference located at the level of ethnicity. As I have argued elsewhere, hegemonic multiculturalism is essentially a culturalist response to dealing with the threat of political instability in the face of changing demographics (first the Europeans – still technically considered White—but later Asians and, more recently, people from the Middle East). 'Culture' is located at the site of ethnic communities that are always imagined as self-contained monocultures (Lo 2000). State multiculturalism is the management of cultural difference based on the premise of unity in diversity; difference is represented as the supplement that enriches the national (White) culture. State multiculturalism is therefore inherently conservative and ethnic differences are used to redefine the centre, but there is little attention given to the promotion of intercommunal dialogue (between various Asian communities, for example) and the formation of minority coalitions (such as Aboriginal–Asian alliances). As Ien Ang and Jon Stratton point out, multiculturalism is a policy that recognises and confirms cultural diversity; it is not specifically designed to combat racism (2001:104). Ghassan Hage goes even further to argue that state, or 'White multiculturalism' as he calls it, perpetuates racist structures of power by continuing to position the ethnic Other as national objects to be moved or removed according to a White national will (1998).

Multicultural studies as a field of research primarily focuses on literature and print and visual media by non-Anglo-Celts. Discourses of migrancy and ethnic pluralism featured strongly in the conceptualisation of multicultural studies and, at the risk of gross generalisation, the research is characterised by critiques of tropes of nostalgia, belonging, and cultural authenticity. The Australian nation as the final destination was the 'ultimate signifier' in multicultural discourse: critical attention focused on how ethnic diversity challenged the boundaries of the national imagined community. A leading multicultural scholar, Sneja Gunew, sought to recuperate agency for ethnic communities by using the Derridean concept of framing. Ethnic writing, she contends, defines and contains Australian writing: 'The exclusion or marginalization of certain writings in fact frame the conditions of existence of those other writings which are included or endorsed' (1994: 28). Aligned closely with Derrida's other concept of the supplement, Gunew repositions ethnic minority writing and culture as a necessary condition for the shaping of Australian literature and national culture.

However, I maintain that the underlying logic of the concept of framing is based on the dominant discourse of the ingestion of cultural diversity for the enrichment of the dominant culture. The idea of 'one nation', albeit one fringed by the smells and bells of multiculturalism, still dominates.

The sublimation of race in multicultural discourse hindered the potential for Australians to critically engage with our colonial past and the continuing presence of racism in society.[6] As Andrew Jakubowicz argues, "multiculturalism functions as an ideology by appearing to act on behalf of the disadvantaged migrants, though in reality it leaves essential social relations and an unequal distribution of power in Australia unaltered" (qtd. in Gunew 1994: 6). Despite the repression of race in official multicultural rhetoric, it continued to surface intermittently in the public domain, particularly in relation to indigenous rights and Asian immigration. The two most notable instances are the immigration controversy in the mid-1980s which was fuelled by historian Geoffrey Blainey's comments that 'too many Asians' would endanger the social, cultural and political structures of Australian society, and the emergence of Pauline Hanson and her One Nation political party in the mid-1990s.

What is important to note in both these cases that led to periods of heightened and sustained racial tensions is the refiguring of racism in culturalist terms. According to Stephen Castles, "(f)ixation on older definitions of racism as notions of biologically based hierarchies allows more subtle racisms based on cultural markers to claim to be benign and progressive" (1996: 29). Following on from Etienne Balibar, he describes this 'new racism' as "racism without race," "one that no longer speaks of superiority, but rather of immutable differences that make coexistence between varying cultural groups in one society impossible" (1996: 29). When Hanson referred to Asians and Asian culture, she was not invoking multiculturalism's ethnic diversity, a diversity that, at least on the *surface*, appeared to distinguish between Vietnamese Australians, Thai Australians and Bangladeshi Australians. On the contrary, these groups were collectively *racialised* by Hanson in order to single them out and amass them as the Other that threatened the national Self (Ang and Stratton 2001: 107). Arguing that Asian culture was culturally unabsorbable into the national culture—that Asianness was incommensurate with Australianness—Hanson invoked traditional binaries of Self/Other, Australian/Asiatic, but presented these binaries in philosophical and cultural terms rather than resorting to racial biology.

This newly racialised environment in the mid- to late-1990s politicised and radicalised many scholars working on ethnic and cultural politics. The inception of Asian Australian studies in 1999 as a field of cultural analysis is located within such a moment of heightened racism and politicisation. This is why I maintain that the critique of race and racism is fundamental to 'doing' Asian Australian studies, and that the category of Asian Australianness is an identity category that enables political solidarity rather than an essentialist mode of identification.

The Asian–Australian Identities conference, and the Alter/Asian conference in Sydney that preceded it, brought together researchers working from a range of disciplines and interdisciplines with a common interest in critiquing the relations between Asian racialisation and cultural production in ways that transcended nation-based methodologies afforded by Multicultural studies. Whereas Multicultural studies focused on ethnicity, biculturalism, migrancy and modes of arriving into Australian-ness, Asian Australian studies focuses on tropes of diaspora, hybridity, heterogeneity, and transnationalism. Rather than Australianness as a single and final destination (however contested), Asian Australian studies emphasises mobility and traveling as major tropes for unpacking the identity formations and knowledge productions of diasporic communities with cultural allegiances and political connections across a number of sites within and beyond the nation.

As mentioned earlier, multicultural studies is premised on the 'unity in diversity' model of imagining the nation. While the recent emergence of 'Critical Multi-culturalism'—which purports to critique specific state formations of multicultural-ism and its impact on gender, racial, ethnic and sexual power relations—attempts to address some of the limitations of the one nation model, I contend that Asian Australian studies offers more innovative ways of (re)mapping the nation in terms of multiple spatialities and histories. In contrast to Gunew's idea of framing margin-alities that imagines the national space and culture in the singular (just as borders frame a central painting), a diasporic framework foregrounding tropes of hybridity and mobility decentres the nation as the ultimate signifier by emphasising the multiple and heterogeneous forms of belonging to, and traveling within and beyond, the nation. Such approaches, therefore, suggest that the concept of the nation is pluralised and hybridised, and that ownership of space (symbolic as well as political) is thus always partial, provisional and open to contestation. This does not mean that the idea of the nation is no longer important within such a global and transnational revisioning. Rather, the idea of multiple mappings serves to foreground the interconnections between uneven histories and unequal power relations within the nation-state: the refugee's mapping of the limits of Australian space is very different to the Aboriginal elder in Arhemland fighting for land rights, to that of the Chief Executive Officer of Australian telecommunications provider Telstra. Such rhizomatic mappings have the potential to diversify the modes of social and cultural intervention and multiply opportunities for the politicisation of minority citizens that go beyond ideas of supplement by challenging notions of a singular or hierarchical national space and narrative.

What I hope to impress with this brief genealogy of Asian Australian studies is, to quote Naoki Sakai, that "it is not because objects of knowledge are prepatorily given that certain disciplines are formed to investigate them; on the contrary the objects are engendered because the disciplines are in place" (qtd. in Chuh and Shimakawa 2001: 16). The constitution of Asian Australian studies is neither preordained nor arbitrary. It has emerged out of specific historical, cultural and political trajectories that in turn produce specific historicised, racialised and politicised objects of study.

State of Play

In the six years following the inaugural Asian-Australian Identities conference, Asian Australian studies as a field has taken on a stronger definition, but it has also lost some of the initial impetus. The racialised political climate that brought scholars together has shifted its focus and this has affected both the momentum and modes of engagement in the field. The political drive appears to be more dispersed as academics struggle to deal with an increasingly commercialised and under-funded Australian tertiary education sector. Many Asian Australian scholars are involved in other unrelated areas of research in the humanities; some no longer work in the field, or even in academia, while others have left Australia to find work elsewhere. Research in the field is, therefore, largely propelled by postgraduate and postdoctoral work, with only a handful of senior scholars acting as mentors. In the past decade, there have been at least thirty postgraduates who have successfully completed graduate qualifications at doctoral and masters levels in Asian Australian-related areas of research across the humanities. Of these graduates, only three have been awarded research-only positions at Monash University, Edith Cowan University, University of Melbourne, and University of Queensland. It should be noted that none of these were advertised as specifically Asian Australian research positions.

While research in this field continues to attract early career researchers, Asian Australian studies has not made a significant impression in terms of claiming curriculum space within the academy. There are, to date, no undergraduate courses in any Australian university devoted to the field, although many Asian Australian texts feature in courses on Australian culture and/or Asian diasporic/migrant cultures. There are a number of Asian Australian-focused coursework programs available at the postgraduate level including a course on Asian Australian cultural production at the Australian National University and a course on Asian diaspora at the University of Melbourne. The scarcity of an Asian Australian presence in tertiary curricula also explains why there has never been a teaching position advertised in this field. Clearly, Asian Australian studies has some way to go in terms of claiming institutional recognition as a legitimate area of undergraduate and postgraduate coursework education.

It is arguably in the area of research that Asian Australian scholars have been making the most impact. Over the past ten years, the national research funding body, the Australian Research Council, has invested large sums of money in this field through a number of leading projects including diasporic Vietnamese women's writing, Chinese Australian masculinities, Asian influences in Australian theatre, and the emergence of Asian Australian cultural politics within the context of Australian nationalism. This research activity is also supported by a number of key conferences where Asian Australian studies featured prominently including the Transforming Cultures/Shifting Boundaries: Asian diasporas and Identities in Australia conference in 2001 and the The Body Politic: Racialised Political Cultures in Australia in 2004. Both conferences were hosted by the University of Queensland under the convenorship of Tseen Khoo. The Locating Asian Australian Cultures symposium held at Monash University (Melbourne) in 2005 has been the only designated Asian Australian studies event to take place in the wake of the 1999 Canberra conference. The fact that this conference was also organised by Khoo is testimony to the vitality, and also the smallness, of the Asian Australian studies community.

Another indicator of the research strength of Asian Australian studies is the growing number of scholarly books and edited collections published since the appearance of pioneering texts such as *Diaspora* (2000) and *Alter/Asians* (2000). The growing archive of Asian Australian studies include monographs as varied as Khoo's *Banana Bending: Asian Australian and Asian–Canadian Literatures* (2003), Ien Ang's *On Not Speaking Chinese* (2001), Shen Yuanfang's *Dragon Seed in the Antipodes: Chinese–Australian Autobiographies* (2001), J.V. D'Cruz and William Steele's *Australia's Ambivalence towards Asia* (2003) and Janis Wilton's *Golden Threads: The Chinese in Regional New South Wales, 1820–1950* (2004). Published collections of essays in the field include Wenche Ommundsen's *Bastard Moon: Essays on Chinese Australian Writing* (2001), Penny Edwards and Shen Yuanfang's *Lost in the Whitewash: Aboriginal–Asian Encounters in Australia, 1901–2001* (2003) and Tseen Khoo and Kam Louie's *Culture, Identity, Commodity: Diasporic Chinese Literatures in English* (2005). There have also been a number of special journal issues focusing on Asian Australian works including *Rubicon* (Ommundsen and Boreland 1995) and *Meanjin* (Cho and Raja 2004), as well as new journal publications such as the online *Journal of Chinese Australia* and community-based publications such as Chek Ling's edited work, *Plantings in a New Land: Stories of Survival, Endurance and Emancipation* (2001).

There is strong correlation between the publication of academic research and the growing general interest in Asian Australian culture. The most significant area of growth in the development of an Asian Australian public profile has been in the area of creative production. Novels and short story collections by writers such as Brian Castro, Lau Siew Mei, Merlinda Bobis, Hsu-Ming Teo, Suneeta Peres da Costa, and Adib Khan have been well received by the wider Australian readership, while musicians like Nicholas Ng and Rendra Freestone, filmmakers like Khoa Do, and visual artists such as Ah Xian, Guan Wei and Aaron Seeto, are increasingly seen as significant players in the national and international arts landscape. The emergence of Asian Australian theatre companies such as Theatre 4a further points to the professionalisation of Asian Australian performing arts, which includes well-known performers such as William Yang, Anna Yen and Mémé Thorne in its ranks. The long-term success of Asian arts advocacy organisations such as the Asia Australia Arts Centre in Sydney and Asialink in Melbourne is also another strong indicator of the growing commercial and artistic value of Asian Australian cultural production in the market place. Both organisations conduct highly effective outreach programs and have strong associations with the academy.

The overall picture of Asian Australian studies is of a field that is growing steadily rather than exponentially. Although the Asian Australian studies community is relatively small, it has a strong sense of identity, which is sustained by regular communication and resource sharing through electronic mailing lists, discussion groups, conferences and informal 'live meet-ups'.[7] Asian Australian studies is not a fully-established discipline in that it has not reached a stage where it is recognised institutionally through specific study programs or the establishment of a designated research centre. Likewise, there is no Asian Australian catalogue in databanks, no defined research field or discipline code recognised by the Australian Bureau of Statistics, and no professional association or designated journal. By most accounts, Asian Australian studies is thus a nascent field of research that is positioned somewhat uneasily between Asian and Australian studies.

Asian studies and Australian studies are area studies in the sense that the object of their analysis is primarily conceived in geopolitical terms. While there is growing interest in Asian studies in the analysis of transnational diasporic histories and cultures, the research reveals its area studies tradition in its search for commonalities and its focus on ethno-national groups (for example, the settlement of the Chinese in Australia)—even if Asian Australian studies is more theoretically suited to exploring intercommunal relations and histories between ethno-national groups. While there are some tentative movements by Asian Australian researchers into Asian studies spaces (for example, two Asian Australian studies panels featured at the 2004 Australian Association for Asian Studies conference) and vice versa, in general terms, Asian Australian studies and Asian studies are affiliated but maintain distinct theoretical objectives. In this sense, Asian Australian studies is perhaps more closely related to Asian Cultural studies which also has an ambiguous relationship to 'mainstream' Asian studies.

Asian Australian studies' impact on Australian studies is similarly muted. There remains some confusion about how Asian Australian studies differs from studies about Australian relations with Asia, and the former's research and creative productions are often placed in the subcategory of multicultural research within Australian studies.[8] While there have been some encouraging turning points, for example, the invitation to present an Asian Australian studies panel at the 2001 annual Association for the Study of Australian Literature (ASAL) conference, there are not enough Asian Australian scholars to create sufficient critical mass to assert whether there is an impact and, if so, in what form. Thus far, it appears that the only influence Asian Australian research has made on Asian studies and Australian studies is a slight stretching of boundaries to accommodate its themes and theories at conferences and occasional publications. It is interesting to note, however, that all the post-1999 Asian Australian studies-related conferences and associated publications have been supported by both Asian and Australian studies centres at the University of Queensland and Monash University.[9] This suggests that there is goodwill and a marked degree of openness to Asian Australian research by the more established disciplines.

There has been much discussion within the Asian Australian studies community about the institutional positioning of Asian Australian studies in relation to both Asian and Australian studies. There appears to be general agreement that it would be unwise for Asian Australian studies to be absorbed into Asian studies as this could be perceived as a mistaken privileging of cultural/ethnic 'origins', thereby emphasising the diasporic subject's alleged foreignness to the 'hostland'. Similarly, there are concerns that forging alliances with the more established Australian studies could result in the weakening of Asian Australian political objectives and interests. I believe that Asian Australian studies is on the right track in not being assimilated into either Asian or Australian studies, and that the field should maintain its productive tensile relationship with these more established disciplines. The dialogic and diasporic energy of Asian Australian studies is best served by nurturing this hybrid location, in much the same ways that Asian American studies has positioned itself in relation to America studies. However, this positioning also entails that the field has to remain vigilant about maintaining lines of dialogue and tracking developments in these adjunct areas of research through a kind of partial membership. This is a challenge for the small community of Asian Australian scholars, who are relatively junior in the academic hierarchy, and already stretched across many disciplines with little institutional infrastructure to support this kind of multiple academic citizenship.

Future Directions

I wish to conclude this essay with some brief observations about some possible future trajectories for Asian Australian studies.

Can Asian Australian Studies Shed its Reactive Politics?

Australians are now implicated in a new political game-plan with an increasing global impetus fuelled by the rhetoric of global terrorism. With the demise of the Pauline Hanson's One Nation party, and the new focus on border security to combat terrorism from the Middle East and Southeast Asia, the politics of domestic racism are not as palpably urgent (that is, unless of course you are 'brown' or of the Muslim faith). In contrast to the late 1990s, when Asian Australian activism was highly visible in the cultural and political arena to combat Hanson-inspired racism, the momentum seems to have eased. To a certain extent, the anti-racist activism of the 1990s has translated into grassroots support for Native Title, human rights and assylum seekers. This slowing down is inevitable, given the fact that Asian Australian activism has largely been reactive. The big challenge now is whether Asian Australian politics should remain strategically racialised for fighting racism domestically, or whether alliances and coalitions can be formed with other minority groups to fight racism and power inequities on multiple fronts, both within and beyond national borders. How will these developments affect the growth of Asian Australian studies?

The Politics of Representation Versus Representative Politics

Thus far, I have maintained that Asian Australian identity is a political strategy to unite Asian Australians of various ethnicities together but, in truth, this is an alliance of unequal partners. At the community level, both the profile and decision-making processes are dominated by the more established communities and by communities with more economic power. This inequality is also present in the academic domain: Asian Australian studies is dominated by the cultural productions of the Chinese and other East Asians. R. Radhakrishnan reminds us that a representational model is also a representative model: 'A representational model raises concerns such as adequacy, fidelity, authenticity, historical veracity, spokespersonship, inclusiveness, and so on' (2001: 251). While it is important that Asian Australian studies should be vigilant about being culturally and politically inclusive of all Asian communities and their interests, I am nervous about the field being charged with the role of being representative of all things Asian in Australia. In my view, Asian Australian studies is not a political lobbying group even though its intellectual objective is closely related to the promotion of social justice and cultural democracy. Asian Australian studies must maintain critical autonomy, even while it may be engaged at various levels with Asian Australian community politics. How is the bind between representational and representative politics to be managed?

The American situation presents some interesting comparisons. Unlike the Australian situation where Asian Australian studies is conceived primarily as an intellectual project, Asian American studies developed out of grassroots community politics. The academicisation of the field in the 1980s introduced new kinds of engagements, most notably with issues of identity that drew on intellectual debates from postcolonial and cultural studies, which called into question the perpetuation of community-based academic work (Dirlik 2003: 167). The tensions between more theoretically engaged research and scholarly work with a community-focus persist. While I am not advocating that Asian Australian studies models itself on its American counterpart, it could be more attentive to the ways in which it negotiates between community interests and intellectual objectives to ensure that the tensions between the community and the academy are productive, rather than debilitating.

Intercommunal Dialogue and Analysis

Most of the work done in Asian Australian studies has tended to focus on specific ethnic communities. While there are good reasons to limit the scope to a particular ethnic group (to allow for historical depth, for instance), I strongly encourage researchers to develop further work in intercommunal analysis. This kind of work is not as well-managed in other affiliated study areas and can be easily achieved under existing theoretical frameworks in Asian Australian studies. One of the main challenges associated with intercommunal analysis is the way in which non-English languages are approached. This is where the academic disciplining of most Asian

Australian studies researchers may be lacking since the study of non-English, and specifically Asian, languages tends not to feature significantly in cultural and communication studies majors at Australian universities. I would also include dialogue with Aboriginal communities and histories under this category of intercommunal dialogue. There is some very important work emerging on how Aboriginality and Asianness have defined and framed discourses of Whiteness, but work on Aboriginal–Asian histories and cultural relations remains relatively under-explored (see Edwards and Shen 2003; Gantner 2006; Shnukal et al. 2004). Academic work in this area is vital to not only broadening Asian Australian research but challenging the racial codification of the Reconciliation process as a largely Black/White matter.

Local Interests and Transnational Perspectives

The lines of kinship between Asian Australian studies and Asian and Australian studies also extend towards other Asian diasporic studies communities such as the Canadian, American, and British. Asian Australian studies has benefited greatly from critical engagement with the theoretical as well as political developments of its international counterparts. One of the ways in which Asian Australian studies might receive institutional approval as a legitimate area for undergraduate teaching is to associate the field with better-established Asian diasporic fields, most notably Asian American and Asian Canadian studies. Although a comparative methodology drawing on theories of diaspora, globalisation, transnationalism and cosmopolitanism would be highly productive, it is important not to be dominated by theories that are abstracted from history and local politics. Asian Australian studies must continue to develop locally specific approaches that are grounded in Australian histories and spaces in order to remain politically relevant to the Australian context, while simultaneously maintaining transnational links and global perspectives.

The tension between addressing local issues and the growing popularity of transnational/diasporic studies has been a feature of Asian Australian studies since its inception, as exemplified by the different approaches taken by the groundbreaking publications, *Diaspora* and *Alter/Asians*. The former was primarily concerned with addressing the politics of race and cultural relations within the nation whereas the latter was informed by a transnational perspective that focused on Asian cultural flows between Australia and the Asia-Pacific region. This tension is also present, in an even more overt way, in Asian American studies. The so-called 'transnational turn' of Asian American studies is said to have occurred in the late 1980s when emphasis on the global dimensions of Asian American studies began to override the original preoccupation with local race-specific relations within the US. Sau-ling Wong asserts that a domestic perspective stresses the status of Asian Americans as an ethnic/racial minority within the national boundary of the US, whereas a diasporic/transnational perspective would perceive Asian Americans as merely "one element in the global scattering of peoples of Asian origin" (1995: 2). One of the main criticisms leveled at a transnational approach is that it runs the risk of homogenising and reifying 'Asianness' and overlooks the specific modes of racialisation deployed by particular nation-states. Wong further avers that "if claiming America becomes a minor task for Asian American cultural criticism and espousal of denationalization becomes wholesale, certain segments of the Asian American population may be left without a viable discursive space" (ibid. 16). While Wong gets to the heart of what is at stake in these different approaches, I am not convinced that the situation in either Asian Australian or Asian American studies is so polarised, or that the appeal of diasporic approaches will expunge local concerns and interests. As Jonathan Y. Okamura (2003) points out, there is significant scope for Asian American studies to negotiate between the two theoretical approaches in ways that may extend current understanding about the imbrication of modes of racialisation between national and transnational contexts. It is therefore important to revoke the perception that intellectual approaches that foreground national interest and specificities are somehow less 'cutting-edge' than diasporic approaches that often purport to be more theoretically sophisticated because they focus on broader global perspectives.

This leads to my final credo. While Asian American studies has been an important referent point for Asian Australian studies, I would caution against seeing the latter merely as a less advanced or more 'junior' version of the former. While Asian Australian studies shares many similar theoretical and political concerns with its American counterpart, there are also significant differences and objectives based on different histories of (post)colonial settlement, race relations and immigration. Rather than assuming a shared teleology, it might be more productive to imagine Asian Australian studies as sharing modes rather than phases of Asian diasporic subjectivity with Asian American studies. Such a framework contests the dominance of the American model as the master-narrative of Asian diasporic studies and recognises the possibility of coexisting modes of academic engagement as well as lines of discontinuities and rupture. More importantly, such a relational approach would open up spaces for a specifically Australian inflection to, and extension of, current theorisations of transnationalism and diasporic subject formations.

Notes

[1] *Burying Mother* premiered at the Belvoir Street Theatre's Festival of Asian Theatre, Sydney, in 1996.
[2] For example, Yana Taylor (1998) focused on the ways in which performance explores various types of temporalities achieved largely through the use of physical embodiment and movement while Keith Gallasch (1996) focused on the transformational qualities of Thorne's performance.
[3] At that point in time, the hyphen was deployed in 'Asian–Australian' to stress the tensile positioning of Asians in Australia who were the targets, along with Aboriginal peoples, of heightened racism in the public sphere. The hyphen has since dropped off from general use, partly as a reflection of the increasing assurance and sense of purpose of the scholarly community, and also to signal the growing internationalisation of the field.

[4] For more contextual and statistical information, see Coughlan and McNamara (1997); Jayasuriya and Kee (1999) and Khoo and Price (1996).
[5] 'Sandstone universities' is a term used to denote the most established Australian universities, all of which are based in the nation's major cities.
[6] Historically, the category of race has been used largely in relation to Aboriginal people in Australian settler culture. This is reflected in the division between multicultural and indigenous politics in Australia which is in marked contrast to countries such as Canada where the obverse is true. Up until recently, Aboriginal affairs and multicultural concerns were managed by different departments within the federal government. This had the effect of further hindering the development of racial coalitions between minority ethnic migrant groups who are perceived to be the beneficiaries of multicultural policies, and indigenous communities.
[7] These informal 'live meet-ups' are the result of active Asian Australian electronic discussion groups wanting to develop a sense of community beyond the virtual realm. There are now regular meet-ups in Melbourne, and similar events have taken place in Sydney and Perth, with plans also for events in Canberra and Brisbane.
[8] See, for example, the electronic gateway to Australian Literature, *AustLit* <http://www.austlit.edu.au/>.
[9] Tseen Khoo's pioneering role in Asian/Australian studies must be acknowledged. She was responsible for organising the aforementioned conferences and associated publications. She also maintains the Asian Australian studies website, *The Banana Pages* <http://www.geocities.com/tseen/>, and moderates the two Asian Australian electronic discussion lists.

References

AustLit: The Resource for Australian Literature <http://www.austlit.edu.au/> (accessed 27 January 2005).
Ang, I. *On Not Speaking Chinese: Living Between Asia and the West*. London: Routledge, 2001.
Ang, I., Chalmers, S., Law, L. and Thomas, M. Eds. *Alter/Asians: Asian–Australian Identities in Art, Media and Popular Culture*. Annandale: Pluto Press, 2000.
Ang, I., and J. Stratton. 'Multiculturalism in crisis: The New Politics of Race and National Identity in Australia.' *On Not Speaking Chinese: Living Between Asia and the West*. Ed. I. Ang. London: Routledge, 2001. 95–111.
Bhabha, H. K. *The Location of Culture*. New York: Routledge, 1994.
Castles, S. 'The Racisms of Globalisation.' *The Teeth are Smiling: The Persistence of Racism in Multicultural Australia*. Eds. E. Vasta and S. Castles. Sydney: Allen and Unwin, 1996. 17–45.
Chek, L. *Plantings in a New Land: Stories of Survival, Endurance and Emancipation*. Brisbane: Society of Chinese Australian Academics of Queensland and Cathay Club, 2001.
Cho, N. and C. Raja. Guest Consultant Eds. 'Meanjin.' *AustralAsian* 63.2 (2004).
Chow, R. *Woman and Chinese Modernity: The Politics of Reading Between West and East*. Minnesota: University of Minnesota Press, 1999.
Chuh, K., and K. Shimakawa. 'Introduction: Mapping Studies in the Asian Diaspora.' *Orientations: Mapping Studies in the Asian Diaspora*. Eds. K. Chuh and K. Shimakawa. Durham and London: Duke University Press, 2001. 1–21.
Coughlan, J. E., and D. McNamara. *Asians in Australia: Patterns of Migration and Settlement*. Melbourne: Macmillan Education Australia, 1997.
D'Cruz, J. V., and W. Steele. *Australia's Ambivalence towards Asia: Politics, Neo-Post-colonialism and Fact/Fiction*. Clayton: Monash Asia Institute, Monash University, 2003.
Dirlik, A. 'Locating Asian American Studies Today: Origins, Identities, and Crises.' *Amerasia Journal* 29.2 (2003): 167–69.

Edwards, P., and Y. Shen. *Lost in the Whitewash: Aboriginal–Asian Encounters in Australia, 1901–2001*. Canberra: Humanities Research Centre, Australian National University, 2003.

Gallasch, K. 'A Body of Words.' *RealTime* 15 (1996): 28–29.

Gantner, R. *Mixed Relations: Histories and Stories of Asian/Aboriginal Contact in North Australia*. Perth: University of Western Australia Press, 2006.

Gilbert, H., Khoo, T., and Lo, J. Eds. *Diaspora: Negotiating Asian–Australia*. Brisbane: University of Queensland Press, 2000.

Gunew, S. *Framing Marginality: Multicultural Literary Studies*. Melbourne: Melbourne University Press, 1994.

Hage, G. *White Nation: Fantasies of White Supremacy in a Multicultural Society*. Annandale, NSW: Pluto Press, 1998.

Hall, S. 'New Ethnicities.' *Stuart Hall: Critical Dialogues in Cultural Studies*. Eds. D. Morley and K. Chen. London and New York: Routledge, 1996. 441–49.

Jayasuriya, L., and P. Kee. *The Asianisation of Australia? Some Facts about the Myths*. Melbourne: Melbourne University Press, 1999.

Khoo, S., and C. A. Price. *Understanding Australia's Ethnic Composition*. Canberra: Department of Immigration and Multicultural Affairs, 1996.

Khoo, T. *The Banana Pages* <http://www.geocities.com/tseen/> (accessed 27 January 2005).

———. *Banana Bending: Asian–Australian and Asian–Canadian Literatures*. Hong Kong: McGill-Queens University Press and Hong Kong University Press, 2003.

Khoo, T. and L. Kam. Eds. *Culture, Identity, Commodity: Diasporic Chinese Literatures in English*. Hong Kong: Hong Kong University Press, 2005.

Lo, J. 'Dis/orientations: Contemporary Asian Australian Theatre.' *Our Australian Theatre in the 1990s*. Ed. V. Kelly. Amsterdam: Rodopi, 1998. 53–70.

———. 'Beyond Happy Hybridity: Performing Asian Australian Identities.' *Alter/Asians: Asian Australian Identities in Art, Media and Popular Culture*. Eds. I. Ang, S. Chalmers, L. Law and M. Thomas. Annandale, NSW: Pluto Press, 2000. 152–68.

Lowe, L. 'Heterogeneity, Hybridity, Multiplicity: Marking Asian–American differences.' *Theorizing Diaspora*. Eds. J. E. Braziel and A. Mannur. Malden, MA: Blackwell, 2003. 132–55.

Morris-Suzuki, T. 'Anti-Area Studies.' *Communal/Plural* 8.1 (2000): 9–23.

Okamura, J. Y. 'Asian American Studies in the Age of Transnationalism: Diaspora, Race, Community.' *Amerasia Journal* 29.2 (2003): 171–93.

Ommundsen, W. and M. Boreland. Eds. 'Rubicon.' *Refractions: Asian/Australian Writing* 1.2 (1995).

Ommundsen, W. Ed. *Bastard Moon: Essays on Chinese Australian Writing*. Special Issue of *Otherland Literary Journal*. 7 (2001).

Radhakrishnan, R. 'Conjunctural Identities, Academic Adjacencies.' *Orientations: Mapping Studies in the Asian Diaspora*. Eds. K. Chuh and K. Shimakawa. Durham and London: Duke University Press, 2001. 249–63.

Shen, Y. *Dragon Seed in the Antipodes: Chinese–Australian Autobiographies*. Melbourne: Melbourne University Press, 2001.

Shnukal, A., G. Ramsay, and Y. Nagata. *Navigating Boundaries: The Asian Diaspora in Torres Strait*. Canberra: Pandanus, 2004.

Spivak, G. C. *In Other Worlds*. London and New York: Routledge, 1988.

Taylor, Y. 'About Time in Performance and Analysis: Streams of Time in Burying Mother.' *About Performance* 4 (1998): 43–55.

Turner, G. 'Discipline Wars: Australian Studies, Cultural Studies and the Analysis of National Culture.' *Journal of Australian Studies* 50/51 (1996): 6–17.

Wilton, J. *Golden Threads: The Chinese in Regional New South Wales, 1850–1950*. Armidale: New England Regional Museum, 2004.

Wong, S. C. 'Denationalization Reconsidered: Asian American Cultural Criticism at a Theoretical Crossroads.' *Amerasia Journal* 21.1/2 (1995): 1–27.

Re-Configuring the Diasporic and Indigenous in the Art of Zhou Xiaoping

Som Sengmany

Ann Curthoys (2000) described the relationship between Indigenous and migrant communities in Australia as an 'uneasy conversation' (21). She pointed to the contested relationship between multiculturalism and Indigenous rights in Australia and highlighted the problematic framing of both these interests under the broader concept of 'cultural diversity' by academics and policy-makers. While Indigenous and Chinese experiences of marginality often intersected, Curthoys argued that they also occupied 'significantly different places on the colonial-post-colonial spectrum' (Curthoys 2000: 32). The re-mapping of Chinese diasporic and Aboriginal histories by historians such as Regina Ganter (2005), Guy Ramsay (2001, 2004) and Sarah Yu (1999) has begun the important process of documenting this 'uneasy conversation'. These historical studies move beyond the 'white/minority' binary to incorporate what Ramsay has called the 'third space of Chinese-Indigenous connections' (Ramsay 2004: 53). In his detailed account of Chinese diasporic and Indigenous communities on Thursday Island, Ramsay identified how these intercultural engagements subverted the colonial structure of Anglo–Australian society:

> the presence on Thursday Island of a longstanding Chinese community, which, while ostensibly subject to the hegemony of White colonial society, subtly undermined the latter's cultural dominance through connections and contentions with an array of other Asian and Indigenous cultures. (Ramsay 2004: 54)

This essay investigates the potential of Chinese diasporic and Indigenous cross-hatchings in the contemporary visual arts to contest the dominant black/white binary. Focusing on the collaborations between Chinese diasporic artist Zhou Xiaoping and Aboriginal artist Jimmy Pike, I situate their artistic partnership within the context of broader debates on the representation of difference in Australia art. My reconfiguration of Zhou and Pike's artistic collaborations within the context of diasporic and Indigenous intersections intervenes and complicates the Aboriginal/Asian framework deployed by Curthoys. The first section of the essay begins by tracing Zhou's intercultural engagement with Indigenous communities and his artistic collaborations with Aboriginal artist Jimmy Pike. It addresses the way Zhou's art opens up new questions about the aesthetics, politics and ethics of cross-cultural representations of Aboriginality. The second section examines how Chinese diasporic and Indigenous cross-hatchings in the visual arts can provide a platform of cultural exchange. Focusing on Zhou and Pike's joint exhibition, *Through the Eyes of Two Cultures* (1999), I discuss how the contested intersection between Chinese diasporic and Indigenous identities can be mediated by a cross-cultural politics of representation. In doing so, this essay attempts to mark out a critical space for visual artists within ongoing debates on diaspora and difference in contemporary cultural theory.

Zhou Xiaoping: From *Guohua* to a Syncretic Aesthetics

> From the beginning, I wanted to communicate with Aboriginal Australians. I had seen their work and while I didn't understand it, I felt it. I felt something for the lines, the landscapes and figures. Particularly the line forms which were somehow related to Chinese painting (Zhou qtd. in Kapetopoulos 1996: 69).

Zhou Xiaoping was part of the cultural diaspora of Chinese artists who arrived in Australia after the Tiananmen Square massacre of 4 June 1989. What distinguishes

Zhou from other post-Tiananmen artists like Guan Wei and Ah Xian, and makes him such a fascinating figure, is his intercultural engagement with Indigenous artists and communities. Zhou was born in the city of Hefei, Anhui Province in China, and became a professional artist trained in the style of Chinese brush painting known as *guohua*.[1] He spent two years at the Anhui Academy of Education, and several years travelling to different parts of China including Huangshan, Guilin and Shanghai to train with *guohua* masters like Zhu Dongren and Yan Wenliang (Wenhui 1993). Zhou first visited Australia in 1988 to exhibit his *guohua* landscape paintings in Melbourne, and was immediately intrigued and fascinated by Aboriginal art and culture. After his exhibition in Melbourne, Zhou headed off to Alice Springs to find out more about Aboriginal art and culture:

> When I got off the bus I saw many black people walking on the streets. That was the first time I saw Australian Aborigines. From that moment I was so excited and wanted to know these people, who they are. So at that time I received help from the Land Council and after that I went to Darwin and they say, Zhou, if you really want to know Australian Aborigines, you should go to Arnhem Land, to see it's a little bit different to the people who are living in the city. So I went to Arnhem Land and met more people and talked to many artists and saw all the rock paintings. I was so excited. (Zhou 2002)

After completing a postgraduate fine arts degree at Northern Territory University, Zhou went on to spend sustained periods of time living with various Aboriginal communities in the Central Australia and the Northern Territory. Between the years of 1989–1994, Zhou spent twenty months living and travelling through Aboriginal communities in Ramingining and Oenpelli in Arnhem Land, Balgo and One Arm Point in the Kimberly, and Yuendumu in Central Australia (Kapetopoulos 1996: 69). While living with these various Aboriginal communities, Zhou attended Aboriginal festivals and gatherings, camped and hunted. He was even given a skin name 'Golok' and bush name 'Wonglu, Wonglu' (Giese 1997: 69).

In 1995, Zhou met Walmajarri artist Jimmy Pike in Fitzroy Crossing, and began a friendship and artistic collaboration that continued until Pike's death in 2002. Originally from the Great Sandy Desert of Western Australia, Pike was a self-taught Aboriginal artist who became famous for his distinctive linear designs of Walmajarri country (Isaacs 2003). Pike worked as a stockman on sheep and cattle stations before he took up painting in his late forties. Zhou speaks of gaining a deeper understanding and appreciation of Aboriginal art and culture from his friendship with Pike:

> I was ready to paint but Jimmy took me into the bush and taught me how to hunt for goanna, how to distinguish birds and how to examine ant hills. He taught about bush tucker and various plants. After a day of walking he decided that we should paint what we saw and experienced. I slowly began to understand, while developing new vision. A completely different interpretation of nature and the Aboriginal spirit was now emerging for me. Things that I had never noticed became more intense and real. (Kapetopoulos 1996: 69)

Zhou and Pike's artistic partnership produced two joint exhibitions. The first, held in Zhou's hometown of Hefei in 1996, was the first exhibition by an Indigenous Australian in China. During this first exhibition, Zhou and Pike travelled together through different parts of China, including the Great Wall and Buddha Mountain, and spent time painting together on a riverbank in Hefei. The second exhibition, *Through the Eyes of Two Cultures* (1999), was held at the National Gallery of China in Beijing, and featured Zhou and Pike's collaborative artworks: *Drew Each Other (1)* (1995), *Drew Each Other (2)* (1995), *Hunting*, (1995) and *Two Artists under a Tree* (1995).

Zhou's art developed in new and interesting ways as the result of his experiences living with Aboriginal communities and his collaborations with Pike. Instead of painting traditional Chinese landscapes, Zhou began to focus on figurative subject matter, specifically the representation of Aborigines and Aboriginal cultures. In 1993, the Beijing Arts and Photography Publishing House published a book titled *Sketches in Australia* (1993), which contained fifty of Zhou's paintings of Aborigines. This monograph featured Zhou's portrait paintings, sketches of Aborigines, and depictions of Aboriginal cultural life. The majority of the paintings in *Sketches in Australia*—for example, *A Woman* (c. 1989–1993) and *Aboriginal Dance* (c. 1989–1993)—featured Aboriginal figures painted in traditional black ink brushwork. Aboriginal portraiture and representations of Aboriginal culture remain the two dominant themes in Zhou's art practice.

Through the Eyes of Two Cultures marked Zhou's development and maturation as a contemporary artist. In it, Zhou combined *guohua* ink brushwork with European materials such as acrylic, and Aboriginal imagery and colours to create compelling artworks like *Land* (1998), *Jimmy in Buddha Mountain, China* (1996) and *Ceremonial* (1998). The mixing of Chinese, Aboriginal and European art styles is evident in *Bush Life* (1998), which features an Aboriginal figure sketched in brushwork on an abstract background that references both the gestural qualities of traditional Aboriginal cave painting and American Abstract Expressionism. In *Jimmy in Buddha Mountain, China* Zhou deployed Aboriginal art techniques to represent mountains in a flat two dimensional perspective, rather than using the traditional multiple perspective of Chinese landscape painting. Paintings like *Bush Life* and *Jimmy in Buddha Mountain, China* show that Zhou is no longer working within the representational codes of *guohua*. For example, missing from these two paintings are the large white spaces or voids that form a large part of the compositional structure of *guohua* (Kwo 1981). Instead, *Bush Life* and *Jimmy in Buddha Mountain, China* are examples of the syncretic aesthetics that Kate McFarlane (2004) suggests underlies the work of Chinese diasporic artists in Australia.

In *Diaspora, Cultural Practice and Syncretic Visuality*, McFarlane analysed the intercultural mixing of visual regimes in the work of two Chinese diasporic photographers, Hou Leong and Yean Leng Lim (2004). She noted that diasporic artists often deployed strategies of hybridisation and cultural mixing in their art practice and identified Leong and Lim's art as examples of 'syncretic diasporic intervisuality' (2004: 175). McFarlane declared that 'Chinese-Australian diasporic visuality' is expressed as neither 'Western nor Eastern but a syncretic mixture of two' (McFarlane 2004: 176). While this statement may be true in relation to Leong and Lim's work, Zhou's art problematises McFarlane's East/West binary model of diasporic visuality. Combining Chinese, European *and* Aboriginal art techniques, Zhou creates an aesthetics that crosses multiple cultural and representational boundaries. His art practice requires us to rethink the concept of 'Chinese-Australian diasporic visuality' within much broader and multi-faceted terms than the East/West model proposed by McFarlane. The next section of this essay examines how Zhou's art opens up a range of new questions about the aesthetics, politics and ethics of cross-cultural representations of difference in Australian art.

Cross-Cultural Representations of Aboriginality in *Sketches in Australia*

Zhou is working within an Australian art discourse grappling with two interconnected issues: a history of colonial representations of Aborigines, and the more recent postmodern artistic practice of the appropriation of Aboriginal imagery. How do we position Zhou within these debates in Australian art? Does his art deploy primitivist tropes of representing Aborigines? Is it possible to differentiate Zhou's appropriation of Aboriginal imagery from that of white contemporary Australian artists such as Imants Tillers and Tim Johnson? In situating Zhou's art within the context of these contemporary debates on Aboriginal representations, the objective of this essay is not to conclude whether Zhou's representations of Aborigines are 'good' or 'bad'. Such a framework of analysis fails to account for the ways that Zhou challenges and problematises these very aesthetic judgements. In her book, *About Face: Performing 'Race' in Fashion and Theater*, Dorinne Kondo reminds us that the unthinking reproduction of the black/white binary 'inevitably erases the complexity of what is better figured as a changing matrix of racialization' (Kondo 1997: 6). While Kondo's point was made in relation to an emergent Asian American cultural politics of representation, her concept of the matrix offers a constructive framework for analysing the potential of Zhou's representations of Aboriginality to expose the limitations of the dominant black/white binary in Australian art.

The representation of Aborigines in Zhou's art falls into two distinct periods: *Sketches in Australia* represents the first period (1989–1993), while *Through the Eyes of Two Cultures* represents the second period (1996–1999). I will focus here on the paintings from *Sketches in Australia* because they present the most challenging aspect of Zhou's art, and are less developed and nuanced than the later artworks in *Through the Eyes of Two Cultures*. Paintings like *Aboriginal Mother* (c. 1989–1993) and *At the Entrance of the Village* (c. 1989–1993) raise the question of whether Aborigines are represented in Zhou's paintings as 'primitive' or 'noble savages'. As Lynette Russell has noted, representations of Aboriginality in Australia have constantly 'wavered between these noble and ignoble constructions, with their assumptions of homogeneity in time and space' (Russell 1997: 231). In *Aboriginal Mother* and *At the Entrance of the*

Village, Zhou depicts Aborigines as barely clothed figures engaged in some sort of gathering activity. The broadening of the face, wild hair and distorted facial features of the Aboriginal figures in these painting are two examples of the problematic representation of the Aboriginal body in Zhou's art. Pat Lowe (1997) has argued that the titles of the paintings in *Sketches in Australia* (1993), such as *An Aboriginal Uncle* (c. 1989–1993), and *A Woman*, reflect Zhou's tendency to objectify Aboriginal subjects as particular types rather than individuals in his art (Lowe 1997: 30).

Before proposing one way of viewing Zhou's art outside of these particular tropes of representation, I want to focus on the issue of why Zhou's representations of Aborigines have elicited so much tension and unease among white art critics. There is no doubt Zhou's representation of Aborigines in paintings like, *Aboriginal Mother* and *At the Entrance of the Village* can be confronting in terms of his racialised depiction of the Aboriginal body. His art breaks many of the taboos surrounding the accepted modes of representing Aborigines in Australia. In one of his earliest exhibitions in Darwin, Zhou was criticised for showing a painting of Jimmy Pike holding a beer bottle (McCulloch 1997). While art critics focused on the perceived negative representation of Aborigines, Zhou explained his reason for painting Pike in this way:

> Pike carries a glass to share beer with others. I would like to paint him when he is drunk. It is part of his life. I drink too much, as them. But I still did some paintings. I really like them. They represent my real feelings. But sometimes I worry about these paintings. People don't want to see what is true. When people are drunk, they become really bastards. (Giese 1997: 72)

Zhou's comments reveal a willingness to depict some of the harsh realities of Aboriginal life in remote communities in Australia. I suggest that the stark depictions of Aborigines in *Sketches in Australia* can be interpreted as Zhou's attempt to represent the destructive effect of European colonisation on Aboriginal communities and individuals. A painting like *Exhausted* (c. 1989–1993), which features an Aboriginal figure crouched down on the ground with his head in his hands, depicts the daily struggles of contemporary Aboriginal life. *Exhausted* powerfully evokes the sense of burden, despair, and despondency that has marked the Aboriginal experience in colonial and post-colonial Australia. Zhou has certainly seen first hand during his experiences living with remote communities in Central Australia, the tough living conditions and struggles faced by Aborigines:

> I got off the bus at Alice Springs and saw black people in Australia for the first time. They looked at me—because I looked at them. These people, you can see from their eyes, the face, not smiling very often, they have so many experiences of life. Their experience is maybe very hard, very difficult. Suffering. (Giese 1997: 68)

In this regard, Zhou's representations of Aborigines in *Sketches in Australia* present a distinct contrast to what Peta Stephenson identified as the 'overly picturesque depictions of Indigenous people favoured by white Australians' (Stephenson 2004).

An interesting comparison can be made between the images of Aboriginality in Zhou's paintings like *Exhausted*, and the work of well-known Chinese Australian photographer William Yang. In his photo-documentary performance *Shadows* (2002), Yang presents a moving account of two communities: Australian Aboriginal people in New South Wales and German migrants in South Australia. Exploring issues of identity, dispossession and reconciliation, Yang's photo-documentary included several confronting images of alcohol abuse at Enngonia, an Aboriginal settlement in New South Wales. Stephenson (2004) has suggested that Yang's images of Aborigines may be uncomfortable viewing for many Anglo-European Australians because they present a reminder of the legacy of colonialism. She argued that for a 'descendent of the Chinese diaspora to challenge white Australians to acknowledge the ongoing ramifications of colonisation and their agency in it, is to contest white national rhetoric that migrants should be forever 'grateful' and not criticise their adopted country'.

Stephenson's remarks point to the underlying issue of authority, the question of who has the right to represent Aborigines, which has marked critical responses to both Yang and Zhou's art practice. In *Astronauts, Lost Souls and Dragons*, Diana Giese noted the critical and unfavourable responses to Zhou's art in metropolitan centres in Australia. She observed that 'there are those who would deny Zhou, as a Chinese man who has been in Australia only eight years, the right to paint Aborigines at all' (Giese 1997: 69). Zhou is aware of these questions of authority and representation:

> Originally, when I exhibited people were questioning my intent. White critics questioned me on my understanding of Aboriginal issues. They thought that the figures were powerful, but too negative. I always sought approval from the communities I work with and they had no problems, yet most of my critics were whites who are completely divorced from any Aboriginal communities. (Qtd. in Kapetopoulos 1996: 69)

In light of such criticism, it is significant to note that Zhou has achieved a level of acceptance and recognition of his art from the Aboriginal communities and artists he works with. For example, Zhou has gained the support of Aboriginal community leaders like Marcia Langton, and his participation in Aboriginal festivals, such as the annual Garma Festival, demonstrates a level of direct engagement with Aboriginal communities. The Garma Festival is an annual cultural festival of the Yolngu— Aboriginal people of northeast Arnhem Land. One of the main Indigenous festivals in Australia, Garma attracts representatives from clan groups all over Australia. At Garma 2003, Zhou was one of the few non-Aboriginal participants invited to contribute to a large collaborative Aboriginal artwork called the *Garma Panel*. More than eighty artists, including Indigenous artists such as Djambawa Marawili, Gawirrin Gumana, and Brenda Croft were involved in the creation of this multi-panelled etching.

How do we read the acceptance and support of Zhou's art practices and representations by Indigenous communities against the suggestions of primitivism levelled as his work by some white critics? While I am not suggesting that the acceptance of Zhou's art by Aboriginal communities makes his work immune from analysis, it does point to the limitations of some white critiques of Aboriginal representations. Graeme Turner has argued that what white people viewed as racist representations were not necessarily seen as racist by Aborigines themselves (1988). In *Breaking the Frame: The Representation of Aborigines in Australian Film*, Turner noted that, 'whites falsely assume that because they can detect the racist agenda underlying so many of their films they are also in possession of the knowledge of what would be a more acceptable agenda to the Aborigine' (Turner 1988: 136). Tseen Khoo, similarly, has labelled the critique of Zhou's art an example of the 'misguided liberal response of attempting to defend the "poor Aborigines"' (Khoo 2001: 100). Both Turner and Khoo's comments suggest an implicit paternalism in Anglo-Australian attempts to construct and define the representation of Aborigines, which often fails to engage with a more nuanced view of the positionality of representation itself. As Stuart Hall so aptly puts it, practices of representation 'always implicate the positions which we speak from or write form—the positions of *enunciation*' (Hall 1993: 222).

Marcia Langton has addressed this relationship between practices of representation and positions of enunciation in relation to the cultural constructions of Aboriginality in Australia (1994). In her essay *Aboriginal Art and Film: The Politics of Representation*, Langton identified three broad categories of cultural constructions of Aboriginality: (i) Aboriginal self representations, (ii) white Anglo Australian representation of Aboriginal based on no direct contact with Aboriginal peoples themselves, and (iii) constructions of Aboriginal generated by Aboriginal and non-Aboriginal people in dialogue (Langton 1994: 100). Adopting Langton's typology of Aboriginal constructions as a framework, I would situate Zhou's collaborative art practices and representations of Aboriginality in the third category of dialogic construction. I suggest that another layer of complexity is present in this third category when analysing non-white, non-Anglo representations of Aboriginality because these representations are situated across sites of difference, rather than framed by the black/white binary. Zhou creates his representations of Aboriginality in direct contact with Aboriginal artists such as Jimmy Pike, producing works like the collaborative self-portrait paintings *Drew Each Other (1)* and *Drew Each Other (2)*. Zhou also often takes slides and photographs of his paintings back to show the remote Indigenous communities he has lived with and visited (Stephenson 2003a: 64). While the critique of the racialised representation of Aborigines within a historical context is still a necessary task, Zhou's art shows us that these critiques must also now engage with the range of representations created by Chinese diasporic and Indigenous cross-cultural collaborations.

Platforms for Cultural Exchange: Chinese Diasporic and Indigenous Cross-hatchings in the Visual Arts

Penny Edwards and Shen Yuanfang have argued that official discourses separating the 'Chinese issue' from the 'Aboriginal problem' have created a black/white binary that has left little space for Asians as active participants in Australia (2003). Edwards and Shen argue that Asian immigrants are trapped in a conceptual conundrum because they are '[e]xcised from popular narratives of colonisation and elided in debates on reconciliation' (Edwards and Shen 2003: 10). I contend that Chinese diasporic and Indigenous collaborations in the visual arts challenge this 'conceptual conundrum' by creating a contemporary site for exploring the connection and contentions between Chinese diasporic and Indigenous narratives in Australia. In doing so, exhibitions like *Through the Eyes of Two Cultures* and *?Lost & Found: A Shared Search for Belonging* (2001) provide a critical complement to the historical re-mappings of Chinese diasporic and Indigenous identities.

Zhou and Pike's collaborative exhibition *Through the Eyes of Two Cultures* represents one dynamic example of how sites for connecting 'Others'—that is, Chinese diasporic and Indigenous cultures—can be created outside dominant Anglo Australian cultural frameworks. The Golden Dragon Museum (Bendigo, Melbourne) organised *Through the Eyes of Two Cultures* specifically for the National Gallery of China in Beijing. This exhibition, which featured individual and collaborative art by Zhou and Pike, generated enormous interest in China because of the lack of exposure of Chinese audiences to Aboriginal visual culture. As well as the two joint exhibitions with Jimmy Pike in Beijing and Hefei, Zhou has also exhibited his paintings of Aborigines at Galerie Dauphin in Singapore (2002) and Qinghua University Arts Centre, Taiwan (1993). Zhou's exhibitions represent the increasing intercultural flow of images of Aboriginality created by artists outside of dominant Anglo-Australian frameworks. As Stephenson (2004) noted, Zhou's collaborations with Pike and intercultural exchange with Indigenous communities in Australia 'seemingly [dis-regard] the self-appointed role of white Australians as mediators or adjudicators of any conversation between 'migrants' and their Indigenous counterparts'.

Moreover, Zhou and Pike's collaborations show the potential of Chinese diasporic and Indigenous cross-hatchings in the visual arts to shift the modes of cultural exchange beyond the dominant Western/Asian and Western/Indigenous paradigms. Such shifts are important and necessary, as the framework for cross-cultural interaction in Australia still seems fixed upon Eurocentric binaries that reinscribe the non-Western as the 'Other'. As Gerardo Mosquera observes, while the 'postmodern interest in the Other has opened some space in "high art" circuits for vernacular and non-Western culture', it has also subsequently 'introduced a new thirst for exoticism' (Mosquera 2002: 269). The representative space for many Asian and Aboriginal artists in Australia has often been mediated through concepts of the exotic Others, or within the framework of cultural exchange with Anglo-Australian culture. Melissa Chiu has identified the operation of this one sided type of cultural exchange within the contemporary Australian art world. In *Rough Trade: Curating Cultural Exchange in Australia*, Chiu (2000) analysed the curatorial strategies in exhibitions such as *Out of Asia* (Museum of Modern Art at Heide, 1990) and the first Asia-Pacific Triennial (Queensland Art Gallery, 1993). She posited that:

> The preoccupation with exoticism as well as European ideas of otherness in [exhibitions like] *Out of Asia* indicates that the debates in Australia in the early 1990s were conceived in binary polarities, where Australia represented the West, and Asia the East. (Chiu 2000: 127)

Chiu's astute analysis reveals the tendency within contemporary Australian art to reposition the 'Other', whether it is Chinese or Aboriginal, as *the* point of difference. The dominance of this 'West versus the Rest of the World' paradigm has created a situation whereby other forms of intercultural exchange are effectively negated in contemporary Australian art.

A number of collaborative exhibitions including *Through the Eyes of Two Cultures*, *Between Remote Regions* (2000), and *?Lost & Found* have attempted to challenge this paradigm by creating a site for direct intercultural exchanges between 'Others'. In *?Lost & Found*, the Immigration Museum and Koori Heritage Trust brought Indigenous and migrant artists together to create individual and collaborative artworks exploring the themes of cultural identity and the search for belonging. Some of the thirty-three participating artists included Donna Brown, Bernardo Duarte, Mami Yamanaka, Le Thanh Nhon and Shin Watanabe. Maree Clarke and Jacqui Geia explained in their curatorial statement that the main objective of the exhibition was to:

> provide a platform for cultural exchange, providing the opportunity for artists form immigrant cultures and Indigenous communities to produce and present singular and collaborative works. We have encouraged the exploration of dislocation from ancestral lands and the notion of leaving the home country, to practice cultural expressions in a new world—a common theme for both the Indigenous and newly arrived Australians.
>
> Many Indigenous artists were shocked by the personal accounts of war, genocide and family fragmentation experienced by migrant families. Many of the artists from migrant backgrounds, often for the first time, heard histories of the First Australians, stories never told in history books, stories of loss, sadness and celebration. (Clarke and Geia 2001: 3)

This comment reveals how the search for cultural identity, belonging and self-determination can be common themes connecting Indigenous and diasporic narratives. Peta Stephenson (2001, 2003a, 2003b) has identified the transgressive potential of diasporic and Indigenous connections to challenge traditional hegemonic narratives of the nation-state. In *Finding Common Ground: Indigenous and Asian Diasporic Cultural Production in Australia*, Stephenson argued that the 'literature and visual arts of Australian Indigenous and diasporic communities play an important role in terms of destabilising traditional, white versions of history, [bringing] new, intra-ethnic histories into the national narrative' (Stephenson 2001: 65). I contend that one way Chinese diasporic and Indigenous collaborations in the visual arts can contest traditional narratives is by creating constitutive sites for a cross-cultural politics of representation.

Zhou and Pike's collaborative self-portraits, *Drew Each Other (1)* and *Drew Each Other (2)*, offer us one example of the potential for diasporic and Indigenous cross-cultural collaborations to challenge dominant codes of representation. To create *Drew Each Other (1)* and *Drew Each Other (2)*, Zhou and Pike worked simultaneously on one canvas, which was passed backwards and forwards between the artists. Zhou described the collaborative process in this way:

> Jimmy Pike, we are very close friends. He drew me, I drew him. Sometimes we just laugh at each other and say, oh gee, you draw me without my hair, I say okay, Jimmy I'm going to draw you with your hair but you have to keep your beard. So it's lots of fun. We really enjoy it, our conversation, our life in the bush. (Zhou 2002)

Drew Each Other (1) and *Drew Each Other (2)* can be read on two levels: first, as Zhou and Pike representing themselves to each other and, second, representing each other to the audience. In *Drew Each Other (1)*, Zhou and Pike depict each other with broad smiles and arms interlinked facing the viewer. In both artworks, Zhou and Pike use cartoon figures to represent one another and, while the result is both humorous and engaging, there is a deeper political resonance to these collaborative self-portraits when viewed against the way that cartoons functioned as a mode for racially stereotyping Aborigines and Chinese in Australia. Racist depictions of Aborigines and Chinese in cartoons were a feature of mainstream Australian newspapers in the late nineteenth and early twentieth centuries. As Marguerite Mahood noted in her study of Australian caricature, *The Loaded Line: Australian Political Caricature*, the Chinese have always been a picturesque cartoon subject in Australia (1973). The *Mongolian Octopus* published in *The Bulletin*, 21 August 1886, is one well-known example of the racialised representation of the Chinese in nineteenth century Australia. Jen Tsen Kwok has observed that cartoons such as the *Mongolian Octopus* represented the Chinese in terms of 'vice, disease and immorality' (Kwok 2004). Zhou and Pike's appropriation of the cartoon form suggest the possibilities for re-countering and resisting such historical codes of representation. In *Drew Each Other (1)* and *Drew Each Other (2)*, Zhou and Pike take the cartoon form and turn it into a humorous and joyous expression of cross-cultural interaction. The critical value and power of such self-representative practices should not be underestimated, especially when viewed within the context of an Australian culture that continues, as Annette Hamilton argued, to represent Aborigines and Asians as objects of both fear and desire (Hamilton 1990).

Stephen Muecke's concept of 'cultural activism' is a useful term to describe Zhou and Pike's cross-cultural self-portraits. In *Cultural Activism: Indigenous Australia 1972-94*, Muecke (1998) defined cultural activism as the 'mobilization of cultural representations as performances' (300), and pointed to the performative nature of the Aboriginal rights movement in Australia. While Muecke focused on cultural activism in relation to Indigenous self-representation, I argue that Zhou and Pike's collaborative self-portraits demonstrate that another strategy of cultural activism, parallel to the one Muecke addressed, is also taking place. Zhou and Pike's collaborative self-portraits, which are part-performance art, show us the potential for diasporic and Indigenous collaborations to challenge positionings of the Chinese and Aboriginal as objects of the Anglo-Australian imagination.

'Lost in the Whitewash'? Reviewing the Debates on the Appropriation of Aboriginality

One of the main critical debates in Australian art in the late 1980s and early 1990s focused on the appropriation of Aboriginal imagery and identity by contemporary white Australian artists such as Imants Tillers and Tim Johnson. Tiller's painting *The Nine Shots* (1985), in which he appropriated Aboriginal artist Michael Nelson Tjakamarra's *Five Dreamings* (1984), exemplified the postmodern aesthetic practice of appropriation. The debates on the appropriation of Aboriginality in Australian art occurred within the wider context of Australia's Bicentennial celebrations in 1988, a year in which Aboriginal relationships with mainstream Australia were very much a contentious cultural and political issue. In *Postmodernism: A Consideration of the Appropriation of Aboriginal Imagery*, a key text published by the Institute of Modern Art in Brisbane (1989), various art critics and artists addressed the contested aesthetic and ethical issues surrounding the practice of appropriation. Two opposing positions were taken by participants in this debate. Art critics such as Henrietta Fourmile, Bob Lingard and Juan Davila viewed the appropriation of Aboriginal imagery as a form of cultural colonialism. Fourmile argued that the 'relations between Aborigines and Anglo-Europeans and their institutions still remain essentially colonial and appropriation should be seen within this context' (Fourmile 1989: 10). Davila was particularly scathing, and he called the appropriation of Aboriginality by artists such as Imants Tillers a form of 'fake marginality' (Davila 1996: 194).

In contrast to this view, Vivien Johnson and Tim Johnson argued for the possibilities of cross-cultural exchange and 'rapprochement' outside the imperialising framework of cultural colonialism. Vivien Johnson suggested that 'the perspective of cultural colonialism is too limiting, to Aboriginal as well as non-Aboriginal actors' (V. Johnson 1989: 14). Tim Johnson agreed and argued that 'the influence of one culture on another is not simply a matter of colonisation within a power/politics equation... all actions are contextual and exchange between cultures must be seen in the context of the mechanism and effects of change' (T. Johnson 1989: 12). Underlying this debate was the confrontation between postmodern art practices and postcolonial theory. The dilemma here is what was theoretically defined and defended as a postmodern art practice could also be viewed as the rationalisation of Western artists to continue the regime of cultural colonisation.

How do we situate Zhou Xiaoping within these debates on Aboriginal identity and appropriation in contemporary Australian art? Zhou also engages in the appropriation of Aboriginal imagery by using traditional Aboriginal symbols and patterns in paintings like *Land* and *Bush Life*. In reviewing these debates, it becomes evident just how strictly the terms of the discourse became structured around the black/white binary. In a text like *Postmodernism: A Consideration of the Appropriation of Aboriginal Imagery*, the 'non-Aboriginal' was constructed exclusively to mean white Anglo-Australian. Sue Cramer identifies in her Introduction that the key issue being examined was the 'white appropriation of Aboriginal culture' (Cramer 1989: 5). What I find problematic is that there is little acknowledgement or reference to the possibilities and realities of non-white non-Anglo-Celtic engagements with Aborigines. A useful comparison can be made between the debates on the appropriation of Aboriginality in the Australian art world, and the Reconciliation debates in mainstream Australia. Both debates, structured around the black/white binary, operated in similar ways to exclude the non-white, non-Anglo-Celtic subject. Scholars such as Minoru Hokari (2003a, 2003b), Peter Read (1997) and Dipesh Chakrabarty (2001) have argued that the framework of Reconciliation in Australia has focused almost exclusively on Anglo-Celtic and Aboriginal relationships. Such frameworks, these scholars argue, are far too limited and negate the necessity of addressing the relationship between Indigenous and migrant communities. Hokari noted for example that documents like *Shared History: A Search for All Australians of Ownership of Their History* (1993), produced by the Council for Aboriginal Reconciliation, contained no statement on Australian non-white migrants' responsibilities for Aboriginal Reconciliation (Hokari 2003b: 88).

These debates on the appropriation of Aboriginality and Reconciliation demonstrate that part of the pervasive power of the black/white binary lies in the implicit nature of its operation. White Australia, as Curthoys observed, does not like to 'address its racial others in a united or coherent discourse, but rather in separate registers at different times' (Curthoys 2000: 24). The critical value of analysing Zhou's art is that his cross-cultural representations of Aboriginality and appropriations of Aboriginal imagery expose the privileged status of this binary. It is interesting to note that Zhou was beginning his intercultural exchange with Indigenous communities at around the same time these debates on Aboriginal identity and imagery were occurring in the late 1980s and early 1990s. Zhou's collaborations with Pike and experiences living with Aboriginal communities are most comparable to that of Tim Johnson. Johnson has worked with Aboriginal artists such as Clifford Possum, as well as Asian and Native American artists to create collaborative artworks such as *Old Man* (1994) and *Judgement* (1993). Zhou and Johnson only paint Aboriginal designs and stories for which they are given permission to use by the Indigenous communities and artists with whom they worked. Despite Johnson's collaborative practices, Lingard argued that 'difficulties still remain at the level of the precise effects and purposes of such appropriation in a society that blatantly continues to oppress and exclude Aboriginal people and their culture' (Lingard 1989: 23).

Lingard's comment points to the wider context of cultural colonialism, within which artists like Johnson work. While agreeing with Lingard, I suggest the cultural context he points to is further complicated in Zhou's case because Chinese diasporic and Indigenous artistic collaborations and appropriations occur across sites of differences. The dominant black/white binary that structures cultural exchange in the work of artists like Tiller and Johnson becomes mediated in non-white, non-Anglo artistic interactions by the issue of difference. Zhou's appropriations of Aboriginal imagery require us to develop nuanced frameworks of analysis that can sufficiently account for, and engage with, the multiple and dynamic intersections of differences.

Conclusion: Points of Departure

In *Indigenous Articulations*, James Clifford proposed that we should 'actively inhabit and explore, not flee from, the mutually constitutive tensions of Indigenous and diasporist visions and experiences' (Clifford 2001: 470). Zhou and Pike's artistic collaborations are one example of how visual artists in Australia have inhabited and explored the 'constitutive tensions' between Indigenous and diasporic visions. The cross-hatching of Chinese diasporic and Indigenous identities in the visual arts has created platforms for cultural exchange, which contest dominant black/white, migrant/settler narratives within Australia. Zhou's ongoing intercultural engagement with Indigenous communities offers us one example of how we can negotiate our differences across often complex and multifocal relationships of power. Zhou's collaborations with Pike challenge the bifurcation of the Chinese and Indigenous identities and histories, and expose the limitations of the black/white binary as a framework for addressing the representation of difference. His art raises a new set of challenging questions about the aesthetics, politics and ethics of Indigenous and Chinese diasporic cross-cultural representations. These questions have no easy answers but, as Hokari reminds us, the ongoing explorations of Chinese diasporic and Indigenous relationships should not be seen as 'an end-product but a point of departure which opens up new and interesting perspectives' (Hokari 2003a: 89). Zhou and Pike's artistic collaborations demonstrate how these points of departure can also produce sites for a constitutive cross-cultural politics of representation.

Note

[1] *Guohua* refers to 'works painted with traditional Chinese pigments on a ground of traditional paper or silk' (Andrews 1994: 50).

References

Andrews, J. *Painters and Politics in the People's Republic of China: 1949–1979*. Berkeley: University of California Press, 1994.

Chakabarty, D. 'Reconciliation and its Histographies: Some Preliminary Thoughts.' *The University of Technology Sydney Review* 7.1 (2001): 6–16.

Chiu, M. 'Rough Trade: Curating Cultural Exchange in Australia.' *Alter/Asians: Asian-Australian Identities in Art, Media and Popular Culture*. Eds. I. Ang, S. Chalmers, L. Law and M. Thomas. Annandale: Pluto Press, 2000. 123–40.

Clarke, M. and Geia, J. 'Curator's Message.' *?Lost & Found: A Shared Search for Belonging*. Ed. J. Geia. Melbourne: Immigration Museum and Koori Heritage Trust, 2001. 3.

Clifford, J. 'Indigenous Articulations.' *The Contemporary Pacific* 13.2 (2001): 468–490.

Cramer, S. *Postmodernism: A Consideration of the Appropriation of Aboriginal Imagery*. Brisbane: Institute of Modern Art, 1989.

Curthoys, A. 'An Uneasy Conversation: The Multicultural and the Indigenous.' *Race, Colour and Identity in Australia and New Zealand*. Eds. J. Docker and G. Fischer. Sydney: UNSW Press, 2000. 21–36.

Davila, J. 'Aboriginality: A Lugubrious Game?.' *What is Appropriation? An Anthology of Critical Writings on Australian Art in the '80s and '90s*. Ed. R. Butler. Sydney: Power Publications and Institute of Modern Art, 1996. 193–96.

Edwards, P. and Shen, Y. 'Something More: Towards Reconfiguring Australian History.' *Lost in the Whitewash: Aboriginal-Asian Encounters in Australia, 1901–2001*. Eds. P. Edwards and Y. Shen. Canberra: Humanities Research Centre, Australian National University, 2003. 1–22.

Fourmile, H. 'Some Background to Issues Concerning the Appropriation of Aboriginal Imagery.' *Postmodernism: A Consideration of the Appropriation of Aboriginal Imagery*. Ed. S. Cramer. Brisbane: Institute of Modern Art, 1989. 6–10.

Ganter, R. *Mixed Relations: Narratives of Asian/Aboriginal Contact in North Australia*. Crawley, WA: University of Western Australia Press, 2005.

Giese, D. *Astronauts, Lost Souls and Dragons: Voices of Today's Chinese Australians in Conversation with Diana Giese*. St Lucia: University of Queensland Press, 1997.

Hall, S. 'Cultural Identity and Diaspora.' *Colonial Discourse and Postcolonial Theory*. Eds. P. Williams and L. Chrisman. Hertfordshire: Harvester Wheatsheaf, 1993. 392–403.

Hamilton, A. 'Fear and Desire: Aborigines, Asians and the National Imaginary.' *Australian Cultural History* 9 (1990), 14–35.

Hokari, M. 'Anti–Minorities History—Perspectives on Aboriginal-Asian Relations.' *Lost in the Whitewash: Aboriginal-Asian Encounters in Australia, 1901-2001*. Eds. P. Edwards and Y. Shen. Canberra: Human Research Centre, Australian National University, 2003a. 85–101.

———. 'Globalising Aboriginal Reconciliation: Indigenous Australians and Asian (Japanese) Migrants.' *Cultural Studies Review* 9.2 (2003b): 84–101.

Isaacs, J. 'Jimmy Pike.' *Art and Australia* 40.4 (2003): 576–77.

Johnson, T. 'Re-Appropriation.' *Postmodernism: A Consideration of the Appropriation of Aboriginal Imagery*. Ed. S. Cramer. Brisbane: Institute of Modern Art, 1989. 11–13.

Johnson, V. 'A White Shade of Palaeolithic.' *Postmodernism: A Consideration of the Appropriation of Aboriginal Imagery*. Ed. S. Cramer. Brisbane: Institute of Modern Art, 1989. 14–18.

Kapetopoulos, F. 'New Lines of Communication.' *Artlink* 16.4 (1996): 69–70.

Khoo, T. 'Re-Siting Australian Identity: Configuring the Chinese Citizen in Diana Giese's *Astronauts, Lost Souls and Dragons* and William Yang's *Sadness*.' *Bastard Moon: Essays on Chinese Australian Writing*. Ed. W. Ommundsen. Victoria: Kingsbury, Otherland Literary Journal (2001): 95–109.

Kondo, D. *About Face: Performing 'Race' in Fashion and Theater*. New York: Routledge, 1997.

Kwo, D. *Chinese Brushwork: Its History, Aesthetics, and Techniques*. New Jersey: Allanheld and Schram, 1981.

Kwok, J. T. 'Anti-Chinese Representations and Governance in Queensland.' *Crossings* 9.3, <http://asc.uq.edu.au/crossings/9_3/index.php?apply=kwok> (accessed 1 December 2005).

Langton, M. 'Aboriginal Art and Film: The Politics of Representation.' *Race and Class* 35.4 (1994). 89–106.

Lingard, B. 'Appropriation of Aboriginal Imagery: Tim Johnson and Imants Tillers.' *Postmodernism: A Consideration of the Appropriation of Aboriginal Imagery*. Ed. S. Cramer. Brisbane: Institute of Modern Art, 1989. 19–25.
Lowe, P. 'Jimmy Pike in China.' *Art Monthly* 100 June (1997). 30–31.
Mahood, M. *The Loaded Line: Australian Political Caricature 1788–1901*. Melbourne, Melbourne University Press, 1973.
McCulloch, S. 'In Praise of Double Vision.' *The Weekend Australian*, 24 May, 1997. 11.
McFarlane, K. 'Diaspora, Cultural Practice and Syncretic Visuality.' *Journal of Intercultural Studies* 25.2 (2004): 175–84.
Mosquera, G. 'The Marco Polo Syndrome.' *The Third Text Reader on Art, Culture and Theory*. Eds. R. Araeen, S. Cubitt and Z. Sardar. London: Continuum, 2002. 267–73.
Muecke, S. 'Cultural Activism: Indigenous Australia 1972–94.' *Trajectories: Inter-Asian Cultural Studies*. Ed. K. Chen. London: Routledge, 1998. 299–313.
Ramsay, G. 'Myth, Moment and the Challenge of Identities: Stories from Australians of Indigenous and Chinese Ancestry.' *Journal of Intercultural Studies* 22.3 (2001). 263–78.
——. 'The Chinese Diaspora in the Torres Strait: Cross-cultural Connections and Contentions on Thursday Island.' *Navigating Boundaries: The Asian Diaspora in Torres Strait*. Eds. A. Shnukal, G. Ramsay, G. and Y. Nagata. Canberra: Pandunus Books, 2004. 53–79.
Read, P. 'Pain, Yes, Racism, No: The Response of Non-British Australians to Indigenous Land Rights.' *The Resurgence of Racism, Hanson, Howard and the Race Debate*. Eds. G. Gray and C. Winter. Melbourne: Department of History, Monash University, 1997. 87–95.
Russell, L. 'Focusing on the Past: Visual and Textual Images of Aboriginal Australia in Museums.' *The Cultural Life of Images: Visual Representation in Archaeology*, Ed. B. L. Molyneaux. London: Routledge, 1997. 230–48.
Stephenson, P. 'Finding Common Ground: Indigenous and Asian Diasporic Cultural Production in Australia.' *Hecate* 27.1 (2001): 59–67.
——. 'New Cultural Scripts: Exploring the Dialogue between Indigenous and 'Asian' Australians.' *Journal of Australian Studies* 77 (2003a).57–68.
——. 'Cross-Cultural Alliances Exploring Aboriginal-Asian Literary and Cultural Production.' *Lost in the Whitewash: Aboriginal-Asian Encounters in Australia, 1901–2001*. Eds. P. Edwards and Y. Shen. Canberra: Human Research Centre, Australian National University, 2003b. 143–162.
——. *Altered States: Indigenous Australian and Chinese Diasporic Alliances*. Paper presented at the 5th Conference of International Society for the Study of the Chinese Overseas, University of Copenhagen, 2004.
Turner, G. 'Breaking the Frame: The Representation of Aborigines in Australian Film.' *Aboriginal Culture Today*. Ed. A. Rutherford. Sydney: Dangaroo Press, 1988. 135–145.
Wenhui, K. 'Preface.' *Sketches in Australia*. Ed. X. Zhou. Beijing: Beijing Arts and Photography Publishing House, 1993.
Yu, S. 'Broome Creole: Aboriginal and Asian Partnerships along the Kimberley Coast.' *Queensland Review* 6.2 (1999): 58–73.
Zhou, X. *Sketches in Australia*. Beijing: Beijing Arts and Photography Publishing House, 1993.
——. 'Interview with Julie Copeland.' *ABC Radio National*, 24 March 2002, <http://www.abc.net.au/rn/arts/sunmorn/stories/s513460.htm> (accessed 1 December 2004).

Telling Stories: The Sacrificial Asian in Australian Cinema

Olivia Khoo

In a documentary entitled *40,000 Years of Dreaming: A Century of Australian Cinema* (1997), director, writer and narrator George Miller (of *Mad Max* fame) boldly connects Aboriginal dreaming and songlines to the idea of Australian national cinema. Miller suggests that Australian films are the 'whitefella's' public dreaming and the songlines that 'sing us into being'. This connection is no doubt a contentious one, opening the film to charges of cultural appropriation and misattribution. However, what is equally conspicuous in Miller's broad sweep of Australian cinema is that it is noticeably devoid of any representations of Asians in or of the national cinema. Asians do not fit comfortably into any of the film's categories such as 'the bushman', 'the convict', 'the digger', 'gays', 'wogs', or 'blackfellas', to list a few of the film's section intertitles.[1] Despite the proliferate categories for the nation's cast of marginal characters, there is a reluctance, or an inability, to make space for Asians within such a seemingly leveling discourse of marginality. It is not that prominent films recounting the stories of Asians in Australia, or of Australians in Asia, do not exist.

Rather, this silence is perhaps due to the fact that the Asian Australian relationship is one that is difficult for many Australians to dream or conceive of fully yet.

To begin the task of writing such a relationship into being, this article traces four key cinematic moments in the Australian encounter with Asia and Asians over the past twenty-five years. Beginning with the seminal portrayal of Billy Kwan by American Linda Hunt in Peter Weir's *The Year of Living Dangerously* (1982) to a role played by Joan Chen a decade later in Stephen Wallace's *Turtle Beach* (1992), the article then analyses what, if anything, has changed in more recent films such as Craig Lahiff's *Heaven's Burning* (1997) and Sue Brooks' *Japanese Story* (2003). Despite various political and economic positionings (or posturings) of Asia as Australia's 'nearest neighbour' and 'friend', in the films discussed the encounter between Asians and Australians inevitably results in violence and ends with the sacrifice of the Asian character. Far from being merely an archaic rite of so-called 'primitive people', sacrifice in the contemporary period also derives its significance as a mode of dealing with conflict and of strengthening a community against a perceived outside threat. Even though it results in a death, sacrifice is also, as Georges Bataille (1986) noted, connected with a generative principle.[2] In contemporary Australian cinema, the sacrifice of Asian characters is tied not only to the birth of a modern-day national identity, but also to the modernity of a national cinema formed through a distinction from its regional 'Other'.

Trying on National Identities

The Australian filmic renaissance in the mid-1970s was the cumulative result of a general growth in support for the arts by the Gorton and Whitlam governments. This more open environment led, for instance, to a series of tax incentives and reforms to promote investment in the industry, giving many new filmmakers the chance to tell their own stories about Australian life. From the fairly static representations of early (colonial) cinema, Jonathan Rayner argues that since the renaissance in the 1970s, Australia has 'resolutely set about problematizing its national identity, taking on, or perhaps "trying on" successive identities, holding together apparently incompatible national and political objectives' (2000: 10). There have been several shifts in Australia's cultural and political sentiments over its relationship to Asia, shifts that have had an impact on the revival of national cinema. In 1973, the final vestiges of the White Australia Policy were rescinded and this was followed by then-Prime Minister Bob Hawke's acceleration of Australia's 'enmeshment with Asia' during the 1980s (see Hawke 1998). Hawke's successor Paul Keating championed Australia's further engagement with Asia in the early 1990s,[3] and the newly instated policy of multiculturalism again changed the shape of the national cinema allowing for new complexities in its definition. A backlash to the Keating years followed, resulting in Labor's devastating defeat to John Howard and the Coalition conservative government in 1996. It is in this political climate that Pauline Hanson and the One Nation party rose to power and media prominence. Hanson's maiden speech in Parliament (as the Independent member for Oxley) on 10 September 1996 called for an abolition of the policy of multiculturalism because she feared that Australia was 'in danger of being swamped by Asians' (Hanson 1996). The present-day Coalition government continues to play on residing fears over an 'invasion' of refugees from the North while at the same time maintaining a desire to capitalise on Asia's perceived economic ascendancy. A year after its induction, the Howard government released a White Paper on Australian Foreign and Trade Policy entitled *In the National Interest*. This White Paper identifies globalisation and the continuing rise of East Asia as the two most profound influences on Australia's foreign and trade policy over the next fifteen years (Downer and Fischer 1997: 17). The Minister for Foreign Affairs Alexander Downer was quick to emphasise: '[C]loser engagement with Asia [does not] require reinventing Australia's identity or abandoning the values and traditions which define Australian society. Australia draws unique strength from the interaction of its history and geography' (Downer and Fisher 1997: iv). In a speech made in Hong Kong later that year, Downer recalculated his approach for a wider regional audience: 'Australia's commitment to and involvement in the affairs of the region extend well beyond the political and the economic and the purely self-interested. Above all else, we do this because these are our friends and our neighbours' (Downer 1997).

Given the geographical proximity of Australia to Asia, and as an official 'neighbour' and 'friend', it is disappointing, though hardly surprising, that there has been a dearth of Australian films that have represented this connection in positive and enriching ways. Australian filmmakers have attempted to work through the anxieties of the national culture and its shifting sentiments, creating films that perform the ideological work of assuaging perceived national, political and economic anxieties regarding Australia's status and role as 'Asia's neighbour'. However, in dominant Anglo Australian portrayals over the last two and a half decades, the question of how to deal with Asia has often been answered unimaginatively with a reliance on death as providing the easy way out of having to sustain any deep or lasting commitment to Asia. Asians have largely been understood in the national cinema within a structure of sacrifice; that is, the deaths function symbolically in the creation of a coherent self-identity for those who witness it. In the repression or exclusion of difference, a perceived national identity and national cinema can find order and expression, and as Australia's nearest neighbour and friend Asia is most frequently, and conveniently, deployed as the excluded ground of this order.

What is further sacrificed in this schema are the national and cultural specificities involved in the category 'Asia', which becomes constructed as a homogeneous region despite differences within the various nations that constitute it. The examples discussed in this essay mark the limits of the dominant Anglo Australian cinematic discourse and the limits of the current imagination for social possibilities between Asia and Australia. It is this breakdown in dialogue, in ways of telling stories, that I want to examine.

During the early years of the filmic renaissance, Australia's engagement with Asia was most commonly explored in the situation of Australians in Asia, rather than representing Asians in Australia. In these scenarios, Australians are able to interact with Asian 'natives' before returning safely home. Asia is figured as something 'out there', as Siew Keng Chua notes, rather than allowing 'Australianness to be inscribed with any kind of Asian ... subjectivity' (1993: 29). This traditional trope of the journey is the subject of two films a decade apart: Peter Weir's *The Year of Living Dangerously* (1982) and Stephen Wallace's *Turtle Beach* (1992). Both films define a bright Australian future against a violent, chaotic Southeast Asian present that threatens to destabilise what it means to be an 'Australian', both at home and abroad.

The Unmet Friend

Peter Weir's *The Year of Living Dangerously* is one of the first Australian films since the 1970s revival to centralise an Asian character. The film recounts a period of intense political turmoil in the history of Australia's nearest neighbour, Indonesia, and in particular the dying days of Sukarno's dictatorship in 1965. Mel Gibson plays Guy Hamilton, a journalist for the Australian Broadcasting Service (ABS) who has just arrived in Jakarta on his first foreign assignment. He soon gains the interest of a cameraman, Chinese Australian dwarf Billy Kwan (Linda Hunt), who senses a 'possibility' in him. Billy speculates, 'Could you be the unmet friend?' Billy supplies the voice-over to the film, framing the various relationships and events that take place, often under his own orchestration, but which ultimately fall outside of his control. With Billy's help Guy soon has access to the top political figures in Jakarta. Billy also introduces Guy to Jill Bryant (Sigourney Weaver), a British consular official, and the two become lovers. When Jill receives confidential information about an arms shipment to the Communists, she passes this information to Guy, hoping that he will leave the country with her and avoid the ensuing civil war. Guy instead uses the information for an exclusive story; he tells Billy: 'This is not just a story, it is *the* bloody story'. This act of betrayal costs him his relationship with Jill and his friendship with Billy. Disillusioned by all those around him, including his political hero Sukarno, Billy takes a banner to a hotel room window painted with the words 'Sukarno feed your people' as a parade car carrying the dictator rolls by. As with his spectacular run in *Gallipoli*—another film made by Weir a year prior to *The Year of Living Dangerously*—Gibson's character runs, this time to the Hotel Indonesia, but is unable to save his friend. Just as the deaths of the young men in Frank and Archie's battalion at Gallipoli was referred to as a sacrifice because their attack was the result of an ill-informed order in a battle they could not possibly win, so too is Billy's death a wasted effort: the banner is removed before Sukarno sees it. Billy's spectacular fall in front of the Hotel Indonesia is also sacrificial in that it is this act that leads to Guy's redemption.

Guy's redemption comes just in time. Indonesia, portrayed as a nation riven by conflict and corruption, provides the backdrop against which Guy's own internal conflicts can be worked out. His personal redemption provides a buffer against the fear that all Australians could potentially succumb to the vices of their Southeast

Asian neighbours. Guy relinquishes his precious news stories to the Indonesian officials at the airport, allowing them to destroy his recordings as he sneaks past them to board a flight to Europe carrying Jill. The film follows the conventions of the classical romance but, here, the future is not so clearly mapped for those who are left behind.

Billy's death provides the trigger to Guy's shift in values and he represents the voice of conscience among the community of foreign correspondents in Jakarta. His idealism, best captured in his Tolstoy-inspired mantra, 'What then must we do?', also registers an anxiety over the future. This future is represented in the film as the future of Indonesia most immediately, but is tied more broadly to the future of the Asian Australian relationship.[4] The 'regional partnership' that Australian governments have all sought to cultivate for economic reasons is precisely the kind of partnership Billy hoped to develop with Guy for far less tangible gains.

The first scene in the ABS newsroom, in which Billy offers Guy an interview with any Indonesian politician he wants, is significant in terms of the way it establishes the road to friendship and betrayal between the two men. Guy is seated at his desk, his back to the camera, and his shadow is projected against the wall like a figure in the *wayang kulit* or traditional Javanese shadow play introduced during the opening credits of the film.[5] The music, lighting and framing of this scene suggests that something ominous is about to happen: beads of sweat form on Guy in the tropical heat intercut with close-ups of water dripping from a leak; a creeping shadow appears as the camera moves slowly behind Guy and the door creaks open to reveal… Billy Kwan. In Weir's direction of this scene, Guy's initial fear or anxiety about being in Indonesia is embodied in his encounter with a Chinese Australian dwarf. Billy, as a go-between figure, most potently represents a threat to the notion of a stable national identity, corrupted by the influence of a chaotic, almost indecipherable Southeast Asia. When Guy later discovers that Billy keeps a file on him, he is immediately suspicious. Billy's response is cleverly disarming: 'You're just going to have to trust me, aren't you? We're a team. We even look alike. It's true. It's been noticed. We've got the same colour eyes'. Billy Kwan is both 'similar'—Chinese Australian and, therefore, also a kind of 'Australian'—and radically different, represented most immediately, and physically, by his short stature. Billy represents both an anxiety-inducing similarity and a radical otherness or difference that needs to be expelled.[6]

The newsroom scene sets up the true nature of the friendship between Billy and Guy, with Billy relinquishing his trust to Guy, an act that is never fully reciprocated. When Guy betrays Billy by using Jill's confidential information for the story, Billy is both distraught and angry: 'I made you see things, I gave you my trust. I created you'.

The growing friendship between Billy and Guy is represented by lines of dialogue that remind us of the fact that Guy is a storyteller, a man of words, with Billy functioning as his eyes and his conscience: 'We'll make a great team old man, you for the words, me for the pictures. I can be your eyes'. In his single-minded pursuit of his career, Guy fails to notice other things; when he says matter-of-factly to Billy, 'You're not a dwarf', Billy replies, 'That's what I like about you Guy. You don't care, do you? Or maybe you just don't see'.

It would be difficult *not* to notice the representation of Billy Kwan by American actress Linda Hunt. The use of a white woman to portray an Asian man is one of the most pernicious in contemporary Australian cinema, particularly as this is not attributable as a case of 'yellowface' but rather occupies a seminal role within Australia's cinematic history and furthermore earned Hunt an Academy Award. Despite the film's voice-over belonging to Billy, Australian audiences are encouraged to identify with Guy—for example, in the newsroom scene, the camera follows Guy's perceptions.[7] The film's use of the eyes as a metaphor for seeing the truth is pushed to its limits when, at the end of the film, Guy must risk losing one of his eyes before he is able to see clearly what is most important to him, having already lost Billy. It is Guy's journey to self-understanding and to seeing 'the truth' that is pursued in this film as *the* story to tell. This is also a gendered narrative; Billy is inherently feminised in his representation by Linda Hunt, but Guy's masculinity is never in question.

As agent and witness to Guy and Jill's romance, Billy can be sacrificed once he has fulfilled his purpose. In fact, an 'aberration' such as Billy *must* be killed off before Guy is able to return home to a white(r) Australia. Guy boards a plane carrying Jill, heading back to 'civilisation' and away from Asia. Guy's Indonesian newsroom assistant Kumar (Bembol Roco) embodies the great disparity between what Guy took from Asia and the relative comfort to which he now returns. Kumar says: 'Think of me, Guy, when you're sitting in some nice café in Europe. In my dreams, I'm always sitting at the table by the footpath, drinking coffee'. Asia becomes a flexible signifier, and 'Chinese' and 'Indonesian' are collapsed as the poor 'others' unable to offer the comforts of the West.

A Friend in Need

A decade after Weir's film, Australia's ambivalent political relationship to Asia is again tackled in Stephen Wallace's *Turtle Beach* (1992), based on a novel of the same name by Blanche D'Alpuget. The film engages with the enduring Antipodean concern with refugees and detention centres, but it does this safely off-shore again, this time in Malaysia.

In the late 1980s and early 1990s, Southeast Asia is still considered Australia's primary threat or 'problem' that needs to be dealt with. These two films were made prior to the rapid capitalist ascendancy of East Asia, which began to pose a new kind of (economic) threat.

The film *Turtle Beach* opens with a white Australian reporter, Judith Wilkes (Greta Scacchi) taking photographs in the midst of the 1969 race riots in Kuala Lumpur. The next cut brings the film forward ten years, with Judith back in Sydney and the mother of two young boys. As in Weir's film, *Turtle Beach* also establishes the main character as an Australian journalist who, despite claims for an investigative depth and interest in Asia beneath its exotic surface, ultimately displays only a gloss on it, with a tourist's gaze aimed solely at self-understanding.[8]

Ten years on from Judith's earlier assignment in Kuala Lumpur, Malaysia is now gripped by a 'refugee problem'. Thousands of Vietnamese boat-people arrive in Malaysia after the fall of Saigon, many landing on the shores of Turtle Beach. Before returning to Malaysia, Judith arranges to meet Lady Minou Hobday, the second wife of Sir Adrian Hobday, the Australian ambassador to Malaysia, and herself the President of the International Refugee Relief Committee. Class, sexuality and gender are collapsed onto the figure of Minou, a Vietnamese woman with three children who has married a much older man in a position of power. When Judith visits Minou in her Sydney hotel room, the background music is generically 'Oriental' as Minou drops her bathrobe, flashes Judith a cheeky smile and tells her to make herself comfortable. Minou is represented as pure sexuality, an Asian seductress in the most stereotypical of ways. This portrayal is reinforced by the inclusion of a later scene with Minou and Sir Adrian in which Minou also plays the Oriental sex kitten and whore, calling her much older husband 'Papa' and referring to herself as 'baby': 'You always protect me, Papa. I'm such a bad girl'. Judith experiences her own version of erotic Orientalism when she becomes involved with a South Asian man, Kanan (Art Malik) who teaches her to let go of some of her fears and prejudices about 'the Orient', only to take on others. Kanan is portrayed as slightly threatening but also thrilling in his dangerous difference; he dances with wild abandon at a religious festival where Judith witnesses cheek piercings and spirit possessions and struggles to let go of her own inhibitions. However, the specificities involved in the category 'Asia' are again disregarded by extending the same mysticism to South Asia as an exotic other.

When Judith and Minou meet again in Malaysia, they forge a friendship based on mutual need and benefit. Judith wants access to the story of the Vietnamese refugees in Malaysia; Minou needs her help in order to expose that story. When she is asked by Minou why she would bother to help, Judith repeats a line earlier uttered by Minou herself: 'No-one helps anyone unless they're getting something out of it'. Minou replies, 'Ah ha, a friend in need'. Significantly, the film makes this an exchange between women over the ground of motherhood (and for Judith, for a story *on* motherhood). Wallace establishes early in the film that Judith is not a good mother or, at least, is more dedicated to her career as a journalist than to the role of motherhood. She would rather leave her sons with her ex-husband to chase the story and, when one of her sons begs her to come home because he has chickenpox, she pleads with their father for a few more days in Malaysia, despite his threats for full custody. Judith begins to accompany Minou on her vigils at Turtle Beach, sharing Minou's hope that one day her own children will arrive by boat. In *Turtle Beach*, motherhood becomes the site for the battle over national identity, which becomes feminised in the process. Australia is portrayed as a land of wealth and abundance, promising a brighter future, while Malaysia is represented as the hysterical, primitive wild woman who will willingly abandon her own. The setting of Turtle Beach, as the last nesting ground of the green turtle, is significant—Minou tells Judith that turtles are terrible mothers, failing to protect their babies from birds and other prey.

On one of their trips to the beach Judith witnesses a brutal massacre of the Vietnamese refugees by the Malaysian villagers. When Minou's three children eventually arrive by boat, the villagers rush out again, ready to attack. Minou sacrifices herself by diverting the attention of the villagers until she drowns. Kanan, Minou's friend and Judith's lover, explains why the villagers won't attack this time: 'You Westerners know nothing about sacrifice... They'll go home and they'll pray the rich Chinese woman's soul will keep the others away. You call it self-sacrifice; it's a very noble act. Judith, they are happy with the sacrifice'.[9] She replies, 'God you talk a lot of crap'. Later, at a press conference, however, she echoes his words: 'It was an act of extreme sacrifice. It was the only way she could save [her children.] Minou Hobday was the bravest woman I've ever met'. After watching Minou sacrifice herself for her children on Turtle Beach, Judith is able to return to Australia with a better understanding of motherhood and an affirmed sense of Asian women as self-sacrificing creatures. In turn, she is able to become a better mother. With this sacrifice taking the place of the need for her own, Judith tells her ex-husband she will take the children out of boarding school and will buy them a bigger house with a yard. Disturbingly, the film restores 'rightful' maternity to the white woman through the sacrifice of the Asian woman, reasserting a gendered national identity with Asia as the pitiable counterpart to the Western mother. The film ends with a statistic that unfortunately rings hollow given the film's superficial treatment of the plight of refugees (and particularly when read in light of Australia's own highly contested policies and practice concerning refugees): 'In the world today, there are more than sixteen million refugees'. The film's sentiment more closely approximates another statement made by Minou to Judith: 'We're all dirty, even you. You profit from the boat people your own way. You've got your story now, haven't you?' As with Billy Kwan, the Asian character in this film is employed to function as the voice of morality, teaching their 'friends' important lessons that can only be driven home by the shock of death.

No Future

More recent Australian films about Asia have shifted their focus from social and political turmoil in Southeast Asia to explore relations with a highly modernised East Asia, particularly Japan. *Heaven's Burning* was made just prior to the 1997 currency crisis in Asia; films made after 2000 engage with an Asia that has been rebuilt economically, thus the figure of the Japanese tourist or businessman—with money and time to spend—appears with greater contemporary currency. There have been three Australian films produced in the last decade that explore the situation of a Japanese character in the Australian outback, that iconic national setting where Australian masculinity is tested to its limits. Two of these films will be discussed in the following sections: *Heaven's Burning* and *Japanese Story*, with a brief comparison made to the third, Clara Law's *The Goddess of 1967* (2000).

Craig Lahiff's *Heaven's Burning* opens with an extreme close-up of a woman's eye reflecting the neon lights of Sydney. To Midori (Youki Kudoh) who is planning to fake her own kidnapping and escape from her new husband Yukio (Kenji Isomura), it seems as though everyone is watching her; she looks up to find ubiquitous surveillance cameras following her every move and even a smile from one of the hotel staff in the elevator appears threatening. Midori's faked kidnapping inadvertently becomes real when she is taken hostage by two Afghani brothers Mahood (Robert Mammone) and Gullbuddin (Salvatore Coco) during a bungled bank robbery. The driver of their getaway car, Colin (Russell Crowe), steps in to save her when the brothers decide to kill her. Colin shoots Gullbuddin, accidentally killing him, and he and Midori are forced to run to escape retribution from Mahood and his father Boorjan (Gheorghiu). Also in pursuit of the pair are two policemen, Bishop (Anthony Phelan), and his young rookie Moffat (Matthew Dyktynski), and Midori's jilted husband Yukio, transformed by rage and shame from reserved businessman into a gun-toting, shaven-headed bikie. The film follows Colin and Midori's journey and developing love affair as they drive from Sydney, through the South Australian saltpans, back towards the beach.

The car is used as the main agent of action in the film and, as Meaghan Morris observes, throughout the history of Australian cinema the car has been deployed as a vehicle through which to think through notions of family and familial space that are often patriarchally structured, but also tied to the landscape and therefore 'naturalised' (Morris 2001). The car is linked to an Australian national identity that has historically been portrayed as masculine, popularised in the contemporary era by the figure of Mad Max. When Colin and Midori arrive at Colin's estranged father's house in the middle of the outback, he asks them what they are doing there. Midori replies, 'Travelling, you know… just travelling'. Like so many others before them, Midori and Colin are unlikely characters in an Australian road movie, reconfiguring the landscape by 'just travelling' through it.[10] The film incorporates many different kinds of 'Australians' and Australian families; however, it is the representation of its Japanese characters as the unassimilated Australians, heading for the beach, which seems most deserving of attention.

As an iconic Australian setting embedded deep in Australia's landscape mythology, the beach is both quotidian and sublime, but what happens when a film inserts Asians into the landscape? Where do Asians fit into Australia's myths of the landscape? In *Australian Cinema After Mabo*, Felicity Collins and Therese Davis (2004) argue that the film is one of the most 'internationally contaminated' in recent years (they borrow this term from Gibson 1988: 31). Jonathan Rayner also suggests that the car (and the genre of the road movie) signifies freedom and a social mobility that can be regarded as analogous to physical mobility. This in turn reflects an increasing internationalisation of the national cinema through imported genres, which are albeit localised (Rayner 2000: 149). Yukio tracks Colin and Midori down to that most time-honoured of outback social gatherings: a Bachelor and Spinsters Ball (a social gathering for youth held in the Australian outback typically involving dancing, drinking and sexual promiscuity). When Yukio pleads with Midori in Japanese, she replies to him in English: 'You don't know what love is'. The final, climactic scene is accompanied by the surging strains of Wagner's *Isolde's Liebestod*, German romanticism juxtaposed with the Australian beach. Despite this 'international contamination', the film is still very much located in the past and rooted in myths of the Australian landscape that are harsh and unforgiving, and that find difference intolerable. They are travelling, but not getting anywhere fast.

Various marginal characters, including a role played by Ray Barrett as Colin's father Cam, are employed to spout racist comments against the Japanese. Cam delivers an extended speech to Yukio on 'karma', warning him that one day Japan and all the 'little people' on its islands will be destroyed as retribution for their role in the Second World War. Ray Barrett has starred in several notable Australian films including Bruce Beresford's *Don's Party* (1976) and Fred Schepisi's *The Chant of Jimmy Blacksmith* (1978); in 2005, he was celebrated with a 'Lifetime Achievement Award' by the Australian Film Industry for his contribution to Australian cinema and television. Thus it is significant that it is Cam, played by the iconic Barrett, who delivers this racist speech to Yukio. Other anti-Japanese sentiments are delivered awkwardly, as when a truck driver in a petrol station diner grumbles to the rest of the patrons, 'Christ, I've never seen one without a camera before' or directs his comments to Colin instead, 'Naughty boy, you let standards slip by breeding with inferior races. And before you know it we'll be breeding half-wits and mongrels'. This fear over the future of Australia jars with the aspirations of those who have arrived in the country hoping to start a new life there. Midori tells Colin that she does not want to return to Japan because she has no future there. Her Japanese lover was supposed to meet her in Australia, and she recalls his words that 'would have a future here'. *Heaven's Burning* offers an extremely doubtful picture of the future of Asians in Australia. Midori's Japanese lover never arrives, and there are no happy endings for those who do make it.

Keeping in mind Morris' earlier comments on the masculinisation of Australian identity through the use of the 'family sedan', and Jonathan Rayner's further observations on the road movie's internationalisation of Australian cinema, it is significant that it is Midori who has final control of the wheels, driving towards the beach with Colin wounded in the seat beside her. For this out-of-place character, the car is her vehicle of action. She reaches the beach and takes her own life. Perhaps due to the excesses of this film (and Crowe's lacklustre performance), *Heaven's Burning* was both a box-office flop and a disappointment to the majority of critics. One of the very few lengthier articles on the film is by Felicity Collins (2000), who recounts that she was compelled to write about the film because she felt 'implicated' by its images of failed father-son connections, which reinscribed for her a (re-)constructed father-daughter relationship. While for Collins the last shot of the film belongs to the policeman Bishop, who is sitting and looking out at the beach as flames engulf Midori and Colin's car, it is a shot of similar length and the last from Midori's perspective that seems equally significant and that implicates me. This is the view from the inside of the overturned car—an upside-down view of the beach. This is Australia, the Antipodes, from a Japanese character's perspective, at the point before death. *Heaven's Burning* depicts one of the bleakest futures in Australian cinema as there is no redemption for any of the characters, just violence spinning out of control.

'People Die in This Country. Often. Lots of People, All the Time'.

Sue Brooks' *Japanese Story* re-activates myths of the Australian landscape, placing the setting of the film in the Pilbara region of northern Western Australia. Toni Collette plays Sandy Edwards, a geologist and partner in a small software company in Perth. She is requested by her colleague, Bill Baird (Matthew Dyktynski) to accompany Japanese businessman Tachibana Hiromitsu (Gotaro Tsunashima) on a visit to one of the iron ore mines in the north of the state since his father is an investor in their company. Sandy is immediately antagonistic: 'I'm not traipsing around the bloody desert with some Japanese prick who doesn't know his ass from his elbow and wants some glorified tour guide. I'm a geologist, not a bloody geisha!' She shows him around reluctantly and unenthusiastically but he insists on driving deeper into the country. When their Jeep gets trapped in the soft sand, they are forced to spend a cold night together under the stars. Thrown together under extreme conditions, the two begin an affair. Hiro's death in an accident brings about the film's emotional denouement. Sandy appears to come to a greater understanding about herself as well as her relationship to this foreign 'Other'. This is Sandy's 'Japanese story', as the film's promotional material tells us.[11]

The screenplay for *Japanese Story* originated from an idea first suggested by Sharon Connolly, the Head of Film Australia, a decade earlier. During its ten years in development, Alison Tilson's script has witnessed the numerous changes in Australia's political climate. However, despite this, the film presents a remarkably static view of Asian Australian relations. Felicity Collins' comments on the film's 'belatedness' are worth revisiting at length:

> Like *The Goddess of 1967* and *Heaven's Burning*, *Japanese Story* was conceived in the mid-1990s when the national agenda was dominated by heated debates over the republic, refugees, reconciliation, One Nation's anti-Asia stance, the report on the Stolen Generation, and the Mabo and Wik judgments on *terra nullius* and Native Title. However, *Japanese Story* was not released until after September 11, after the Bali bombing and the 'Coalition of the Willing's' war on Iraq. This belated release has created a time lag, producing an altered context for the reception of Australian films over the past two years. Many films conceived in the pre-September 11 era continue to address the inward-looking national agenda of the 1990s described above. Yet they have been released in the post-September 11 era, producing an odd effect of belatedness as filmmakers face the task of accompanying their finished films into a changed national and global context. The sense of an inward-looking gaze, despite the cross-cultural plot in *Japanese Story*, arises from its revival of familiar Australian landscapes (remote, desert, outback) and character types (brash,

laconic, independent) as the bedrock of an Australian identity based on white settler masculinity. In this regard, *Japanese Story* reprises an unmarked, Anglo-Celtic, rather than cosmopolitan or multicultural, concept of Australian-ness. (Collins 2003)

The film employs the figure of the Japanese tourist and businessman against which to define this static view of Australian national identity. The film's initial premise of cultural dislocation and transnationalism is not developed further after the opening sequence, which begins with a shot of a long, winding road as a car approaches. Inside the car, a Japanese man in a business suit listens to music by indigenous Australian band Yothu Yindi. All around are empty stretches of desert land. The Japanese man looks anxious, his brow furrowed, and he tightens his grip on the steering wheel. He decides to walk into the bush to take a photograph of himself using the self-timer on his camera.[12] When he returns to the car he changes the Yothu Yindi CD for some traditional Japanese music. Now, he loosens his shirt and drives off, away from the camera, leaving a trail of red dust. Apart from this opening sequence, Hiro's perspective is almost wiped from the film. He often appears puzzled, secretive, and audiences are given little indication of what he is feeling until after his death (and, even then, his feelings are only conveyed in a voice-over commentary as he reads a letter written to Sandy but which almost never makes it to her). The opening sequence was removed from the version of the film made for American release. As she discusses in the audio commentary accompanying the DVD, director Brooks felt that this opening would have been too confusing to an American audience; instead, Brooks made the decision to open the film from Sandy's point of view since it was really 'her movie', her story.

As with the figure of Guy Hamilton in *The Year of Living Dangerously*, the 'masculinised' Anglo Australian 'hero' in the film is represented by the character Sandy. Her masculinity, in the form of a self-sufficiency and capacity for action, comes at the expense of Hiro's. However, her gradual 'self-discovery' is implicitly linked to the formation of a national identity that is softer, more feminine in its openness to vulnerability, going some way towards a rethinking of purely masculinised Anglo Australian national identity.

To accomplish this, *Japanese Story* elicits audience identification with Sandy; we are invited to join her emotional journey and to experience our own 'Japanese story'. However, the fact that this journey is predicated on an affective relationship with two stereotypes ('brash, laconic' Australian and reserved Japanese businessman and tourist) seriously undercuts its cause. 'Journey films', where a character attempts to find him or herself by meeting an 'Other' along the way, can only be as interesting as that 'Other' is allowed to be. In this sense, the shallow, fetishised representation offered by the character Hiro does not aid what we might understand to be Sandy's journey of self-discovery. Hiro functions merely as a cipher for Sandy's own process of self-discovery and, like Billy Kwan in *The Year of Living Dangerously*, is conveniently eliminated once he has served his purpose.

Throughout most of the film, Hiro's only line is a conciliatory '*Hai*' ('yes'), unless he is commenting on how much space there is in Australia. At moments where the film attempts to be self-reflexive, by deriding Sandy's attempts at cultural or linguistic translation, it again falls into old traps. When Sandy is told that she has to accompany Hiro into the desert, she implores her best friend for advice: 'So, tell me about the Japs'. Unbelievable as her total ignorance may seem in a contemporary, educated Australian woman living in a major metropolitan city in Australia (and working as a geologist in the Japanese-dominated mining industry), Sandy endeavours to find out more about 'the Japs' through her intimate engagement with one of them. The first sex scene shows Hiro lying naked (presumably) under the bed sheets while Sandy puts on his pants and gets on top of him. The scene is yet another example within (Australian) cinema of the feminisation of the Asian man, so painfully obvious that it begs for a reading of some more complex form of gender play. Sue Brooks is not ignorant of the curiosity and confusion aroused by this scene and, in the director's commentary on the American-release DVD of the film, she answers the often-asked question of why Sandy would wear Hiro's pants with the comment, 'Why not?... Millions of miles from anywhere, people do strange things'. She adds that the scene 'speaks for itself', that 'it's transgressive, about crossing boundaries, about trust... [it is] a moment of madness, a moment of exploration, of intimacy, of crossing over into becoming one with him. To explain a set of reasons takes the magic out of it' (Brooks 2003).

Brooks' unwillingness to engage with the 'reasons' again marks the limits of the Anglo Australian discourse giving shape to Australian Asian relations. Asian self-representations have made some attempt to provide the answers, with varying degrees of nuance and success. Clara Law's *The Goddess of 1967*, for instance, is an ambitious attempt to complicate the notion of a singular Australian national identity. Many critics have drawn parallels between *Japanese Story* and *The Goddess of 1967*, and structurally the two films are very similar. In *Goddess*, Rose Byrne plays a blind Australian girl who convinces an eccentric Japanese man to travel across the country with her in search of her father. He agrees because he wants to buy the 1967 Citroen DS in the girl's possession, which is his reason for travelling to Australia. Again, the sex scene between the two characters is rendered as a site of 'connection', with Rose Byrne 'on top'. Cross-cultural exchange and understanding is made to be hetero-sexually resolvable, but only through a reconfiguration of gender relations applied to a hierarchy of race.[13]

However, Hiro is never active in his moments of intimacy with Sandy. Sandy always touches him (his face, his arms, his chest) and it is she who holds him while they are asleep in the bush. Hiro is the object of Sandy's gaze: she watches him towel off at the beach, not necessarily erotically, but with a curiosity that is penetrating. Hiro's objectification is further revealed in a slip made by Baird when he refers to Hiro as 'it' after his death: 'The consulate's shut so we won't be doing anything tonight to it... to him'. At this moment of reduction, Hiro's death is revealed as a sacrifice; no longer valued as a human being, his body is placed in the cooler of an outback petrol station. One scene in the film does attempt to recuperate a corporeal presence for Hiro: directly after his death at the billabong, Sandy attempts to haul Hiro's body into the back of the truck before driving back into town. It was then that the materiality of his body, as something physical and palpable, was portrayed. For once, he becomes a 'real' body, not just a fetishised representation, and we are made to feel the weight of that implication. It is a pity that he has to be dead for this to happen.

The second half of the film explores Sandy's grief and her coming to terms with feelings of guilt. Tellingly, the music playing during their first sexual encounter is the same as that used at the end of the film after Hiro has died.[14] This traditional Japanese music becomes almost anthemic for Sandy's emotional journey, the overpowering strains playing on the audience and reminding them that this is Sandy's 'Japanese story', where sacrifice and death are ineluctably tied to eroticism and sex. Collins and Davis also highlight the significance of Sandy's act of grieving, suggesting that *Japanese Story* 'bring[s] grief-work into the public sphere of Australian cinema as a way of overcoming historical amnesia' (2004: 174). The authors argue that collective mourning is one way of dealing with the aftershock of the Mabo decision (as a defining moment in Australia's history recorded through its cinema) and that public testimony and grief work is a way of engendering affect that can then lead to action. In *Japanese Story,* that task becomes 'how to turn Sandy's grief and guilt into an act of reparation' for the injustices experienced by Indigenous Australians (178). Although Hiro's death *is* in many ways symbolic, it also represents a significant and enduring breakdown in Asian Australian relations, which Collins and Davis fail to address in their analysis. Of the four examples discussed in this paper, all (apart from *Japanese Story*) are very public sacrifices. In *The Year of Living Dangerously,* Billy Kwan's fall is witnessed by the wealthy foreign patrons at the Hotel Indonesia; in *Turtle Beach,* Minou's drowning occurs not only in front of Judith Wilkes and the Malaysian villagers but also before the eyes of her own children; in *Heaven's Burning,* Midori and Colin's car burns up spectacularly at the beach before the two policemen in their pursuit. These sacrifices are all spectacles, needing to be witnessed in order for there to be redemption gained by those who experience it. What becomes public in *Japanese Story* is the grieving, the aftermath, which also provides the act of 'reparation' leading to redemption. However, this same space is never afforded to other Asian characters. They are not 'saved' by the act of grieving. For example, Hiro's wife Yukiko (Yumiko Tanaka) is not afforded any space for grieving (either publicly or privately); there is only one brief shot of her covering her face with her hands as her car drives away. She remains silently suffering ('inscrutable') and self-sacrificing, and her only line in the film is 'Thank you' (spoken in English) in response to Toni Collette's apology delivered in faltering Japanese. Sandy's redemption comes in the form of a letter handed to her by Yukiko, written by Hiro while he and Sandy were together. Hiro tells Sandy that during their time together his 'heart [was] open'. For both Hiro and Midori in *Heaven's Burning,* Australia and its wide open spaces allows for a new-found freedom which in turn allows their Australian counterparts to view the landscape of their own country through different eyes. Sandy's mother (Lynette Curran) cuts and pastes death notices from the newspaper into her scrapbook, reminding Sandy that 'death is a part of life'. Sandy returns to her mother's home to understand this 'universal' act of mourning. However, such glib 'universals' do not allow for a present, specific or inhabitable relationship between Australia and Asia. At the end of the film, Sandy is crying in the airport lounge as she watches a casket-shaped package being loaded onto the plane; Hiro is being returned to Japan like a faulty item or a bad import that was never welcome in the first place. The film speaks of a utopic vision for Asian Australian relations, where Asia is 'in' Australia, but Asians are not *of* Australia.

Japanese Story does very little to shift prevailing cultural stereotypes about the Japanese. Beautifully shot, the film is a more sophisticated version of the Australian films discussed earlier that have also emptied their Asian characters out onto the landscape only to have them disappear into all that space. In the four prominent Australian films discussed from the last two and a half decades, the Asian characters are 'sacrificed' for the sake of the white protagonists' emotional fulfillment, continuing a long tradition in Australian cinema whereby Asian characters are denied autonomy as characters on their own right.

The logic of sacrifice requires that difference be sacrificed so that order and identity can be attained. This is the foundation for so much of contemporary theory—from feminist philosophy to deconstruction to psychoanalysis—all of which are structured around sacrificial economies that suggest that order and identity are necessarily sacrificial. Is it possible to find a non-sacrificial order for Australian (national) identity and Australian (national) cinema, or to recognise difference rather than identity as the social bond; that is, to find ways of expressing rather than repressing difference? What would this mean for Australian cinema? There are exceptions to the sacrifice of Asian characters within Australian cinema, such as Solrun Hoaas's *Aya* (1990) based on the experiences of a Japanese war bride, although this paper has chosen to focus on more prominent examples, particularly those invested with the kind of 'star' power that can bring mainstream acceptance (again contributing to the *public* display of the sacrifice of their Asian characters). At a time when critics are decrying the sorry state of the Australian film industry, each year hopes are pinned on one or two breakout hits. *Japanese Story* was that hit in 2003, praised for 'reviving' the national cinema through a 'cross-cultural love story' amidst what was otherwise a dismal year of feature filmmaking. Two years later, 2005 rested its hopes on yet another story of cross-cultural relations: Rowan Woods' *Little Fish* (2005). The film is set in Cabramatta, near Sydney, where there is a large community of groups from the Vietnamese diaspora. It contains several Vietnamese characters, including Dustin Nguyen playing Cate Blanchett's boyfriend, who are 'assimilated' in ways that are *non*-sacrificial in their maintenance of difference (although the characters are still somewhat ghettoised in their Cabramatta surroundings).[15]

Little Fish shifts the previous setting of Asian Australian encounters from the outback to a more urban centre such as Cabramatta, charting, along a different axis, another movement in Anglo Australian anxieties about Asia and its people. What is now overriding are *urban* fears and anxieties, of terrorists, street gangs, and drug dealers. The shift from the outback to the urban centres, however, might also allow for greater dialogue between Asians and Australians and open up new possibilities and new relationships. *Little Fish* promises to portray the 'little stories', the everyday interactions, friendships and relationships that can be found in a 'neighbourhood' where there can be both 'maintenance' *and* 'change' in what Morris calls 'stories of contact' regarding Australia's cinematic engagement with Asia (Morris 1998).

Counter-representations are beginning to emerge as Asian Australian filmmakers begin making films about their own experiences, attending more to the specificities of what it means to be 'Asian' and the constituencies that comprise it. For example, there is Clara Law's *Floating Life* (1996), Tony Ayres' documentaries *Sadness* (1999) and *China Dolls* (1997), and most recently, Khoa Do's remarkable *The Finished People* (2003). It is no wonder that *Floating Life*, Australia's first subtitled film, ends with a pregnancy; a sign of hope and regeneration for the Asian diaspora in Australia amidst so much loss.[16]

These self-representations contribute to the modernity of an Asian Australian cinema that both supplements, yet remains distinct from, 'Australian national cinema' as the majority of writers on the topic have so far conceived of it.[17] At a time of rampant fear and panic, and increased border control against the threat of 'foreign invaders', the release of more 'Australian stories'—of all kinds—is not only welcome, but vital.

Notes

[1] 'Blackfellas' and 'whitefellas' refer to the indigenous inhabitants of Australia and to white settler colonists (and their descendants), respectively. The term 'digger' is used to denote an Australian war veteran while a 'bushman' represents those who live or work in outback or rural areas of Australia. The term 'wog' was originally used as a pejorative to refer Australians of Southern European or Middle Eastern ancestries but has been reclaimed by the communities themselves following successful television, stage and film productions by Greek-Australians using the term.

[2] Connecting death and sacrifice to eroticism, Bataille writes: 'It is common business of sacrifice to bring life and death into harmony, to give death the upsurge of life, life the momentousness and the vertigo of death opening on to the unknown. Here life is mingled with death, but simultaneously death is a sign of life, a way into the infinite...' (1986: 92).

[3] See Keating (2000) for Paul Keating's personal account of his years as Prime Minister and the policies concerning Asia that characterised his leadership.

[4] Although Billy Kwan is coded Chinese in the film, he is also very much linked to the local Javanese people, conversing to them in their native language and 'adopting' a Javanese woman and her child whom he cares for.

[5] For more on the symbolism of the wayang kulit, see Campbell (1994). When Billy explains the tradition of the wayang to Guy using his own puppets, Guy is established as the figure of the 'Prince', with Billy as the dwarf who will serve him.

[6] In his study on ritual violence, Rene Girard observed that sacrifice often becomes more meaningful when the victims bear some similarity to the sacrificing community (1972: 11). There can hardly be one closer than a neighbour or a friend.

[7] This would be true also for the majority of American audiences. In the film Guy is Australian American whereas in the Christopher Koch novel of the same name on which the film is based, Guy is Australian British. This change was no doubt affected in order to capture a larger North American audience, but it also adds a dimension of brashness and ambitiousness to Guy's character that is reminiscent of the lead actors from classical Hollywood romances from which the film derives some of its aesthetics.

[8] John Duigan's *Far East* (1982) also places an Australian journalist in Manila in the Philippines.

[9] Note that Kanan refers to Minou as 'the rich Chinese woman' although she is Vietnamese in the film. This slip in the dialogue again collapses ethnic distinctions into a generic 'Asianness' that is particularly striking in the Malaysian context where racial sensitivities continue to exist between the Malays, the Chinese and the Indians. The 1969 riots were a violent outbreak of these racial differences but this is only superficially foregrounded by opening the film with Judith amidst these riots.

[10] See for example Stephen Muecke (2001) on Philip Noyce's *Backroads* (1977). Muecke argues that the aesthetics of the film, in which a white Australian man and an indigenous Australian man drive through the Australian outback, allow spectators to make open-ended connections in 'the intervals between events', which are also moments of exchange.

[11] The film was a critical success and arguably the most lauded Australian feature of 2003. It won eight Australian Film Industry (AFI) awards and was also praised at international film festivals from Cannes to Toronto to Pusan. Toni Collette won Best Actress at the AFI Awards, the Independent Film Awards, and the Film Critics Circle of Australia Awards. Although Gotaro Tsunashima was nominated for Best Actor at several of the same festivals, he did not win any award.

[12] This is an echo of a similar scene that occurs at the beginning of Clara Law's *The Goddess of 1967*.

[13] Although the Japanese character in *Goddess* provides his Australian counterpart with some redemption, their relationship also brings about his own moral redemption and he is allowed to 'live'.

[14] For Georges Baitaille, the closest we come to an experience of sacrifice in contemporary life is in eroticism. Michael Richardson explains, 'Baitaille's linkage of sacrifice with eroticism may appear tendentious, for in eroticism there is no victim... Yet Bataille's perception asks us to consider not the outward forms that sacrifice takes, but rather the internal necessity to which it responds... [W]hat is offered up in a relationship between the two lovers is themselves— they mutually offer themselves to one another, give up their own identities, if only momentarily. It is experienced within us as a loss, though welcomed as such...' (Richardson 1998: 387). *Japanese Story* takes the relationship between eroticism and sacrifice (as death) to its literal extreme.

[15] Woods' film won Best Actor, Best Actress, Best Supporting Actress, Best Sound and Best Editing at the respective year's Australian Film Awards. It also won Best Box Office Achievement at the Independent Film Awards. As with the other films discussed, no Asian actors received any awards; Gotaro Tsunashima received only nominations, suggesting that these actors, and the roles they play, are still very much marginalised in status.

[16] In *Turtle Beach*, a mother is sacrificed. In *Heaven's Burning*, it is a bride. Billy Kwan represents an almost asexual dwarf: he loves Jill and asked her to marry him, but was rejected. Hiro is both a father and husband, although we do not see his children except a glimpse of a photograph. No Asian families are allowed to exist in these films, which constitutes another violent act of representation.

[17] See for example Dermody and Jacka (1987), O'Regan (1996), and Rayner (2000).

References

Ayres, T. (Director) *China Dolls*, 1997. Film.
——. (Director) *Sadness*, 1999. Film.
Bataille, G. *Eroticism, Death and Sensuality*. Trans. M. Dalwood. San Francisco: City Lights Books, 1986 (originally published as *L'Erotisme*, 1957).
Beresford, B. (Director) *Don's Party*, 1976. Film.
Brooks, S. (Director) *Japanese Story*, 2003. Film.
Campbell, F. 'Silver Screen, Shadow Play: The Tradition of the *Wayang Kulit* in *The Year of Living Dangerously*.' *Journal of Popular Culture* 28.1 (1994): 163–70.
Chua, S. K. 'Reel Neighbourly: The Construction of Southeast Asian Subjectivities.' *Media Information Australia* 70 (November 1993): 28–33.
Collins, F. '*Heaven's Burning* aka You Don't Know What Love Is.' (Craig Lahiff, 1997). *Senses of Cinema*, 2000 <http://www.sensesofcinema.com/contents/00/9/heaven.html> (accessed 28 January 2006).
——. *Japanese Story*: A Shift of Heart. *Senses of Cinema*, 2003 <http://www.sensesofcinema.com/contents/03/29/japanese_story.html> (accessed 28 January 2006).
Collins, F., and T. Davis. *Australian Cinema After Mabo*. Cambridge: Cambridge University Press, 2004.
Dermody, S., and E. Jacka. *The Screening of Australia: Anatomy of a Film Industry*. Sydney: Currency Press, 1987.
Do, K. (Director) *The Finished People*, 2003. Film.
Downer, A. *Australia, Asia and Globalisation*. Speech by the Hon. Alexander Downer MP, Minister for Foreign Affairs, to the Asia Society and AUSTCHAM, Hong Kong, 1997, 15 October, <http://www.dfat.gov.au/media/speeches/foreign/1997/austcham15october97.html> (accessed 28 January 2006).
Downer, A. and Fischer, T. *In the National Interest. Australian Government White Paper on Australia's Foreign and Trade Policy*, 1997, August, <http://www.dfat.gov.au/ini/> (accessed 28 January 2006).
Duigan, J. (Director) *Far East*, 1982. Film.
Gibson, R. 'Formative Landscapes.' *Back of Beyond: Discovering Australian Film and Television*. Ed. S. Murray. Sydney: Australian Film Commission, 1988. 20–32.
Girard, R. *Violence and the Sacred*. Trans. P. Gregory. Baltimore and London: The Johns Hopkins University Press, 1972.
Hanson, P. *Maiden Speech*, 1996, 10 September <http://www.nswonenation.com.au/parliamentryotherspeeches/paulinhansosnspeech.htm> (accessed 28 January 2006).
Hawke, R. J. L. *A Confident Australia*, The Inaugural Hawke Lecture. University of South Australia, 1998, 12 May, <http://www.hawkecentre.unisa.edu.au/speeches/lecture1.htm> (accessed 28 January 2006).
Hoass, S. (Director) *Aya*, 1990. Film.
Keating, P. *Engagement: Australia Faces the Asia Pacific*. Sydney: Pan Macmillan, 2000.
Lahiff, C. (Director) *Heaven's Burning*, 1997. Film.
Law, C. (Director) *Floating Life*, 1996. Film.
——. (Director) *The Goddess of 1967*, 2000. Film.
Miller, G. (Director) *40,000 Years of Dreaming: A Century of Australian Cinema*, 1997. Film.
Morris, M. 'White Panic, Or *Mad Max* and the Sublime.' *Trajectories: Inter-Asia Cultural Studies*. Ed. K. Chen.. London and New York: Routledge, 1998. 239–62.
——. 'Fate and the Family Sedan.'. *Senses of Cinema*, 2001 <http://www.sensesofcinema.com/contents/01/19/sedan.html> (accessed 28 January 2006).
Muecke, S. *Backroads*: From Identity to Interval. *Senses of Cinema*, 2001 <http://www.sensesofcinema.com/contents/01/17/backroads.html> (accessed 28 January 2006).

Noyce, P. (Director) *Backroads*, 1977. Film.
O'Regan, T. *Australian National Cinema*. London and New York: Routledge, 1996.
Rayner, J. *Contemporary Australian Cinema: An Introduction*. Manchester and New York: Manchester University Press, 2000.
Richardson, M. 'Seductions of the Impossible: Love, the Erotic and Sacrifice in Surrealist Discourse.' *Theory, Culture and Society* 15.3/4 (1998): 375–92.
Schepisi, F. (Director) *The Chant of Jimmy Blacksmith*, 1978. Film.
Wallace, S. (Director) *Turtle Beach*, 1992. Film.
Weir, P. (Director) *The Year of Living Dangerously*, 1982. Film.
Woods, R. (Director) *Little Fish*, 2005. Film.

'The Tyranny of Appearance': Chinese Australian Identities and the Politics of Difference

Carole Tan

Introduction

Literature located within the burgeoning field of Chinese Australian and Asian Australian studies highlights salient issues the descendants of Asian migrants face as a racialised minority living in dominant white Australia. This literature has often been inspired by a growing array of visual and textual narratives written and produced by multi-generational Asian Australians who explore what it means to be a gay/straight, male/female person of Chinese/Asian descent living in Australia (Ayres 1998, 1999, 2000; Chan 2000; Leong 2000; Shun Wah 1999; Wang 1998; Yang 1994, 1995, 1996). Emerging from this, Australian academics and scholars have begun to interrogate the construction of contemporary hybridised Asian Australian identities (see Ang et al. 2000); gendered representations of Asian Australian identities within Australian literature (Khoo 1999, 2003a, 2003b; Louie 2002; Louie and Low 2003; Tucker 2000); and the nature of identity politics Asian Australians are forced to engage in as a racialised minority within dominant white Australia (Ang 2000, 2001; Khoo 1999, 2001, 2003a, 2003b; Luke and Carrington 2000; Luke and Luke 1998, 1999). While these works are extremely valuable, there is still room for extensive research to be carried out in this field.

This essay seeks to contribute to this field by examining the racialised experiences of the descendants of the longest established Asian migrant community in Australia—the Chinese. Chinese migrants first began to arrive in Australia from the Pearl Delta region of South China in the mid-1800s. Although stringent immigration laws restricted the entry of Chinese to Australia under the White Australia policy (1901–1966), small numbers of Chinese migrants settled and established families in Australia leading to the development of an Australian-born Chinese community (Choi 1975; Fitzgerald 1997; Giese 1997). Using cultural studies approaches, this essay interrogates issues of race and identity facing the second, third and fourth generation descendants of these early Chinese migrants (henceforth referred to as 'multi-generational Chinese Australians'). Drawing on close analysis of oral history interviews and personal narratives, it investigates how multi-generational Chinese Australians negotiate their identities in response to encounters of 'difference' and 'Otherness' within mainstream Australian society.[1] In so doing, it seeks to draw attention to exclusionary mechanisms that continue to obstruct the complete acceptance of Chinese Australians as Australians despite rights of birth and citizenship, generational longevity and strong national and cultural identities grounded in Australia. At the same time it demonstrates how 'Chinese' (and 'Asian') identities become externally imposed on Chinese Australians, whether they like it or not, despite their attempts to create collective and individual identities of their own fashioning. Although the essay focuses exclusively on the experiences of one specific group within the wider Chinese and Asian Australian diasporic community, the issues it draws attention to are likely to resonate with more recent Chinese and Asian migrants who have arrived in Australia,[2] whose experiences are similarly shaped by race and racialisation processes operating in Australia (Ang 2001; Luke and Carrington 2000; Luke and Luke 1998).

While the perspectives presented within this essay cannot be said to represent the experiences of all Chinese/Asian Australians, they provide valuable insights into the nature of racialised processes operating within Australian society at the micro-sociological level of everyday life. In particular, they highlight the significant role of racial appearance and 'looks' in demarcating the boundaries between those who are unconditionally accepted as 'real' Australians, and those who are constituted as 'foreign' and forever cast beyond the pale of the Australian nation. Before looking more closely at the experiences of Chinese Australians as revealed within oral history interviews and personal narratives, it is pertinent to examine the role of race and the racialisation of 'looks' within discursive national boundary-making processes which seek to delimit membership of the Australian nation.

Race Matters

Although race only exists as a social construct, the ongoing power of race in ordering social relations and classifying, categorising, and designating the 'Other' has been well established (Ang 2001; Brah 1996; Gilroy 1998, 2000; Kibria 2000; Luke and Carrington 2000; Luke and Luke 1998; Mercer 1994; Pettman 1992, 1995; Stratton 1998; Tuan 1998; West 1990, 1994). Race studies suggest that the key to understanding the ongoing power of race in configuring power relations lies in the ineradicability of visible 'racial' markers (such as skin colour, hair type and eye shape) carried in the body (Brah 1996; Jackman 1994; Mercer 1994) and the genetic transfer of these markers across generations (Banton 1998; Gilroy 2000). Michael Banton (1998) suggests that the highly visible and ineradicable nature of racial 'difference' creates an ongoing problem for the descendants of racialised migrants who become bound by the same race categories as their parents despite their acculturation and assimilation into dominant society. This problem is exacerbated by racialisation processes that encode racial markers carried in the body with specific societal values and meanings (Kibria 2000; Mercer 1994). As a result, racial bodily markers become 'signs' and 'cues' that involuntarily give off information to others about various aspects of a person's identity (Kibria 2000: 78).

Asian American studies suggest that for people of Asian descent living in the United States, having 'Asian looks' (marked by phenotypical features such as skin colour, hair type and eye shape) serves as a 'cue' denoting perpetual 'foreignness' and 'Otherness' that precludes their unconditional acceptance as 'American' (Yamamoto 1999; Yu 2001). This essay proposes that the experiences of multi-generational Chinese Australians revealed within oral history interviews and personal narratives appear remarkably similar. While informants carry strong national and cultural identities grounded in Australia, they continually encounter challenges to the legitimacy of their 'Australianness' on account of their 'Asian looks' that give rise to 'assumptions of foreignness' (Tuan 1998) and the permanent fixing of informants' identities in 'another place' outside of Australia.

Australian scholar Fiona Nicoll provides insights into the nature of these racialising processes in her work *From Diggers to Dragqueens: Configurations of Australian National Identity* (2001). In this volume Nicoll describes the 'metonymic fusion of race, face and nation' (131) within Australian discourse as a result of 'whiteness' and 'Australianness' being viewed as synonymous. Consequently, Nicoll proposes, people of non-white, non-Anglo Celtic stock living in Australia become subject to racialisation—or 'facialisation' as she prefers to call it—as 'foreign' and 'un-

Australian', on account of the fact that they do not visibly 'fit' the image of a 'real' Australian. In *Race Daze* (1998), Jon Stratton makes a similar point, arguing that it is easier for a new migrant of white Anglo-Celtic stock to be accepted as a 'real' Australian than it is for a person of Asian descent whose family has lived in Australia for generations. This is due, he suggests, to 'Asian-looking' people looking 'different' from the popular image of a 'real Aussie', who is typically white. The insidious effects of 'facialisation'/racialisation on people of Chinese descent in Australia is referred to as 'the tyranny of appearance' by William Yang (1994: 90) and 'the corporeal malediction of Chineseness' by Ien Ang (2001: 28). The way in which these differential processes have shaped and moulded the diverse experiences of other Chinese Australians and their struggle to gain acceptance as Australians is explored below.

'Where Are You From?'

Oral history interviews and personal narratives reveal that one of the most common ways informants have experienced the legitimacy of their 'Australianness' being called into question, has occurred in social encounters with Anglo Australians who ask the ubiquitous question 'Where are you from?'[3] While this question may be well intended and appear harmless, it represents an 'assumption of foreignness' by the inquirer, who assumes that since informants *look* 'Chinese' and/or 'Asian', they must be foreign to Australia.[4]

A clear example illustrating this is provided in an account by Robyn On,[5] a (4, 2)[6] generation Chinese Australian, who speaks about her experiences as a university student in Perth, Western Australia, during the 1980s. Having moved from Darwin in the Northern Territory to complete her studies, Robyn recalls that it was in Perth that she first experienced her 'Australianness' being challenged ostensibly because of her Chinese 'looks' and the assumption that she was 'foreign'. She ascribes this to the wide acceptance of racial and cultural diversity in Darwin[7] whereas Perth's predominantly white population was still coming to terms with the arrival of 'new' Asian immigrants. One of the results of this was that people of Chinese and Asian descent in Perth were often regarded as a source of curiosity for white Australians. Robyn recalls how this curiosity resulted in her constantly being questioned about her 'nationality'. She notes:

> When someone says what nationality are you, I can only say Australian, because I was born here. But they'll go, 'No, but where were you born?' And I go 'Darwin'. 'Well, where were your parents born?' And I go 'Well, my dad was born in Katherine, my great-grandparents were born in Pine Creek'. They go 'No, no, no. Where did they originally come from?' I'm going, 'Oh, you mean what's my cultural background?' And they go, 'Yeah, okay'. They do it all the time.[8]

As demonstrated here, despite the fact that Robyn can trace her Australian heritage back four generations to when her great-great-grandparents arrived in Australia in the late 1800s, her claims to 'Australianness' are not readily accepted by white Australians who insist she must be from 'another place'. Robyn describes the sense of frustration she experiences as a result of her 'Australianness' continually being called into question by others, particularly when she recognises the probability that their families are likely to have migrated to Australia more recently than her own.

Lyn Fong, a (3, 3) generation Chinese Australian who currently works as a doctor in Queanbeyan, also finds being constantly questioned about where she is from a source of annoyance and frustration. She observes:

> For most Australians an Asian person or a Chinese person is unfamiliar, strange, people from a strange culture and something very alien to Australia. So when people would speak to me and say, you know, 'Where are you from?' that used to incense me. And I thought, 'What are you talking about?', you know, 'I'm as Australian as you'. So I felt quite hurt that even though you [sic] were born in Australia, people keep asking you [sic] where you are from. And then it finally dawned on me what they were trying to say. Because I was thinking 'Where are you from? Where else could I be from—Mars?' And then it dawned on me that they were really talking about being Chinese. So you must be Chinese or you are from China.[9]

Lyn's account demonstrates the assumed connection between 'looks' and 'place of origin' within Australian popular discourse, which results in the identities of Chinese Australians being perpetually fixed in China and/or Asia. Lyn described the insidious effects of this practice on her own life, recounting several racist encounters she experienced as a result of the assumption that she is a 'foreigner'. On one occasion, for instance, Lyn's neighbour yelled out across the fence: 'Why don't you people go back to wherever you are from?' On another occasion Lyn recalls:

> I can remember walking across a street in Sydney, Elizabeth Street—and I was almost at a crossing and the light had changed so I was just stuck there. So there were people crossing the road and these boys just said something like, you know, 'Asians out!' and were shouting at me. It's really tragic. This was extremely hurtful and I also felt it was dangerous. You know, had this been in the evening or at night these people would have been quite capable of attacking a person they don't know...[10]

Lyn recounts that not long after this incident, a person of Asian descent was actually beaten up in nearby Hyde Park. This, she felt, justified her sense of vulnerability and wariness when walking Sydney streets, believing that her 'foreign looks' mark her out as a target of anti-Asian sentiment and racism.[11] Lyn suggests that this problem has become aggravated in recent years as a result of Pauline Hanson's comments concerning Asians in Australia.[12] For Lyn, this has been a painful time, which has shaken her unconditional sense of belonging to Australia and forced her to confront her Chineseness in new ways.

In considering Lyn's and Robyn's experiences, it is pertinent to note that what they found most disturbing, frustrating, and hurtful is that, despite rights of birth, generational longevity, and strong national and cultural identities and identifications firmly grounded in Australia, their claims to Australianness are not readily accepted as valid or legitimate by white Australians. Instead, regardless of whether or not they identify as 'Chinese' and/or 'Asian', their identities become 'spatially incarcerated' (Jackman 1994: 107) in China and Asia. Although oral history accounts and personal narratives indicate that not all informants interpret the question 'Where you are from?' as an affront to their Australianness (many simply viewing this as a result of 'ignorance'), the assumption that Chinese Australians are 'foreign' and 'un-Australian' has significant ramifications for all people of Chinese/Asian descent in Australia. Evidence of this is found in the volume *On Not Speaking Chinese: Living between Asia and the West* by Ien Ang (2001), where Ang notes the 'dangerous quandary' of being 'yellow' and having "slanted eyes" (28–29) places Chinese Australians in due to the collective racialisation of people of Asian descent in Australia who become 'lumped' together as 'one and the same'. As will be shown in the discussion below, this process has had important implications for multi-generational Chinese Australians, who are frequently mistaken as tourists or 'new' migrants, despite their birth and generational longevity in Australia.

Mistaken Identities

Oral history accounts and personal narratives reveal that while being mistaken as a tourist or a 'new' migrant may seem innocuous, at times informants have found themselves implicated in community tensions and public hostility towards other Asian groups simply on account of their 'Asian looks'. For example, while informants are commonly thought to be 'new Asian migrants'[13] to Australia, at various times they have also been mistaken to be Japanese and/or Vietnamese. Although encounters in which informants are mistaken in this way are often harmless, on occasions when Japanese and Vietnamese have been the focus of heightened tensions within the Australian community, it has at times led to informants becoming targets of racism. While examples illustrating these aspects are provided below, it is interesting to note the frequent slippage that occurs between specific categories such as 'Japanese', 'Vietnamese', and 'Chinese' and the broad category of 'Asian', as informants themselves inadvertently switch between these terms.

In considering the processes through which Chinese Australians are mistaken to be from 'somewhere else' and confused with other Asian groups in Australia, it is pertinent to note that while these experiences may have become more frequent as a result of recent Asian immigration to Australia, they are not completely new. Even during the Second World War, for example, it was possible for people of Chinese descent in Australia to be mistaken as Japanese (for example, see Fitzgerald 1997: 141). An interesting example illustrating this is provided in a captivating story that was recounted in an informal dinner conversation with Ben and Vincent Wong Hoy, two elderly gentlemen who live in Cairns, Northern Queensland.

Ben and Vincent recount an incident that took place at a time when many Australians believed Japanese troops would almost inevitably invade North Australia. They tell the story of how one day they were riding their motorbikes up to the Atherton Tableland when suddenly they were accosted by a group of locals. Although they were naturally bewildered by what was happening, Ben and Vincent soon discovered that locals thought they were 'Japanese invaders' who had to be stopped and restrained. Fortunately, it did not take long for Ben and Vincent to be set free since their broad 'Aussie' accents clearly demonstrated that they were not Japanese. This story was recounted with a great deal of humour and shows the bemusement Chinese Australians often feel when they are mistaken to be 'foreigners' in the land of their birth. Nevertheless, it also provides an example of the dangerous quandary Chinese Australians have been placed in at times on account of looking 'Asian'.

Informants' recollections of more recent encounters in which they are mistaken as Japanese often take place in locations that attract a lot of Japanese tourists. For example, several informants recollect occasions when they were approached by strangers (mostly of Anglo-Celtic descent) and spoken to v-e-r-y s-l-o-w-l-y in v-e-r-y s-i-m-p-l-e English. For example, Robyn Lee Long, a (2, 3) generation Chinese Australian, recounts an incident that took place when she was a schoolteacher in Cairns and was taking her class on a trip to Green Island. Robyn describes at one point having to locate a missing student, and notes:

> So I was walking along the wharf trying to find this lost child to mark him off on my roll and the [tour group] hostess came and said [very slowly] 'M-a-y I h-e-l-p y-o-u?' And I thought, 'What am I going to say?' And she said, 'A-r-e y-o-u g-o-i-n-g to G-r-e-e-n I-s-l-a-n-d or F-i-t-z-r-o-y?' And I couldn't stop laughing. And she was looking at me really strangely. And I said 'I'm a school teacher and I've lost one of my students'. And she said, 'Oh, good luck to you'.[14]

Robyn explains the assumption that she was 'foreign', saying:

> [H]ere in Cairns, people pass everybody as 'Asian' basically. And then... because the Japanese are such good tourists—they assume that you must be Japanese. So they just treat you like that.[15]

Although Robyn and other informants generally responded to such incidents with good humour, at times they express frustration that others should immediately assume they are 'foreign' on account of their 'looks'. They also object to the patronising responses of inquirers who, upon discovering informants speak perfect English, proceed to compliment them on speaking '*so well*'. Although these kinds of encounters may appear innocuous, the fact that informants' 'looks' continue to be 'read' as a sign of 'un-Australianness' and 'foreignness' has significant ramifications on their everyday lives. These encounters are particularly significant as visible ineradicable 'racial' markers they carry in their bodies, which mark them out as 'different' and 'Other' within mainstream Australian society, force informants to confront Chineseness (and Asianness) as an undeniable 'fact' or 'reality' in their lives.

Moreover, these encounters serve to destabilise and subvert informants' unconditional sense of belonging in Australia while they become tired of continually being expected to 'prove' the legitimacy of their claims.

In addition to the ostensibly harmless (but nonetheless powerful) ways being mistaken as Japanese impacts on informants, these encounters can also have traumatic and disturbing effects. This is particularly the case when being mistaken as Japanese or a new Asian migrant marks informants out as targets of racism. For example, Annette Shun Wah, a (3, 2) generation Chinese Australian who is a well-known radio and TV presenter, recollects several racist incidents she encountered in Sydney in the mid-1980s. Annette notes:

> Around 1986 I had a couple of quite racist incidents happen to me. There was a really strong anti-Asian sentiment at the time, partly because of this sort of anti-Japanese thing that was happening in Queensland, the Japanese buying up a lot of the real estate... [S]o for the first time I was faced with really bitter, hateful racist comments...[16]

Annette also describes an incident that took place when she and her boyfriend were waiting in her car at some pedestrian lights in the city. She observes:

> I don't know if I'd sort of had a bit of a peck on the cheek from him or something and I had my hair really short so maybe I looked like a boy. These skinheads walked past and said 'Asian poofters'... and I was mortally offended. One, that they thought I was a boy and two, you know, that they took exception to the fact that I was Asian...[17]

Annette found these incidents shocking and disturbing, particularly as they were totally unprovoked. Furthermore, while Annette identifies strongly as 'Australian', these racist encounters confronted her with the highly visible and ineradicable nature of her Chineseness on account of phenotype and 'looks'. Annette's account also demonstrates the complex entanglement between race, gender and sexuality (Anthias and Yuval-Davis 1992; Brah 1996) within Australian discourse. For Annette's appearance marked her out not only as 'foreign' and 'undesirable', but also as 'gay'. Although this was a case of mistaken identities, Annette's account illustrates the doubly precarious position of homosexuals who are marked by race within mainstream Australian society. This is reiterated in the work of William Yang (1996) and other queer Chinese Australians such as Tony Ayres (1999, 2000) and Greg Leong (2000, 2002), who draw attention to the sexualised nature of racialised processes and practices operating in Australia.

Lyn Fong's account provides a further illustration of how being mistaken as Japanese can cause informants to become targets of racism. In describing some of the racist incidents she has encountered as an adult (some of which have been noted earlier), Lyn notes concerns she holds about appearing in public on Anzac Day precisely because her 'looks' could lead to her being mistaken as Japanese. In explanation of this, Lyn observes:

> [O]f course, Anzac Day doesn't in reality represent anything that's racist... It's really something about peace... But on a superficial level, things like Anzac Day can be periods of hostility. Like, a lot of Chinese, including myself, would be very cautious to even walk on the streets during times like Anzac Day. Why should that be? Why should I feel that I shouldn't be as evident on that day or as upfront about, you know, being an Australian? It's because there are people who say, 'Well we fought you during the War'. And we say, 'Who did you fight during the War? You mean the Japanese? I'm not Japanese'. 'Oh sorry'. This kind of conversation. It's just pathetic. Even if I were Japanese... what difference should it make? So I know that mistaken identity or not it really represents a kind of racist undercurrent that's always there.[18]

Lyn's account not only demonstrates ongoing hostility towards Japan within some sectors of Australian society, but also illustrates the lack of public awareness and recognition of the personal sacrifices made by Chinese Australians, who contributed to the defense of Australia during the Second World War (see Giese 1999; Loh 1995; Loh and Winternitz 1989). It also demonstrates that the collective racialisation of people of Asian descent in Australia can have harsh effects on the lives of Chinese Australians when they become the scapegoats of public hostility toward other Asian groups.

This is further demonstrated in oral history accounts and personal narratives that describe racist encounters informants have experienced as a result of being mistaken as Vietnamese. For example, Ernie, a (3, 3) generation Chinese Australian from Darwin, notes:

> [T]he Vietnamese, I think, have created a problem for us. Now, I've got nothing against Vietnamese, right. They're very hard working people... But I can remember down the casino... I was just going to the bar to get a drink and here's this bloke about thirty years old, mumbling to me that I should 'go home', 'Vietnamese slope', ra, ra, ra. And I had to grab him by the throat and say, in good plain Australian English, that I am not a Vietnamese slope and I live in this country and have probably been here longer than him...[19]

In talking about this and other racist encounters he and other family members have encountered, Ernie remarks that while people who know him personally accept him as an 'Aussie', those who do not know him always treat him by the colour of his skin. Hence Ernie declares, 'I can live in this country for five hundred years... but I'll always be Chinese'.[20] Ernie notes that this is not because he himself identifies strongly as Chinese but because of the ineradicability of his 'Chinese looks'.

Robyn Lee Long's account provides a further illustration of how Chinese Australians become the targets of racism towards Vietnamese. Recollecting some of her experiences as a schoolteacher, Robyn notes several occasions when parents explicitly asked that she not be allowed to teach their children because she was 'Asian'. She remarks:

> I was surprised at that. I really had thought that racism was on the way out but there were just these few people who'd just say things like that. You know, 'My

husband fought in Vietnam so therefore I don't want my child being taught by an Asian'—things like that.[21]

Besides Chinese Australians becoming the scapegoat of public hostility towards Vietnamese, oral history accounts and personal narratives reveal concerns that the Vietnamese presence jeopardises the already tenuous position of multi-generational Chinese Australians. For example, Daryl, a (4, 4) generation Chinese Australian from Darwin, comments:

> A lot of bad things do come from this Asian immigration. We [Chinese Australians] feel the effects of the bad things that come from it, because we are tarred with the same brush... For instance, if you look at the situation in Cabramatta at the moment with the Vietnamese... They haven't assimilated very well with the rest of the community. They have their gangs. They bring all of their fighting with them... [Interviewer: And you feel that the stigmatisation of them passes over into the older communities?] Exactly—that's right.[22]

Interestingly, Daryl's account reflects popular images of Vietnamese refugees circulating within mainstream Australian society that stereotype Vietnamese as prone to violence and crime. In talking about the 'problem' of Vietnamese in Australia, Daryl also refers to the 'handouts' Vietnamese received from the government, which provided them with housing and social security benefits, mirroring negative stereotypes of Vietnamese refugees as poor, unemployed, and a drain on the Australian government and people.[23] Concomitantly, Daryl's comments mirror concerns within the Chinese Australian community that Chinese Australians become 'tarred with the same brush' as Vietnamese newcomers. This was seen to jeopardise the already fragile acceptance and tolerance the descendants of early Chinese migrants have worked so hard to achieve within mainstream Australian society (compare Fitzgerald 1997: 154).

While on the one hand multi-generational Chinese Australians become targets of racism towards Vietnamese on the basis of negative stereotypes outlined above, they also become ambivalently and contradictorily constituted in accordance with class stereotypes of 'new' Chinese and Asian migrants to Australia. In contrast to Vietnamese refugees and migrants who are perceived to be very poor, 'new' Chinese and Asian migrants are perceived as being extremely wealthy and 'successful'.[24] As Ernie Chin observes:

> They look at a Chinese or an Asian [and] say, 'Oh, that bastard's got more money than me'... [or] 'You Chinamen have always got money'... They all think we're rich.[25]

These ambivalent and contradictory stereotypes constituting 'Asians' in Australia as both poor and dependent and incredibly rich and 'successful' ultimately have similar outcomes—in both instances they constitute Asians as 'undesirable' and a threat to the social and economic well-being of white Australians.

These accounts demonstrate how ineradicable racialised markers carried in the body, embodied by 'Asian looks', become imbued with a range of societal meanings and associations signifying not only 'foreignness' but also 'undesirability'. Furthermore, as a result of collective racialisation and the homogenisation of all 'Asian-looking people' as 'one and the same' (Ang 2001), Chinese Australians find that their already tenuous position within mainstream Australian society has become further attenuated as they become the target of community tensions, hostility and racism towards more recent Asian arrivals in Australia.

Chinese Australian Responses

Here it is pertinent to look at various ways multi-generational Chinese Australians have responded to racialising processes, which perpetually cast them as 'foreign' and 'un-Australian'. As the voices of Chinese Australians represented below clearly demonstrate, informants are not afraid to stand up for their rights and actively assert the legitimacy of their claims to be recognised as bona fide Australians in the land of their birth. Oral history accounts and personal narratives indicate that informants have done this in several ways.

One of the ways some informants have responded to encounters where they feel their Australian identities are called into question, is by resolutely refusing to fit into the 'box' others seek to place them in on account of difference. Robyn On notes:

> I think I gave up a few years ago trying to fit into a box—because people ask me this question all the time. 'So where do you think you fit then?' And I go, 'Well I don't need to fit any more'. There doesn't need to be a special little box for me to say that this is what I am. I don't need to have that little box any more. Because I don't think there is one that you can fit perfectly into—because everybody's different anyway. So whether I am Chinese or whether I'm Australian I am still going to be different to the next person that I'm sitting next to. I don't feel the need now to try and decide whether I'm Chinese or Australian, or Chinese Australian or whatever.[26]

Adam Lowe, a (3, 2) generation Chinese Australian from Darwin, expresses a similar response, observing:

> I think that in some ways, in some instances, being Chinese made me dare to be different. Not that I was trying to show any superiority or that. But I guess I was trying to say, 'Well, I'm just as good as anybody else. And all I ask is that I be treated with the same level of respect as everybody else in this room'. I don't make any pretensions that I am better because I am Chinese, and on the other hand, I never have the attitude of 'poor bugger me' because I am Chinese, you know. I just look other people in the eye and say, 'Well, here I am, take me for what I am'.[27]

While Robyn and Adam responded to attempts to 'pigeon-hole' their identities by 'daring to be different', other informants choose to interpret challenges to their

'Australianness' as a reflection of ignorance and narrow-mindedness. Annette Low, a (2, 2) Chinese Australian who lives in Townsville, North Queensland, says:

> I feel that if any one makes a racial remark or mistakes you for something else it's only because they don't know any better. People who are educated, or who travel, know better. But people like that don't know any better so there's no point wasting your time.[28]

Daryl Chin holds a similar view, remarking:

> My attitude is that I feel sorry for them. They are ignorant, they're not aware of the situation—so I feel sorry for them… Let's face it… as Australians… we're a nation of immigrants anyway. And myself, I say our family has been here longer than a lot of the Anglo immigrants. So who are they to say they are more Australian than I am?[29]

The 'situation' Daryl refers to in this account concerns the longstanding nature of the Chinese Australian community as the descendants of early Chinese migrants to Australia which, if fully recognised and acknowledged, would give Chinese Australians more status as Australians than more recent migrants to Australia from white Anglo-Celtic backgrounds. From Daryl's point of view, however, 'ignorance' and 'lack of awareness' allows these later arrivals to Australia to think they are the 'real' Australians while Chinese Australians continue to be cast as 'foreign' and 'un-Australian'.

Such views are widely held within the Chinese Australian community. This has led to some informants being resolutely determined to challenge and subvert the ignorance and narrow-mindedness of others. For example, Elizabeth Chin Seet, a (4, 4) generation Chinese Australian from Darwin, is very assertive about her right to belong in Australia. Furthermore, she is not afraid to openly challenge others' attempts to judge her on face value as 'Chinese' and therefore 'foreign' and 'un-Australian'. She notes:

> [O]ccasionally in the street, if people would call out names or tell you [sic] to go back where you [sic] came from, I'd just turn around and say, 'Well, I've been here a lot longer than you, why don't *you* go back?' And that quickly stops them short because I think, one, they don't expect an innocent-looking Chinese person to turn around and abuse them back, and two, with a very valid argument.[30]

Some Chinese Australians are also keen to 'educate' the wider Australian community regarding the longstanding nature of the Chinese Australian community and the contributions early Chinese migrants and their descendants have made to Australian life. Lyn Fong states:

> I am Australian, so the fact that my fellow-Australians are racist or have racist notions—you know, that's not just a static state. I can contribute to that. I can say to them, 'What are you talking about? You're really right off the air. We have been here as long as you have' and so on. Of course you can't fight with people in the

street—it's not worth wasting your breath. But in terms of your own life, in your own profession, in your education, you know, with fellow students, you can change people. You can talk about being Chinese. And I think part of that desire to research my own family history is to be able to prove their contribution to Australia and to write about it and for them to have some acknowledgment of Chinese in Australia. You know, if they are outstanding people, which I believe they are, then that's a story worth telling. So in a way I think that we as Chinese in Australia we can contribute to the formation of the Australian identity. It's time that some of it was questioned.[31]

The accounts above demonstrate some of the passive and assertive responses informants exhibit in dealing with racism they interpret as a result of 'ignorance' and a 'lack of awareness' of the long-standing establishment of the Chinese Australian community to which they belong.

In some cases, however, informants have responded in more aggressive and volatile ways to racism they and other family members have encountered. Ernie Chin describes the rage he experienced when a stranger at a pub where Ernie had taken the family to eat called his twelve-year-old son a 'slope'. He says:

> I didn't think I'd feel the sort of anger that I would feel. I mean, here was my son twelve years old telling me some adult person was calling him a slope and he was only a kid and picking on him. I walked over to the table and there was about eight guys sitting there... [a]ll bikie types and one guy wearing a cowboy hat and a patch on his eye. And I didn't even look at the other fellows. I walked up to this bloke and I just slapped him right across the back of the head. You know, just bang. I just slapped him with the back of my hand. He jumped up and he said, 'What's going on?' I said, 'Listen, mate, I'm a slope... The young fellow with me is a slope too... But I'm a man... You call *me* a slope and see what happens'. Well, I just lost my temper... [and] slammed his face into the dishful of bloody salad... The whole pub came to a standstill.[32]

These responses demonstrate the open assertiveness of Chinese Australians who tenaciously defend their right to be accepted as 'real' Australians and not only challenge racism, but also actively seek to redefine the boundaries of 'Australianness' in an effort to have their claims to Australianness recognised and validated.

Conclusion

This essay has demonstrated the 'tyrannising' power of race and 'looks' in not only shaping the experiences and identities of multi-generational Chinese Australians, but also obstructing their unconditional acceptance as 'real' Australians within mainstream society. This tyrannising power stems from the conflation of 'race, face and nation' within Australian discourse in which 'whiteness' and 'Australianness' are seen as synonymous and 'Asian looks' become invested with notions of 'foreignness' and 'un-Australianness'. As a result, regardless of rights of birth and citizenship, generational longevity and strong national and cultural identities grounded in Australia, and regardless of whether they willingly choose to identify as Chinese (or Asian) or not, multi-generational Chinese Australians find their identities are permanently incarcerated in China (and Asia) while their claims to Australianness are constantly challenged and invalidated.

The ramifications of this are significant, particularly, as has been seen, when it leads to Chinese Australians becoming targets of hostility and racism. Additionally, oral history interviews and personal narratives indicate that even while multi-generational Chinese Australians unequivocally consider Australia to be 'home', failure to find complete and acceptance within Australian society can unsettle their sense of national belonging and cause them to set out in search of their 'Chinese roots'.[33] Nevertheless, as this essay has sought to demonstrate, Chinese Australians continue openly to assert their rights to gain recognition as Australians and strive to push back the boundaries of racism and exclusion that circumscribe their lives. If they are to be successful, however, it is imperative that the boundaries of the Australian nation be extended and made more inclusive so that *all* national citizens can find unconditional acceptance as 'real' Australians regardless of racial and cultural background or appearance. Only once this transformation has occurred can Australia be justified in calling itself a 'multicultural' nation.

Notes

[1] Although this essay focuses specifically on issues of race and identity that informants experience within mainstream (white) Australian society, my other work further examines these issues within the context of Chinese diasporic spaces that informants inhabit (including the family and the wider diasporic Chinese community). See Tan (2004).

[2] Following the abolition of the White Australia policy and the relaxation of immigration restrictions in the 1970s, increasing numbers of Asian migrants began to arrive in Australia from Taiwan, Hong Kong, mainland China, Malaysia and Singapore as well as parts of Southeast Asia.

[3] Compare Thomas (1999) and Ang (2001) who also make mention of the ubiquitous nature of this question and its effects on individuals from non-white non-Anglo-Celtic backgrounds in Australia.

[4] A number of scholars make mention of the assumed connection between 'looks' and 'place of origin' in dominant white discourse. See Bauman (1997), Brah (1996), Tuan (1998), Yamamoto (1999) and Yu (2001).

[5] In order to respect the privacy of informants, personal details other than names are not disclosed in this essay.

[6] Generational indicators denoted here identify both paternal and maternal sides of informants' heritage and index their generational distance from China. The paternal indicators are located on the left, and maternal indicators located on the right within brackets. (4, 2) generation thus denotes that the informant is fourth-generation on their paternal side, and second-generation on their maternal side. A detailed explanation of reasons for doing this can be found in the methodology chapter of my dissertation (see note 1).

[7] This assertion is supported by historians who have investigated the Chinese experience in the Northern Territory. For example see Giese (1995, 1999) and Jones (1997).

[8] Interview with author in Darwin, Northern Territory, 4 September 2000.

[9] Interview with author in Queanbeyan, ACT, 25 September 2001.

[10] Interview with author, 25 September 2001.
[11] It is interesting to note that evidence provided in the *Report of the National Inquiry into Racist Violence* carried out by the Human Rights and Equal Opportunities Commission in 1991, indicates that increasing numbers of Asians entering Australia corresponded with an increase in racism against people of Asian descent in Australia (see Jayasuriya and Kee 1999; Vasta 1996).
[12] For a discussion of Hansonism and attitudes towards Asians in Australia see Ang (1999, 2000), Jayasuriya and Kee (1999), Perera (1999, 2000), and Stratton (1998).
[13] Here emphasis is placed not on a single country of origin but on the assumption that Chinese Australians are both 'new' to Australia and 'undesirable' on account of their 'Asianness'.
[14] Interview with author in Gordonvale, North Queensland, 12 August 2000.
[15] Interview with author, 12 August 2000.
[16] Interview with Diana Giese in Sydney, NSW, 24 May 1995. *Post-War Chinese Australians Oral History Project* TRC 3261, National Library of Australia (NLA). Also see Giese (1997: 160–161).
[17] Interview with Giese, 24 May 1995. Also see Giese (1997: 160–61).
[18] Interview with author, 25 September 2001.
[19] Interview with Diana Giese in Darwin, Northern Territory, 14 December 1993, *Post-War Chinese Australians Oral History Project*, TRC 3007, NLA.
[20] Interview with Giese, 14 December 1993.
[21] Interview with author, 12 August 2000.
[22] Interview with Diana Giese in Darwin, Northern Territory, 14 December 1996, *Post-War Chinese Australians Oral History Project*, TRC 3540, NLA.
[23] For further discussion of the negative stereotypes seen as typifying Vietnamese in Australia see Moss (1986), Thomas (1999) and Luke and Carrington (2000).
[24] Wang Gungwu makes mention of these stereotypes in The Chinese Overseas: From Earthbound China to the Quest for Autonomy (2000: 100).
[25] Interview with Giese, 14 December 1993.
[26] Interview with author in Darwin, Northern Territory, 4 September 2000.
[27] Interview with author in Darwin, Northern Territory, 31 August 2000.
[28] Interview with author in Townsville, North Queensland, 3 August 2000.
[29] Interview with author in Darwin, Northern Territory, 28 August 2000.
[30] Interview with Diana Giese in Darwin, Northern Territory, 9 September 1993, *Post-War Chinese Australians Oral History Project*, TRC 3006, NLA.
[31] Interview with author, 25 September 2001.
[32] Interview with Giese, 14 December 1993.
[33] Although it is not possible to provide evidence of this in this essay, these aspects are explored in my doctoral thesis where I examine various ways in which Chinese Australians seek to 'rediscover' their 'Chinese roots' through making trips to China and so on.

References

Ang, I. 'Racial/Spatial Anxiety: 'Asia' in the Psycho-Geography of Australian Whiteness.' *The Future of Australian Multiculturalism: Reflections on the Twentieth Anniversary of Jean Martin's The Migrant Presence.* Eds. G. Hage and R. Couch. Sydney: Research Institute for Humanities and Social Sciences, University of Sydney, 1999. 189–204.

———. 'Transforming Chinese Identities in Australia: Between Assimilation, Multiculturalism, and Diaspora.' *Intercultural Relations, Cultural Transformation and Identity: The Ethnic Chinese. Selected Papers Presented at the 1998 ISSCO Conference.* Ed. T. Ang See. Manila: Kaisa Para Sa Kaunlaran, 2000. 249–58.

——. *On Not Speaking Chinese: Living Between Asia and the West*. London: Routledge, 2001.
Ang, I., Chalmers, S., Law, L. and Thomas, M. Eds. *Alter/Asians: Asian-Australian Identities in Art, Media and Popular Culture*. Annandale: Pluto Press, 2000.
Anthias, F. and Yuval-Davis, N. *Racialised Boundaries: Race, Nation, Gender, Colour and Class and the Anti-Racist Struggle*. London: Routledge, 1992.
Ayres, T. 'Undesirable Aliens.' *HQ* March/April (1998): 110–15.
——. 'China Doll—The Experience of Being a Gay Chinese Australian.' *The Journal of Homosexuality* 36 (1999): 87–97.
——. 'Sexual Identity and Cultural Identity: A Crash Course.' *Diaspora: Negotiating Asian-Australia*. Eds. H. Gilbert, T. Khoo and J. Lo. Brisbane: University of Queensland Press, 2000. 160–63.
Banton, M. *Racial Theories*. Cambridge: Cambridge University Press, 1998.
Bauman, Z. 'The Making and Unmaking of Strangers.' *Debating Cultural Hybridity: Multicultural Identities and the Politics of Anti-racism*. Eds. P. Werbner and T. Modood. London: Zed Books, 1997. 46–57.
Brah, A. *Cartographies of Diaspora: Contesting Identities*. London: Routledge, 1996.
Chan, D. 'The Dim Sum vs. the Meat Pie: On the Rhetoric of Becoming an In-between Asian-Australian Artist.' *Alter/Asians: Asian Australian Identities in Art, Media and Popular Culture*. Eds. I. Ang, S. Chalmers, L. Law and M. Thomas. Annandale, NSW: Pluto Press, 2000. 141–51.
Choi, C. Y. *Chinese Migration and Settlement in Australia*. Sydney: Sydney University Press, 1975.
Fitzgerald, S. *Red Tape, Gold Scissors – The Story of Sydney's Chinese*. Sydney: State Library of New South Wales Press, 1997.
Giese, D. *Beyond Chinatown: Changing Perspectives on the Top End Chinese Experience*. Canberra: National Library of Australia, 1995.
——. *Astronauts, Lost Souls and Dragons: Conversations with Chinese Australians*. St. Lucia: University of Queensland Press, 1997.
——. *Courage and Service: Chinese Australians and World War II*. Sydney: Courage and Service Project, 1999.
Gilroy, P. 'Race Ends Here.' *Ethnic and Racial Studies* 21.5 (1998): 838–47.
——. *Against Race: Imagining Political Culture beyond the Color Line*. Cambridge: The Belknap Press of Harvard University Press, 2000.
Jackman, M. *The Velvet Glove of Paternalism and Conflict in Gender, Class and Race Relations*. Berkeley: University of California Press, 1994.
Jayasuriya, L. and Kee P.K. *The Asianisation of Australia? Some Facts About the Myths*. Melbourne: Melbourne University Press, 1999.
Jones, T. *The Chinese in the Northern Territory*. Revised edition. Darwin: Northern Territory University Press, 1997.
Khoo, T. *Banana Bending: Asian–Australian and Asian Canadian Literature*. Unpublished PhD thesis. Brisbane: University of Queensland, 1999.
——. 'Re-Siting Australian Identity: Configuring the Chinese Citizen in Diana Giese's *Astronauts, Lost Souls and Dragons* and William Yang's *Sadness*' *Bastard Moon: Essays on Chinese Australian Writing*. Special Issue of *Otherland Literary Journal* 7 (2001): 95–109.
——. *Banana Bending: Asian-Australian and Asian-Canadian Literatures*. Hong Kong: McGill-Queens University Press and Hong Kong University Press, 2003a.
——. '"Angry Yellow Men": Cultural Space for Diasporic Chinese Masculinities.' *Asian Masculinities: The Meaning and Practice of Manhood in China and Japan*. Eds. K. Louie and M. Low. London: RoutledgeCurzon, 2003b. 220–43.
Kibria, N. 'Race, Ethnic Options, and Ethnic Binds: Identity Negotiations of Second-Generation Chinese and Korean Americans.' *Sociological Perspectives* 43.1 (2000): 77–92.

Leong, G. 'Remembering Chinese.' *Diaspora: Negotiating Asian-Australia*. Eds. H. Gilbert, T. Khoo and J. Lo. Brisbane: University of Queensland Press, 2000. 58–66.

———. 'Internalised Racism and the Work of Chinese Australian Artists: Making Visible the Invisible World of William Yang.' (Representing Identities). *Journal of Australian Studies* 72 (January) (2002): 79–93.

Loh, M. 'Fighting Uphill: Australians of Chinese Descent and the Defense Forces, 1899–1951.' *Chinese in Australia and New Zealand: A Multidisciplinary Approach*. Ed. J. Ryan. New Delhi: Wiley Western, 1995. 59–66.

Loh, M. and Winternitz, J. Dinky-Di: 1989 *The Contributions of Chinese Immigrants and Australians of Chinese Descent to Australia's Defense Forces and War Efforts 1899–1988*. Canberra: Australian Government Publishing Service, 1989.

Louie, K. *Theorising Chinese Masculinity: Society and Gender in China*. Cambridge: Cambridge University Press, 2002.

Louie, K. and Low, M. Eds. *Asian Masculinities: The Meaning and Practice of Manhood in China and Japan*. London: RoutledgeCurzon, 2003.

Luke, C. and Carrington, V. 'Race Matters.' *Journal of Intercultural Studies* 21.1 (2000): 5–24.

Luke, C. and Luke, A. 'Interracial Families: Difference within Difference.' *Ethnic and Racial Studies* 21.4 (1998): 728–54.

———. 'Theorising Interracial Families and Hybrid Identity: An Australian Perspective.' *Educational Theory* 49.2 (1999): 223–49.

Mercer, K. *Welcome to the Jungle: New Positions in Black Cultural Studies*. London: Routledge, 1994.

Moss, I. 'Chinese or Australian? Growing up in a Bicultural Twilight Zone from the 1950s on.' *Survival and Celebration: An Insight into the Lives of Chinese Immigrant Women, European Women Married to Chinese and their Female Children in Australia from 1856 to 1986*. Eds. M. Loh and C. Ramsay. Melbourne: Morag Loh and Christine Ramsay, 1986. 11–20.

Nicoll, F. *From Diggers to Drag Queens: Configurations of Australian National Identity*. Sydney: Pluto Press, 2001.

Perera, S. 'Whiteness and its Discontents: Notes on Politics, Gender, Sex and Food in the Year of Pauline Hanson.' *Journal of Intercultural Studies* 20.2 (1999). 183–198.

———. (2000) 'Futures Imperfect.' *Alter/Asians: Asian-Australian Identities in Art, Media and Popular Culture*. Eds. I. Ang, S. Chalmers, L. Law and M. Thomas. Sydney: Pluto Press, 2000. 3–24.

Pettman, J. *Living in the Margins: Racism, Sexism and Feminism in Australia*. Sydney: Allen and Unwin, 1992.

———. 'Race, Ethnicity and Gender in Australia.' *Unsettling Settler Societies: Articulations of Gender, Race, Ethnicity, and Class*. Eds. D. Stasiulis and N. Yuval-Davis. London: Sage, 1995. 65–94.

Shun Wah, A. 'Being Chinese in Australia: A Personal Journey.' *Imagining the Chinese Diaspora: Two Australian Perspectives*. Canberra: Centre for the Study of the Chinese Southern Diaspora, The Australian National University, 1999. 19–29.

Stratton, J. *Race Daze: Australia in Identity Crisis*. Sydney: Pluto Press, 1998.

Tan, C. '*Chinese Inscriptions*': Australian-born Chinese Lives. Unpublished PhD thesis. Brisbane: University of Queensland, 2004.

Thomas, M. *Dreams in the Shadows: Vietnamese-Australian Lives in Transition*. Sydney: Allen and Unwin, 1999.

Tuan, M. *Forever Foreigners or Honorary Whites? The Asian Ethnic Experience Today*. New Brunswick: Rutgers University Press, 1998.

Tucker, S. 'Your Worst Nightmare: Hybridised Demonology in Asian-Australian Women's Writing.' *Diaspora: Negotiating Asian-Australia*. Eds. H. Gilbert, T. Khoo and J. Lo. Brisbane: University of Queensland Press, 2000. 150–157, 234–36.

Vasta, E. 'Dialectics of Domination: Racism and Multiculturalism.' *The Teeth are Smiling: The Persistence of Racism in Multicultural Australia*. Eds. E. Vasta and S. Castles. Sydney: Allen and Unwin, 1996. 46–72.

Wang, G. *The Chinese Overseas: From Earthbound China to the Quest for Autonomy*. Cambridge: Harvard University Press, 2000.

Wang, L. (Director) *Reunion*, 1998. Film.

West, C. 'The New Cultural Politics of Difference.' In: R. Ferguson, M. Gever, T. M. H. Trinh and C. West (Eds.) *Out There: Marginalisation and Contemporary Cultures*. New York: The New Museum of Contemporary Art, 1990.19–36.

——. *Race Matters*. New York: Vintage Books, 1994.

Yamamoto, T. *Masking Selves, Making Subjects*. Berkeley: University of California Press, 1999.

Yang, W. 'I ask Myself, Am I Chinese?' *Art and Asia Pacific*, April (1994): 89–95.

——. 'My Chinese Identity.' *From Yellow Earth to Eucalypt: Stories and Poems from China and Australia*. Ed. N. Whitfield. Melbourne, Longman, 1995. 28–30.

——. *Sadness*. Sydney: Allen and Unwin, 1996.

Yu, H. *Thinking Orientals*. New York: Oxford University Press, 2001.

The Aesthetics of Simplicity: Yang's *Sadness* and the Melancholic Community

Gilbert Caluya

His face still haunts me. This face I have seen a hundred times and yet have never seen. His name is Allan, I am told, and although he haunts me, I do not know him. I remember first encountering him in high school. I was so distraught that I was led out of the classroom to sob outside. I wasn't quite sure why I was so upset. Perhaps it was the way his eyes refused to (or couldn't) look back at the camera in what Peggy Phelan calls the claustrophobia of a shrinking vision, 'the failure to have one's deepest gaze returned' (1997: 165). Perhaps it was the way his mouth, slightly open, suggested a pained, laboured breathing. The clinical whiteness of the pillow gives him an almost angelic glow, but maybe this is my way of sanitising the image, of neutralising the

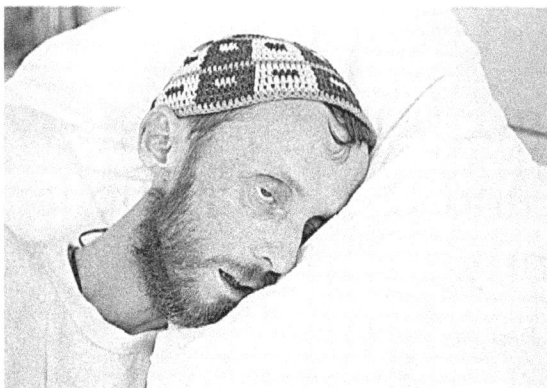

Figure 1 'Allan. Sacred Heart Hospice' (1990) © William Yang

painful act of witnessing. The smoothness of the pillow foregrounds the textures of Allan's face, the growing beard, the 'sleep' in his eyes and the spots on his face. When I remember this image in my mind, there are two things that strike me: his half-closed eye and the curve of the pillow pressed against his face.

This photograph comes from William Yang's performance *Sadness* (1992), a monologue with slides. Yang has worked as a 'social photographer' in Sydney for over thirty years, using his photographs of Sydney's gay subculture to create what he calls 'a documentary diary of the times' (1996: i). A third-generation Chinese-Australian, he was born William Young in northern Queensland, Australia. *Sadness* combines projected images, spoken word and live music into a multilayered performance that deals with the thematics of death and grief. It documents the loss of his gay friends and his mother during the 1980s and early 1990s. Simultaneously, *Sadness* interweaves a murder-mystery focusing on the shady circumstances surrounding the death of his uncle-in-law, William Fang Yuen.

Originally created and performed in Australia, *Sadness* has since travelled internationally to New Zealand, Hong Kong, England and the USA. During 1996, the work was transposed into a book, published by Allen and Unwin and, in 1999, it was adapted as a film directed by Tony Ayres (who is also the director of *China Dolls*). The film version has since received seven awards in Australia, and was a documentary finalist in the 1999 New York Festivals Television Programming Awards (Leong 2002: 83).

I first encountered the above photograph at high school in a book *Don't Leave Me This Way* (Gott 1994). It was one in a series of photographs following Allan's deterioration from AIDS-related diseases. Coming across the film version of *Sadness*, I realised it was part of a larger work and it was during Yang's 2003 retrospective performance that I was finally able to see him perform it at the Downstairs Belvoir St, Theatre in Sydney, Australia (where it originally premiered on 1 October 1992).

During the performance I was struck by how powerful this image was and continues to be. I was struck by how it continued to move me, how I seemed to react palpably, despite having already seen it. It is not just this one photograph, however, as *Sadness* as a whole has a way of emotionally affecting the viewer. This essay attempts to grapple with this phenomenon, to understand how *Sadness* affectively engages its audience. In particular, how does it function as an art work, one that not only portrays loss but viscerally conveys it? To be able to broach these questions, this essay mobilises an aesthetically-grounded, performative reading in order to tease out the complex interrelations between sadness, aesthetics and loss. What aesthetic practices are employed in *Sadness* and to what effect? The effect of any work of art relies also on the viewer and, in recognition of this fact, I attempt a performative reading practice to consider the interrelation between audience and art. If a performative reading foregrounds the engagement with the text, then it is here that one may make an ethical-political intervention. How can *Sadness* be put to work? What sort of work can it do, for whom and to what end?

Reframing William Yang's *Sadness*

Reviews of *Sadness* have often approached it through the lens of identity. In such readings, *Sadness* appears as a journey towards self-discovery, interpreting the artwork as the exploitation, repudiation, denial, or reconciliation of Yang's Chinese heritage. For example, Christine Choo observes that *Sadness* 'disturbed [her] greatly' (2002: 5). She describes her engagement in terms of 'unease' and 'impatience' because, as she states, 'Yang uses Chinese props publicly' (2002: 5). According to Choo, Yang exploits symbols 'such as joss sticks, an altar and other overtly Chinese props to signify 'Chineseness',' and this exemplifies 'the paradox embodied in his being and identity' (2002: 136). Her unease and impatience stems from a perceived artificiality of Yang's Chineseness, as if his performance of ethnicity betrays his own ambivalent positioning. Similarly, Paul Hayes reads *Sadness* in terms of a search for identity. In his review for *Outrage* (an Australian gay magazine), Hayes writes: 'After years in the wilderness of denial, Yang's identity was coming together' (1996: 57). Furthermore, Bryce Hallett observes that Yang 'emerges like a detective trying to make sense of his own identity' (2003).

This search for identity—an instability that fluctuates between the lack of identity and its excess, between anxiety over the lack of one and its artificial over-compensation—is destabilised within *Sadness* itself. At one point, Yang jokes that now he makes a living out of being Chinese, to which the audience laughs hesitantly. Read against the prior narration of the painful realisation that he is Chinese when teased by a white student—a moment that echoes Franz Fanon's own discovery of his objecthood in *Black Skin, White Masks* (1967)—the joke becomes extraordinarily self-reflexive. On one level, the joke acknowledges his own staging of ethnicity and functions to critique his own desire for identity, but on another level it questions the audience's complicity in this, by forcing us to confront our own desire to see an Asian or a gay artist. Yang questions the authenticity of identity at the same time that he questions our desire to see it performed.

Thus, when Greg Leong finds Yang's use of a Taoist alter, 'rather stagey' whereas for his 'Euro-Australian friends ... it was both moving and exotic' (qtd. in Chan 2000a: 54), what I argue is that, despite the different responses, both regulate what counts as authentically Chinese. The regulation of ethnic authenticity is made explicitly clear when, in reference to the use of the alter, Leong claims it is 'something which we older Chinese remember with awe' (54). Choo's response is provoked by her review of Shen Yuanfang's book *Dragon Seed in the Antipodes: Chinese-Australian Autobiographies* (2001). For Shen, Yang's work can be interpreted in the context of Chinese Australian autobiographical writings: 'Central to the autobiographical approach of Australian-born Chinese is the question of "Who am I?", a question that reflects constant identity crises' (2001: 129). Thus, she argues, Yang's work exemplifies a way of recreating or restaging his Chineseness in an Australian context: 'It is by telling a Chinese past with roots in Australia that William Yang conceptualises his Chinese-Australian identity and demands a rightful place in Australia' (130). As opposed to Choo, Shen's formulation is a little more generous in recognising the creativity of the diasporic subject.

Dean Chan extends a welcomed critique of the racially essentialist art criticism circulating around Yang's work. As a rejoinder to the ethnic determinism that delimits exoticist readings of Asian Australian artwork, Chan concludes that 'the current interpretative pitfalls stem from the fact that narratives on Asian Australian art have yet to move very far from the loaded discourse of *race*, and the arena of ontological absolute truth claims' (2000b: 150, emphasis in original). Beneath this, he proposes a number of strategic questions to redirect our critical energies:

> one could be prompted to ask, for example, about the ways and means by which a third-generation Chinese-Australian artist like Yang negotiates the reclamation of a sense of Chineseness within Australia. Which aspects or versions of Chineseness are aspired towards; and which are seemingly de-privileged in this particular 'search for identity'? (2000b: 150)

Whether Chan moves away from an ontologically absolute truth towards an ontologically relative truth does not, in my argument, negate 'the loaded discourse of race'.

In the abstraction to understand the impetus of the work by the question 'Who am I?', the aesthetics of *Sadness* is lost (as is Yang's 'gay identity'). The focus on identity is a direct consequence of analysing *Sadness* through the genre of autobiography. This mis-categorisation effaces the innovative aesthetic contribution Yang makes, particularly since this contribution can be rendered as a disruption and synthesis of other genres. Some of these genres are already established within different art histories: portrait and landscape photography, dramatic monologues, contemporary music, biography. It also destabilises the high/low art dichotomy by incorporating everyday genres: the family slide show, oral testimonies and the documentary. To complicate this further, he also incorporates found objects from the historical archive, whether it is old family photos not taken by him, historical photographs of past landscapes and even a written document found in a local court archive. These artifacts, found objects from the past, serve to layer his stories of loss historically. On another level, the 'auto' in autobiography does not really do justice to the others in Yang's work: his photographed subjects.

I want to acknowledge that this identitarian framework of interpretation can be read in part as an attempt to respond critically to the political and psychic consequences of varying histories of oppression; these consequences are often hinged on the identification of racial and sexual others. Part of my contention with identity politics is not with its political impetus but rather its consequences. Specifically, that it often unwittingly reinscribes the same field of forces that produces racial and sexual identities as problems in the first place.

This is made clear in the context of racial identity by Kelly Oliver's reading of Fanon. Ever since Fanon's appropriation of the Hegelian master-slave dialectic in *Black Skin, White Masks* (1967), colonial and postcolonial studies have been haunted by a recurring politics of recognition framed by questions of identity. Oliver extends Fanon's analysis to 'interpret the recognition model of identity as the particular pathology of colonial or oppressive cultures', arguing that the struggle for recognition 'itself is part of the pathology of oppression and domination' (2001: 23). A wider critique of identity politics is articulated by Wendy Brown in *States of Injury*. Through the notion of 'wounded attachments', Brown explores the 'logics of pain in the subject formation process' (1995: 55). She argues that disenfranchised subjects are wounded by histories of domination and oppression, and consequently seek to have such injuries recognised and redressed. This demand for recognition, however, often works through a logic of *ressentiment*, in which the wounded subject seeks a site to redress their injury: the oppressors. In doing so, the rightfully resentful, because wounded, subject effectively 'fixes the identity of the injured and the injuring as social positions' (27), through reiterating the identity categories originally employed in the constitution of the injured subject. In other words, identity politics works through *ressentiment*, which restates the structures of domination, rather than neutralising the injured identity itself. The notion of 'wounded attachment' thus denotes a paradox, whereby an identity constituted by an injury, at the very moment of attempting to redress that injury, replicates the binary logic of 'us versus them', which enabled the injury in the first place (66–69).

To be fair, Chan's questions are important, particularly when juxtaposed against the exoticist (why not heterosexist?) readings that he is criticising and they constitute a progressive political move. Yang draws explicitly on his Chinese heritage, particularly Daoism. He employs a Daoist shrine at the end of his performance and cites Lao Tzu. When he narrates his discovery of Daoism, it is clearly couched as a return to his roots. As I have already mentioned, Yang was born William Young and he changed his name later, a gesture of reclamation in itself. I do not doubt that these elements point to a search for identity but, when read within the context of *Sadness* as a whole, this search for identity takes on a melancholic hue. A constitutive loss mars his search for identity. To the extent, argues Judith Butler, that the 'history of race is linked to the history of diasporic displacement it seems to me that melancholia is there, that there is, as it were, inscribed in "race" a lost and ungrievable origin, one might say, an impossibility of return, but also an impossibility of an essence' (qtd. in Bell 1999: 170).

The notion of melancholia opens up another angle from which to view our wounded attachments. Briefly put, for Sigmund Freud, both mourning and melancholia are similarly reactions 'to the loss of a loved person, or to the loss of some abstraction which has taken the place of one' such as an ideal (Freud 1984: 252). However, where the work of mourning processes the loss of the loved object by withdrawing from it and sometimes reinvesting in a new love, the melancholic turns away from reality by clinging to the lost love object (253). This clinging establishes 'an *identification* of the ego with the abandoned object', in which the ego 'wants to incorporate this object into itself' (258).

In *The Melancholy of Race*, Anne Anlin Cheng points out that although much academic attention is aimed at the deconstruction of categories of gender, race and sexuality, little focus 'has been given to the ways in which individuals and communities remain invested in maintaining such categories' (2000: 7). This investment, Cheng suggests, can be understood through 'racial melancholia'. For Cheng, racial melancholia helps to explicate the complex psychodynamic processes of racial rejection and desire. As 'a theoretical model of identity', racial melancholia 'provides a critical framework for analyzing the constitutive role that grief plays in racial/ethnic subject-formation' (Cheng 2000: xi).

What I find useful in Cheng's model of subjectivity is that it recognises the paradox at the heart of identity that Brown explicates without surrendering agency. Racial melancholia exists as both 'a *sign* of rejection and as a psychic *strategy* in response to that rejection' (Cheng 2000: 20). Read from this angle, the sadness in Yang's *Sadness* can begin to resonate with new political meanings, and it is from within this framework that I want to explore the aesthetic shape it gives to this melancholia.

An Aesthetics of Simplicity

In order to discuss this notion of melancholia, we need to address how loss is figured in the artwork itself. On one level, *Sadness* can be read as Yang's creative response to loss. If, in melancholia, traces of the lost object are incorporated into the psychic landscape then, as Susette Min argues, in the attempt by the melancholic to reinstate the lost object, such traces might re-emerge in certain contemporary artworks (2003: 234).

Yang's signature artwork is a new genre: the 'monologue with slides'. In this form, images are projected onto two screens located behind him, which he combines with a spoken monologue. It would appear something akin to the slide show often employed in narrating family holidays, but if this is a journey, it is a profoundly painful one involving death, loss and sadness.

Tseen Khoo (2001) and Belinda Smaill (2002) have already noted that *Sadness* as a whole is structured by two trajectories portraying different types of losses, which are interspliced through an episodic narrative. One trajectory traces the death of his gay friends from AIDS-related diseases. Visually, this is represented by photographic case histories in which he tracks the debilitating effects of AIDS on his friends. The other trajectory narrates his journey to north Queensland, where he investigates the circumstances surrounding the death of his uncle-in-law. By the end of this investigation, we discover that Yang's uncle-in-law was murdered but, since he was Chinese, the police failed to investigate the circumstances properly. In this narrative, Yang employs photographs of people he interviewed, the cane-field his uncle-in-law once owned, and a police document. Towards the end of *Sadness*, the death of his mother serves as the fulcrum that hinges his dénouement.

What is most evident about Yang's photographs is their realistic aesthetic. Of course, such realism is inherent in the photograph. However, many visual artists have employed photography specifically to question its supposed relation to reality. Processing techniques such as superimposition or attempts to incorporate painterly aspects (such as in Bill Henson's images), as well as 'doctored' photographs through desktop publishing, have all affected the contemporary viewer's relation to photographed reality. Within this contemporary postmodern context, Yang's photographs might lack stylisation and, for the most part, any romanticisation, so his approach could strike the viewer as naïve. I would suggest, however, that Yang's realist aesthetics are central to the type of experience he is trying to portray. A large number of the photographs in *Sadness* can be read within the tradition of portraiture. These portrait photographs, employing close-ups that zoom in on the face, engage the viewer in direct contact with his subjects. His subjects often directly face the camera, and this makes it almost impossible to objectify them fully. Since the eyes look back at you, regard you, it is difficult not to recognise that one faces another subject, another being. For Roland Barthes, the photograph carries its referent in a way that no other image does: 'in Photography I can never deny that *the thing has been there*' (2000: 76, emphasis in original). The photographs' indexical relation to realism, what Barthes figures through the phrase 'the-thing-that-has-been' (76), is further expanded by Susan Sontag. As opposed to other images that interpret the real, the photograph 'is also a trace, something directly stencilled off the real, like a footprint or a death mask' (2002: 154). Yang employs this inherent realism of photography in order to re-create the experience of his photographed subjects; that is, the experience of being in their presence.

In a 1996 interview Yang comments on his style, 'I think the particular talent that I have is that I see things really simply ... The simpler it is, the more effective it is' (qtd. in Hayes 1996: 58). I read this simplicity as the paring down of his life experiences to tell a story that is unique to him. In an interview for Company B, Yang pays tribute to one of his inspirations: 'Isaac Bashevis Singer, the novelist, said that you should strive to tell the unique story that only you can tell, and that idea has been an inspiration for me' (Yang 2003).

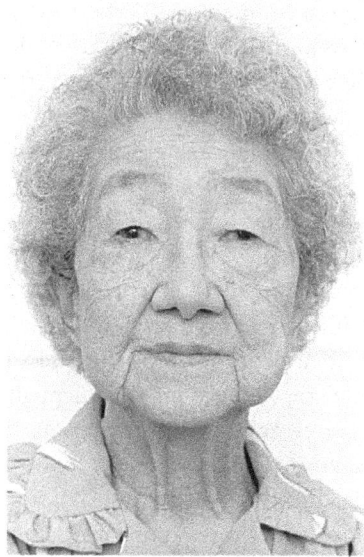

Figure 2 'Mother' (1988) © William Yang

This search for a unique story is described by Yang in quasi-phenomenological terms. In an earlier interview he states:

> I just try to examine things as really and honestly, as I can. Then you start peeling back those social attitudes towards them. If you can get close to the essence of things, if you could get back to a truthful base, or an essential base of things, then I think that is what people will respond to. And that then doesn't need to be presented in a big way because it's basically a very simple thing, and you can present it in a simple way (qtd. in Wong 1998).

His simplicity is a way of striving for the truth, the essence and the uniqueness of his subjects: gay friends, family members, but also people he meets in transit. Although, for the most part, he photographs them in natural lighting and domestic settings, the subjects are almost always looking at the camera. They are aware, they recognise the camera and, as a photographic effect, they can stare back at the viewer.

Barthes reads the photograph as a literal emanation of the referent or the subject of the photograph. He states that '[f]rom a real body, which as there, proceed radiations which ultimately touch me ... the photograph of the missing being ... touch[es] me like the delayed rays of a star' (2000: 80-81). In this luminous connection between the viewer and the photographed subject, light becomes a 'carnal medium, a skin I share with anyone who has been photographed' (81). It is through this relation that Barthes is able to find the 'air' of a singular being in the photograph, which he describes as 'the expression, the look' (107). The air of the face is akin to the soul of the other, 'is a kind of intractable supplement of identity, what is given as an act of grace ... the air expresses the subject' (109). Yang's striving for simplicity can be seen in terms of this air, as an expression that 'captures' the soul of his family and friends. It is this air, this direct representation of the other, that the audience is called upon to respond to in *Sadness*. For example, the humble shine in Allan's eyes, the intensity of Nicolaas' stare, the dignified distance of his mother (see Figure 2) or the quizzical expression of Aunty Kath. In this sense, portrait photography becomes 'an act of sharing where we are exposed to each other and to being-in-common when we expose ourselves to the camera lens' (Kaplan 2001: 7).

The visual simplicity of Yang's photographs have their corollary in his narrative and voice. Helena Grehan argues that Yang's performance style can be characterised as 'stillness'. For Grehan, Yang's stillness provokes the intrigue of the audience, by allowing them to 'revel' in the absence of an explicit interpretive framework provided by Yang (2002: 152). This stillness is partially the stylistic effect of his voice. While Choo views his delivery as 'deadpan' (2002: 136), I suggest that this is partially because Yang's voice sounds rather affectless. This consideration fails to recognise the multiple qualities of his voice. Besides being softly-spoken, Yang's voice has a soft-hued texture and a mellow timbre and, while this may not be something he intends, it nevertheless contributes to the serene atmosphere of the piece. Furthermore, reading him as affect-less or deadpan gives too much focus to his mostly even pitch. However, through the rhythm of his speech, he conveys a sombre tone, or a light-hearted, casual one. Since both the film and performance require our visual and auditory attention (it also incorporates music), Yang's delivery may arguably be a strategic choice that allows the viewer to maintain focus within a multi-sensual experience.

Yang's narrative is episodically structured around anecdotes: the verbal equivalent of the photograph. If the 'still photograph is a privileged moment' in time (Sontag 2002: 18), one might also say this of the anecdote. Just as the photograph turns anything into an art object—each bottle, cup or chair leg—so, too, the anecdote can turn any incident into a story worth telling. These anecdotes in Yang's performance represent particular moments and gestures as events in and of themselves. Like the photograph, the anecdote can give a heightened awareness to the experience of the everyday. In this way, *Sadness* blurs the boundaries between art and the everyday, since Yang's aesthetic form has the appearance of everyday actions—taking photographs and telling stories. Indeed, the straightforward phrasing of his anecdotes again reflects his aesthetics of simplicity. If, as he describes himself during a radio interview, he is a 'diary-ist' (Yang 1996: i), then his journal entries combine succinct, compressed observations with sharp, microscopic detail.

Yang explains another thing that he likes about Isaac Bashevis: 'I find I like warm-hearted people and I like charming people, like writers who charm you with their view of the world and it's in the detail and the way they see it' (qtd. in Cavenett). This attention to detail in anecdotes, coupled with Yang's previous statement on simplicity, gives meaning to the apparent minimalism of its form.

Through the work of Barthes, I want to figure the affective capacity this attention to detail engages in the viewer. For Barthes, the detail, or what he calls the *punctum*, in the photograph is what gives it the capacity to wound. In *Camera Lucida*, Barthes makes a distinction between *studium* and *punctum*. The former refers to the socio-cultural meaning of the photograph, which includes not just the context of the photograph but also the intentions of the photographer. However, there is a second element that breaks through or punctuates the *studium*, which Barthes calls the *punctum*. It is a photographic detail 'which rises from the scene, shoots out of it like an arrow, and pierces me' (2000: 26). This rising movement of the *punctum*, or detail, and its capacity to wound are brought together in Barthes' affective phenomenology of the photograph.

For Barthes, one must close one's eyes to let the photograph speak for itself: 'to say nothing, to shut my eyes, to allow the detail to rise of its own accord into affective consciousness' (55). Thus, the detail carries an affective capacity to wound, provoking an embodied response: 'I see, I feel, hence I notice, I observe, and I think' (21). In this formulation, the detail provokes a chain of responses tying vision to thought, a process that renders the viscerally-felt relationship one has to Yang's photographs and anecdotes.

Despite his everyday, conversational tone, Yang's anecdotes function to capture details about his friends and family. Take, for example, an anecdote regarding his friend, Nicolaas. In discussing how 'immaculate' Nicolaas' will was, Yang remembers one idiosyncrasy. He writes, '[Nicolaas] was from Johannesburg and he had a large collection of ethnic jewellery. He requested that the ivory be sent back to be buried in the soil of Africa' (Yang 1996: 8). Why notice this? Why remember this? Who cares? In this case, remembering *is* caring; taking notice of the other is a form of caring, a patient attention to the other. Yang is drawing on the everyday importance of the anecdote. We usually have our favourite ones about friends and family that we tell and re-tell, precisely because it reveals something particular about that person. Insofar as the anecdote carries details in the form of idiosyncrasies, what Yang is portraying is the uniqueness of these individuals. Like the photograph, which is always already a reduction (through framing, editing, and selecting, but also through timing), the anecdote reduces the history of a relationship into a particular incident. Like the portrait photograph, which one face only could have made, the anecdote functions as an idiosyncrasy that represents that particular person or relationship.

The aesthetics of simplicity in *Sadness* is important on another level. One soon learns that many of Yang's photographed subjects (friends and family) have since died—since, that is, the photograph was taken. For Sontag, photographs inherently expose 'the vulnerability of lives heading toward their own destruction, and this link between photography and death haunts all photographs of people' (2002: 70). Photography intrinsically exposes us to the being-towards-death.

For Barthes, the *punctum* is refined in his meditation on the relationship between photography and death. In Part Two of *Camera Lucida*, he narrates how, after his mother's death, he sifts through photographs of her, trying to 'find' her. The Winter Garden Photograph achieves this for Barthes, since in it he discovers her '*as into herself*' (2000: 71, emphasis in original). In finding the essence of his mother in the Winter Garden Photograph, Barthes then uses this to explore the essence of photography itself in relation to death. As Derrida points out, the Winter Garden Photograph becomes the *punctum* of *Camera Lucida*, which 'irradiates the entire study' (2001: 58). From this point on, Barthes' affective phenomenology develops a melancholic overtone.

Through this photograph Barthes locates a second *punctum*: time. The photograph, he argues, attests to what has existed. We see 'reality as in a past state' (2000: 82), but this reality is '*without future*' (90, emphasis in original). In other words, time is immobilised in the photograph, and it is from this that Barthes derives the photographs' pathos and melancholy. In describing the 1865 photograph of Lewis Payne, which pictures him awaiting his hanging in a cell, Barthes realises the *punctum* is 'he is going to die'. This leads him to realise simultaneously, '*This will be* and *this has been*; I observe with horror an anterior future of which death is the stake' (96, emphasis in original). By superimposing the time of the spectator with the time of the photograph, Barthes locates in every photograph 'a catastrophe which has already occurred' (96).

While Sontag argues that '[p]hotographs may be more memorable than moving images, because they are a neat slice of time, not a flow' (2002: 17), what is central to *Sadness* is time. Yang's performance *is* temporal; his photobiographies stage a chronology of his subjects. Like memory, however, these life histories are reconstructed in hindsight from privileged moments in their relationship expressed in photographs and anecdotes. In a way, the artistic process of selecting, rearranging, reordering these images and stories parallels the process of re-membering itself, and thus becomes a way of preserving his loved ones.

From the point of view of the spectator, however, these photobiographies disrupt time. *Sadness* weaves together multiple stories into a multi-layered artwork of loss. The logic of haunting pervades *Sadness* as a whole since it is permeated by the fact that most of his subjects are already dead. This fact, which one soon discovers, becomes the precondition for the work as a whole, which ultimately disrupts the time of the artwork. The photobiographies of his gay friends are presented as a chronological series of photographs tracking the effects of AIDS, following them towards their death, but this movement towards death is haunted by the realisation that they are already dead. In the time of the spectator, the actual death has already occurred, but within the time of *Sadness*, their death is yet to come. I also want to suggest that something else is at play or, more precisely, being replayed. Yang's loss of his friends is being recited, rehearsed and re-enacted, suggesting the melancholic's repetitive attempts to invoke the lost love object.

There is another type of *punctum* that is captured in Yang's non-portrait photography. The landscape photographs, pictures of rooms and of food affect the viewer differently, a factor that needs to be read in light of the movement of his photobiographies. Their power derives from what is missing; their *punctum* consists of the metonymic absence of the loved one. Alphonso Lingis argues that 'the mortality of the other concerns me' because 'I find the shape of my own destiny in the outline of enterprises that the others traced in the world but did not have the time or

Figure 3 'Peter Tully's Room' (1990) © William Yang

the power to realize' (1994: 171). Through the photographs of the Australian landscape, of the empty rooms of Yang's friends and in the rose his mother grew, Yang's *Sadness* traces the resonance of his friends and families in the world around us. These non-portrait photographs resonate as material objects and dwellings left to us by the dead. They metonymically represent the dead. However, this metonymic association simultaneously denotes the absence of their presence: they become ruins, altars or vigilant candles.

What I have argued in this essay is that realism is thus employed in *Sadness* as part of an aesthetics of simplicity, an aesthetics that enables Yang to represent the uniqueness and particularity of his subjects. To point out that realism is a fabrication, an aesthetic convention that gives the effect of the real, does not undo its potency. Neither does it address why this aesthetic is employed. I would argue that it is part of Yang's ethical imperative to represent his subjects honestly, to bear witness to their loss, and to document their suffering.

The Melancholic Community

My reading of Yang's aesthetics focuses on shedding light on how *Sadness* intervenes into the politics of communal mourning. In one sense, Yang transposes the political act of 'coming out' into an aesthetic process of grief. If coming out is a political defiance against the strictures of who one is or is not allowed to love, then Yang's *Sadness* defies the social regulation of who one can or cannot grieve. *Sadness* questions what losses count as losses by puncturing the social fabric that defines legitimate grief.

I want to consider this by reflecting on the conclusion of *Sadness* itself. The last photograph he shows is of an AIDS Candlelight Vigil. During the performance back-lighting slowly lights up a Daoist shrine at the back of stage, and Yang proceeds towards it as if to pay homage. At this point, the light fades out. An initial reading could stress how this conclusion brings the two halves of his identity together in a narrative of reconciliation and redemption. This conclusion/resolution is haunted,

The Aesthetics of Simplicity: Yang's Sadness and the Melancholic Community 95

Figure 4 'Candlelight Vigil' (1994). © William Yang

though, by the irreplaceable loss to which we, as an audience, have just borne witness. This is encapsulated by the paradoxical request that Yang makes of the audience. While showing the photograph of the AIDS Candlelight Vigil he suggests: 'We should not pull them back to this physical world with our sadness. Let them go. They have a new journey to travel' (1996: 78). However, directly after this, Yang concludes that '[l]oved ones are never lost. They are always here, in the heart' (79). What Yang advocates then is to let the lost loved object go by remembering that it still remains within us.

While this reminder might be an attempt to mitigate the sadness felt at their loss, it can also be read as a ghostly remembrance. The double imperative—to let them go but to hold on—points to the ambivalence of melancholia itself, a condition in which the dead continue to haunt the living as unfinished business. This occurs precisely because 'melancholia is brought about by the subject's inability to work out the problems or contradictions the object and its loss produce' (Muñoz, 1997: 351).

This ambivalence begins to resonate with political overtones within *Sadness*. Where Freud argues that the successful work of mourning returns the mourner to normal life, José Muñoz argues that normal life for some minorities can be a life of ungrievable loss. He emphasises that:

> melancholia, for blacks and queers of color, is not a pathology but an integral part of everyday lives. The melancholia that occupies the minds of the communities under siege ... is part of our process of dealing with the catastrophes that occur in the lives of people of color, lesbians and gays (1997: 355).

This ungrievable loss is evident in two of the cases Yang presents. The first example is Peter Tully, a Melbourne artist, who died without leaving a will. Yang narrates: 'There was a struggle for control between David and the family. By New South Wales law the estate went to the family, but not without a great deal of bitterness from both parties' (1996: 52). Here, the law refuses to recognise same-sex relationships as forming anything like a family. In contrast to this, Yang observes how Tully 'asked that his ashes be divided in two—half going to his biological family and the other half going to the gay and lesbian family' (52). This directly references the number of cases within the gay community in which one is not able to legitimately, publicly grieve since the law defines what counts as a family.

If gay relationships are not recognised by the state, the law or the public, then grieving for a gay lover is foreclosed in the public eye. How does one grieve a love that does not exist? The painful logic of this question not only has legal ramifications in terms of the distribution of the estate of the dead, but consequences for our own psychic processes of mourning. The very fact that Tully has to request that he be divided in death points to the unevenness in the right to grieve publicly. This irresolvable loss is often a part of normal life for many gay men.

The second example Yang narrates is the murder-mystery of Yang's uncle-in-law, in which he travels to Queensland interviewing people about the incident. His search for the truth behind this death falters around circumstance and hearsay. The archival discovery, a local court record, does not point Yang to the truth, but reveals another deception: it records his mother as having given testimony. Rather than continue his search, Yang refuses to press his mother about something on which she has chosen to remain silent. We are left with the speculative conclusion that his uncle-in-law was murdered. The case embodies the impossibility of publicly grieving past injustices that are hidden behind official stories, a condition many diasporic communities face. There is a gap between the oral testimonies that affirm his murder and the court record, between oral histories that reveal a darker story and the state archives. His mother's silence metonymically parallels the silence of the archive, while symbolically embodying the impossibility of successful mourning for Yang.

These cases highlight the troubled relation that gay men and Chinese Australians have towards mourning. By giving faces to these cases, Yang reveals how the politically-invested social legitimisation of mourning is played out in the private sphere of mourning. Thus, if Yang's *Sadness* performs grief, it does so in a way that questions the work of mourning as both a public and private venture.

I want to make clear here that this reading goes against the expressed intentions of Yang, who has described *Sadness* in the familiar terms of catharsis: 'I felt that by talking out this piece, through the ritual of theatre, that I have been able to tap into and in some ways purge society's suppressed sadness' (Yang 2003). This affective exorcism of sadness undercuts what allows *Sadness* to become an important exploration of the ethics and politics of mourning: namely, its examination of foreclosed grief in minority communities.

The question, as Butler succinctly puts it, 'is whether one can survive without the possibility of grief' (qtd. in Bell 1999: 172). She argues:

> grief needs its public rituals. If there's a public foreclosure of the possibility of grief and the recognition of loss, then it's not that an individual fails to grieve, it's that there's a public foreclosure of the possibility of grief, instituting melancholia throughout that culture. (qtd. in Bell 1999: 172)

Muñoz draws on and expands Michael Moon's notion of collective mourning to consider melancholia as a structure of feeling within minority communities and their cultural products. For Muñoz, Isaac Julien's *Looking for Langston* can be read as a photography of mourning supplying 'a necessary history to a collective struggle ... in the form of identity-affirming "melancholia"' (1997: 356). Melancholia thus becomes a mechanism 'that helps us (re)construct identity and take our dead to the various battles we must wage in their names—and in our names' (356).

This notion of collective mourning usefully questions the everyday assumption of mourning as a private psychological process. By situating the work of mourning within the public sphere, Muñoz enables an engagement with the politics of mourning. I want to question this from the viewpoint of an ethics of alterity.

If *Sadness* presents to the audience the specificity of Yang's subjects through an aesthetics of simplicity, then it is possible to approach a feeling of loss when one finds they are dead. The presence of Yang, however, undercuts this easy appropriation of loss. Whether in physical or narrative form, Yang's commentary functions to make the audience constantly aware that these are *his* losses: his friends, his mother, his uncle-in-law. Instead of an appropriation of loss, the audience is moved to a sympathetic grief in which an affective bond is formed between Yang and his audiences through sadness.

Jean-Luc Nancy's warning about the absorption of death into the service of community is worth noting here. We should be suspicious, he argues, of 'the retrospective consciousness of the lost community' (1991: 10), in which a nostalgic logic takes hold of mourning such that what is lost becomes the foundations of that very community. What the community has lost 'is lost only in the sense that such a "loss" is constitutive of the "community" itself' (12).

The contention that Nancy has with this nostalgic move is that it absorbs the other's death into the work of the community, effacing their singularity, their alterity. This is evident in Muñoz's conceptualisation of collective mourning, in which mourning Langston Hughes, for example, 'is about mourning for oneself, for one's community, for one's very history' (355). The repetition of 'one' in this passage should make us suspicious of the political move that is at play: what has happened to the other? In other words, viewed from the perspective of an ethics of alterity, Muñoz's argument risks effacing the singularity, the uniqueness of the individuals and their deaths. Muñoz's notion of collective mourning risks not just appropriating Yang's loss as one's own but also effacing the uniqueness of Yang's friends and family.

I want to conclude by returning to the AIDS Candlelight Vigil photograph in order to think more carefully about the kind of bond that is being built between Yang and his audiences. For me, the photograph invokes both the individual burden of grief and its collective form. It holds these two in tension, just as *Sadness* holds grief in Asian Australian communities and gay communities in tension. The photograph of the candlelight vigil depicts a night where surviving friends and families of people who have died from AIDS-related diseases congregate to grieve together. This communal grieving, itself a socio-political act of defiance, is captured in this photograph as both a private and public act as a necessarily individual but also collective work of mourning. This event forges a connection in the affect of collective sadness without, however, effacing the specificity of our separate losses. Similarly, the episodic narrative enables Yang to juxtapose different stories of loss without making them equivalent.

What *Sadness* helps facilitate is the connection between losses. These are not connections made through substitution or appropriation, but through recognition of the other's loss. By exposing the audience to the individuality of his own lost family members and friends, Yang provokes us to reflect on not only our own losses, but also those of our neighbours. In recognising the other's loss there opens up a space for connecting through a sympathetic sadness in what I call the melancholic community. We may bond through the affect of sadness despite not having the same loss. The melancholic community describes a sympathetic, affective alliance with the other's sadness without claiming the other's specific loss as one's own. Similar to Lingis' (1994) notion of the community with nothing in common, the melancholic community does not attempt to efface the alterity of the other, and it works across and disrupts already-formed communities. Through its episodic structure and the juxtaposition and intertwining of stories of loss, *Sadness* opens up a space for building bridges not just between individuals, but also across communities. If, as Cathy Beadnell (1999) writes, '[t]here are two sides to this story ... the Chinese and the gay and they have come together over grief', then I would argue that they have come together over grief without effacing their specific grievances or eliding their particular loss.

If cultural critics have written about strategic alliances formed from separate grievances, what about the possibilities for affective alliances formed from separate losses? If we begin to build affective alliances, is there the possibility of forging connections with those who do not share a particular grievance? An affective alliance might enable a political coalition not simply from within sexual or racial minority groups who—supposedly because of a presumed correspondence between identity and political interest—have the same grievances, but also from those who do not share these grievances, yet who are nevertheless impelled to respond to injustice because they are affectively moved by suffering. While this essay can only gesture toward these questions, what *Sadness* reveals to us, at the very least, is that this ethical imperative rests on being able to recognise the other's loss, a process that is partially enabled by the affective contagion of sadness.

Acknowledgements

I would like to thank profusely my supervisor Elspeth Probyn and associate supervisor, Natalya Lusty, who have been generous and supportive throughout the history of this essay. I would also like to acknowledge colleagues and ex-students in the Gender Studies Department of the University of Sydney who have kindly read and insightfully commented on various versions: Linnell Secomb, Jane Simon, Kym Chapple and Damon Young. Thanks also to Josh Wright whose question 'What about the object?' has continued to haunt and challenge me. All images were generously provided courtesy of William Yang who retains copyright.

References

Barthes, R. *Camera Lucida: Reflections on Photography*. Trans. R. Howard. London: Vintage, 2000.
Beadnell, C. *Sadness: A Monologue by William Yang*, 1999 <http://home.vicnet.net.au/~artsaliv/film_review/sadness.html> (accessed 30 November 2003).
Bell, V. 'On Speech, Race and Melancholia: An Interview with Judith Butler.' *Theory, Culture and Society* 16.2 (1999): 163–74.
Brown, W. *States of Injury: Power and freedom in Late Modernity*. Princeton: Princeton University Press, 1995.
Cavenett, W. *William Yang:* Sadness, The North. <http://www.thei/aust.com/isite/btl/btlinyang.html> (accessed 30 November 2003).
Chan, D. 'The Poetics of Cultural Theory: On Hybridity and the New Hierarchies.' *Diaspora: Negotiating Asian-Australia*. Eds. H. Gilbert, T. Khoo and J. Lo. Brisbane: University of Queensland Press, 2000a. 52–57, 229–30.
———. 'The Dim Sum vs. the Meat Pie: On the Rhetoric of Becoming an In-between Asian-Australian Artist.' *Alter/Asians: Asian Australian Identities in Art, Media and Popular Culture*. Eds. I. Ang, S. Chalmers, L. Law and M. Thomas. Annandale, NSW: Pluto Press, 2000b. 141–51.
Cheng, A. *The Melancholy of Race*. Oxford: Oxford University Press, 2000.
Choo, C. 'Floods of Memory.' *Meanjin* 61.1 (2002): 132–36.
Derrida, J. *The Work of Mourning*. Eds. P. Brault and M. Naas. Chicago and London: The University of Chicago Press, 2001.
Fanon, F. *Black Skin, White Masks*. Trans. C.L. Markmann. New York: Grove Press, 1967.
Freud, S. *On Metapsychology: The Theory of Psychoanalysis*. Eds. A. Richards. Trans. and J. Strachey. London: Penguin, 1984.
Gott, T. (Ed.) *Don't Leave Me This Way: Art in the Age of AIDS*. Canberra: National Gallery of Australia, 1994.
Grehan, H. 'Stillness and Intrigue in *The North* and *Sadness* by William Yang.' *Journal of Australian Studies* 73 (2002): 151–59.
Hallett, B. 'Sadness, William Yang.' *Sydney Morning Herald*, 2003, 2 May, <http://www.smh.com.au/articles/2003/05/01/1051382048540.html> (accessed 30 November 2003).
Hayes, P. 'Yang at Heart.' *Outrage* 161, October (1996), pp. 54–58.
Kaplan, L. 'Photography and the Exposure of Community: Sharing Nan Goldin and Jean-Luc Nancy.' *Angelaki* 6.3 (2001): 7–30.
Khoo, T. 'Re-Siting Australian Identity: Configuring the Chinese Citizen in Diana Giese's *Astronauts, Lost Souls and Dragons* and William Yang's *Sadness*.' *Bastard Moon: Essays on Chinese Australian Writing*. Special Issue of Otherland Literary Journal 7 (2001): 95–109.
Leong, G. 'Internalised Racism and the Work of Chinese Australian Artists: Making Visible the Invisible World of William Yang.' *Journal of Australian Studies* 72 (2002): 79–88.
Lingis, A. *The Community of Those Who have Nothing in Common*. Bloomington: Indiana University Press, 1994.
Min, S. 'Remains to Be Seen: Reading the Works of Dean Sameshima and Khanh Vo.' *Loss: The Politics of Mourning*. Eds. D. Eng and D. Kazanjian. Berkeley: University of California Press, 2003. 231–50.
Muñoz, J. E. 'Photographies of Mourning: Melancholia and Ambivalence in Van Der Zee, Mapplethorpe, and *Looking for Langston*.' *Race and the Subject of Masculinities*. Eds. H. Stecopoulos and M. Uebel. Durham and London: Duke University Press, 1997. 337–58.

Nancy, J. *The Inoperative Community*. Eds. P. Connor. Trans. P. Connor, L. Garbus, M. Holland and S. Sawhney. Minneapolis and London: University of Minnesota Press, 1991.
Oliver, K. *Witnessing: Beyond Recognition*. Minneapolis: University of Minnesota Press, 2001.
Phelan, P. *Mourning Sex: Performing Public Memories*. London and New York: Routledge, 1997.
Shen, Y. *Dragon Seed in the Antipodes: Chinese-Australian Autobiographies*. Melbourne: Melbourne University Press, 2001.
Smaill, B. 'Disorientations: Sadness, Mourning and the Unhomely.' *Journal of Australian Studies* 73 (2002): 161–69.
Sontag, S. *On Photography*. London: Penguin Books, 2002.
Wong, A. 'William Yang: Real Fiction.' *Transmissions* 2.1 (1998), <http://www.rumble.org/trans/transmissions2-2.htm> (accessed 3 November 2003).
Yang, W. *Sadness*. Sydney: Allen and Unwin, 1996.
——. *The Journeys of William Yang: Interview for Company B.*, 2003 <http://www.belvoir.com.au/sadness.html> (accessed 30 November 2003).

Grafton to Guangzhou: The Revolutionary Journey of Tse Tsan Tai

Rodney Noonan

The early years of the twenty-first century have witnessed a renewed interest in the activities and accomplishments of Tse Tsan Tai (pinyin: Xie Zuantai). Wendy Siuyi Wong's *Hong Kong Comics* (2002) proclaimed Tse's *The Situation in the Far East* the first cartoon created by a Chinese artist in Hong Kong. The *South China Morning Post* celebrated its centenary in November 2003 with a feature-length profile of Tse as its founder. Although these studies acknowledged the political dimension to Tse's cartooning and newspaper enterprises respectively, neither referred to his association with secret societies. Furthermore, both pieces were written for a Hong Kong audience and made only passing reference to Tse's Australian upbringing. This essay seeks to re-assert the importance of Tse's Australian background and not only situate it within the context of his revolutionary activities, but also use it as a catalyst to explore his relationship with Chinese secret societies.

By his own admission, Tse's political awakening occurred in Australia through the influence of his father who was a leading figure within one such society. Tse's affiliation with secret societies would constitute an increasingly important part of his political development, culminating in the unique role of these societies in his failed 1903 Guangzhou uprising. Tse's secret society membership in Australia and its significance for his later revolutionary activities emerged as a contentious issue in Australia in the 1930s following the claims of fellow Chinese Australian V.Y. Chow that Tse Tsan Tai rather than Sun Yat-sen was the founder of Republican China.

The intersecting transnational histories of Tse and Chow simultaneously contribute to two growing trends in Asian Australian studies. Their stories foreground efforts to recuperate diasporic community heritage by researching the history of individuals, thereby supplementing traditional research that predominantly focused on the presence of such groups in specific regions, particularly the goldfields. They also point to the complex ongoing relationship between diasporic communities in Australia with communities overseas. Tse's and Chow's respective published works subvert populist notions of docile, inarticulate Chinese miners, cooks and market gardeners, and illuminate a dynamic heterogeneous community whose political engagement with China is informed, rather than negated, by its Australian context.

Tse Tsan Tai was born in Sydney in 1872. His parents arrived in Australia in the late 1860s and his elder sister was born in Sydney in 1870. His father, Tse Yet Chong, worked as a merchant for an import-export firm in Sydney's Chinatown district (Tse 1924: 6). His mother Kwok Shi was one of only twelve Chinese women living in New South Wales at the time (Yong 1977: 275). Soon after Tse's birth, the family moved north and settled in Grafton, the major town on the Clarence River. The Clarence is the largest river between Sydney and Brisbane and served as an important site for trade and transport. Although Grafton never boasted a large Chinese population, Chinese miners frequently travelled through the town on their way to either the goldfields on the upper Clarence or the goldfields and tinfields further west in the New England region.

Tse Yet Chong operated a general store in Grafton's main street. He used the Anglicised surname of See and was known locally as John See. Tse Tsan Tai was known as James See. Tse's younger brother Tse Tsi Shau, who was known in Grafton as Thomas See and joined his brother as a revolutionary in the 1903 Guangzhou uprising, was born in Grafton in March 1876. The Clarence River flooded four months later and the trapped Tse family were rescued by reporters from the newspaper office adjoining their store. The reporters lowered a rope from the second floor balcony of the *Clarence and Richmond Examiner* office to the front door of the single-storey shop and hoisted the family to safety. The family and reporters remained in the newspaper office for two days, surviving on canned food from Tse Yet Chong's store until the floodwaters had sufficiently receded for them to leave (*Daily Examiner* 1932a: 4).

With the exception of the flood rescue, Tse had an unremarkable childhood in Grafton. However he recalled his years there with great fondness in his political memoir *The Chinese Republic* (1924). Tse attended Grafton public school and was baptised at the Church of England by Bishop Greenway in November 1879. Greenway, who was the son of the convict-architect Francis Greenway, was also Tse's godfather and the pair corresponded for many years after Tse left Grafton. Tse attributed his 'strict moral rectitude and conduct in life' to Greenway's influence and his schooling in Grafton (1924: 6). His Christianity and Western education were an integral part of his make-up and later gave him much in common with the revolutionaries and reformers with whom he collaborated, such as Sun Yat-sen, Yang Quyun and Yung Wing (pinyin: Rong Hong).

One of the very few other Chinese in Grafton at the time was King Jung Sao. He too operated a general store. Much more significantly, King was reputedly the leader of the Revolutionary and Independence Society of Australian Chinese. According to King's grandson, V.Y. Chow, the party was founded by Loong Hung Pung in Sydney in 1850 and Loong remained its leader until succeeded by King in 1878 (Chow 1933a). Tse Yet Chong was also a leading figure in the party (Tse 1924: 7). Despite the negligible Chinese population living in Grafton, King Jung Sao and Tse Yet Chong were able to use the town's strategic location to disseminate their views to the vast numbers of Chinese miners travelling through the region and shopping at their stores. Unsurprisingly, Tse Tsan Tai was exposed to anti-Manchu thinking at an early age and claimed that his political convictions were born in Australia. Tse further stated that in his pre-teens he vowed to return to China and overthrow the Qing dynasty (1924: 7). Fifty years later, V.Y. Chow contended that Tse's emerging political consciousness coupled with King's association with Tse (and his father) in Grafton was a critical juncture in the development of the revolutionary movement. Chow (1933b: 430) argued that leadership of the Chinese Australian revolutionary movement passed from Loong Hung Pung to King Jung Sao to Tse Tsan Tai and that Tse had been the movement's 'spiritual head and spokesman' since 1887 (*Daily Examiner 1932b*: 4). In Chow's view, Tse presented a tangible link between underground Chinese political organisations in Australia and the early revolutionary movement in China.

Later historians exploring Chinese secret societies in Australia have paid minimal attention to these figures. Although Yong (1977: 157–58) mentions the existence of Loong Hung Pung, King Jung Sao and Tse Yet Chong, he is sceptical of the source material and, lacking any further documentation, focuses on a rival history of other society leaders. Cai (2004) does not refer to them at all. Yong and Cai acknowledge that the birth of Chinese secret societies on the goldfields coincided with political turbulence in China, as evidenced by the Taiping rebellion, but neither suggests any politicisation of the Chinese secret societies in Australia until after Federation. Furthermore, their use of terminology is non-political: they refer to the societies as the Hung League, the Yee Hing and the Chinese Masonic Society. Chow frequently uses the latter term as well, but he and Tse both use explicitly political titles in their description of the societies in the nineteenth century. Tse (1924: 7) refers to the Chinese Independence Party of Australia, while Chow constantly refers to the Revolutionary and Independence Society of Australian Chinese. While not denying the heightened sense of Chinese nationalism among Chinese Australians in the post-Federation period, particularly in light of the passing of the 1901 Immigration Restriction Act and the distinguished reformer Liang Qichao's six-month fundraising tour in support of the Baohuanghui (Protect the Emperor Society), Tse and Chow point to a complex and hitherto under-explored politicisation of nineteenth century Chinese Australian communities.

Tse's family returned to Hong Kong in 1887. Despite his initial sense of alienation, he quickly adapted to his new surroundings and enrolled in Queen's College in preparation for joining the Hong Kong civil service. During this period he established a close network of friends who shared his political outlook. Foremost among them was Yang Quyun with whom Tse founded the Furen Wenshe (Literary Society for the Promotion of Benevolence) in 1890. Yang was born in Hong Kong in 1861 and educated in missionary schools. Like Tse, he was an English-speaking Christian with a Westernised education (Hsüeh 1960: 307). Yang worked as a chief shipping clerk and played a leading role in the revolutionary movement until his assassination in January 1901.

The Furen Wenshe contained just sixteen members and was more reformist than seditious in nature. Nonetheless, it created a supportive environment for activists with like-minded ideological concerns and provided a platform for their later revolutionary activities. The group held regular meetings at which they promoted a reformist programme and Tse wrote a number of newspaper articles propagating these views, including pieces opposing 'feng-shui, foot-binding, opium-smoking and mui-tsai (bonded maid servant system)' (Tsai 1993: 98). His articles did not pass unnoticed and in May 1894 Tse was reprimanded by the colonial secretary 'for "dabbling in politics" whilst in government service' (Tse 1924: 8)

The shift from reformist newspaper articles to active revolution coincided with the latter stages of the Sino-Japanese war. In early 1895, the Furen Wenshe amalgamated with Sun Yat-sen's fledgling Xingzhonghui (Revive China Society), which lent its name to the newly-formed entity. The merger was not surprising as the two organisations shared many similarities. Both were comprised of young men: at thirty-three, Yang was the oldest member of either party. All members had received a Westernised education. All were Christian. All shared a desire to overthrow the Qing dynasty (Rhoads 1975: 39). However, the two leaders apparently differed in their views on China's political future. Only Yang was firmly committed to a republican form of government. Sun was vehemently anti-Manchu but was still prepared to accept a 'monarchical institution if the emperor was Chinese' (Hsüeh 1960: 310).

Tse (1924: 9) first met Sun on 13 March 1895 at a meeting with Yang Quyun and Huang Yongshang in which they discussed plans for an attack on Guangzhou. Huang was a wealthy new recruit whose father had served in Hong Kong's Legislative Council (Schiffrin 1968: 48). Although not previously a member of the Furen

Wenshe, Huang nonetheless aligned himself with Tse and Yang. As the Xingzhonghui had insufficient members to launch the attack alone, it was agreed to recruit fighters from secret societies and bandit gangs. Yang, Tse and Huang 'formed the triumvirate which managed the financial and other aspects of the Hong Kong phase of the plot', while Sun and his closest supporters were responsible for recruitment and fundraising in Guangzhou (Schiffrin 1968: 70).

The Xingzhonghui leadership also held covert meetings with the editors of the English-language newspapers the *China Mail* and the *Hongkong Telegraph*, both of whom promised to support the revolutionary movement. Part of the Xingzhonghui's propaganda campaign included an open letter to the Guangxu emperor printed in the major English-language newspapers imploring him to follow the Japanese example and adopt reform on 'approved Western lines' (*China Mail* 1895: 3). Tse claimed authorship of the letter, which appeared on 30 May 1895, and called upon the emperor to introduce six major social and political changes: implement a constitutional government; remove all incapable officials; abolish the queue; prohibit footbinding; prohibit opium-smoking; and ensure freedom of the press.

Logistical arrangements for the uprising proceeded throughout 1895. The two branches of the Xingzhonghui were engaged in recruitment and fundraising initiatives in Hong Kong and Guangzhou respectively but without a designated leader. Neither Yang nor Sun had relinquished leadership when the two groups merged. On 10 October, just two weeks before the scheduled uprising, the members of the Xingzhonghui elected Yang as their leader. Sun's supporters were bitterly disappointed but were forced to accept Yang as leader 'because of his control of the movement's finances' (Schiffrin 1968: 70). Not only did Yang have the vast personal wealth of his Xingzhonghui ally Huang Yongshang at his disposal, he had secured the financial support of a rich Hong Kong business figure outside the Xingzhonghui. Although Sun's followers begrudgingly accepted Yang's election, they were infuriated by his defeat. The ongoing leadership tension between Yang and Sun generated considerable enmity and bitterness between their respective supporters for the next five years. Yang's supporters were equally aggrieved when he was deposed as leader by Sun in 1900. Tse formed an unfavourable opinion of Sun in 1895 and campaigned vigorously for Yang during the leadership battles. When Sun assumed leadership of the party in 1900, Tse initially refused to work under him and soon after nominated Yung Wing as a compromise leader. Tse's animosity towards Sun is evident throughout *The Chinese Republic* and reflects the disruptive factionalism that existed within the early revolutionary movement and that was exacerbated by the failure of the 1895 October uprising.

Although the authorities had been informed of a probable uprising and were already on the alert for any suspicious activity, the revolutionaries were thwarted by a delay in their Hong Kong arrangements. On learning of the delay, Sun attempted to postpone the operation, but Yang received notification too late and the police were waiting when his recruits eventually arrived in Guangzhou. Between forty and fifty rebels were arrested while the rest scattered in the crowd (Schiffrin 1968: 84–87). This incident added to the extant bitterness between the two factions, and Sun and his supporters blamed Yang for the failure of the uprising.

Following the exposure of their plot, most of the leading revolutionaries fled overseas. Sun was famously kidnapped in London before establishing a revolutionary base in Japan. Yang travelled to South Africa, where he founded a branch of the Xingzhonghui in Johannesburg. He left South Africa in early 1898, and briefly returned to Hong Kong for a meeting with Tse before joining the main revolutionary body in Japan. Throughout his travels, Yang frequently corresponded with Tse who urged him to cultivate relations with secret societies in Malaya and Singapore during his return journey. This policy is indicative of the ongoing link in Tse's thinking between secret societies and the revolutionary struggle. The concept grew out of Tse's own experiences in Australia and he reiterated it to Yang at their reunion in Hong Kong in March 1898 when Tse emphasised 'the importance of obtaining the cooperation and support of the anti-Manchu secret societies' in the aforementioned regions (Tse 1924: 10).

With the other leaders in exile, Tse was the most senior Xingzhonghui figure remaining in Hong Kong. Isolated from his revolutionary colleagues, he used the opportunity to cultivate closer relations with the leading figures in the reform movement. Tse met Kang Youwei's younger brother Kang Guangren on 21 February 1896, just four months after the failed October uprising. Tse and Kang Guangren held several meetings and exchanged correspondence between 1896 and 1898 in which they constantly reiterated the need for the two groups to unite and cooperate. Tse (1924: 11) also held a meeting with Kang Youwei on 4 October 1896 in which they reportedly decided to 'unite and cooperate' but nothing eventuated. Kang Guangren advised Tse that Liang Qichao also supported the concept of unity and cooperation. This is particularly pertinent given Liang's role in later unity discussions with Sun Yat-sen in Japan. Furthermore, Tse's close relationship with the reformers, especially Liang, laid the platform for their cooperation in the 1903 Guangzhou rising.

In his analysis of the relationship between the revolutionaries and the reformers, Hao Yen-p'ing asserted that 'during the Hundred Days of Reform in 1898, the two parties were not on good terms' (1961: 95). However the estrangement between the camps did not preclude contact between individuals. Kang Guangren wrote to Tse on 24 July 1898, urging him to arrange a meeting with Yang Quyun (1924: 13). Kang had previously expressed his desire to meet Yang and as early as September 1897 Kang confided that he was enthusiastic about working with Yang but would not unite with somebody as 'rash and reckless' as Sun Yat-sen (Tse 1924: 12). Despite Tse's and Kang's enthusiasm, no meeting was ever arranged. The Empress Dowager Cixi deposed her nephew in a bloody coup on 21 September 1898: the emperor was imprisoned; Kang Youwei and Liang Qichao fled to Japan; and six of the reformers were arrested and beheaded, including Tse's friend Kang Guangren.

The period following the Hundred Days was one of intense activity and negotiation between the revolutionary and reform movements. Most of the leading revolutionaries and reformers were in exile in Japan where some members explored the possibility of cooperation and unification. Tse was still based in Hong Kong and therefore more isolated than ever before from the party machinations. It was then that he created his cartoon *The Situation in the Far East*. Now regarded as the first cartoon by a Chinese national, Tse intended it to 'arouse the Chinese nation, and to warn the people of the impending danger of the partitioning of the Empire by the Foreign Powers' (1924: 15). The cartoon depicted the conquest of China by foreign nations, while simultaneously condemning the complicit behaviour of Qing officials and the complacency of the general populace. It was initially banned in China but was published in Japan in July 1899. Tse was again reprimanded by the Colonial Secretary for his political views. The cartoon was widely published in China during the early twentieth century without credit to Tse, and the work has often been erroneously attributed to another artist (Wong 2002: 13).

Tse (1924: 17) also devoted himself to the cause of the exiled reformer Jing Yuanshan. Jing was wanted by the Qing authorities and had been arrested in Macao on what Tse regarded as fraudulent charges. Jing had a longstanding reputation for political liberalism and in 1897 established plans for the first girls' school in China. Tse's reformist friends Kang Guangren and Liang Qichao both assisted Jing in this venture (Qian 2003: 402). Tse used his contacts in the foreign community in Hong Kong to lobby the Portuguese authorities to release Jing rather than hand him over to the Qing authorities. Tse persuaded the editors of the *China Mail* and *Hongkong Daily Press* to offer their public support for Jing. He also used his involvement in the anti-footbinding movement to heighten awareness of Jing's plight and apply diplomatic pressure for Jing's release. Alicia Little is regarded as the person most 'responsible for the abolition of footbinding in China' (Hoe 1996: 19) and she extended her Natural Foot Society to Hong Kong in 1900 (Hoe 1996: 188), Tse and his wife were among its supporters. Tse (1924: 13) publicly campaigned against footbinding while in the Furen Wenshe and founded a society for its suppression in March 1898. The Hong Kong governor Sir Henry Blake's wife and daughter were also members of Little's Natural Foot Society. Given Jing's commitment to female education, he found immediate sympathy from the Blakes and Little. Jing's safe release in 1901 was attributed in large part to the political and media campaign Tse coordinated on his behalf (Armentrout 1976: 96).

Tse used the period following the Hundred Days as productively as possible, but his isolation from Japan meant that he was unable to effectively support Yang Quyun in a renewed leadership struggle with Sun Yat-sen. Yang had arrived in Japan in March 1898. Although in a weakened position of power, Yang continued to serve as the nominal leader of the Xingzhonghui and Liang Qichao made a particular point of including Yang in negotiations between the reformers and revolutionaries. However, by the end of 1899, Sun had finally wrested the leadership from Yang (Hsüeh 1960: 313–14). Yang travelled to Hong Kong in January 1900 to confer with Tse before submitting his resignation as leader. Tse (1924: 16–18) agreed it was the best course of action but vowed that he would not serve under Sun's leadership. Despite this threat, Tse remained active within the Xingzhonghui for another twelve months.

However, he made one final attempt to dislodge Sun from the leadership in March 1900. Within three weeks of first meeting Yung Wing, Tse nominated him as a compromise leadership candidate. Yung was not a member of the Xingzhonghui but shared many of their political concerns. He too was a Christian with a Westernised education. Yung was born in a small village near Macao in 1828 and educated in Macao and Hong Kong before leaving for the United States in 1847. Yung entered Yale University in 1850 and four years later became the first Chinese student to graduate from an American university (Worthy 1965: 267–70). He returned to China during the late 1890s and served as Under Secretary for Foreign Affairs during the Hundred Days Reform. Although Tse's efforts to install Yung as leader of the Xingzhonghui failed, Yung was to become an increasingly important figure in the broader anti-Manchu movement. He was elected president of the reformers' National Assembly in Shanghai in July 1900, and was one of the primary organisers of the reformers' Hankou uprising one month later (Wong 1986: 18–21). Tse continued to correspond with Yung and intended to install Yung as president if his Guangzhou uprising had succeeded.

Despite being deposed as leader, Yang Quyun was still part of the Xingzhonghui's inner circle. On 18 April 1900, Yang briefed Tse (1924: 18–19) on plans for a new uprising in southern China to coincide with the reformers' uprising in Hankou. Four days later, Tse recruited Li Jitang to the Xingzhonghui. Li's wealth and factional alignment made him a natural replacement for Huang Yongshang who died two years after the 1895 uprising. Li devoted his entire fortune to the revolutionary cause and his presence helped re-establish the Tse-Yang powerbase within the Xingzhonghui. He not only provided substantial funding for the Xingzhonghui's Huizhou uprising in 1900, but was a major financial contributor to Tse's Guangzhou uprising in 1903. Li also provided financial assistance to the *Zhongguo ribao* (*China Daily*), the newspaper founded and edited by Sun Yat-sen's supporter Chen Shaobai (Rhoads 1975: 66–67).

Before either the reformers or revolutionaries were ready to act, the Boxer Rebellion inspired an alternative plan. The Boxer siege of the foreign legations in Beijing generated fears in southern China of foreign intervention there as well. A scheme emerged whereby several of the southern provinces would declare their independence. The plan required the revolutionaries to act in conjunction with the southern authorities, most importantly Li Hongzhang, governor of Guangdong and Guangxi. Seizing this unexpected opportunity, Sun arrived in Hong Kong harbour on 17 June 1900 and held a one-hour meeting aboard the SS *Indras* with Tse, Yang, Chen Shaobai, Zheng Shiliang and their Japanese supporter Hirayama Shu. It was Tse's first joint meeting with the other leading Chinese revolutionaries since the failed 1895 uprising. They decided that three Japanese supporters should meet Li Hongzhang's advisor Liu Xuexun to ascertain Li's intentions. On 17 July, the revolutionaries met again and drafted a letter to Li Hongzhang outlining their proposed social and political changes. Tse, Yang and Sun were among the nine signatories. Their efforts were ultimately futile as Li joined with two other provincial governors in refusing to recognise the validity of the imperial court's declaration of war (Rhoads 1975: 42–43).

Following the failure of these negotiations, the revolutionaries then reverted to their original scheme of dual uprisings. However, the two uprisings did not coincide as planned. The reformers' Hankou uprising was exposed in late August. Several of the leaders were executed and many others, including Yung Wing, were wanted by the Qing authorities. The revolutionaries' Huizhou uprising commenced in October 1900. Under Zheng Shiliang's leadership they fought a series of battles against government troops for over two weeks but when promised Japanese funding failed to materialise, the rebel force was disbanded. Retribution for the Huizhou uprising was swift and severe, with Yang Quyun as the prime target. Since returning to Hong Kong in early 1900, Yang had been teaching English at his home. A gunman entered Yang's home in the early evening of 10 January 1901 and shot him in front of his students. He died in hospital the following morning (Hsüeh 1960: 317). Yang's assassination served as a catalyst for Tse to break finally with the Xingzhonghui and pursue his own revolutionary agenda independent of Sun.

Tse planned to launch his Guangzhou uprising on Chinese New Year 1903. His fellow organisers were Li Jitang and Hong Quanfu. Tse was responsible for cultivating support among the foreign community, Li was responsible for finances, and Hong was responsible for the military aspects of the campaign. Hong was a senior Hung Men leader to whom Tse had been introduced by his father in November 1899, reinforcing the central role of secret societies in Tse's revolutionary activities. Hong was also the nephew of the Taiping leader Hong Xiuquan and had served in the Taiping campaign. In fact, there were echoes of the Taiping rising in some of the Chinese-language proclamations issued by the rebels. Hong had lived in exile for many years after the Taiping rebellion, including a period in Australia where he almost certainly would have been in contact with the secret societies because of his own society membership (Armentrout 1976: 88).

The revolutionaries planned to attack Guangzhou on 28 January 1903. The uprising would begin with an assault on the Temple of Longevity, which would be blown up once all the leading Qing officials had gathered there for the New Year festivities. Three separate militia bands comprised of recruits from secret societies would then launch simultaneous attacks throughout Guangdong. One contingent would destroy the provincial arsenal in Guangzhou while two other contingents would rise up to combat the provincial army and navy respectively. The three rebel groups would then jointly converge on Guangzhou to battle any remaining Qing forces and seize the city (Armentrout 1976: 94).

Several leading reformers were also closely involved with Tse's plot. Yung Wing had been Tse's compromise leadership candidate of the Xingzhonghui in 1900 and was now Tse's choice to serve as president. Yung endeavoured to raise funds in the United States to help equip and train the revolutionary force. He also developed plans to 'promote mining, reorganize the tax and banking system, and encourage industry' (Armentrout 1976: 102). Ou Qujia and Liang Qichao were also heavily involved in the preparations. Unsurprisingly, they were the same two leading reformers Kang Youwei had reprimanded for becoming too close to the revolutionary cause in Japan in 1899 (Schiffrin 1968: 164). Ou edited both reformist and Hung Men newspapers in San Francisco. These publications enabled him to promote the revolutionaries' cause and solicit funding from Chinese Americans. Ou's treatise *Xin Guangdong* (*New Guangdong*) advocated a separate state for Guangdong and was disseminated through these publications (Armentrout 1976: 99–100). Liang offered similar support for Tse's revolutionary cause in his Tokyo publications and also published Ou's *Xin Guangdong*. Liang had joined the Hung Men in Hawaii in 1900, strengthening his ties with the other leading figures in the rising. Liang corresponded with Yung Wing about the rising during the planning stages (Armentrout 1976: 90) and after meeting Yung in 1903, Liang expressed his admiration for Yung's patriotism and sophisticated political ideology (Worthy 1965: 286).

In the months preceding the uprising, Tse (1924: 21) wrote several articles for the English-language press opposing Manchu rule and advocating change. He had the support of *China Mail* editor Thomas Reid and *Hongkong Daily Press* editor Alfred Cunningham, both of whom had lobbied for the release of imprisoned reformer Jing Yuanshan. Reid had supported the Xingzhonghui's 1895 uprising, but Cunningham was the more active participant in Tse's scheme. He even printed the revolutionaries' *Proclamation of Independence* on Christmas Eve 1902.

The plan was not dissimilar to the Xingzhonghui's plan to seize Guangzhou in 1895: the attack was scheduled to coincide with a major festival; fighters were recruited from secret societies; most of the leaders were Christian; and the foreign press had demonstrated its support. The similarities were so pronounced that Edward Rhoads declared the only difference 'in 1903 from 1895 and 1900 was the absence of Sun Yat Sen' (1975: 68). However, as Eve Armentrout (1976) has cogently argued, the uprising did not merely replicate earlier Xingzhonghui uprisings but was a unique fusion of revolutionary, reformist and secret society principles. Whereas the revolutionaries and reformers simply attempted to coordinate their Hankou and Huizhou uprisings in 1900, the revolutionaries and reformers worked together in Tse's uprising to raise funds, disseminate propaganda and organise the military strategies. Furthermore, the Xingzhonghui had merely recruited members of secret societies as fighters for the 1895 and 1900 uprisings cited by Rhoads. Tse acknowledged that his plans 'depended upon the anti-Manchu secret societies to furnish the fighting material for the revolution' (1924: 21) but the fundamental difference is that all the leaders in Tse's uprising actually belonged to secret societies: Tse Tsan Tai, Hong Quanfu, Li Jitang, Liang Qichao and Ou Qujia.

Tse Tsan Tai was not the only member of the Tse family involved in the plot. His politically-minded father Tse Yet Chong was still active in the Hung Men, had introduced Tse to Hong Quanfu in 1899 and assisted in the planning stages. Tse's Grafton-born younger brother Tse Tsi Shau was expected to play an active military role in the campaign and Tse (1924: 22–23) appointed him as his deputy when he arrived in Hong Kong from Singapore on Christmas Day 1902. Two days later, Tse Tsi

Shau accompanied Hong Quanfu to a crucial strategy meeting with eight militia leaders in Guangzhou to finalise preparations for the uprising. Tse Tsan Tai, his father and brother held a meeting in Hong Kong on 20 January 1903 to discuss and finalise their plans. Five days later, Tse Tsi Shau and Hong Quanfu set out together for Macao. Within hours of their departure, the plot had been uncovered and police raided Hong's quarters in Hong Kong. Tse Tsan Tai sent warnings to his rebel forces through a Christian minister in the Berlin Mission. Tse Tsi Shau returned safely to Hong Kong on 27 January but that same day more than twenty of Tse's rebels in Guangzhou were arrested and executed (Armentrout 1976: 101).

Fearing execution, Hong Quanfu fled overseas. Six weeks later a Guangzhou peddler who closely resembled Hong was lured to Hong Kong on the pretext of a job offer. The peddler was murdered and his corpse was handed over to Chinese authorities on a gunboat just outside of Hong Kong harbour, enabling his killers to collect the reward being offered for Hong. Details of the crime emerged just as one of Yang Quyun's assassins was being tried for murder. The two crimes, both relating to Tse's political allies, aroused diplomatic concerns about infringements of British sovereignty and the Hong Kong governor Sir Henry Blake protested to Guangdong officials. The Guangdong authorities then launched an investigation into both the murder and the uprising. Their report included a list of Chinese residents in Hong Kong suspected of involvement in the uprising. Among those named were Tse Tsan Tai, Tse Tsi Shau and Li Jitang. Sir Henry Blake refused to accept that any of those named in the report had participated in the uprising and Li Jitang 'was given extensive protection by the Hong Kong police' (Chan 1990: 62–63). As Tse and his wife were both friendly with the Blake family through their membership of the Natural Foot Society, it is highly probable that the Tse brothers were afforded the same offer of protection.

Disheartened by the failure of the uprising and the death of his father two months later, Tse abandoned active revolution. Tse claimed that his decision would allow 'Sun Yat-sen and his followers a free hand' (1924: 24) while Tse pursued a pro-reform path through the English-language press. For this purpose, Tse and Alfred Cunningham founded the *South China Morning Post*. Despite Tse's overt political intentions, the *Post's* board of directors did not share Tse's commitment to reform and sought only 'a paper "very much better and more interesting" than its rivals' (Hutcheon 1983: 15). Despite its longevity and continued existence, the *South China Morning Post* never fulfilled Tse's reformist ideals. It struggled financially during its early years of operation and by 1907 neither Tse nor Cunningham remained with the paper. Cunningham was dismissed for financial mismanagement and Tse was retrenched in a cost-cutting exercise (Hutcheon 1983: 28).

Thereafter, Tse had little involvement with the revolutionary movement. He continued to correspond with Yung Wing in America and twice met with Sun Yat-sen following the downfall of the Qing dynasty. Their first meeting was an informal greeting aboard the SS *Devanha* in Hong Kong harbour on 21 December 1911 as Sun prepared to travel north to assume the provisional presidency. Their second meeting was at a function held in Sun's honour in Hong Kong on 24 April 1912 where Tse was asked to introduce prominent Hong Kong society and business figures to Sun. However, Tse was no longer an active figure in the movement and bid his farewell to the revolutionary scene in 1924 when the *South China Morning Post* published his memoir *The Chinese Republic: The Secret History of the Revolution*.

Tse's political legacy and his role in the revolutionary movement became an unlikely source of public debate following the arrival of V.Y. Chow in Australia in 1932. Chow was the grandson of the former Grafton storekeeper King Jung Sao who had been a party colleague of Tse Yet Chong. Chow was born and raised in Lismore, near Grafton in New South Wales, but left Australia as a young adult and worked as a journalist and foundation editor of the Shanghai-based English-language political journal *United China Magazine*. The magazine was extremely critical of the ruling Guomindang, whom Chow accused of being 'traitors to the nation' and in a fiery editorial he stated the magazine's intention to 'expose the source of the origin of the revolutionary movement ... and the ungracious hero-worship of Dr Sun Yat-sen as the one and only Chinese revolutionary worthy of remembrance' (1932: 150).

As previously mentioned, Chow believed that the 1911 revolution was the culmination of organised political dissent and revolutionary thought that originated with the founding of the Revolutionary and Independence Party of the Australian Chinese by Loong Hung Pung in 1850. Chow argued that Sun 'was really a mild diversion in the great record of the Chinese revolution' and that Tse was 'more truly the father of modern Chinese republicanism than Sun Yat-sen could ever be' (1933b: 430). Chow not only venerated Tse's role in the revolutionary movement at the expense of Sun, he also accused Sun of plagiarising his Three Principles from Loong Hung Pung. Chow (1933b: 427) claimed that Sun acquired a copy of Loong's *The Reconstruction of China as a Modern State* sometime after Tse retired from revolutionary activity. Unable to transcribe it all before it was destroyed in a fire, Sun re-produced Loong's treatise from memory and published it as *The Three Principles of the People*.

Chow's visit and his polemic theories generated a vitriolic response within the pro-Sun, Chinese Australian community in Sydney. He was debated and denounced at various public meetings and social functions. Despite their obvious political differences, Chow (1933c: 442) lent his only copy of Tse's *The Chinese Republic* to the Chinese Australian business figure and community leader William Liu. It was returned to him just as he was leaving Sydney for Grafton. Chow claimed that all comments critical of Sun Yat-sen had been excised and in some cases entire pages had been removed. Chow also stated that he had been under surveillance while staying with his mother and sister in Sydney (*Daily Examiner 1932c*: 2). He further claimed that a Chinese spy followed him to Grafton but immediately left town when Chow (1933c: 442) confronted him. Although these claims of surveillance cannot be independently verified, a file in the National Archives of Australia (1935) confirms that Chow was being monitored by Australian authorities on a subsequent visit to Sydney and one Federal politician unsuccessfully sought to have him deported.

Sydney's Chinese-language press paid close attention to Chow's visit. Chow accused the Guomindang-backed *Chinese Times* of a 'scurrilous attack' on him (Chow 1933c: 441) and claimed that it deliberately mistranslated an interview he had conducted with the *Sydney Morning Herald*. He expected similar treatment from the Sydney Chinese Chamber of Commerce-backed *Tung Wah Times*, but to his surprise the paper 'printed what amounted to a defence in their next issue' (Chow 1933c: 441).

Chow's visit also garnered publicity in the broader non-Chinese community. The Brisbane press interviewed Chow upon his arrival there on 18 September 1932 and the Sydney newspapers offered similar coverage when he arrived there three days later. The *Sydney Morning Herald* (1932) published an extensive feature article on him later in the month and not only reported his views on Tse and Sun but also his belief that unless the Guomindang 'rehabilitated itself', China would eventually fall under communist rule. Chow strategically positioned himself as an authoritative voice to his readership: 'I was brought up at once an Australian and a Chinese. I can speak for my Australian-Chinese comrades and also for the Chinese Republican Movement' (Chow 1933c: 436). He couched his theories in a manner amenable to the Australian public and employed the emotive rhetoric of Anzac and Gallipoli to relate the struggles of the Chinese Australian revolutionaries, at once acknowledging their patriotism and loyalty to Australia, but also invoking their valour and sense of sacrifice in China (Chow 1933a: 423, 426).

Chow's visit and theories influenced the work of John Sleeman whose *White China* was published while Chow was still in Australia. Sleeman dedicated his book to Sun Yat-sen and clearly disagreed with Chow's anti-Sun pronouncements. Nonetheless, Sleeman devoted an entire chapter to Tse, whom he declared the 'greatest Australian-born Chinese' (1933: 137). Sleeman praised the early history of the Revolutionary and Independence Party of the Australian Chinese and the leadership roles of Loong Hung Pung and King Jung Sao, but refused to accept links between the party in Australia and later revolutionary activity in China. Sleeman criticised some of Tse's actions, particularly those relating to Sun. He also allowed William Liu an opportunity to refute Chow's theories in his book's thirty-four page appendix.

Nowhere was the interest in Chow's theories greater than in Grafton, where local residents expressed a parochial pride in Tse. The visit to Grafton enhanced Chow's research output and was unquestionably the public relations highlight of his Australian trip. Chow (1933c: 442–443) was greeted by the mayor upon his arrival at Grafton railway on 3 November, and regaled community groups with tales of how a former Grafton resident had liberated China. Chow inspected Tse's baptism certificate at Christ Church Cathedral, met one of Tse's former schoolteachers and interviewed one of the journalists who rescued the Tse family from floodwaters in 1876.

Upon leaving Grafton, Chow (1933c: 445) wrote to the mayor convinced that 'the citizens of your fine city will not forget that the founder of the Chinese Republic ever regarded Grafton as his "hometown"'. Yet there are no monuments to Tse in Grafton, nor in Hong Kong or Guangzhou. Despite his marginalisation, Tse remains a seminal figure in the early revolutionary movement: he was a foundation member of the Furen Wenshe; a strategist in the 1895 and 1900 Xingzhonghui uprisings; an impassioned negotiator for unity between the reformers and revolutionaries; and the central figure behind the 1903 Guangzhou uprising. Furthermore, Tse's pioneering ventures into cartooning and newspaper publishing were both driven by a political imperative. Tse's political journey may have concluded in Guangzhou, but it began in Grafton and his Australian background was fundamental in framing his later revolutionary activities.

References

Armentrout, L. E. 'The Canton Rising of 1902–1903: Reformers, Revolutionaries, and the Second Taiping.' *Modern Asian Studies* 10.1 (1976): 83–105.
Cai, S. 'From Mutual Aid to Public Interest: Chinese Secret Societies in Australia.'. Trans. D. Campbell. *Otherland* 9 (2004): 133–51.
Chan, L. K. *China, Britain and Hong Kong, 1895–1945*. Hong Kong: Chinese University Press, 1990.
China Mail 'Constitutional Reform in China.', 1895, 30 May: 3.
Chow, V. Y. 'The Party's or the People's Dictatorship?' *United China Magazine* 1.4 (1932): 149–151.
——. 'In 1850 the Revolution Was Born.' *United China Magazine* 1.11 (1933a): 423–26.
——. 'Sun Yat Sen's "Fatherhood" of New China.' *United China Magazine* 1.11 (1933b): 427–30, 491.
——. 'Odyssey in the South.' *United China Magazine* 1.11 (1933c): 434–47.
Daily Examiner 'Tse Tsan Tai: The Chinese Revolutionary.', 1932a, 24 September: 4.
——. 'Chinese Leader: Ex-Grafton Boy.', 1932b, 4 November: 4.
——. 'New Chinese Movement.', 1932c, 7 November: 2.
Hao, Y. 'The Abortive Cooperation between Reformers and Revolutionaries (1895–1900).' *Papers on China* 15 (1961): 91–114.
Hoe, S. *Chinese Footprints: Exploring Women's History in China, Hong Kong and Macau*. Hong Kong: Roundhouse Publications, 1996.
Hsüeh, C. 'Sun Yat-sen, Yang Ch'ü-yün, and the Early Revolutionary Movement in China.' *Journal of Asian Studies* 19.3 (1960): 307–318.
Hutcheon, R. *SCMP: The First Eighty Years*. Hong Kong: South China Morning Post, 1983.
National Archives of Australia *(Communism): Re Meetings Held in Leigh House, Sydney by Mr V.Y. Chow*, 1935. A467, SF42/273.
Qian, N. 'Revitalizing the Xianyuan (Worthy Ladies) Tradition: Women in the 1898 Reforms.' *Modern China* 29.4 (2003): 399–454.
Rhoads, E. *China's Republican Revolution: The Case of Kwangtung, 1895–1913*. Cambridge: Harvard University Press, 1975.
Schiffrin, H. *Sun Yat-sen and the Origins of the Chinese Revolution*. Berkeley: University of California, 1968.
Sleeman, J. *White China: An Austral-Asian Sensation*. Sydney: J. Sleeman, 1933.
South China Morning Post (Centenary Supplement) 'The Idealist who Founded a Paper.', 2003, 6 November: 12.
Sydney Morning Herald 'China: Menace of Communism.', 1932, 29 September: 13.
Tsai, J. *Hong Kong in Chinese History: Community and Social Unrest in the British Colony, 1842–1913*. New York: Columbia University Press, 1993.
Tse, T. T. *The Chinese Republic: Secret History of the Revolution*. Hong Kong: South China Morning Post, 1924.

Wong, J. Y. 'Three Visionaries in Exile: Yung Wing, K'ang Yu-wei and Sun Yat-sen, 1894–1911.' *Journal of Asian History* 20 (1986): 1–32.

Wong, W. S. *Hong Kong Comics: A History of Manhua*. New York: Princeton Architectural Press, 2002.

Worthy, E. H. Jr. 'Yung Wing in America.' *Pacific Historical Review* 34.3 (1965): 265–87.

Yong, C. F. *The New Gold Mountain: The Chinese in Australia 1901–1921*. Richmond: Raphael Arts, 1977.

'No Place Like Home': The Ambivalent Rhetoric of Hospitality in the Work of Simone Lazaroo, Arlene Chai, and Hsu-Ming Teo

Deborah L. Madsen

> Hospitality is culture itself and not simply one ethic among others. Insofar as it has to do with the ethos, that is, the residence, one's home, the familiar place of dwelling, inasmuch as it is a manner of being there, the manner in which we relate to ourselves and to others, to others as our own or as foreigners, *ethics is hospitality*; ethics is so thoroughly coextensive with the experience of hospitality. (Derrida 2001: 16–17)

Introduction

The traditional song says, 'Home, home, sweet sweet home/There's no place like home'. Home is an incommensurable place, a place of safety and security that cannot be replicated. For migrants, refugees, and seekers of asylum, the difficulties of locating such a space, a place like home, are insurmountable. For the deterritorialised or deracinated subject, there can be *no* place like 'home'. In this essay, I would like to rehearse some of the conceptual scenarios offered by Derrida as he considers what is at stake in the debate concerning hospitality and cosmopolitan rights of abode, within the context of Chinese Australia, a place which Ien Ang has compellingly written about as an ambivalent scene of hospitality: offering reluctant tolerance and an unhomely home, where the Other can live, but cannot belong.

In the essay *The Curse of the Smile: Ambivalence and the 'Asian' Woman in Australian Multiculturalism* (from *On Not Speaking Chinese*, 2001), Ang perceptively describes the condition of individuals of Asian descent in contemporary Australia - when she writes: 'racially and ethnically marked people are no longer othered today through simple mechanisms of rejection and exclusion, but through an ambivalent and apparently contradictory process of *inclusion by virtue of othering*' (2001: 139, emphasis in original). Ang's analysis focuses on the image of an East Asian woman's smiling face ('the stereotypical submissive smile of the exotic oriental woman traditionally so enchanting and pleasing to westerners' (149)) that featured in an Australian government poster campaign to promote the taking-up of citizenship. This woman's face appeared with the slogan 'Come and join our family'. 'Why should this representative face be Asian and feminine?' Ang asks, while wryly noting that 'in a peculiar way, Asians have, by the mid-1990s, become Australia's pet people' (139– 40). Ang's use of the term 'pet' here is interestingly similar to Jacques Derrida's use of the term 'hosti-pets' in the essay *Foreigner Question: Coming From Abroad/from the Foreigner* (in *Of Hospitality*, 2000). Derrida inserts the hyphen into the word *hostipets*—signifying the host who welcomes a stranger into his house—that creates within the term the word 'pets' and suggests the relationship of power inequality that is always inscribed in the concept of hospitality (2000: 5).

Ang's response to her question concerning the representative 'multicultural' quality of the feminine Asian smile is located precisely in the cultural dynamic that permits the emergence of a 'pet people', a dynamic that is situated at the limits of liberal-pluralist discourses of diversity and multicultural tolerance. Ang encapsulates this positioning as the contradictory and paradoxical understanding that 'tolerance itself is irrevocably dependent on intolerance, insofar as it can only establish itself through a fundamental intolerance towards intolerance' (141). So, majority groups that hold the power 'to tolerate' effectively objectify as Other those minority groups that are structurally placed within the culture as those who are 'tolerated'. This relationship between the tolerated and the tolerator, then, 'perpetuates the self-other divide which is the epistemological basis of the very possibility of racism' (142).

The ambivalence of tolerance has implications for the concept of hospitality: as Ang comments, the question 'Where are you from?' also encodes a set of assumptions about 'here' and 'there', (non)belonging, that objectifies a person as ethnically marked and situates them as Other. This is not an innocent question. It is a question which implicitly states that the person to whom the question is addressed somehow 'belongs' elsewhere and cannot 'be at home' where they reside. In the preface of his book, *Thinking Orientals*, Henry Yu writes:

> This study has been an attempt to answer why it is that an Asian American in the United States, no matter how long and for how many generations he or she might have been here, will still be regularly asked 'Where are you from?' The inquisitors are never satisfied with the answers of Los Angeles, or Vancouver, or Canada. You are seen as an 'Oriental' of some sort, and they need to sort you according to some foreign distinction. (2001: vi)

The positive connotations of the word 'distinction'—as different by virtue of being good, better or even the best—are taken up by Ang when she refers to Australia's desire to embrace its geographical proximity to an increasingly prosperous Asia. The perception of Asia not simply as different to Anglo-Celtic Australia but as more interesting, more spiritual, more exotic, grounds Ang's argument that in contemporary Australia 'Asians are no longer excluded (...), nor are they merely reluctantly included *despite* their "difference", but *because* of it! What we have here is acceptance through difference, inclusion by virtue of otherness' (2001: 146, emphasis in original).

The ambivalence that Ang identifies as occurring on the level of daily intercultural exchange, Derrida finds inscribed in the very concept of 'hospitality'. In his essay *On Cosmopolitanism*, Derrida (2001) explores the relationship of dependence that exists between the duty (*devoir*) of hospitality and the right (*droit*) to hospitality. He finds an ambivalent relationship of dependence between this duty and this right in Immanuel Kant's *Perpetual Peace* (1795), where hospitality is characterised as a natural and inalienable law. However, the right to occupation of all parts of the surface of the earth is set against the right to possess that which lies upon or above that surface: culture, social institutions, the State. Hospitality is a right of visitation only, a temporary sojourn, but not of permanent residence; residence would be a concern of treaties between states rather than an issue of human rights. Hospitality then, although a human right, reveals the public nature of the public space, which is regulated by the State through the law (international and domestic) and is controlled by the police. There is a relationship of dependence between the moral law of unconditional hospitality extended a priori to all foreigners and the conditional laws that govern the right to hospitality.

Hospitality, like tolerance, is at once offered and withheld; it necessarily remains incomplete, compromised by the proximity of political and juridicial forces, and power relationships. Home, as a place of security and acceptance, is likewise compromised and rendered ambivalent for the migrant subject when hospitality is always conditional and tolerance is inseparable from a process of othering. We might add to Ang's description of patronising acceptance and intolerant tolerance the observation that Australia's reluctant surrendering of the White Australia Policy in the face of inadequate northern European emigration, in the middle part of the twentieth century, signifies a highly compromised and economically motivated form of hospitality extended to those Asian migrants who were permitted the right of residence to counter negative demographic trends. The offer of citizenship, of complete belonging—indeed, the offer of a 'home'—to these Asian migrants was always already inscribed with the absence of true hospitality, the promise of which was betrayed by self-interested motivations. How the experience of such migrants has been transmuted in literary terms is the subject of the following discussions.

I want to argue that the emerging canon of Anglophone Chinese Australian literature shares with much of the Chinese diasporic literary canon what I would call the 'neither here nor there' motif. The migrant truly belongs neither 'here', in the hostland, Australia, nor 'there' in the homeland or nation of origin. Of this literary canonical context, David Palumbo-Liu observes that 'the reading of ethnic literature can be seen to set a stage for the performance of difference ... complex differences cross-hatched by gender, class, race, ethnicity, sexual orientation, and so on, are subordinated to the general category of experience of the unfamiliar' (1995: 11). To this I would add the observation that, in the case of Anglophone Chinese diasporic literature, such differences are reconstructed under the rubric of the unfamiliar as that which is not 'family', and which does not belong. This failure to belong completely to a new home, or to return to the home left behind, is powerfully characterised by the diasporic motif of 'neither here nor there'. This motif expresses rhetorically within the individual text the realisation on the part of the Chinese diasporic subject that s/he belongs 'neither here nor there': as a consequence of nationalistic social formations, s/he is fully integrated into neither Australian nor a greater Chinese culture. This motif is repeated in many canonical texts of Chinese Australian, Chinese American, and Chinese Canadian literature; the frequency of the repetition suggests that this motif is more than just a characteristic of the individual texts themselves, but is one of the shaping principles of the developing canon of Anglophone diasporic Chinese literature.

The simplistic opposition of nationalisms so that one must be either 'Australian' or 'Chinese', 'American' or 'Chinese', 'Canadian' or 'Chinese', both asserts the legitimacy of these national categorisations and at the same time 'naturalises' them. I find it discomforting that the literary texts selected for canonical status should repeat the same exclusionary formulations as the legal and social exclusions that are condemned in those same texts. Writers like Brian Castro, who avoids the 'neither here nor there' dichotomy and its poetics of exclusion, is not a part of this emergent canon. However, Simone Lazaroo's 2000 novel, *The Australian Fiancé*, directly confronts the exclusionary White Australia Policy and her first novel, *The World Waiting to Be Made* (1994), depicts a society only partially evolved away from that historic legacy;

Arlene Chai's novels *On the Goddess Rock* (1999) and *The Last Time I Saw Mother* (1995) enact a rhetorical failure to belong by representing protagonists that are not truly at home either 'here' in Australia or 'there' in Asia. Hsu-Ming Teo's first novel *Love and Vertigo* (2000) powerfully depicts a failure to belong, to find a true home for the narrator's mother, whose act of suicide opens the narrative. The inability of these texts to represent a complete sense of being-at-home is a consequence of the ambivalent hospitality inscribed within the social formation of Chinese Australian experience.

In what follows, I want to highlight the ambivalence that surrounds ideas of 'home' in three recent novels chosen because they at once invite us to think carefully about issues of diaspora and belonging, and they also explore these issues in a range of different diasporic contexts: the context of migration (Lazaroo), the return to 'homeland' (Chai), and refugee experience (Teo), as nationalism asserts itself as a force that denies true belonging to those who are nonetheless 'hosted'.

Imminent Home: *The World Waiting to be Made*

In the preface to her translation of Derrida's two seminars *Foreigner Question* and *Step of Hospitality/No Hospitality*, Rachel Bowlby points out that the French word *l'étranger*—the multiple meanings of which Derrida plays upon throughout the two texts—signifies at once both 'the stranger' or 'the foreigner' and also the concept that in English we call 'abroad' or 'foreign lands'. Another meaning that Bowlby does not use in her translation is the term by which the title of Albert Camus' novel *L'étranger* is most often translated into English: 'the outsider'. This is an important concept evoked in Derrida's text, particularly in the opening sequences of *Foreigner Question*, when Derrida evaluates the power of the stranger-outsider (*l'étranger*) to pose questions that are feared for their destructive force by those in authority within the society the outsider would enter. For the foreigner as an outsider, a subject external to the social structure s/he has entered, arrives in possession of knowledge and epistemological privilege that empowers her/him to question the phallogocentric authority that governs her/his new 'home'.

It is for this reason that Derrida, in his discussion of Plato's *Sophist*, asks why the foreigner, the *Xenos*, asks not to be identified as a 'parricide'. Derrida observes how

> (t)he Foreigner shakes up the threatening dogmatism of the paternal *logos*: the being that is, and the non-being that is not. As though the Foreigner had to begin by contesting the authority of the chief, the father, the master of the family, the 'master of the house', of the power of hospitality, of the *hosti-pets* ... (2000: 5)

Plato's foreigner, like the migrant in Chinese Australian writing, is an expatriate in a patriarchal culture, an ex-patriate: s/he has left behind or separated from the Father and the phallogocentric authority of the Father. In this separation lies the threat and the freedom of the expatriate: to ask the question that cannot be asked by those who are 'at home' in the Father's symbolic domain. The epistemological freedom to ask the question implies also the ethical freedom to deliver judgment, and in this lies the threat posed by *l'étranger*, 'the Outsider', who is now ambivalently located 'Inside'.

It is in this dynamic relationship of threat and authority that we can interpret Lazaroo's use of the motif of the repeated question as she characterises the ambivalent friendship between her unnamed Eurasian migrant protagonist-narrator and the narrator's Anglo-Australian school friend, Sue. The character of Sue epitomises all that the patriarchal Australian culture-of-the-Father demands of the adolescent feminine subject. She is blonde, bronzed, and part of the surfing subculture that Lazaroo depicts as a pseudo-sacred artefact of contemporary Australian cultural values.

At school, the narrator is not so much ostracised as simply ignored by Sue and her popular crowd of friends. However, it is Sue who greets the narrator, on her first morning at the new school, 'Hullo, Tropical Barbie Doll' (77), just loud enough for the whole class to overhear. This is a reference to the childhood Barbie games these two girls, then neighbours, would play. Early in the narrative, the narrator tells how Sue had a California Barbie that bore an uncanny resemblance to Sue's own mother, and how, in order to make the doll resemble the narrator more closely, Sue 'squashed the small purple (lilly pilly) fruit onto her Barbie doll's protuberant breasts ... "This is how they dress in Oobla-Oobla land where you come from", she explained' (29). The significance of popular material culture in the novel has been addressed by Dorothy Wang (2000); here, I want to draw attention to the way in which the unthinking racism of the child, as she objectifies her friend in this way, is offset against the qualified reassurance she offers when the words 'ASIANS GO HOME' appear emblazoned on the bus shelter across the street from the narrator's house. 'Don't worry, you don't look like a slope or a boong', Sue tells her (27). As Robyn Morris remarks, in Lazaroo's work 'white dominance remains paramount to conceptions of 'the nation' and 'foreignness" (2005: 286). The internalised perception of somatic racial difference and of differences within that difference (Asians opposed to Aborigines, 'slopes' opposed to 'boongs') that inflects Sue's reported response to the imperative that Asians 'go home' signifies the complex intercultural space within which the narrator is situated, and within which her Anglo-Australian neighbours situate themselves.

When Sue unexpectedly telephones to invite the narrator on a trip to the beach, the question that immediately arises is: why? The narrator does not know; the boys who crowd around Sue do not know. As Shirley Tucker observes, the beach functions as a liminal space 'for the negotiation of the narrator's Eastern and Western ethnicities' (2003: 185). While the narrator lies on the beach watching Sue 'do what Australian girls were supposed to do' (111),

> (n)ormally cool boys squatted sweating at her feet and made conversation with her, pausing only to give me their odd puzzled glance.
> They didn't know why I was there, why Sue had me along.

> I was as bewildered as they were. Was a bit of fun to be had with someone who didn't know her place? (111)

But if the narrator does not know her place—and so much of the narrative traces her various efforts to find or create a 'place' for herself, to 'make' this world of hers that is 'waiting to be made'—then Sue knows for her. For this question follows another, as the encounter between these two girls is structured around Sue's desire to ask her companion—the migrant, the foreigner, the outsider—a single question. The asking of this question comes out of a moment of silence and solemnity, as befits a defining moment in their relationship:

> When Sue spoke again, she spoke as if she was depending intently on my reaction to her question, but her eyes were averted: 'Do you think girls who have *done it* are sluts?'
> I was alarmed by her question. I had never thought about such things in these terms, but something beseeching about her tone of voice warned me that it was important that I reply, as sincerely as I could, 'No'. (106, emphasis in original)

Though the question that would destroy the system of patriarchal sexual values is not articulated by the ex-patriate, it is the narrator as an Outsider who possesses the authority to make this judgement. Sue makes this clear when, in her relief at receiving the answer she wants to hear, she confesses that she has asked this question of the narrator because of her perceived difference: 'It must be the Asian in you' (107), she confides. It is the Asianness, the Eurasian difference that marks the narrator as an outsider, that also gives her the authority to judge, to contradict the advice of her father that sexual activity is sanctioned only within marriage. According to her father, girls who '*do it*' are indeed 'sluts'. The foreigner, the ex-patriated outsider possesses, in her very Otherness, the power to say other than what is scripted by the Father. Sue attributes to the narrator the authority to judge but Sue scripts the judgment.

Later in the narrative, when Sue (again unexpectedly) invites the narrator to stay with her at her family's beach shack, this same question is posed again, but this time in the context of Sue's desire to confess her pregnancy. '"Do you think girls who have done it are sluts?" she asked me suddenly, for the second time that I could remember' (156). And although Sue adds defiantly, 'I am not a slut', the narrator hears the panic in Sue's voice as she says, 'Just pregnant'. Sue panics because she has placed herself beyond the 'edge': she is beyond the pale, the dangerous place where the narrator describes herself and her family as located. While speculating about the reasons why the neighbourhood turned so hostile towards her mother after her father abandoned the family, the narrator considers that 'we, her exotic-looking children, were evidence that she'd already made her own bed a long time ago in a dangerous place, beyond the pale' (144). Sue has transgressed gender norms, the narrator's mother has transgressed racial norms, and both women are consequently located by the narrative in a space of exclusion.

This place, beyond the 'pale' (a term that carries with it connotations of white cultural norms), lends the narrator both the authority and the threat of the Outsider but it is also a place of non-belonging. Rejected by her own mother for marrying a Chinese-Malaysian man, the narrator's mother is also rejected by her husband's family. She enacts the double exclusion experienced by her daughter in the next generation, belonging neither 'here' in Australia nor 'there' back in Malacca. The tone of the novel, as Lazaroo addresses the issue of cross-cultural marriage, is bleak. The symbolism of the multicultural festival parade in Broome, where the narrator dresses as a mermaid for the Pearl Queen float, is one of many narrative vehicles that conveys Lazaroo's pessimism. As Tucker, in her essay on 'demonology' in this and other novels by Asian Australian women, rightly remarks:

> (Lazaroo's) use of the mermaid as a familiar signifier of uncontrolled female sexuality conjures up that which should remain hidden in this context—the mythology of female sirens who lure men to their destruction, and Orientalist anxieties about Asian femmes fatales. By associating mermaid imagery with ethnic diversity, Lazaroo invokes deeper fears of cross-species intercourse and nineteenth-century debates about miscegenation (2000: 154–55).

Throughout the novel, the dangers of cross-cultural marriage are twinned with the danger of romanticising 'Asia', of making Asians a 'pet' people. This is what Sue does, as she transforms the narrator into her 'pet'—a token outsider or ex-patriate who will lend her the legitimation she desires by speaking words other than those scripted by the Father in this phallogocentric Australian culture.

The narrator is herself aware of her own earlier tendency to find self-worth in her Oriental difference and so, as she travels to Singapore and Malacca in the attempt to 'find herself', she is aware that living for a time in the houses of her Asian relatives will not provide her with a sense of 'being-at-home'. The return to the putative 'homeland' to find a sense of belonging and true hospitality is always already doomed to failure. The implied emphasis upon 'where you're from' is a rhetorical strategy of exclusion enacted by the dominant culture, a strategy that obscures the fact that members of overseas communities can never simply or easily return to 'where they are from'. This crystallises a double exclusion, this sense of no longer belonging in the putative 'homeland' or in the 'hostland'. The novel ends with a lyrical passage that mourns the loss of 'recognition' as the migrant scrambles to acquire the material comforts associated with belonging to 'the Australian way of life', ironically symbolised for the narrator by 'the vision of Gloria, the Pearl Queen, on her way to a marriage with Jeff, the Municipal Works King' (275). The narrative's conclusion is ambivalent; it endorses nothing (as Wallace Stevens might say, 'the nothing that is not there and the nothing that is' (Stevens 1923)). Lazaroo's conclusion emphasises the constitutive absence of migrant experience, as she follows negative with negative: '... and so much of our past was not shared with anyone, and never handed down to our children, who play and skip in the surf with the neighbours' children, and are not torn so much by a feeling of belonging elsewhere' (275).

The Undiscovered/Rediscovered Home: *The Last Time I Saw Mother*

The storyline of Arlene Chai's first novel uses a strategy familiar in Anglophone Asian diaspora texts: the migrant's return to the homeland in order to discover some long concealed secret knowledge that is fundamental to the individual's sense of identity. In such texts, like Dewi Anggraeni's *The Root of All Evil* (1987), Arlene Chai's third novel *On the Goddess Rock* (1999), and most famously Amy Tan's novels, historical agency is surpassed by transcendent blood identity. Home participates in the illusion of a 'pre-culture'; that is, of a subjective condition that precedes culture and which is somehow identical with the homeland, the 'roots' or blood-basis of identity. The discovery specifically of a family secret underscores the 'blood' nature of the connection that is found in the return 'home'. In fact, I want to argue that these narratives of return assert what David Leiwei Li calls 'the mystic and genetic inheritance of the kind for which Amy Tan is famous' (2004: 110) but this assertion is undermined by a lack of corresponding transnational kinship or a sense of belonging in more than one homeland. Indeed, a cultural disjunction between homeland and hostland is opened by the migrant's unsatisfactory return to a home that is no longer homely, even in these texts that set out to celebrate 'mystic and genetic' diasporic identities.

What the narrative of migrant return emphasises is inevitably the historical disjuncture that characterises all migrant experience: the culture to which one returns cannot be the culture one left. The chronological displacement between 'here' and 'there' cannot be bridged but only obscured by narrative rhetoric that emphasises timeless, often mythical, symbolic elements (the ancestral curse that must be exorcised on the Goddess Rock in Chai's novel of that name and the myth of authentic kinship in *The Last Time I Saw Mother*). In such texts, the revelation of secret blood kinships serves to obscure the difficulty of return by emphasising the necessity of such returns.

In *The Last Time I Saw Mother* the protagonist, Caridad, learns from her elderly mother that she is in fact the blood daughter of her supposed aunt, her adoptive mother's sister. This revelation is represented by Caridad as the resolution of questions and uncertainties about her origins that have shadowed her life. In the early part of the narrative, when Caridad confesses her insecurities and suspicions that her aunt may be more to her than an aunt, the instability of personal family identity is twinned with the representation of 'home' as an unstable and contested concept. When Caridad is suddenly summoned from Sydney by her mother in Manila, she thinks about her changing understandings of the concept of home. She recalls that, although Australia has become her adopted home (a nationalistic parallel to her adopted mother), she is often asked 'Where's home?' (19). It is worth a pause here: many migrants report that they are asked the same question but differently phrased as 'Where are you from?' Indeed, this phrase forms part of the title of Paul Gilroy's influential 1990 essay *'It Ain't Where You're From It's Where You're At': The Dialectics of Diasporic Identification*. But Chai chooses to use the term 'home' here when her protagonist recalls being asked 'Where's home?' and Caridad goes on to wonder why it is that she persists in thinking of Manila as home:

> In my mind, I have two homes. Manila, where my past is. And Sydney, where Jaime and I came to live in search of better opportunities and a safer place to raise our child. So no matter which home I am going home to, I am always leaving another one behind. Some part of me is always absent. Missing the sights and smells of one as I go rushing to the other. Migrants, I think, are people who are never whole, never completely in one place. Ours is a fractured existence. (20)

The absence that is constitutive of migrant experience is given a particular historical specificity not only by Chai's references to the disturbances that led to the end of the Marcos regime in the Philipppines and the transformation of the society Caridad left but, more importantly, by references to the history of diasporic Chinese communities in the Philippines. Absence is inscribed in Caridad's family history, by the father she never knew and the China to which he and his family are never able to return.

As I stated above, the migrant can never 'return'; blood cannot bridge the chasm of time that separates departure from any return. The implicit claim of the 'neither here nor there' motif that one can authentically be 'Chinese' or 'Australian' or 'American' or 'Canadian' is a rhetorical strategy by which subjects are only partially interpellated (in the Althussurian sense of the term) into the national narrative of Australia, America, or Canada. Recall the lament by Chai's protagonist Caridad, who finds herself at home neither in Manila nor in Sydney: 'no matter which home I am going home to, I am always leaving another one behind. Some part of me is always absent' (20). The complaint that one belongs 'neither here nor there' is a restatement of the desire to belong 'either here or there': it is a profoundly nationalistic sentiment. In the absence of any political or cultural content to this nationalism or patriotism, however, an appeal to the mystical power of 'blood' must cement a putative relationship with 'home'.

A narrative detail that dramatises this mystical power of blood is the description given by Caridad's natural mother, Emma, of what happened after the birth of her first child, Ligaya: 'We kept the afterbirth in a box which we buried under the house to make sure she would grow up to love her home and would not wander off to strange places' (120). In contrast, Caridad's birth is attended by a different superstition: the tears swallowed by her newly widowed mother would reach her in the womb and nurture her on sadness. When Ligaya discovers that Emma has given the child away to Thelma she screams at her mother, 'How can you give your child away? ... Your own blood' (265). Where Emma has carefully preserved Ligaya's blood connection to 'home', she severs this connection between Caridad and 'home' when she gives away 'her own blood'. This, the narrative suggests, enables Caridad to become a migrant, shuttling between worlds. She is able to live this 'between worlds' condition, where she is always incomplete, always leaving one home behind, because she is incomplete from the time her mother separates her from her blood family. That constitutive estrangement from her mother is underlined when Thelma tells Caridad that of all her seven children it was only Caridad who was not breastfed by her mother.

The importance of blood kinship is emphasised further in the story of Thelma's childlessness. She is reluctant to adopt a child that is not of her husband's blood; when her sister-in-law asks her, 'You want only his son. His blood', Thelma responds, 'Yes... yes, of course' (347). Because she shares the commitment of her husband and his family to the concept of pure blood inheritance, Thelma is able to accept Raoul's illegitimate son as her own, even though his mother is a Filipina, and to mourn his death as if he was her own son. The death of the mixed-blood son is congruent with the rest of the narrative which endorses the idea of ethnic purity and same-race marriage within the overseas Chinese community of the Philippines.

The 'Chineseness' of Chai's narrative is not at all obvious. With names like Caridad, her parents Raoul and Thelma, her birth parents Alfonso and Emma, it is not clear at first that the characters of this novel are ethnic Chinese. Chai plays on the written nature of her text to conceal the somatic features of Chineseness that are nonetheless key to her storyline. It is the memory of Alfonso's lonely childhood, as a motherless child taken from China and brought to the Philippines by his father at the age of eight, together with his desire that his own children should not be lonely, that Emma offers as partial explanation of why she had so many children—too many to care for after Alfonso's death only weeks before Caridad's birth. The size of her family and the difficulty of caring for so many children in the years immediately following the Japanese Occupation causes Emma to give up the new-born Caridad to her wealthier sister. If Emma, like Thelma, had not belonged to a family that insisted on marrying its daughters to 'pure' Chinese husbands, however, the secret adoption of Caridad by her aunt would not have been possible. Philippine society is described in this narrative as voluntarily racially segregated, with Spaniards marrying into other Spanish families, Chinese marrying other Chinese, leaving only the Filipino community to associate with other ethnic groups. As a consequence of this *de facto* segregation, both Thelma and Emma marry Chinese men. Unlike the baby who preceded her adoption, the son who is half Filipino and only half Chinese, Caridad is of pure Chinese descent. She is said to have inherited her father Alfonso's eyes, but otherwise she bears the physical appearance of a child who 'belongs' to her parents. This somatic resemblance, this Chineseness, enables Thelma to insist that Caridad never be told of her true parentage and, until she feels she must honour Raoul's wish that Caridad know the truth about herself after his death, Thelma's secret is preserved. The idea of blood kinship is, then, key to the operations of Chai's story: without the insistence on the importance of blood relationships not only would the storyline be implausible but so too would the character of Caridad and the constitutive 'absence' of her migrant experience, which can only be filled with 'blood'.

The Horizon of Home: *Behind the Moon*

One of the major protagonists of Hsu-Ming Teo's second novel, Tien Ho, finds that far from providing a basis for belonging, her mixed-blood background underlies her failure to belong. The cousins with whom Tien must live, after her mother gives up her place in the refugee boat for her own father and is stranded in Vietnam, continually tease Tien about her dark skin colour and her black American GI father. Sexual impropriety is enmeshed with racial difference as Tien thinks of her mother always as both a bar-girl and a woman who has known many GIs. In the absence of a father who perhaps does not know she exists and a mother she is led to believe has died in Vietnam, Tien identifies with Dorothy, the heroine of *The Wizard of Oz*, and wishes that she could find a place where she belongs, a home 'behind the moon', that is neither Australia nor Vietnam.

When Tien develops romantic feelings for her Singaporean Chinese friend Justin, she is reminded by his mother, Annabelle, of her own mixed blood. Annabelle tells Tien that Justin will marry a 'pure Chinese girl' and Tien wonders whether she is being given a coded warning. Indeed, in this respect Tien repeats the experience of her mother who, being only part Chinese and part Vietnamese, finds herself at the age of sixteen in an arranged marriage with a Chinese Vietnamese man whose family use this marriage to comply with government policies to 'Vietnamise' society. As the fourth son of a wealthy Chinese family, he is made to marry a woman perceived to be Vietnamese and he deeply resents the racial insult he reads into this symbolic marriage. His brothers had been married to 'pure' Chinese wives and he expected no less. After only a year of marriage, he abandons Linh and their sickly infant daughter, running away to Hong Kong with his Chinese mistress.

Abandoned by her husband, who tells her as he leaves that because their marriage was only a Buddhist ceremony it has no legal status, and later abandoned by Tien's father, who goes missing in action, Linh is in important symbolic respects a refugee long before she actually leaves Vietnam. She is betrayed and abandoned by her country, just as she was abandoned by her husbands, when she is forced to do hard field labour, clearing jungle for agricultural use and later when she is forced into prostitution to earn enough to keep herself alive. She lives within the borders of the nation state but she is not 'of' the state. As a stateless person, she has no protection from a national government. As a stateless refugee Linh cannot be at home in the place where she finds herself: whether it is in Vietnam or Australia.

As part of his exploration of asylum as a human right, in the essay *On Cosmopolitanism*, Derrida (2001) turns to the medieval principle that 'who is in the state is the state' which leaves only two options for foreigners: repatriation or naturalisation. Either a refugee becomes a naturalised subject citizen or s/he must leave to be repatriated to the state of origin. This principle has, in the modern era, become subject to international laws and treaties, which produce a network of sovereign nation states with no sphere of authority that is separate from and transcendent to the international network of nations. Unlike the ex-patriate who is able to ask the deadly symbolic question because s/he is Outside, separate from and transcendent to the 'hostland' s/he would enter, there is no privileged Outsider in the international network of nation states. This means that the duty of hospitality is always impure and compromised. The right to hospitality is subject to international diplomacy, to written treaties and agreements among nation states. The refugee, who repudiates a national identity within the scope of a prior nation state, can only request a hospitality that is subject to the diplomatic interests of that nation and the host or 'asylum nation'. This hospitality, then, must always be compromised and incomplete; a constitutive absence lies at the heart of the concept of hospitality for the refugee or asylum seeker, the subject whom we might intuitively think is most worthy of unconditional hospitality.

Nationalism and not internationalism controls access to hospitality for the asylum seeker; the sovereignty of the nation is expressed both in a diplomatic willingness to surrender a citizen to another state and in that other state's willingness to respect international treaty relations and extend hospitality to the refugee. The 'Australianness' of refugees—particularly Asian and Vietnamese refugees—is always in question, together with the ambivalent hospitality that is extended to them. A frequent insult hurled at Justin, because of his somatic Chineseness, is the abbreviation of 'boat person', 'boatie'; ironically, Tien is not called this because of her dark skin—she is Vietnamese but does not look like it. However, she is insulted as an Aboriginal person, a 'boong'. The insults shouted at the three friends, Tien, Justin and Nigel, on an Adelaide tram by a drunken man are echoed later at the 'Dead Diana Dinner', when Nigel's father Bob Gibson loses his temper and in a drunken rage calls Justin's family 'chinks' (133).

Domestic ethnic groups provide the material for personal insults; the 'otherness' within 'Australianness' is dramatised by a nationalism that defines itself by patterns of exclusion. The Adelaide drunk tells Justin 'Go back to where you came from, you commie bastard boatie' and when Tien intervenes, the drunk turns on her, snarling 'Go climb back up ya tree' (64). These insults encode a desire that the Other should 'go back'—go back 'home' to a place of belonging but to a lesser place: a refugee boat, a tree—and it is the disruption of *his* sense of belonging that triggers Bob Gibson's loss of control. Olivia Khoo remarks in her essay *Whiteness and* The Australian Fiancé: *Framing the Ornamental text in Australia* that a complement to the prominence of femininity in recent Asian Australian writing is an increasing emphasis upon masculine whiteness (2001: 69). Bob feels 'out of place' in the place he regards as his and takes revenge on the Singaporean family that seems to belong in Australia in his stead. He thinks of them as:

> (p)erfectly multicultural, holding on to the best of the old Chinese ways ... and good-humouredly adopting the occasional ockerism, but always with that self-deprecating smile of awareness to show that they were quoting Australianness ironically; that they were cultured and sophisticated enough to play these multicultural games and win. Oh yes. My word, they actually believed they were winners and that he, Robert Gordon Gibson, had a problem. (133)

It is the perception that the power dynamic underlying hospitality has been reversed that enrages Bob. He is being 'hosted', literally, by Annabelle and her husband Tek, who have invited the three friends and their families to a memorial dinner on the evening of Princess Diana's televised funeral. Bob is the guest, and his Singaporean friends are the hosts. Teo uses the dinner to encapsulate and dramatise the emotional complexity of hosting, of offering hospitality across the cultural divides that criss-cross Australian multiculturalism. Bob is willing to tolerate, to host, to offer hospitality to these Singaporean and Vietnamese families—but on his terms. When he finds himself tolerated, hosted, offered hospitality by these same families he suddenly perceives the condescension that underlies these relationships of hospitality, and he does not like it. It is not just that Bob is white and his friends Asian: when Justin is hosted in Malaysia by his boyfriend Jordie he is shocked to be criticised as an Australian. 'Justin felt incredulous anger that this Malaysian had the gall to criticise an Australian' (147) and, by feeling scandalised in this way, Teo suggests that Justin is at his most 'Australian'. He adopts the subject position of a true Australian when he resents any challenge to his authority mounted by an 'Asian'.

The lack of true hospitality is endemic in a racist society. This is why when Tien asks Miss Yipsoon, who has an ambiguous relationship with the Gibson family, if Gibbo is really Chinese, her response is so unsatisfactory. Miss Yipsoon replies, 'We're all Australians now' (60). But what does this mean? None of the characters in the novel feel at home in Australia. That Nigel Gibson, the son of a first generation British migrant mother, Gillian, and a father, Bob, who prides himself on being a 'true blue Aussie', should feel the need to claim an Asian identity in order to overcome his sense of loneliness, of being-alone, raises the question of nationalism and national belonging. To return to Ang's discussion of the smiling Asian female face that invites the viewer to embrace Australian citizenship: she is included by virtue of her otherness. By representing the Asian face that somatically inserts difference into the Australian self-conception of multicultural community, the smiling, unthreatening Asian woman is simultaneously objectified as Other and accepted into the 'multi-cultural family' of Australian citizens. Gibbo cannot feel truly Australian while he is the ordinary son of white British migrants; he must be 'multicultural' in a society that assumes whiteness has neither colour nor ethnicity to contribute to this Australian 'family of all colours'.

Conclusion

In these three novels by Asian Australian women, there is no place like home. Australia is represented as a place where, for Chinese migrants from throughout the diaspora, home is an aspiration and hospitality is offered conditionally and ambivalently. This should not be surprising. The Immigration (Restriction) Act of 1901, which inaugurated the White Australia Policy, was passed into legislation at the same time that the Commonwealth of Australia came into being. Asian exclusion and Australian national identity have been virtually synonymous from that time until the reforms of the Whitlam Government in the 1970s. The essays collected in Ang's book *On Not Speaking Chinese* make a powerful case for the reluctant and provisional nature of Australian hospitality in relation to Asian migrants. It is the force of Australian nationalism, a national identity built historically upon the foundation of Anglo-Celtic culture, that denies the possibility of true hospitality, of true belonging, to Asian Australians. The 'neither here nor there' motif of non-belonging explored in these three narratives takes an ironic turn in Teo's novel, where the force of nationalistic exclusion is so strong that it condemns even white Australians like Gibbo to a condition of not-belonging, but, we might ask, is this irony an innovation?

The double exclusion experienced by the characters and promoted by the narratives of these novels play to established cultural myths of authenticity and entrenched narratives of racial discrimination. As Lyn Jacobs has argued, the works of Lazaroo and Teo challenge national imaginaries through the representation of diversity (2002). However, it remains that to belong 'neither here nor there' is to desire a home *either* here *or* there, to be Australian *or* Chinese, Australian *or* Malaysian, Australian *or* Filipino, and so on. The destructive power of nationalism that cuts across the internationalism regulating asylum, refugees, and migrants is sustained by literary texts that insist upon a spurious originality, a place 'to go back to', a mythical authenticity. If, as Derrida (2001) claims, 'hospitality is culture itself' (16), such narratives of exclusion, and the literary canon that enshrines them, form a questionable inheritance for a culture that seeks to call itself genuinely multicultural and truly hospitable.

References

Ang, I. *On Not Speaking Chinese: Living Between Asia and the West*. London: Routledge, 2001.
Anggraeni, D. *The Root of All Evil*. Melbourne: Indra Publishing, 1987.
Chai, A.J. *The Last Time I Saw Mother*. Sydney: Random House, 1995.
——. *On the Goddess Rock*. Sydney: Random House, 1999.
Derrida, J. *Of Hospitality: Anne Dufourmantelle Invites Jacques Derrida to Respond*. Trans. R. Bowlby. Stanford: Stanford University Press, 2000.
——. *On Cosmopolitanism and Forgiveness*. Trans. M. Dooley and M. Hughes. London and New York: Routledge, 2001.
Gilroy, P. '"It Ain't Where You're From It's Where You're At": The Dialectics of Diasporic Identification.' *Third Text* 13 Winter (1990): 3–16.
Jacobs, L. 'Remembering Forgetting: Love-stories by Nicholas Jose, Simone Lazaroo and Hsu-Ming Teo'. *Intersections* 8 October (2002), <http://wwwsshe.murdoch.edu.au/intersections/issue8/jacobs.html> (accessed 13 January 2006).
Kant, I. *Perpetual Peace: A Philosophical Sketch*. Trans. T. Humphrey. Indianapolis: Hackett, 2003 [1795].
Khoo, O. 'Whiteness and *The Australian Fiancé*: Framing the Ornamental Text in Australia.' *Hecate* 27.2 (2001): 68–85.
Kwok, J. T. 'Anti-Chinese Representations and Governance in Queensland.' *Crossings* 93 (2004), <http://asc.uq.edu.au/crossings/9_3/index.php?apply=kwok> (accessed 1 December 2005).
Lazaroo, S. *The World Waiting to be Made*. Fremantle: Fremantle Arts Centre Press, 1994.
——. *The Australian Fiancé*. Sydney: Picador, Pan Macmillan, 2000.

Li, D.L. 'On Ascriptive and Acquisitional Americanness: The Accidental Asian and the Illogic of Assimilation.' *Contemporary Literature* 45.1 (2004): 106–34.

Morris, R. '"Many Degrees of Dark and Light": Sliding the Scale of Whiteness with Simone Lazaroo.' *Culture, Identity, Commodity: Diasporic Chinese Literatures in English*. Eds. T. Khoo and K. Louie. Hong Kong: Hong Kong University Press, 2005. 279–98.

Palumbo-Liu, D. Ed. *The Ethnic Canon: Histories, Institutions, and Interventions*. Minneapolis: University of Minnesota Press, 1995.

Stevens, W. *The Harmonium*. New York: Knopf, 1923.

Teo, H. *Behind the Moon*. Sydney: Angus and Robertson, 2005.

——. *Love and Vertigo*. Sydney: Allen and Unwin, 2000.

Tucker, S. 'Your Worst Nightmare: Hybridised Demonology in Asian-Australian Women's Writing.' *Diaspora: Negotiating Asian-Australia*. Eds. H. Gilbert, T. Khoo and J. Lo. Brisbane: University of Queensland Press, 2000. 150–57, 234–236.

——. 'The Great Southern Land: Asian-Australian Women Writers Re-View the Australian Landscape.' *Australian Literary Studies* 21.2 October (2003): 178–88.

Wang, D. 'The Making of an 'Australian' 'Self' in Simone Lazaroo's *The World Waiting to Be Made*.' *Diaspora: Negotiating Asian-Australia*. Eds. H. Gilbert, T. Khoo and J. Lo. Brisbane: University of Queensland Press, 2000. 44–49, 229.

Yu, H. *Thinking Orientals: Migration, Contact, and Exoticism in Modern America*. New York: Oxford University Press, 2001.

Touring the Phantom Agent: Recognition, Defacement and the Vietnamese Australian War Memorial

Scott Brook

This bronze memorial was donated by the Community of Cabramatta to commemorate the comradeship shared by Australian and Vietnamese soldiers during the Vietnam War 1962–1972 and was officially unveiled by the Governor of

New South Wales His Excellency Rear Admiral Peter Sinclair A.O. on 31st August 1991. (Cabravale Park War Memorial plaque, Cabramatta (see Figure 1))

[A] memorial to locals who died in the Great War and to the legend of Anzac—that cast the suntanned, loyal and laconic white Australian male as the Australian national type—has been revised. The unknown warrior citizen of the old nation has been joined by latter-day freedom fighters. In this representation all of the men in Australia become 'diggers'. ('On Not Belonging: Memorials and Memory in Sydney', Paula Hamilton and Paul Ashton 2002: 25)

I love Australia (Graffiti, Cabravale Park War Memorial)

Reading the Digger

Nhon Do's bronze sculpture occupies the centre of a small amphitheatre that is depressed about three feet below ground level. Two seated soldiers, one representing the ill-fated Republic of Vietnam (1955–1975), the other Australia, gaze at the grass in front of the tiered pool around their feet. Directly opposite the site is another war memorial: a commemorative Anzac Gazebo erected in 1919. Hamilton and Ashton's reference to a revision of Anzac iconography would be one kind of approach to interpretation, although the digger as 'suntanned, loyal and laconic' is perhaps better known from Peter Weir's 1981 film *Gallipoli*, rather than 'the unknown warrior-citizen' of commemorative statuary. The 'digger' (a colloquial term for Australian soldiers, especially those who fought World War 1) is a complex figure in Australian national mythology, one that constitutes 'mateship' around an ethos of survivalism and acts of self-sacrifice. Fiona Nicoll notes that the 'digger-sign' has regularly been the subject of contested revisions and controversy has most often focused on the digger's face (Nicoll 2001: 97–122).

A close reading would have to note that, strikingly, these are public figures of introversion. Instead of the blank gaze that might signify the afterlife (the Classical Digger; 'the unknown warrior citizen') or a focused attention on this world (the digger as can-do Aussie, such as Mel Gibson's character from the iconic film *Gallipoli*), the facial expressions on the sculptures are despondent. Instead of the idealised male bodies of those who have made the supreme sacrifice and are fit subjects of commemoration, Nhon Do's figures represent those who must perform this act of recollection. As temporally complex figures for both the act *and* object of collective memory, their body posture seems neither disciplined to the attention of the public nor quite 'at ease'. It is precisely here, as the body of the Vietnam Veteran as popular trope emerges, and a potentially celebratory reading of the sculpture's *use* of the language of the digger might appear, that a close reading would seem to fail me. One could read the sculpture as existential rather than heroic, revising a nationalist idiom in order to articulate national with *migrant* loss, a 'becoming minor' of a major mythology, or a splitting of a unified national temporality. I want to write that these bodies appear 'awkward', but sense that this risks projecting onto the statues a well-rehearsed discussion about 'ambivalence' and public memory after the Vietnam

War. That is, sitting in Cabravale Park it would be the heritage tourist, perhaps, who feels awkward.

Vietnamese Australian Public Culture

Despite the boom of social memory studies mapping the effects of the Vietnam War for populations in both Vietnam and Western countries, studies have rarely addressed the post-1975 Vietnamese diaspora (Curthoys 1994; Tai 2001). In the Australian context, though significant social anthropological, sociological and media studies on Vietnamese Australians have been structured around memory, identity and 'homeland politics' (Carruthers 2001; Cunningham and Nguyen 2000; Thomas 1999; Viviani 1996), they focus on contexts that are linguistically and ethnically specific. They tend to occlude consideration of Vietnamese Australians as agents for what might be called the 'public historical sphere'. 'Public historical sphere' is a term developed in Cultural Studies to refer to institutions, texts and sites such as public museums, monuments, broadcast television and radio documentaries, films, plays, art exhibitions, published novels and memoires that enact public forms of historical consciousness (Bennett 1988: 3); they are forms of 'public culture' that circulate meanings about the past for a 'general or mixed audience' (Morris and McCalman 1998: 4).

The Cabravale Park memorial is located in Cabramatta in Sydney's southwest, a suburb with a high percentage of Indochinese businesses and residents that has become a key site of academic discussion on Australia's transformation under the government's stated policy of multiculturalism. During the 1990s, the area was also the site of regular moral panics in popular media over 'ethnic gangs' and drugs (Teo 2000). The memorial is at once an example of community-specific place-making, as well as a strong example of public heritage (a war memorial) that attempts to historicise a relation between Vietnamese Australians and the Australian nation. In terms of the history of Vietnamese migration to western nations, this would be a diasporic Vietnamese memorial that might usefully be compared to memorials in Dandenong (Melbourne) and Westminster (California), where veterans of the Southern regime who later escaped as refugees have developed similar iconographies of war-time alliance in monumental sculptures. Although it is a site where this symbolically privileged group within the diaspora have successfully incorporated their representations into the idiom of public culture, it needs to be noted that discussions about the site remain strongly ethnically marked. In his survey of national statuary, Ken Inglis notes the memorial is 'a novelty in the landscape', as it is a tribute 'to Australian war dead offered in the name of immigrants—*Asian* immigrants— [...] commemorating a common lost cause' (1998: 387, emphasis in original).

By thinking about the Cabravale park memorial as 'public culture', I want to highlight its engagement with the symbolic capital of 'Official Culture'—being both endorsed and partly funded by the local government. While the War Memorial Committee raised $150,000 through donations to pay for the design and casting of the bronze figures by prominent Cabramatta-based artist Nhon Do, Fairfield City Council contributed through extensive site-development. It is also a space of 'public culture' in the sense that it is collectively inscribed and subject to multiple uses. My opening epigraphs were by the memorial committee whose chairman in 1991 was local Alderman Phuong Ngo (a prominent local councillor whose position enabled him to combine both Vietnamese Australian community and local municipal rhetorics), two non-Vietnamese public historians, and an anonymous graffiti writer. This way of thinking about the space of public culture focuses on the forms of exchange and reinscription it facilitates. Meaghan Morris and Iain McCalman suggest such a dynamic model for public culture when they write:

> [P]ublic culture is an array of more or less 'porous' spaces open to a variety of commercial and popular as well as governmental uses. This means it is not coextensive with the state-sponsored affirmations of identity and heritage that it none the less crucially includes, any more than it subsumes the community and commercial activities that both draw on and expand its resources. (1998: 7)

'Public culture' and 'popular uses' here have a mutually productive force. The popular both draws on and expands the resources of public culture through occupying its 'porous spaces', while public culture, a field of cultural reserve that harbours the symbolic capital of a 'National Culture', is nevertheless inhabited and utilised by the popular. There is a trace of Michel de Certeau's distinction between 'State strategies' and 'popular tactics' here, yet the relation is refigured as mutually expansive, rather than agonistically mutually definitive (de Certeau 1984).

This essay, then, makes a close reading of the various forms of rhetoric that would seek to respond to and mediate the Cabravale Park memorial as a site of 'Vietnamese Australian public culture'. In particular, I focus on the recent suggestion by two eminent public historians Hamilton and Ashton that it 'doesn't belong' (2002). A reading of Hamilton and Ashton's article would be significant for Asian Australian studies more broadly as they read the site as an ethnicity-based 'call for recognition'. The term 'recognition' has been referred to in influential cultural policy discussions of how community groups are able to effect changes in the public historical sphere (Bennett 1988). The discipline of public history has regularly relied on the terms 'recognition' and 'identity politics' to describe an increasingly diversified field of social memory that exceeds those Australian settler-colonial and nationalist narratives that sustain the symbolic centrality of Anglo-Celtic heritage. Yet, despite social theory's turn to 'recognition' in the 1990s, many critics argue that the discourse is an ambivalent good. Nancy Fraser argues that the appeal of 'recognitive justice' for a 'postsocialist', identities-based critique risks eclipsing a focus on 'redistributive justice', while Wendy Brown demonstrates that identities-based claims articulate identity negatively, as always already 'wounded' (excluded or misrepresented), and hence run the risk of inculcating collective identities around an experience of Nietzschean *ressentiment* (Brown 1995; Fraser 1997). More recently, Alexander García Düttman argued that, although the discourse of recognition might secure 'legal, social, institutional, and political equality of status and treatment', struggles for recognition are always potentially stymied through '[disappearing] in a reformism which admits of differences only to the extent that they can be considered *valid* differences, that is, as differences justified by their relation to a fundamental unity' (Düttman 2000: 105). However, as most critics agree, such 'reformism' cannot sensibly be reneged. Given 'recognition' is not so much a universal solution as a *rhetoric* that may be useful for achieving particular, context-specific outcomes, it follows that critical attention needs to be paid to specific instances in which it is used. An emergent discipline in the 1990s, public history seeks to apply the training of historians for 'real world' effects, to position itself as capable of advising institutions and influencing policy outcomes relevant to the management of the public historical sphere and, in particular, heritage sites. Further, Hamilton and Ashton are key agents in the institutional reproduction of this field, being the editors of the journal *Public History Review* in which the article I am discussing appears. It is significant that *they* rely on the discourse of 'recognition' to suggest that the memorial does not belong.

To put their conclusion in context: Generalising rather than ethnographic, their article was an occasional piece that compared three Sydney memorials in a mode Dean MacCannell might describe as 'negative sightseeing' (1989: 40), a term that describes an itinerary that is made up of those sights the tourist feels do not, or should not, belong. For MacCannell, the tourist's itinerary is not motivated by perversity, but by a need (foundational for the modern Western subject) to recuperate the experience of social differentiation for a renewed sense of society as *fundamentally* an explicable totality. It is for this reason that MacCannell posits the ideology of modern tourism as related to the emergence of the social sciences, and containing within itself the solution to the problems it causes. That is, the tourist always has the potential to be a social planner. Hamilton and Ashton's objective is not to read the memorial in its specificity—a case study in social memory—but to illustrate their critical warnings against the boom in 'community-based public history' under multiculturalism and, in particular, the danger of critics aligning themselves unproblematically in a power-sharing, remedial relation to communities whose struggle to articulate and reconnect identity through history and place might lead the critic to elide difficult questions of what constitutes community in the first place. Their article is therefore a reformer's pedagogy, in which the memorial functions as an example by which to demonstrate the over-accumulation of community specific memory-sites since the 1970s, and an exercise in how the public historian might discern, at a glance, which ones appear 'out of place' (2002: 23). Their engagement with the memorial is the first and longest of the three examples (the other two being an inner-city aerosol mural, and an Aboriginal mural in Hyde Park), and includes a full-page and slightly out-of-focus photograph. It also provides this particular edition of *Public History Review* with half of its catchy 'Asia Australia Issue' title, *Changi to Cabramatta—Places and Personality*.

In framing their article, Hamilton and Ashton write:

> We have chosen to examine memorials and monuments to groups that do not quite work in the sense that they are out of place, or for a variety of reasons seem odd, jarring our sense of expectation or failing to communicate their message. This may be said of many memorials that seem irrelevant to the years they endure, but those which we consider here are all in fact of much more recent origin . . . . They reveal much about the changing nature of memorial practices in contemporary society in that they bear witness to the power of identity politics; to the claims of recognition by and for groups on the basis of ethnicity and race. (2002: 23)

Somewhat conveniently for my argument, the preposition 'of' in 'claims of recognition' introduces a semantic uncertainty here. There are claims by groups, and claims for groups; that is, 'claims by groups of recognition', and 'claims of recognition for groups', almost as if the discourse of recognition could make the claim. '*Calls for* recognition by and for groups' would have removed this doubling-up of the meaning here, and yet what we have are 'claims *of* recognition. As this sort of resistant if opportunistic reading might suggest, I want to ask whether it is recognition *itself*—as a structured relation in discourse—that is staking a claim here? And, if so, what does it want?

Framing the site as a solicitation for recognition 'on the basis of ethnicity or race' enables Hamilton and Ashton to focus on the discrepancy between the agents who are empowered to inscribe a group's collective identity, and what Tony Bennett (1992) has influentially described in the context of museum politics as 'phantom agents'. By 'phantom agents', Bennett refers to the *representations* of abstract collective subjects such as 'the Vietnamese Australian community', 'the working class' or 'local residents' that are utilised by *actual* social agents who may or may not identify with the interests of such groups. Bennett's point with such a distinction was to argue that Cultural Studies should not be mistaken in invoking such rhetorical figures as agents of social change themselves, but that they only have real-world utility as rhetorical constructs of collective interest when deployed by actual agents:

> [O]ne would find neither classes nor 'the people'—or, for that matter, races or genders—active as identifiable agents in the sphere of museum politics. What one *would* find, of course, are claims to *represent* class or popular interests, claims which might be advanced by a whole range of effective social agents—museum critics, sectional pressure groups like WHAM [Women's heritage and museums], committees of management, teams of designers, curators, sometimes even boards of trustees. (1992: 31, emphasis in original)

For Bennett, the fact that such claims are rhetorical is not a criticism (i.e. *merely* rhetorical), but a reminder that such claims cannot themselves effect the changes sought. Although Hamilton and Ashton do not use the phrase 'phantom agent' in their article, the 'negative revelations' that rhetorically make their argument persuasive rest upon showing the disconnect between the *claims* of actual Vietnamese agents and the condition of the site itself. The spectacularly abject re-presentation of the memorial in their article, comparable to the sort of tabloid television that mediated national concern about Cabramatta during the 1990s, is offered as evidence for their suggestion that there is no real community behind the site's claims. The use of the discourse of recognition to restrict attention to the normative rhetorics of public cultural address (i.e. who is this donation from? who speaks?) permits not only the pre-cued answer of 'those who have power speak' (Chow 1993: 384), but also the exclusion of popular forms of practice from the account of the memorial's value. Constructing the site as properly addressed *from* 'the Vietnamese Australian community' *to* a representative National Subject—who they gloss as 'white Anglophone Australia' (Hamilton and Ashton 2002: 33)—permits the public historian not only to debunk such an address, but to substitute their own common sense readings as white, Anglophone visitors (the proper addressee) in lieu of any ethnographic data on actually existing subjects whose experiences might be addressed at a level of intimacy beyond that of a heritage tourist attraction. Furthermore, this allows the public historian to avoid accounting for those mediating practices, such as tourism and tabloid media consumption, that generate such 'common sense' in the first place. As I seek to demonstrate in what follows, the discourse of recognition here has little to do with articulating minority claims for inclusion in the public historical sphere, nor subjecting such claims to critical scrutiny, and a lot to do with the rhetorics of a scandalous exposure that might accumulate the authority to manage.

Rhetorics

Hamilton and Ashton writes:

> [s]uch cultural activity is also as much about hope as it is history. By materially inscribing their story on the landscape, these people have expressed a collective desire to be part of the 'Public [or Official] Culture', that 'great drama, endlessly playing', as Donald Horne put it, that maintains 'definitions of the nation and its social orders. (2002: 28)

In support of their argument, they quote an article by Phuong Ngo published in a local newspaper, the *Fairfield Champion*, the week after the monument was unveiled. Here, Ngo glosses the memorial:

> The Vietnamese community of the Cabramatta area have always wanted to give recognition to the Australian servicemen who gave their lives fighting on behalf of the Vietnamese people. And to the Australians who supported the Vietnamese struggle for freedom and democracy ... It is of course tragic that the struggle for a free Vietnam was lost. But the very fact that Australia then welcomed Vietnamese refugees into the community after 1975 only makes the Vietnamese people appreciate Australia's efforts even more. (Qtd. in Hamilton and Ashton 2002: 25)

Let us consider, here, how Ngo positions the monument as an historical statement. As well as the equation of 'Vietnamese People' and 'Vietnamese struggle' with the fate of south Vietnam, Ngo also links the historical moment of 'comradeship' in the plaque's dedication with the acceptance of Vietnamese refugees after 1975. This is the year Vietnam was reunified under the North and the first wave of political refugees fled to the West. It is for these reasons widely promoted by community organisations and the media as marking the genesis of a Vietnamese community in Australia. Similarly, 'community of Cabramatta'—as it is in the plaque's dedication—becomes '*Vietnamese* community'. Ngo mediates a relation between Vietnamese and non-Vietnamese Australians that connects two historical moments (war and migration) to the present, conjoining local expressions of sentiment ('Vietnamese of Cabramatta wanted to give recognition') to a national frame of reference ('Australians welcomed').

Significantly, the orientation of 'recognitive justice' in Ngo's text runs in the opposite direction to that in Hamilton and Ashton's reading. For Hamilton and Ashton, it is not a case of the 'Cabramatta community' recognising the comradeship between Vietnamese and Australian war veterans (as it is in the plaque), or Vietnamese Australians recognising Australians who fought in Vietnam and/or welcomed refugees (as it is in *The Fairfield Champion* article). It is that Vietnamese Australians are *seeking* recognition from a broader national subject ('white Anglophone Australia') on the basis of ethnic difference. By contrast, Ngo's statement seems to articulate what Ghassan Hage has recently described as 'migrant participatory belonging'. For Hage, the migrant's affective relation to the host society might be read as symbolically structured around a gift economy for which the gift of a new social life that comes with migration might incur, if 'well given', a form of symbolic debt (Hage 2003: 100).

Hamilton and Ashton's version of 'recognition' would seem to derive from Charles Taylor's influential essay, 'The Politics of Recognition', a model for which the appeal to race or ethnicity is central (Taylor 1994). Taylor states that recognition can only be achieved by 'human cultures that have animated *whole* societies over some considerable stretch of time' and that are entitled to their share of universal value, as brokered by the State, in that they 'have something important to say to all human beings' (Taylor 1994: 66, emphasis added). This relation is what allows Hamilton and Ashton to posit the State as the final addressee for the site with themselves as public historians who are capable of adjudicating on whether such solicitations are successful.

Homi Bhabha notes Taylor's necessary exclusion of what Bhabha calls 'partial cultures' whose identity is read under the sign of historical rupture rather than the *longue durée* of racial or ethnic identity (Bhabha 1998). I suggest that 'partial cultures' are a useful way of thinking about culture in terms of historical contingency, which also means challenging the possibility of knowing what constitutes a culture in its totality. Such a concept is crucial in considering the multiple historical trajectories that contribute to a post-1975 Vietnamese diaspora. Taylor's model of 'recognition' would here work to effect an ontological difference between host and migrant culture in which the former would be in full possession of its historical identity, and to which minority solicitations would issue from a fundamentally other history. If 'recognition' might be criticised for referring difference to a 'fundamental unity', we can see how it may have trouble with the sort of historical *involvement* the memorial wants to recall.

Hamilton and Ashton suggest the memorial is 'out of place' for two reasons, each corresponding to a different mode of 'belonging'. The first reason reflects a general critique of the ideological work behind the idea of 'community', the means by which agents represent a group's experience of belonging to each other. The second relies on imagining Cabramatta itself as a zone of social displacement, a spectacular failure of belonging to place. They argue that the memorial's claim to represent 'community' is inauthentic, a ruse of local elites, due to the fact that public monuments *in general* are funded by subscriptions from eminent individuals, organisations and businesses. Yet they do not provide examples of memorials that *do* belong, where the mobilising of 'community' is 'authentic. 'Community' here, like ethnicity, becomes the burden of the other, a totality that can always be shown to be wanting. When the migrant other turns out to be like the host culture (i.e. not a given totality, but partial, with their elites sponsoring public cultural statements just as the host culture's do), then the imputed solicitation for recognition can be rebuffed. Hamilton and Ashton conclude that '[u]ltimately, the memorial could be read as either an expression of a group of expatriate Southern Vietnamese capitalists and their hatred of communism, or the desire of local ethnic leaders to gain social standing, civic legitimacy and access to power' (2002: 29). The rhetoric of 'community' is exposed as a discourse available for elite manipulation.

Mandy Thomas notes the role of Vietnamese Australian organisations and particularly Vietnamese Australian veterans who were the first wave of post-1975 migrants, in attempting to anchor representations of 'community' in an exile narrative. This narrative seeks to connect the historical legitimacy of the South Vietnam regime with a specifically refugee exodus and, finally, with a continuing non-acknowledgement of the current government in Vietnam. Thomas' study includes a picture of the Cabravale Park memorial as a general illustration to her chapter on the use of Tet celebrations (Vietnamese New Year) at Cabravale Park to inscribe this narrative within community events (1999: 146). Of course, considering the site under the rubric of 'public culture', such politics are not exceptional. Meaghan Morris quotes Donald Horne to the effect that 'the public culture' is produced by institutions that 'sustain a 'mirage that can float over a society, purporting to be its national life, serving some interests and suppressing the very existence of others" (Morris 1998: 9).

Given that Hamilton and Ashton's form of ideology critique inheres in the very concept of public culture, what *would* be significant is how their argument is justified not through reference to local debate about the site, but through reference to the site itself. In their concluding passage, the park expands to take in the whole suburb, almost becoming an *exposé* of Cabramatta's defrauding of Australian civic space:

> The monument rests—symbolically—on the periphery of a scruffy, suburban syringe-littered park that is in an out-of-the-way place. Two blocks away, in the centre of town, a pedestrian mall reminiscent of an Asian market sits like a floating world in a classic 1920s bungalow suburb. The long-term presence of Vietnamese gangs and drug trafficking led the state government in 2000 to launch in Cabramatta a public campaign around the extension of police powers in relation to narcotics. Graffiti and neglect—expressions of 'vernacular' culture—indicate this memorial is out of place. (Hamilton and Ashton 2002: 29)

This passage works in a similar way to tabloid TV journalism. Here, the voice of critical evaluation gives way to a concerned voice-over that narrates a sequence of visuals that might tell their own story: an establishing shot of the park fades to a close-up of syringes on the ground, cut away to a nearby Asian Market, insert file footage of police arrests and government announcement as 'background' story, cut back to original site with a second close up of 'graffiti and neglect'.

Given the strong critique of Sydney-based media for their articulation of 'Cabramatta' with the semantic string 'Vietnamese-heroin-gangs' (Teo 2000), critique that has gained currency in Sydney media itself (Kremmer 2005), the completely unqualified appearance of this passage in an academic context summons the rhetorical force of the public secret erupting in the space of (what then becomes) polite discourse: as if the after media-critique, the empirical truth behind such scandalously prejudiced associations is at last free to circulate. For one can surely ask what relevance 'Vietnamese gangs and drug-trafficking' has for a discussion of the memorial? I ask this not as a rhetorical question, one that might preface a defence of Vietnamese Australians from such racialist attacks. That is, I think this question *does* have an answer in their article, one which reveals the force of public secrecy in circulating these kinds of images and how 'the popular' might inhabit public culture as what anthropologist Michael Taussig describes as 'the verge' of such open secrets (Taussig 1999: 8). I want to draw attention to the fact that Hamilton and Ashton group the presence of graffiti with 'neglect' rather than as evidence of continuing significance. This seems a premature conclusion, one based on not actually having read what the graffiti says. Although they may be referring to graffiti at the site that has since been removed (their photo does not reveal any), current graffiti is confined to several carved inscriptions on the sandbags beneath the figures and facing the wall. These include a name in a love heart, 'I love Australia', 'Long Tan Battle' and 'Nui Dat'.[1] The only writing on the front of the memorial is Nhon Do's maker's mark at the soldier's feet.

A more recent intervention into the memorial's significations, however, draws our attention to the real public secret at work in Hamilton and Ashton's article, one that provides the semiotic link between Cabravale Park and the tabloid image of Cabramatta they reproduce. This concerns the public profile of Phuong Ngo, the memorial committee's chairman, whose name has been partly cut away from the bronze plaque. After seven years of prolific media speculation and two mistrials, Ngo was finally convicted in 2001 with a life-sentence for conspiracy to murder John Newman, a local Labour Party MP, who had been shot outside his Cabramatta home in 1994. In the extensive media coverage of this period, both figures developed dramatic public profiles. Ngo was regarded as a sort of mafioso political heavy-hitter, Cabramatta Alderman and founder of the Mekong Club (where he allegedly recruited the killer[s] for what was dubbed Australia's first 'political assassination'). The late John Newman was reputed to be tough on crime, willing to take on the 'Asian gangs', and Ngo's local political rival.[2] When Hamilton and Ashton published their article in 2002, I find it difficult to believe they did not make this connection. I suggest that their non-engagement with this media history returns, nevertheless, in a displaced form *via* their representation of Cabramatta. Such 'not-speaking' produces the same disfiguring effects in their article as the physical attempt to remove Ngo's name has had on the plaque, an erasure of Ngo's public profile that is rendered all the more conspicuous by the logically unmotivated associations of the memorial with crime.

In *Defacement: Public Secrecy and the Labor of the Negative*, Taussig suggests that the public secret—that which is generally known, but not easily spoken about—is intimately related to the act of 'defacement', considered as both iconoclasm and profane revelation. For Taussig, the act of defacement harnesses the social power of sacrilege, an unmasking of the sacred that produces its own magical effects. As 'unmasking', defacement exposes the falseness of a thing, even as it re-enchants the space of representation through the power of negation. It is here that I want to turn from the normative grammars of recognition to consider Hamilton and Ashton's article as itself a form of defacement that testifies to a curiously intense form of participation. Defacement, like recognition, is a theory that attempts to think the circulation of symbolic violence as generative of sociality yet, unlike recognition, it does this for a sociality that has no normative conclusions and in which power lies in knowing how to 'work' the public secret, rather than morally justified positions in discourse. I still want to use the idea of defacement, in its everyday sense, to draw attention to what Hamilton and Ashton *do* with the memorial; that is, defacement is a popular form of protest at sites of civic culture such as war memorials. However, Taussig's theoretical account lets us read Hamilton and Ashton's article as a kind of *ritual* of unmasking that would channel the power of the public secret for its own effects, including the statecraft of the heritage critic who is empowered to make such pronouncements. It is significant that in the first edition of *Public History Review* the term 'recognition' comes up several times in relation to the struggle of public historians to achieve professional acknowledgement for their expertise (Curthoys and Hamilton 1992).

Taussig suggests the ritual of defacement works with the power of the negative immanent to the object to be defaced. Given this, one would have to also ask: beyond the public fate of one of its key agents, how might the Cabravale Park memorial *already* effect a negation, a defacement/exposure, of national iconography? Taussig draws on the figure of the Vietnam veteran as a walking defacement of the national sacred. Locally, Nicoll has argued that the Vietnam War is a period during which Australian nationalist iconography publicly 'lost face' not because of military defeat but because it so transparently served US interests (Nicoll 2001: 113). Such defacing power might attract the heritage critic. Yet we might also ask what defacing power is released through the representation of an Asian soldier in the space of Australian public culture, a power that might provoke the tonally awkward phrase, at once protective and amused, of 'all of the men become "diggers"'?

Getting There

Fairfield City Council's promotion of Cabramatta as a 'Day Trip to Asia' does not include the Cabravale Park war memorial, although a visitor who walked along Park Street might find themselves there.[3] Walking past the monumental sculptures in Freedom Plaza and under the Pai Lau gate—recognisable from the tourist websites—the Cabramatta sightseer might continue to be guided by the street itself, following the footpath as the gift and fabric shops give way to suburban homes. After all, getting *off* the tourist route is precisely what tourists desire to do. According to MacCannell (1989), the figure of the tourist is a canny consumer of attractions, one who actively seeks out the 'back regions' of the sights and precincts they are presented with. Cabravale Park might then become a function of what MacCannell describes as the tourist's search for 'authenticity', a 'backstage' area where the combination of local recreations (open parkland, a basketball court, legal graffiti on an amenities block) and an absence of tourist markers from the Day Trip itinerary might be read as a guarantee of the Real.

There is another itinerary, however, that may bring the interested visitor. Having read about the memorial in a book such as *Sacred Places: War Memorials in the Australian Landscape* (Inglis 1998) or been directed here by listening to the Liverpool Museum's driving tour on audio CD *Tune In to Fairfield*, the heritage tourist would have found Cabravale Park in a street directory and driven here by car. Unlike the figure of the tourist-shopper for whom Cabramatta is advertised as a site of culturally exotic and inexpensive consumption, for the *heritage* tourist the war memorial would be a specific destination; the experience of 'authenticity' is underscored by research, rather than contingency. It is an itinerary for which the memorial may be either a reaffirming or deflating experience, a good or bad surprise.

In considering the tourist circuits in which the site is activated, I want to displace the question of 'who speaks?' with a question of practice; that is, what brings us to Cabravale Park in the first place? In place of cultural civics, we might pose Chow's question of 'cultural surplus', or 'what plays?', for tourism as a spatial practice (Chow 1993). Morris provides a useful summary of Chow's critique:

For Chow, the problem with 'who speaks?' is that 'the emphasis of the question is always on 'who'... Designed to elicit the answer that those who have power speak, this question disavows the power and the technology that enable it to be put, and simplifies oppression by 'trying to understand the world in the form of a coherent narrative grammar, with an identifiable (anthropomorphic) subject for every sentence'. (Morris 1998: 229)

As Morris points out, tourism emerged in the 1980s as both a long-term governmental solution to Australia's economic survival and as a catalyst for debates over a viable national self-image in which the question of 'viable for whom?' emerges as a point of struggle (Morris 1995). As a phase of intensely conflictual 'economically motivated cultural restructuring', the period produces a nation space both physically and symbolically circumscribed by domestic and international itineraries, and substantially renovates the field of practices and objects that public history seeks to describe. Yet Cabramatta is a particularly quirky site in this regard. Its original articulation as a site of 'Asia-in-Australia' domestic tourism in the late-1980s was due to local council and Indochinese community groups' strategies of combining 'place making', economic development and a positive image campaign (Dunn 1998, 2003). This would suggest that a 'nationalist commercial project' (Turner qtd. in Morris 1998: 9) of 'manufacturing traditions for tourism' (Morris 1995: 181) may coincide not only with government policy on multiculturalism and tourism, but also with what Stephen Frost (1997) has described as 'centreing Asia'. That is, as a local tourist strategy it is also partly enabled by the moment of the Garnaut Report (Garnaut 1989) in which understanding Asia was promoted as part of a national program to 'change the culture' in the name of a regional economic future. This moment in which Asia/Australia relations become a site of extensive governmental reform, which would later be implicated in (as Frost and Morris note) a populist backlash, has been a catalyst for a new space of Asian Australian critique.

Although the Cabramatta tourist is not addressed explicitly in Hamilton and Ashton's article, it is present as a problematic speaking relation that is schematically implied by their argument. They suggest that it is 'white Anglophone Australia' that local Vietnamese Australians hail in the civic language of national belonging. Although such an addressee would concur with the *invoked* subject of Ngo's statement in the *Fairfield Champion* article, it does not necessarily follow that this subject and the intended audience for *the statement* are one and the same. Such a subject may perform a purely ceremonial function for a local constituency, such as 'His Excellency Rear Admiral Peter Sinclair A. O.', who came to Cabramatta to perform the unveiling and whose name is inscribed on the plaque. Similarly, while 'white Anglophone Australia' may be hailed by Cabramatta's 'Day Trip to Asia' promotion—the non-local shopper for whom a generalised space of 'Asia' as a consumable ethnicity is attractive in its very alterity, but with the thrift-factor of geographic proximity because it is no more than a 'Day Trip'—there are other kinds of tourists and tourist relations in Cabramatta. Kevin Dunn notes how Cabramatta has become a significant regional shopping and recreational centre for Vietnamese

Australians throughout the state (Dunn 1998: 12). The first time I visited the area was when I was staying with a Vietnamese Australian friend who had recently moved from Melbourne. My friend lived on the other side of the city, but occasionally went to Cabramatta to browse the shops, take documentary photographs (he is a professional photographer), and to show it to friends when they were passing through town.

Reading the public historian read the site in terms of an 'identifiable (anthropomorphic) subject for every sentence', we could regard such a proper addressee as the counterpart to the site's 'phantom agent' in whose name it speaks. A normative tourist relation could be regarded as the public historian's 'medium', in both the everyday and arcane sense of this word. Tourism does not only direct and facilitate field-work but, through producing sites of public culture, it might sustain the image of a proper addressee—*the* tourist as National Subject, not just anyone who passes by—that the public historian might listen *through*, but (being historians) not speak as.

Conclusions

In replying to Hamilton and Ashton's article, I have not made a case for 'the contra' in two important senses. First, I have not argued that the memorial does not solicit recognition. I have merely focused on how the discourse of recognition might be used to limit, rather than expand, the public historian's engagement. Secondly, I have avoided producing an ethnography that would account for current users of the site for whom it has positive value (minimally, the Vietnamese Australian ex-servicemen and their families who commemorate national Vietnam Veteran's day here). This is not to suggest such an ethnography would not be significant but as a response to this particular engagement of public history, it would run the risk of suggesting the memorial should be recognised, or that it does belong, which is not my argument either. Heeding Bennett's call for better attention as to how claims are *placed* (Bennett 1992), such a plea would not need to be made by me, or made in this context. Community agencies such as the Vietnamese Community Association (which has strong links to veterans groups) are perfectly capable of promoting and defending the interests of this particular constituency. Such a defence concedes that there is a case that needs to be answered, which I do not think there is. Most significantly though, to defend the site in terms of the rights of a particular constituency may (however crucial in one context) ignore the fact that the site may be ambivalent for others. It would suggest that the significance of memory-sites can be restricted in this way. This would be problematic as a 'rights discourse' implies that the articulation of social memory, like the accumulation of authority to speak, is not subject to multiple claims and renegotiations over time.

In terms of the public historical sphere serving as the 'critical resource' Bennett once feared could be threatened by the ascendancy of tourism (Bennett 1988), further research on public history at Cabramatta could look past the rhetorics of recognition in order to consider how Vietnamese Australian agents have both brokered and renegotiated the kinds of unequal relations that come with tourism and media interest more generally.[4]

For public history, my argument would strike a note of caution in terms of the confidence with which the discipline seeks to mediate the value of memory-sites between local and national contexts, and a note of critical adventurousness, in terms of encouraging more focused attention on the pedestrian practices and unruly forms of dialogue that animate both the critic's discourse and their objects.

Notes

[1] 'Nui Dat' was the location in Vietnam of an Australian personnel base, while 'Long Tan' has become enshrined in Australian war mythology as the site of an engagement which left the highest number of Australian causalities of any single encounter.

[2] Scott Poynting and Tim Anderson have been prominent critics of the role of the media in the case. See their articles at the *Free Phuong* campaign website <http://home.iprimus.com.au/dna_info/phreephuong/>. See also Dunn (2003).

[3] Cabramatta is promoted by Fairfield City Council (FCC) on its website, as well as on numerous tourism websites. See FCC's *Cabramatta Spotlight* link <http://www.fairfieldcity.nsw.gov.au/>.

[4] Tanja Dreher (2002) has made some steps in this direction. Khoa Do's (2003) independent feature film *The Finished People* might be an interesting starting point. Utilising 'fictodocumentary' techniques, the film incorporates the kinds of 'issues' that mediated national concern about the area and enabled the film to find a sympathetic audience. It references Vietnamese Australian place-making and historical identity in numerous sequences. The film also includes a scene at the foot of the Cabravale Park Vietnam memorial that responds directly to the racialising of local heroin dealers and users. Significantly, the director's production company is called Post 75 productions.

References

Cabramatta Spotlight <http://www.fairfieldcity.nsw.gov.au/default.asp?iSubCatID=297&iNavCatID=1> (accessed 28 January 2006).
Free Phuong <http://home.iprimus.com.au/dna_info/phreephuong/> (accessed 10 March 2005).
Bennett, T. *Out of Which Past? Critical Reflections on Australian Museum and Heritage Policy. Cultural Policy Studies, Occasional Paper No. 3*. Brisbane: Institute for Cultural Policy Studies, Griffith University, 1988.
———. 'Putting Policy into Cultural Studies.' *Cultural Studies*. Eds. L. Grossberg, C. Nelson and P. Treichler. New York and London: Routledge, 1992. 23–37.
Bhabha, H. K. 'Culture's In Between.' *Multicultural States: Rethinking Difference and Identity*. Ed. D. Bennett. London and New York: Routledge, 1998. 29–36.
Brown, W. *States of Injury: Power and Freedom in Late Modernity*. Princeton and New Jersey: Princeton University Press, 1995.
Carruthers, A. 'National Identity, Diasporic Anxiety, and Music Video Culture in Vietnam.' *House of Glass: Culture, Modernity, and the State in Southeast Asia*. Ed. Y. Souchou. Singapore: Institute of Southeast Asian Studies, 2001. 119–49.
Chow, R. 'Listening Otherwise, Music Miniaturized: A Different Type of Question About Revolution.' *The Cultural Studies Reader*. Ed. S. During. London: Routledge, 1993. 382–99.

Cunningham, S., and T. Nguyen. 'Popular Media of the Vietnamese Diaspora.' *Floating Lives: The Media and Asian Diasporas*. Eds. S. Cunningham and J. Sinclair. St Lucia: University of Queensland Press, 2000. 91–135.

Curthoys, A. "Vietnam": Public Memory of an Anti-War Movement.' *Memory and History in Twentieth Century Australia*. Eds. K. Darian-Smith and P. Hamilton. Melbourne: Oxford University Press, 1994. 123–130.

Curthoys, A., and P. Hamilton. 'What Makes History Public?' *Public History Review* 1 (1992): 8–13.

De Certeau, M. *The Practice of Everyday Life*. Trans. S. F. Rendall. Berkeley and Los Angeles: University of California Press, 1984.

Do, K. (Director) *The Finished People*, 2003. Film.

Dreher, T. 'Intersections: A Transdisciplinary Approach to Identity, Media, and Place.' *Australian Journal of Communication* 29.1 (2002): 67–80.

Dunn, K.M. 'Rethinking Ethnic Concentration: The Case of Cabramatta, Sydney.' *Urban Studies* 35.3 (1998): 503–25.

——. 'Using Cultural Geography to Engage Contested Constructions of Ethnicity and Citizenship in Sydney.' *Social and Cultural Geography* 4.2 (2003): 153–65.

Düttman, A.G. *Between Cultures: Tensions in the Struggle for Recognition*. Trans. K. B. Woodgate. London and New York: Verso, 2000.

Fraser, N. 'From Redistribution to Recognition? Dilemmas of Justice in a 'Postsocialist' Age'. *Justice Interruptus: Critical Reflections on the 'Postsocialist' Condition*. New York and London: Routledge, 1997. 147–161.

Frost, S. 'Negotiating Asia.' *The UTS Review* 3.2 (1997): 23–45.

Garnaut, R. *Australia and the Northeast Asian Ascendancy: Report to the Prime Minister and the Minister for Foreign Affairs and Trade*. Canberra: Australian Government Publishing Service, 1989.

Hage, G. *Against Paranoid Nationalism: Searching for Hope in a Shrinking Society*. Sydney: Pluto Press, 2003.

Hamilton, P., and P. Ashton. 'On Not Belonging: Memorials and Memory in Sydney.' *Public History Review: Changi to Cabramatta—Places and Personality* 9 (2002): 23–36.

Inglis, K. *Sacred Places: War Memorials in the Australian Landscape*. Melbourne: Melbourne University Press, 1998.

Kremmer, C. Generation V. *Sydney Morning Herald*, News Review, 2005, 30 April, <http://www.smh.com.au/news/National/Generation-V/2005/04/29/1114635756057.html> (accessed 27 January 2006).

MacCannell, D. *The Tourist: A New Theory of the Leisure Class*, Revised edition. New York: Schocken Books, 1989.

Morris, M. 'Life as a Tourist Object in Australia.' *International Tourism: Identity and Change*. Eds. M. Lanfant, J.B. Allcock and E.M. Bruner. London: Sage, 1995. 171–91.

——. *Too Soon, Too Late: History in Popular Culture*. Bloomington and Indiana: Indiana University Press, 1998.

Morris, M. and McCalman, I. 'Public Culture'. *Knowing Ourselves and Others: The Humanities in Australia into the 21st Century, Vol. 3: Reflective Essays*. Canberra: Department Of Employment, Education, Training and Youth Affairs, 1998. 1–20.

Nicoll, F. *From Diggers to Drag Queens: Configurations of Australian National Identity*. Sydney: Pluto Press, 2001.

Tai, H. H. 'Commemoration and Community.' *The Country of Memory: Remaking the Past in Late Socialist Vietnam*. Ed. H. H. Tai. Berkeley and Los Angeles: University of California Press, 2001. 227–71.

Taussig, M. *Defacement: Public Secrecy and the Labour of the Negative*. Stanford: Stanford University Press, 1999.

Taylor, C. 'The Politics of Recognition.' *Multiculturalism: Examining the Politics of Recognition*. Ed. A. Gutman. Princeton and New Jersey: Princeton University Press, 1994. 25–73.
Teo, P. 'Racism in the News: A Critical Discourse Analysis of News Reporting in Two Australian Newspapers.' *Discourse and Society* 11.1 (2000): 7–49.
Thomas, M. *Dreams in the Shadows: Vietnamese-Australian Lives in Transition*. Sydney: Allen and Unwin, 1999.
Viviani, N. 'The Indochinese in Australia 1975–1995: From Burnt Boats to Barbecues'. Melbourne: Oxford Oxford University Press, 1996.

Figure 1 Cabravale Park War Memorial, sculpture by Nhon Do. Photograph by Scott Brook

'Growing up an Australian': Renegotiating Mateship, Masculinity and 'Australianness' in Hsu-Ming Teo's *Behind the Moon*

Robyn Morris

> Let us stop deceiving ourselves that we were cast in the mould of Bligh, Wentworth, Ned Kelly, the ANZACS, and other tough, devil-may-care characters of historical fact and fiction. (Brian Penton 1943: 1)

In constructions of 'Australianness', the cast is, historically, male dominated. Archetypal and heroic, hyper-masculinised, white and heterosexual—figures such as the stoic bushman, brash bushranger, or the fearless ANZAC soldier[1] are routinely resurrected in cultural celebrations of Australian nationhood. Writing from culturally hybridised spaces such as Malaysia and Australia, Hsu-Ming Teo addresses the raced, gendered and sexualised basis of such constructions of nationhood in her second and most recent novel, *Behind the Moon* (2005a; hereafter referred to as *BM*). The novel articulates a politicised poetics of resistance through its renegotiation of an institutionalised and singularised model of Australian identity, one that focuses on these deeds of, and relationships between, white, heterosexual males. The narrative makes central a dysfunctional and triangulated 'mateship' between characters who have been traditionally 'othered' in stories of nation. Teo's critique of normative models of identity and the centring of characters whose countenance is not favoured, or desired, under the policing eye of whiteness because they are of Asian or African American ancestry, are gay or overweight, are too dark or too light—characters who are definitely and defiantly not like white—signals a timely arrival on the Australian literary scene. The novel is important in its examination of how individuals negotiate the gendered and raced binaries underscoring the concept of mateship while presenting this site as one of much needed complication and disavowal.

Creating a palimpsestic text in which the historical, the iconic and the real are overlaid, Teo also invokes, both in the novel's title and early in its narrative, two seemingly disparate but iconic filmic texts: Peter Weir's *Gallipoli* (1981)[2] and Victor Fleming's *The Wizard of Oz* (1939). *Behind the Moon* narrates a journey of three friends who are male and female, one of whom is gay and one who, to paraphrase Homi Bhabha (1994), is 'not quite white'. They live, as the novel's title with its direct reference to *The Wizard of Oz* suggests, somewhere behind the moon, over the rainbow (Judy Garland begins singing the film's signature song 'Somewhere Over the Rainbow' just after she utters these lines in the movie). The Land of Oz for these friends is a place far from the mythologised beach at ANZAC Cove; the novel is set in an inner Western suburb of Sydney called Strathfield. However, the correlation between a contemporary Asian Australian novel, an iconic Australian 'war' film and a Hollywood musical fantasy rests on the way each text complicates the dynamics that pattern and underscore conceptions of 'mateship'.

It is significant that Teo reintroduces her readers to *Gallipoli* though the eyes of one of the novel's central characters, Justin Cheong, who is a gay, Chinese Australian male. This reference to *Gallipoli* prompts a return to and (re)reading of this iconic story of nation through a narrative that explores how the formation of a seemingly unitary national identity is embedded in a stereotype that privileges the white, heterosexual male—characteristics that are embodied by *Gallipoli*'s central characters Frank Dunne (Mel Gibson) and Archy Hamilton (Mark Lee). Ideologically-driven from its first sweeping frame of the desert to its carefully controlled three-part structure, *Gallipoli* sets out to define what it means to be an Australian, what it means to be a mate and what it means to be a hero, specifically linking Australian heteromasculinity to war and landscape.

The film revives what Amanda Lohrey has noted as 'one of the most suspect and outdated aspects of the [Australian] Legend, namely the myth of rural virtual' (1982: 29). Lohrey suggests that the film's sentimental nationalism circulates around 'the legend of the bushman and its post-war transmutation into the ANZAC myth' (29). The ANZAC, as Tony Ayres observes, 'has always been one of the cornerstones of Australian national identity' (2000: 162). Justin watches the underwater, nude male swimming scene from *Gallipoli* in a history class at school and later purchases a poster of the film picturing Gibson and Lee. When Justin's father, Tek Cheong, sees it hanging in his son's bedroom he reads this image as a sign 'that Justin was growing up an Australian' (*BM* 6). Jane Freebury has commented that the film is an extended definition of 'what is intrinsically Australian—mateship, endurance, the outback and a nationalistic belief in an as yet unrealised potential' (1987: 7). While *Gallipoli* operates simultaneously as excessively nationalistic and anti-imperialistic, it is also exceedingly gendered and raced in its implication that mateship is a game that only white men can play.

Aimed straight at the heart of a white, nationalist culture, *Behind the Moon* tackles the pervasiveness of this sentimental heroism and truth status surrounding a myth that is so well known and deeply embedded in the national psyche that it is commonly regarded as an assumed truth. The reference to *Gallipoli* in a contemporary Asian Australian novel signals a need for a reassessment of the film's ideological underpinnings, particularly of what it means to be 'an Australian' in terms of race, sexuality, and gender. The narrative circulates around the lives of Justin, his friends Tien Ho and Nigel 'Gibbo' Gibson, and their immediate families. Tien is a Vietnamese refugee and the daughter of a Chinese Vietnamese mother and an African American, Cajun father. She prefers to be called Tina and identified as 'a normal, everyday Australian' (*BM* 56). Anglo Australian Gibbo, son of a doctor who is also a Vietnam veteran, is bullied by his classmates for being non-athletic, scholastically obtuse and overweight. Gibbo fails to live up to 'the impossible ideals of Australian masculinity laid down by [his father] Gordon Gibson' (*BM* 282) and could be read, alongside of his friends Tien and Justin, as the antithesis of the stereotypical Australian male characters played by Gibson and Lee in *Gallipoli*.

Behind the Moon begins by introducing Justin and his mother Annabelle Cheong and her obsession with toilet hygiene. The novel is characterised by its playful prose and is also peppered with vaudeville-like moments from the disastrous 'dead Diana dinner' (a reunion of Justin, Tien, Gibbo and their families to watch the funeral procession of Princess Diana) when Justin's homosexuality is revealed to his parents, to Tek's karaoke nights, Gibbo's mother Gillian's interpretation of the unspoken rules of political correctness, Tien's move to California and introduction to the pubic hair shaving ceremony of the Gaia Goddess cult, and Gibbo's unrequited love for, vomiting upon, and relentless stalking of Linh, Tien's mother. The move from parody to politicised reality within the novel occurs with the massacre of seven people by a deranged gunman in the Strathfield Plaza shopping centre, a place frequented by Justin, Tien and Gibbo as teenagers. At the precise moment of carnage, Tien and Gibbo are in a supermarket shopping for hairspray while Justin, keeping in mind his mother's admonishment never to touch a toilet seat, is otherwise occupied in his first homosexual encounter in one of the shopping centre's toilets.

While this moment hints at the first splintering of the group, it also catapults Justin's life-story into prominence. The novel's dramatic peak ends with another toilet block, more sex and again, Justin. His search for love and identity, however, results in him being beaten almost lifeless. His attackers call him a 'Fucking Asian faggot' (*BM* 333) and Justin is doubly punished for his sexuality and for his visible Asian-ness. The quest for Justin—and for Gibbo and Tien—is articulated in Justin's last coherent thought before he enters a coma and this is a wish to live a life where he is not 'reducible to his ethnicity or his sexuality or his occupation or geographical location or even his family' (*BM* 334). It is the very positioning of a dominant and desired subjectivity on to and from the markers of race, sexuality and gender that is perpetuated in *Gallipoli*. By making reference to a film that is intrinsically tied to a sense of white, national (masculine and homosocial) identity in a novel driven by non-white, gay, female and effeminate characters, Teo creates a timely collision between the discourses of nationalism, mateship gender and race.

'Oddness' in the Suburbs, Mateship in the Dardanelles

The point of intervention in contemporary representational politics for *Behind the Moon* is the (re)focus on the lives and mateship of three friends who have been thrown together because of their status, not as heroes, but as social misfits. From their formative years at primary school, Justin, Gibbo and Tien are labelled as physically different and this form of social othering propels them to unite as 'a gang' (*BM* 54). Gibbo proudly labels them 'the Three Musketeers' (*BM* 54). Their tenuous stand against social ostracisation allows them to negotiate the fraught arena of playground politics. Tien befriends Gibbo at school, the boy who sat alone every lunch hour while waiting expectantly for an empty drink carton or apple core to be hurled in his direction: 'he was used to being the schoolyard reject, the fat kid everyone picked on' (*BM* 28). As a new arrival in Gibbo's classroom, Tien is immediately aware of his loneliness. Made strange by her own lack of English language skills, and her towering height over her new class mates (she is two years older than them), she instantly recognises that 'they were the two class rejects' (*BM* 27).

When Justin, whom Gibbo has met through shared piano lessons every Saturday afternoon since they were six, is expelled from his private school and joins Tien and Gibbo mid-way through high school, Gibbo is ecstatic: 'his two best friends—his only two friends—with him in school, fortifying him against his own oddness, demonstrating to the rest of his classmates that he was no longer an outsider' (*BM* 54). Stigmatised as not 'normal' or not belonging, Gibbo 'didn't seem a proper man, a real Aussie' (*BM* 8). As an adult Gibbo still struggles with the role of masculinity that is expected of him at the level of the family and the social. He resorts, at the age of twenty-one, to a group dating service in order to 'observe and learn the dating and mating habits of the average Aussie male' (*BM* 102). This is a failure and his first evening ends with him drunk and vomiting over Tien's mother Linh. On the eve of his twenty-first birthday (which his parents have incidentally forgotten) Gibbo, not considering himself 'in any way normal' (*BM* 102) looks in a mirror and describes himself as a 'self-confessed friendless loner and lard-arse freak, an athletic philistine who tripped over his tongue as well as his feet' (*BM* 106).

Tien experiences a similar sense of corporeal outsiderness because of her African American, Chinese Vietnamese ancestry. A motherless refugee transplanted to Sydney from Vietnam at the age of five, Tien struggles against both gendered and racialised stereotypes. She retreats to sullenness in order to cope with her hostile social world, and describes her racial and cultural hybridity as 'her mongrel roots' (*BM* 72). Read by her family and school peers as physically bi-cultural, Tien straddles the rather uncomfortable divide that Bhabha has defined as 'the ambivalent world of the not quite/not white' (1994: 92). Rejected by her Vietnamese Australian family because of this 'multi-racial' heritage, by her skin which, in summer, 'tanned to a crisp, dark shade of honey soy chicken wings' (*BM* 28), Tien struggles for recognition outside of a stereotype that 'fixes' her as different and non-white. The description of Tien's skin as honey-soy coloured is a reflection on a representational process in which coloured subjectivity is inscribed not only through a culturally specific process of visualisation, but in comparison to a fictitious white and Western norm.

Tien's story is arguably paralleled with that of *The Wizard of Oz*. Teo complicates the very notion of 'belonging' and being 'at home' in what may be a subtle reference to the oft-repeated phrase to Asian migrants in Australia. Newly-arrived or decades old, people of visible Asian ancestry are routinely told to click their red shoes like Dorothy, and 'go home'. Ien Ang notes that 'for the migrant it is no longer "where you're from", but "where you're at" which forms the point of anchorage'. Ang further observes that 'so long as the question "where you're from" prevails over "where you're at" in dominant culture, the compulsion to explain, the inevitable positioning of yourself as deviant *vis-à-vis* the normal, remains' (2001: 30). *Behind the Moon*, in part, reflects upon this process. It complicates and reviews the way culturally entrenched and politically endorsed dichotomies of difference, which fix and exclude colour, sexuality and race from the normative model of white hegemony, are reproduced in Western visualising practices. An integral part of such practices is the way whiteness positions itself as a marker of power, while simultaneously marking specific forms of embodiment as strange, alien and visible signifiers of a subordinated difference. Skin difference, as Sara Ahmed notes, 'is radically unstable given its dependence on multiple regimes of difference and identification' (1998: 27).

Teo's connection between the practice of fixing corporeal difference and the cultural reproduction of whiteness as non-different is an important intervention in contemporary identity politics in Australia. The narrative deliberately displaces both the mateship model of white male duos and embedded models of family and heterosexual romance, with shifting sites of queerness and hybridity in the suburbs. Despite the novel's reference to the embedded hierarchies of raced, gendered and sexualised differences operating in *Gallipoli*, *Behind the Moon* is not a study on whiteness. As Richard Dyer, who admits to being filled with dread at the thought of reproducing white privilege through pedagogical practices, states: 'My blood runs cold at the thought that talking about whiteness could lead to the development of something called 'White Studies' (1997: 10). Whiteness is only made visible in *Behind the Moon* through its reference to *Gallipoli's* scopic privileging of the white male body.

If, in an Australian context, prowess in war has been linked to the construction and adulation of the white male, it is not surprising that within the exhibition spaces of a popular icon of Australian nationalism, the Australian War Memorial, there is, as Fiona Nicoll has observed, a 'striking' and 'virtual absence of female bodies' (Nicoll 2001: 70). Nicoll further notes that in comparison to war memorials and art spaces in Britain and Canada this gendered scarcity is 'unusual' (2001: 70). Visitors to the Australian War Memorial are bombarded with images of male bodies in paintings, sculptures and dioramas. Heroic in theme, execution and performance, there are repeated images of 'shooting diggers, swimming diggers, marching diggers, standing diggers, mounted diggers and flying diggers [who] are all represented playing their respective parts within various theatres of war'[3] (Nicoll 2001: 70). The War Memorial makes the white male body the axis of its story and, as if taking the Memorial's cue, Weir's *Gallipoli* veers little from this gendered and raced scripting of war. *Gallipoli*, however, does more than simply make the male body visible. The film constructs a specifically white (Australian) masculinity; one that is not raced, that is not queer, and one that in representations of its very normativity implies that difference is an undesirable form of otherness. Being a woman and non-white, Tien has no place in such a story of nation and, in aligning her story with that of the adventure undertaken by Dorothy in *The Wizard of Oz*, Teo is perhaps prompting a questioning of *Gallipoli's* insistent, singularised and masculinised visual and narrative focus.

In their introduction to *Gender and War: Australians at War in the Twentieth Century*, Joy Damousi and Marilyn Lake suggest that, while 'masculinity found its best expression in war, war engendered a crisis in masculinity' (1995: 11). This sense of 'crisis', however, is simply not explored in *Gallipoli*. Instead, the film is celebratory in the way it depicts war as a learning field, where young, rural and urban Australian males like Archy and Frank can practice acts of courage, stoicism, bravery and physical feats far from their Australian environment. The film shows how war is associated with whiteness, youth, athleticism and masculinity while all 'others', including Archy's Aboriginal jackeroo, his mother, and also younger siblings and uncle, remain on the domestic front. Despite being underage, Archy is accepted into the esteemed and prestigious Light Horse regiment for his exceptional horse riding skills. It is the character of Archy rather than Frank who is consistently associated with divinity, whiteness and light, from his blond hair, to his pristine shirt cuffs in the desert of Cairo. Dyer's work on representations of whiteness questions the way whiteness remains, in dominant discourse, as un-raced, un-named and unseen. Normalising whites works to eliminate whiteness from any categories that mark difference such as gender, class or sexuality. In the unbalanced dynamics of racism, 'race is something only applied to non-white peoples, as long as white people are not racially seen and named, they/ we function as a human norm' (1997: 1). Dyer explores the way in which film is a codified example of identity politics and suggests that in order to decentre whiteness, 'whiteness needs to be made strange' (1997: 10). *Gallipoli's* lighting repeatedly favours Archy, giving him this divine glow while Frank's face and body are often shadowed. This continual build-up of light around Archy explodes (literally) in the final scene where he hurls himself over the trenches to face the gunfire of the Turks. Beauteously white, he dies in a Christ-like pose, with arms outstretched, and bathed by light in what is otherwise a field of smoke, mayhem and carnage.

However, as Claudia Benthien's study on 'skin' shows, 'just as the European gaze was long regarded as neutral in cultural history, "white" skin is still seen as nonsignificant and is therefore not considered to be a construct' (2002: 153). Part of *Behind the Moon's* politics of representation is the decentring of whiteness so that characters previously 'made strange' rather than heroic in stories of nation are given presence and voice. In (re)focussing the audience gaze upon white male bodies diving, swimming, running, wrestling and dying (heroically) in the Dardanelles, the film draws upon the idea of carnival and this focus of young men at play in a battle-zone, is an 'example of what Lacan called 'the male parade', pleasurable male pin-ups dispensing *jouissance* for both the female and the male viewer' (Walsh 2004: 213). If the appeal of a film such as *Gallipoli* is pitched to white audiences as a way of affirming a sense of cohesive nationhood then Teo's depiction of a gay Chinese Australian male, desiring the white on-screen body of these soldiers, is not only a pointed critique of how white maleness is routinely represented as ideologically attractive, but also unsettles the structuring of the policing eye of whiteness. The novel reverses the inward-looking, racialised and gendered gaze associated with the construction of a singularised national identity, one that is inextricably tied to homogenising cultural practices as exemplified and celebrated in *Gallipoli*.

Mateship in the Land of Oz

While *Gallipoli* is about a war fought on foreign shores, Teo takes her story inland and to what appears, on the surface, the monotony of life in suburban Strathfield. Teo comments that Strathfield is

> the region I grew up in and where I still live. It is a place of endless fascination to me in its multicultural hybridity and middleclass suburban mundanity; its complete lack of 'cool' and unfashionable 'westiness'; the tragicomic dramas of my neighbours and the quiet tales of heroic Cold war survivors and postcolonial migrants. This is the Australia that I know intimately, but it is not one that I encounter in many Australian novels (2005b: 1).

By tracing the conflicted lives of three suburban and 'othered' teenagers whose stories are otherwise negated in stories of nation, Teo shows that the classic bush myth of Oz has no place in the reality of a suburban Australian existence. It is, however, a pervasive myth that, as Neil Rattigan observes, dominates images pertaining to national identity in the visual arts (1991: 16). The bushman/drover is envisioned, through the depiction of his strength, determination and exceptional horse riding skills, as the embodiment of Australian masculinity. If the 'Australian character' (male) is formed by responses to experiences in a harsh environment then 'these experiences have given rise to a set of perceptions, of myths, around the notions of egalitarianism, mateship, and collectivisation in a loose populist sense' (Rattigan 1991: 16) and mateship, as Rattigan further observes, is, perhaps 'the single most important mythic element in the cultural identity of Australia' (1991: 27). Brian McFarlane similarly notes that 'the sentimental ideal of mateship may well be Australia's chief contribution to the history of human relationship. Like most images which together constitute a national identity, the image of men as mates derives from the blurred territory between myth and reality' (1987: 54). This notion of an intense homosocial bonding in an environment that revolves around the relationships forged between men, one where women play no part, is important in the process of readdressing the model of mateship put forward in *Gallipoli*. Early discussions about *Gallipoli* also focussed on its representation of a homosocial mateship, with Lohrey suggesting that *Gallipoli* 'has no real faith in the old ANZAC myth of mateship [instead promoting] the view of mateship as a substitute sexual bonding' (1982: 33).

In a recent analysis of *Gallipoli* and Peter Jackson's *The Lord of the Rings* trilogy, Ian Henderson suggests substituting the term 'fellowship for 'mateship' in an attempt to move from the fixed definitions surrounding this ideal:

> fellowship may be plotted somewhere along that section of Kosofsky Sedgwick's continuum which provokes the greatest unease, where any fixed sexual identity is bamboozled by indefinite and/or variable behaviour over time: fellowship is thus understood here as a unique way of *one man relating to another* for which sex acts are beside the point... fellowship denotes a precise and imprecise, non-substantiating way of relating, provisional in that it is conditioned by the adventure, and variable over time: it is fundamentally queer. (2005: 1, emphasis added)

Despite Henderson's recognition of the need to locate the concept of mateship as shifting and variable, and his underscoring of the suppressed queerness of the relationship between males in both *Gallipoli* and *The Lord of the Rings*, this redefinition still fails to make problematic manifestations of power other than sexuality operating under the umbrella of mateship. While *Gallipoli* operates simultaneously as excessively nationalistic and anti-imperialistic, it is also exceedingly gendered and raced in its implication that, as I mention above, mateship is a game that only white men can play.

While *Behind the Moon* problematises the very notion of mateship as the domain of white heterosexuality, *Gallipoli* takes the ideal of (platonic) mateship and links the development of Archy and Frank's friendship to the desert landscape. It is in this geographical space where these characters cement their deep and abiding (until death do us part) mateship. Any embers of queerness are quickly smothered by the narrative.

Masculinity in *Gallipoli* is defined more by mateship than by heterosexuality, and this is encapsulated in the pyramid scene. The men, gazing into each other's eyes, cement their devotion to one another, not through a rough hug, a light shoulder punch or even a virtuous kiss on the cheek, but through a handshake. Given the geographical and historical reality (these boys are after all sitting on top of a pyramid on the eve of their move to the front line), the chasteness of this action appears incongruous when compared to the overwhelming emotion of the moment. The handshake, intimating a 'manly' physical closeness, an emotionless, heterosexual contact of male skin, is an important edict in the script of Australian mateship reinforcing the idea of an egalitarian, sexless, classless mateship. This handshake is the only socially-accepted expression of physicality that men can do and the image speaks volumes, especially when read against Teo's text, for what is denied and suppressed.

Teo exposes the falseness of this ethos by having Justin and Gibbo take a camping trip together after the completion of their Higher School Certificate exams. After a day of sun and surf, a half-cooked barbeque dinner and too many beers, they lay wrapped in individual sleeping bags next to a dying fire and 'grinned idiotically at each other and felt exhilarated by enacting the sheer normality of being two Aussie adolescents smashed at the beach' (*BM* 90). This moment of fellowship is shattered when Justin leans over and 'kisses Gibbo long and hard' (*BM* 92). Gibbo responds with 'an explosion of fists on his face' (*BM* 92). This reaction occurs because Gibbo subscribes to the same script of masculinity that is encoded in *Gallipoli*. There is only one form of mateship—one which keeps a physical distance—and his violent response to Justin's homosexuality prefigures the reaction of Justin's three attackers that results in his eventual coma. While Justin lies comatose, Gibbo replays the campfire scene in his mind:

> He wished he had kissed Justin just once that night. If he could go back, rub out the past and rewrite his life, this was the thing he would change. He wished he'd had the maturity, the compassion and courage to kiss Justin back, hug him tightly, then ease away and say with a smile, 'Jus, if I was gay you'd be for me. Maybe in our next lives, mate. Let's drink to that, eh?' (*BM* 337)

Justin's momentary lapse in the suppression of his queer identity is parallelled with his pretence at heteronormativity with Tien. However, when Tien asks him to partner her to their school formal, she not only excludes Gibbo (reducing the trio to a heteronormative male/female duo), but she also inadvertently catapults Justin's struggle with his homosexuality to the fore. Justin is torn by what he perceives as his betrayal of his friendship with Gibbo—'He was angry with Tien. She had placed him and Gibbo in the position of being rivals. Instead of best friends, they were now winner and loser; the chosen and the rejected' (*BM* 75)—and his desire for a platonic rather than sexual friendship with Tien. Justin's angst exemplifies a deep guilt over his sexuality. By being gay, he feels he is rejecting the script of heterosexual romance that Tien, through her endless reading of women's gossip and beauty magazines, believes is paramount.

In searching for the mythical Land of Oz where she can be surrounded by the love and affection espoused by these beauty and lifestyle magazines, Tien accepts a marriage proposal from Stan Wong, the first boy who had ever asked her out. In an uncanny echo of Justin's incredulousness over being accepted as a lover by the character of Dirk, Tien believes the proposal was a sign 'that she was loved and wanted by a man' (*BM* 164). She leaves with Stan for America, but, rather than finding friends and adventure, Tien feels isolated in the hippy culture of California and is betrayed by Stan who embarks upon an affair. Essential to her journey of growth is the realisation that 'she hadn't landed in Oz after all because she didn't have the Scarecrow, Tinman and Cowardly Lion with her, and what use was Oz without her friends?' (*BM* 323). Tien's discovery that Oz/Australia is the place she feels she belongs is empowering. It is her group of friends in which she finds true love, and she accepts her divorce from Stan as liberating rather than socially disabling. As a newly single woman she is admonished by Annette Cheong, who tells her that marriage 'is like buying a new pair of shoes ... at first new shoes pinch and hurt ... then you break them in' (*BM* 341). However, Tien discards the ideology underscoring this sentiment. Unlike Dorothy whose red shoes bound her to the patriarchal social order of home (and, if *The Wizard of Oz* had a sequel, to the binds of heterosexual romance/marriage), Tien replies: 'I can always buy a nice new pair of shoes' (*BM* 341).

Desiring 'Normality'

Tien's realisation that the accruements of identity are sometimes less than a perfect fit and can require remodelling indicates the transient rather than fixed nature of identity. However, to survive in a world that fixes queerness and Asianness as symptoms of abnormality, Justin presents a façade of 'fitting in'. This is why his father Tek is so pleased to see the *Gallipoli* poster in his son's bedroom, reading it as a badge of Australianness, one that complemented Justin's sporting trophies and school text books. These outward trappings of normality belie Justin's inner turmoil and he is described as a boy without essence, somewhat akin to the Tin Man in *The Wizard of*

Oz. Justin is described as simply a 'skinful of flesh and bone that did not seem to connect to the feelings or fantasies he harboured' (*BM* 13). He is consumed by guilt over his queerness and is psychologically traumatised by continually 'mak[ing] himself normal for his parents—the good son—and then tr[ying] to make himself normal for his friends' (*BM* 141). What Justin eventually realises is that this is an impossible task, 'because he didn't know what normality was' (*BM* 141). Stuart Hall uses Fanon's *Black Skin, White Masks* to elucidate the fracturing of identity that occurs under white regimes of power (1990: 231). The presence of whiteness is dependent on exclusion and imposition but, Hall warns, although this appears to be an external process, the psychological scarring, powerfully revealed in *Black Skin White Masks*, is another facet that must be reconsidered in articulations of resistance to the imposition of fixity that emanates from the imperial eye of whiteness (233).

That Justin's story and point of view is made prominent is a significant and politicised move given that, in the dominant Western pecking order of masculinity, it is the gay Asian male who is read as a symbol of national difference, a corporeal and cultural alien who is to be both feared and mocked. Tseen Khoo argues that in 'the histories of Western nations such as Australia and Canada, diasporic Chinese and/or Japanese men are figurative and material threats to the integrity of perceived Australian—or Canadianness' (2003: 120). These threats perpetuate a range of stereotypes: from the model minority, to the opium dealer, from the cheap labourer and sexual threat to white women, to the effeminate affront to heteromasculinity. Justin is fully aware of these stereotypes and Teo writes that he 'struggled with his Asian oddness and resented the knowledge that he was contaminated. He did not want to be Asian. He did not want to be gay' (*BM* 88). Ayres (2000) also comments on this sexualised and racialised hierarchy:

> Most gay Caucasian men in Australia have their earliest experiences with other Caucasians. This is the template by which desire is, initially at least, stamped. When desire is further shaped by public representations of what is considered 'desirable', there's a marked absence of Asian men both within the gay and mainstream media. (162)

In a study on Asian American masculinity, Jachinson Chan observes that images of Chinese American men as submissive and sexually inferior to the white, American male are reified in American culture through stereotypical and controlling images such as Fu Manchu and Charlie Chan. These images become the inheritance for contemporary Asian American males as this Charlie Chan stereotype

> functions as a cultural icon that situates Chinese American men in a social position, such that marginalised men constantly fall short of a hegemonic heteromasculinity. Consequently, Chinese American men are forced to prove their heterosexual masculine identity, or risk the stigmatisation of being further subordinated as effeminate, sexless or gay. (2001: 53)

In a society that normalises white heterosexual masculinity, Justin finds it very difficult being gay: 'Being gay was a complicated affair. Gayness was an identity and, if you got it right, it was a means of belonging. If you didn't, if you were an Asian gay, it was practically an oxymoron' (*BM* 141). In the white gay scene, Justin's Asianness is seen as undesirable: 'he furtively bought gay magazines and responded to the classifieds. Nobody got back to him when he identified himself as Asian' (*BM* 149).

When he is finally accepted by the investment banker Dirk Merkel (a middle-aged, divorced, father of two), he is incredulous. Justin simply cannot believe that 'he was accepted, wanted, loved, *by a white man*. He didn't deserve it' (*BM* 162, emphasis added). Dirk is also aware of not just the Orientalist, but also the ageist, hierarchy at work in constructions of Australian masculinity and reciprocates Justin's incredulity that 'this exotic oriental youth with his beautiful dark looks and well-toned body actually desired him' (*BM* 158). Justin hides his homosexuality from his family and is tormented by the fear that they should accidentally find out that he was not the 'good boy' (*BM* 362) they thought him to be: 'In his mind he rehearsed endless conversations with his family and relatives. In reality, he had yet to rev up his courage to declare himself gay' (*BM* 151). Playing the filial son is the paramount concern for Justin, and he leads a schizophrenic existence donning 'separate masks, one for his friends and another for his family' (*BM* 145).

While Weir's *Gallipoli* imagines the construction of a white Australian identity that is focussed on males, on mateship, on heterosexuality, *Behind the Moon* shows that what Australian culture idealises as 'normal' and masculine is far from the reality of Justin, Gibbo or Tien. *Gallipoli's* representation of masculinity creates a dichotomy in which those falling outside this paradigm of constructed normality are feminised and othered as women, as gay, as Black, Asian, Muslim, or as Buddhist, for example. Indeed, as Kenneth MacKinnon observes, hegemony needs heroic, mythical, figures (and while he does not refer to *Gallipoli*, the characters of Frank and Archy are guiding examples of such creations) 'to embody its particular variety of masculinity' (2003: 9). Robert Connell writes that

> hegemonic masculinity can be defined as the configuration of gender practice which embodies the currently accepted answer to the problem of the legitimacy of patriarchy, which guarantees (or is taken to guarantee) the dominant position of men and the subordination of women. (1995: 77)

Connell stresses that although hegemony is historically mobile it does 'relate to cultural dominance in the society as a whole. Within that overall framework there are specific gender relations of dominance and subordination between groups of men' (1995: 78). This is particularly prevalent to the hierarchical relationship between heterosexual and homosexual men. In addition,

> oppression positions homosexual masculinities at the bottom of a gender hierarchy among men. Gayness, in patriarchal ideology, is the repository of whatever is

symbolically expelled from hegemonic masculinity ... from the point of view of hegemonic masculinity, gayness is easily assimilated to femininity. And hence—in the view of some gay theorists—the ferocity of homophobic attacks. (Connell 1995: 78)

The tragic attack on Justin results in Tien, Gibbo and their families being reunited around Justin's hospital bed after several years of estrangement. It also signals an important shift in Justin's sense of self. This scene is the culmination of Teo's continual interweaving of the issues of gender and sexuality and a raced/racist sense of nationhood exemplified through Justin's search for an answer to the vexed question of what it means to be an Australian of Asian descent, living in a predominantly white community and being gay. This questioning process makes visible the hierarchy of difference operating at the level of the social in Australia. When Justin's attackers ask him what he is, Justin replies, 'I am me' (*BM* 333), and this is an epiphany—and defining moment—in that it takes this attack and this question to make him realise 'that he no longer needed the external markers of identity' (*BM* 333).

The Best Friends (Ever)

This defining moment indicates Justin's connection and disconnection from the discursive processes of naming corporeal difference. Until this point, the essence of friendship between Justin, Gibbo and Tien has not been validated because none of the three have discovered or acknowledged their own sense of self. They take on the nomenclatures of difference that are socially decreed and name themselves as other, odd or abnormal to the dominant Anglo culture within which they circulate. Despite the duration of their friendship, the three only reveal 'slivers of the self' (*BM* 361) to each other and this is, in part, an act of self-protection from a hostile social world but it is also motivated by a desire to fit in or belong. It is Gibbo who realises that 'the people all around him—even those he was closest to—only ever presented amputated selves to him. He would never see them as they really were' (*BM* 361).

Returning to Australia, Tien and Gibbo reunite after Justin's bashing. Echoing Dorothy in *The Wizard of Oz*, Tien tells Gibbo, 'You're the best friend anyone could ever ask for' (*BM* 360). Gibbo acknowledges this gesture of friendship but also knows its transient nature. He understands that 'their friendship could not be snap-frozen at this point' (*BM* 360). Gibbo realises that friendship competes with the patriarchal constructions of family and heterosexual romance and he muses 'for whatever the strength of their friendship now, he knew they would not resist the pull of romantic love and the promise of a special partner if and when one came along' (*BM* 361). The idealised friendships depicted in *The Wizard of Oz* and *Gallipoli* are fantasy-based, and it is Gibbo who is the first to realise that friendship is cyclical rather than linear and that the truth of friendship is growth and fracture, love and loss, and quite a bit of regret. The novel forces a collision between the discourses of race, sexuality, gender and mateship, suggesting that identity is a fluid process, open to constant revision and translation in spite of the encroachment of dominant historical, social and representational practices. Sneja Gunew writes that

> for the first time in 200 years, perhaps, a space is opened up for alternative gestures of recognition and a consequent identity... In all these spaces which echo the discursive effects of 'multiculturalism' there remains the need to disrupt dominant categories and identities without at the same time containing the non-dominant within the same classificatory logic. (2004: 106)

Teo's depiction of a triangulated, dysfunctional, non-idealised model of mateship detours from that depicted in *Gallipoli*, where the intensity of a relationship forged through the shared experience of war is frozen with the death of one of the main characters. Stepping into contemporary Australian representational politics, Teo's character-driven novel prompts a re-evaluation of what is a deeply embedded and stagnant national mythology of mateship and masculinity. The novel re-visions the 'familiar' white (heterosexual male) body that is at the centre of racist and gendered discourse in Australia. Emphasising notions of differentiated otherness, the novel is strategically interventionist in its examination of the fixed binds of difference perpetuated by dominant political and social power structures. In this sense, *Behind the Moon* is a timely intervention in the debate about national identity precisely for the way it contests an established topography of race, sexuality and gender. The exploration of the friendship between Justin, Gibbo and Tien reconsiders the way Australianness is costumed as heterosexual, white, and male. Teo's exploration of 'other' models of mateship allows a critique of the cultural constructedness of identity in an Australian context.

Notes

[1] Richard White notes that in the 1880s 'the bush worker, rather than the urban or agricultural worker, gave Australia its identity in the empire' (1988: 103). The bushman/drover refers to a horse rider who moves and herds animals, such as cattle and sheep, from one territory to the next. In contrast, the bushranger or outlaw 'herds' humans or animals with a gun or with the threat of violence for personal (and usually illegal) gain. ANZAC is the acronym for Australian and New Zealand Army Corps while also referring to any soldier from both countries.

[2] Inarguably, one of the most enduring and revered myths of the birth of Australian nationhood circulates around the ANZAC soldier, and *Gallipoli*, written by the award-winning Australian playwright David Williamson, and starring Mel Gibson and Mark Lee, is a potent cultural instance of such essentialised perceptions. The film's title functions only as an incidental reference to what is a specific historical event in World War I and that is the ill-fated landing of the ANZAC troops in Gallipoli as part of the allied attack on the Dardanelles of Turkey. Indeed, so pervasive is the myth of Australian soldier's heroism at this landing and in the protracted campaign in the Dardanelles that Australian audiences back in the 1980s required little explanation as to the actual historical event the film's title referred to. What remains important in the context of rereading the film through Teo's novel is how Australia

has come to celebrate a historical moment associated with huge losses and eventual defeat of its soldiers with the birth of nationhood and a venerated form of Australian masculinity.

[3] The term 'digger' was once used in England to refer to coal minors but was revived in World War I as an informal name for ANZAC soldiers—perhaps a reference to trench warfare—while also meaning 'mate' or 'friend'. After the landing at Gallipoli the digger emerged as the national hero: 'He held a special place in the national identity because he could be seen as the ideal expression of the "Australian type". It was with a mixture of relief and pride that patriotic Australians could regard the national type as tested and not found wanting. With those credentials, the digger soon came to stand for all that was decent, wholesome and Australian. Not only did he embody Australianness, but [the digger] was its greatest protector' (White 1988: 125).

References

Ahmed, S. 'Tanning the Body: Skin, Colour and Gender.' *New Formations* 34 (Summer 1998): 27–42.

Ang, I. *On Not Speaking Chinese: Living Between Asia and the West*. London: Routledge, 2001.

Ayres, T. 'Sexual Identity and Cultural Identity: A Crash Course.' *Diaspora: Negotiating Asian-Australia*. Eds. H. Gilbert, T. Khoo and J. Lo. St Lucia: University of Queensland Press, 2000. 160–63.

Benthien, C. *Skin: On the Cultural Border Between Self and The World*. Trans. T. Dunlap. New York: Columbia University Press, 2002.

Bhabha, H. 'Of Mimicry and Man: The Ambivalence of Colonial Discourse.' *The Location of Culture*. London: Routledge, 1994. 85–92.

Chan, J. *Chinese American Masculinities: From Fu Manchu to Bruce Lee*. New York: Routledge, 2001.

Connell, R.W. *Masculinities*. Los Angeles: University of California Press, 1995.

Damousi, J. and Lake, M. Eds. *Gender and War: Australians at War in the Twentieth Century*. Cambridge: Cambridge University Press, 1995.

Dyer, R. *White*. London: Routledge, 1997.

Fleming, V. (Director) *The Wizard of Oz*, 1939. Film.

Freebury, J. 'Screening Australia: Gallipoli—A Study of Nationalism on Film.' *Media Information Australia* 43 (February 1987): 5–8.

Gunew, S. *Haunted Nations: The Colonial Dimensions of Multiculturalism*. London: Routledge, 2004.

Hall, S. 'Cultural Identity and Diaspora.' *Identity: Community, Culture and Difference*. Ed. J. Rutherford. London: Lawrence and Wishart, 1990. 222–37.

Henderson, I. 'The Ethics of Fellowship in Two Antipodean War Films: *Gallipoli* (1981) and *The Lord of the Rings* (2000, 2001, 2003).' *Australian Humanities Review* 34, Jan–Feb, (2005), <http://www.lib.latrobe.edu.au/AHR/archive/Issue-Jan-2005/henderson.html> (accessed 1 November 2005).

Khoo, T. *Banana Bending: Asian-Australian and Asian-Canadian Literatures*. Hong Kong: McGill-Queens University Press and Hong Kong University Press, 2003.

Lohrey, A. '*Gallipoli*: Male Innocence as a Marketable Commodity.' *Island Magazine* 9/10 (1982): 29–34.

MacKinnon, K. *Representing Men: Maleness and Masculinity in the Media*. London: Arnold, 2003.

McFarlane, B. *Australian Cinema 1970–1985*. Melbourne: William Heinemann, 1987.

Nicoll, F. *From Diggers to Drag Queens: Configurations of Australian National Identity*. Sydney: Pluto Press, 2001.

Penton, B. *Advance Australia—Where?*. Sydney: Cassell and Company, 1943.

Rattigan, N. *Images of Australia: 100 Films of the New Australian Cinema*. Dallas: SMU Press, 1991.

Teo, H. *Behind the Moon*. Sydney: Allen and Unwin, 2005a.

——. *Reading Group Notes: Behind the Moon*. Sydney: Allen and Unwin, 2005b.

Walsh, J. 'Elite Women Warriors and Dog Soldiers: Gender Adaptations in Modern War Films.' *Gender and Warfare in the Twentieth Century: Textual Representation*. Ed. A. Smith. Manchester: Manchester University Press, 2004. 195–215.
Weir, P. (Director) *Gallipoli*, 1981. Film.
White, R. *Inventing Australia: Images and Identity 1688–1988*. Sydney: Allen and Unwin, 1988.

Travelling Theory, Reshaping Disciplines? Envisioning Asian Germany through Asian Australian Studies

Mita Banerjee

How does an academic field come into being? This essay explores the paradoxical possibility of trying to create an academic field from scratch; of creating a discipline or sub-discipline where academia (and the wider, mainstream public) do not see the necessity for such a creation. I explore the political and historical context of present-day Germany and the problem of addressing the increasing heterogeneity of its population, a heterogeneity of which its Asian communities are only one example. Within this context, ethnic communities—and Asian Germans more specifically—have been granted only a somewhat bizarre, token inclusion into Germanness. For the purposes of this essay, 'Asian' will be used as an umbrella term, which must in turn be negotiated against the generic use of 'ethnic' or, rather, 'foreign', as it permeates contemporary German discourse. At the same time, it is crucial to note that given the recent influx of Indian professionals into Germany, the South Asian component of this umbrella Asianness is currently the most visible in German popular culture, which is why the examples used in this essay will mainly be concerned with South Asianness in German popular culture. On the other hand, in order to gain a historical perspective of this new visibility as well as a basis for opposing the generic dismissal (or tentative inclusion) of 'foreignness' into the German nation, it is necessary to relate this South Asian presence and the discourse that surrounds it to the presence and histories of other Asian communities currently living in Germany.

In a recent TV campaign designed to help boost Germany's self-esteem in the face of a persistent economic downturn, a campaign entitled *Du bist Deutschland* (*You are Germany*), a few non-white faces have been included among faces that, in the narrative logic of the commercial, are more representative of 'Germanness'. These 'ethnic' faces hence seem to have been included as mere tokens, as markers of a commitment by the German nation to multiculturalism. Yet, it is crucial to examine not only the fact of ethnic inclusion, but also the framework that governs this inclusion; a framework that has largely gone unnoticed. Significantly, the media campaign *You are Germany* addresses Germany's economic, not its cultural, insecurity. Sponsored by leading German corporations (Axel Springer, Bertelsmann, Burda), the campaign, in a strikingly neo-liberal fashion, calls on Germans not to blame the state for the economic downturn but to take matters into their own hands: 'Regardless of where you work, regardless of what position you have, you keep the nation running', the spot assures its German TV audience. What is interesting here is the intersection between the (multi)cultural and the economic. From the narrative logic of the commercial, it would seem that the effort to include non-white representatives of Germanness is motivated by the acknowledgment that, in an effort to regain economic strength, Germany may well need its migrant workers. It is in this sense that including, for instance, the face of African German soccer player Gerald Asamoah may be symptomatic of subordinating the cultural to the economic or, perhaps, of employing the cultural in the service of the economic.

This subordination notwithstanding, the campaign may nevertheless serve to exemplify the shift in official debates from the slogan 'We are not an immigrant country' (Chiellino 2000: V-VII) to its reluctant negation. Starting with a groundbreaking reform in naturalisation law in 2000, which for the first time since 1913 substituted *ius sanguinis* (the granting of citizenship solely on the basis of German descent) with *ius soli* (which grants citizenship to people born in Germany), the ethnic migrant, *officially*, has no longer been considered a sore in the eye of the German nation. Yet, this shift has not been a facile one. If no longer an eyesore, the ethnic presence may still be a speck in the mirror of Germanness that may cause the dominant culture to look twice at the ethnic in its midst. A call for an Asian German studies at this historical moment may do well to remember Tseen Khoo's observation that Asian Australian studies has always had to contend with the idea that the Asian is a 'chink' in the armor of a white nation. Khoo's comment could not be more pertinent to the current German situation:

> [T]he 'chinks' in Australia's armour could be taken quite literally as the presence of its racial minority citizens. An unanswered question is whether Australia as a nation has the ability to include these citizens as a part of the multicultural present, in all its cultural and political structures. (2003: 13)

The similarities in official rhetoric that link Germany to Australia seem to point to a structural logic of white identification, or the identification of the nation as white, which may transcend national lines.

In this sense, I am arguing that an Asian German studies may do well to take its cue from Asian Australian studies in a variety of ways. This essay will be concerned with trying to counter the *absence* of Asian German studies through the alternative framework of Asian Australian studies. Khoo's *Banana Bending: Asian-Australian and Asian-Candian Literatures* (2003) is doubly significant for my considerations, not only because it makes a case for an Asian Australian studies that links the Australian context to Asian diasporic studies as a larger paradigm, but because it draws attention to the metatheoretical implications of calling a field into being. If *Banana Bending* is situated on the brink towards a fully fledged academic field (Asian Australian studies), I find myself on the other, the wrong side of this brink in trying to call for an Asian German studies that does not yet exist.

So far, the only way to address Asian presences as they haunt German popular culture and contemporary canon debates has seemed to be through an Asian diasporic studies framework. For instance, in her study of South Asian diasporic cinema, Jigna Desai calls for a framework whose vision of a 'Brown Atlantic' would be modelled on Paul Gilroy's model of diasporic blackness:

> My hope is that this study will interrupt certain types of narratives (e.g. national, heteronormative, masculine, bourgeois) as it maps the space of the 'Brown Atlantic', paying particular attention to the contours of global capital, migration, colonialism, and empire in the global cities of New York, London, Toronto, and Bombay. (2004: 3)

While Desai notes the crucial distinction between the black and the brown Atlantic (namely the fact that South Asian migration, for the most part, was a voluntary one), her idea of a South Asian diasporic studies informs this essay through the concept of a transnational perspective on the ways in which (South) Asian migrant bodies have been shaped in a variety of national contexts. The question is, however, what tension between the national and the transnational would emerge from this critical framework. It could be argued that such a framework may fail to address the specificity of national context (a pitfall that Desai's study is well aware of), and that there would thus be a need for addressing, for instance, the Asian German experience more specifically.

At the same time, for a variety of reasons (one of them being that even the concept of hyphenated subjectivity has not been officially acknowledged and has not made it into either academic discourse or everyday language in Germany), to speak of an Asian German experience in the first place currently seems impossible. The issue of demography may be only one side of the coin: of a total population of 82.6 million people, there are currently 826,504 people of Asian descent living in Germany. As a comparison, the Turkish community in Germany is the largest migrant community in Germany with 1,764,318 people. The attempt to establish an Asian German studies hence seems to be *demographically* impossible. Yet, even if Asian Germans have no political clout and, given their lack of demographic visibility, there seems to be no justification in calling for a new paradigm through which their (small) presence could adequately be addressed or described, the stereotypes through which Asians are ridiculed in German popular culture, for instance, *are* culturally specific. It is this specificity that an Asian German studies might be able to address. At the same time, it is important to note that while, for instance, Turkish German writers have been much more visible in the public arena, their contributions to the narrative of the nation—a contribution that may be backed by the demographic presence of the Turkish German community—seems to have failed to transform substantially the discipline of German Studies, whose interest in 'difference' has been informed by the pedagogical category of comprehending that which is 'foreign'—a point that I will elaborate upon in more detail below.

If a potential Asian German studies might take its cue from the field of Asian Australian studies, however, it is also important to note key differences in the way in which Asian communities have been racialised in Australia and Germany, respectively. If in Australia, 'Asians' have for a long time been configured through 'invasion narratives' and have hence been highly visible (although in a very problematic sense) in the public debate, the reverse seems to be true in Germany. Rather, German post-war history has been marked, since the 'invitation' of guest workers from Turkey, Greece and Italy in the 1950s in particular (Yano 2000), by the discourse of the 'guest worker problem'. This discourse has focused almost exclusively on these three ethnic communities, especially the Turkish migrant group that was perceived to be culturally incompatible with the German dominant culture. 'Asians' were hence absent from public discourse because, with their numbers being negligible, they did not seem to constitute a problem. What is significant here, however, is that this has changed with the recent influx of computer professionals especially from India; the question, then, is how this new history of 'Asianness' can be negotiated with other, already existing discourses on ethnicity within the German nation.

At the same time, the *tension* between demographic visibility and academic necessity may nevertheless link Asian presences in Germany to their Australian counterparts. Khoo observes that it has often been suggested that 'the small population of Asian communities in Australia, in addition to the enduring "whiteness" and resistance confronting racism in Australia, result in an environment that is not conducive to the growth or institutionalization of Asian-Australian studies' (6). It is for this very reason that it seems possible to call an Asian German studies into being through a reference to Asian Australian studies after all, because in Australia, demographic facts have not obstructed the creation of an academic field addressing Asian Australian cultural production.

For sheer lack of visibility and the requirements of what Samir Dayal (1998) has called the 'numbers game' of the political process (the need for small communities to enter into an alliance in order to be publicly visible), ethnic German activists and writers alike have hence found it necessary to resort to a panethnic coalition, using 'ethnic Germanness' as an umbrella term. Ilija Trojanow's anthology of ethnic German literature, *Döner in Walhalla: Texte aus der anderen deutschen Literatur* (*Döner in Valhalla: Texts from the Other German Literature*) (2000), to which I will return in more detail below, gathers writings by Indian German, Turkish German and Bulgarian German writers alike. Trojanow's endeavor to establish ethnic German literature as *German* literature is thus indicative of a specificity of the German debate. Because ethnicity as such is not acknowledged as German, there has been the need for a *panethnic* effort.

Such an umbrella framework, however, may also serve to erase cultural specificity. For this very reason, I believe that there may be a need for a variety of paradigms: panethnic, Asian diasporic, and Asian German. It is with regard to the latter two possibilities in particular that the framework of Asian Australian studies seems especially significant. Khoo writes in the introduction to *Banana Bending* that, *Banana Bending* is concerned with mapping, interrogating, and creating critical pathways for diasporic Asian literary studies. The book argues that in order to examine the disciplines and production of Asian-Canadian and Asian-Australian literatures, work needs to be considered within layers of nation, community, and the gendered self... To this end, the chapters chart a progression of these concerns by, first, explicating the national contexts for Asians and racialised writing in Australia and Canada and then shifting to examine specifically the significance of these layers for Asian-Australian and Asian-Canadian texts and their construction (1).

It is thus significant that Khoo's study seeks to balance Asian diasporic with national (Australian and Canadian) contexts. Such a balance would also be of critical importance in trying to establish an Asian German studies.

The paradox, in contemporary Germany, is the fact of ethnic diversity and the absence of a language in which to address it. The piecemeal endeavour of creating an Asian German studies from scratch is possible only through a reference to other fields within Asian diasporic studies that have only quite recently been established or acknowledged as integral parts of both academic and national contexts. For me, the emergence—and the parameters of emergence—of Asian Australian studies are of key importance in believing that such a field of Asian German studies may eventually come to exist. To call only for an inclusion of Germany's Asian population into the framework of Asian diasporic studies would fail to address the obstacles to acknowledging an Asian German presence within German political, cultural and academic discourse. All these obstacles are specific to German national history, it is for these historical reasons that it seems necessary to call not only for an inclusion of Germany into Asian diasporic studies, but for an Asian German studies more specifically. I am thus interested in Khoo's stressing of the balance between 're-siting' a particular discipline such as Asian Australian studies, while at the same time inserting it into a larger, even global cultural and academic framework: 'Looking outside Australia, to similar national formations and other histories of diasporic Asian literature, offers Asian Australian studies the opportunity to re-site national arguments within global perspectives' (34). Such a balance, I believe, would be especially crucial in the current German context.

Similarly, Asian Australian studies, and this is significant for my argument here, has come into being through a comparative cultural and academic framework. Khoo's study explores Asian Australian literature in conjunction with Asian Canadian literature. I am interested, then, in the nature of this conjunction in which the Australian context is at once present and 'transcendable'. For instance, this conjunction is present in Khoo's reminder that, in the context of (Asian) Australian history, a particular writer's exploring of the *benefits* of assimilation cannot be reduced to the claim, by now well established in both Asian Canadian and Asian American studies, that to speak of the need for assimilation is either a failure of cultural logic or an indication of the cultural belatedness of one's own national context. Khoo has observed with regard to Hsu-Ming Teo's *Love and Vertigo*,

> In cultural histories, assimilation is a term which has taken on only negative connotations. It most often signifies loss of homeland cultures and languages, compromise of self, and 'selling out' to dominant cultural mores. Teo herself has made the observation that her assimilative upbringing, and the cultural capital accrued because of it, is what allows her the ease to occupy a variety of employment and social spaces. (157)

Khoo reminds us that, to simply impose the critical consensus that could be said to exist, for instance, in Asian Canadian studies (a consensus which holds that assimilation is inevitably a deeply problematic concept), to adopt uncritically this view prevalent in Asian Canadian studies on the Australian literary and academic context, would be short-sighted.

It is also significant for the purpose of this essay that Khoo aligns Asian Australian studies not with Asian American studies—a field which has long been perceived as Asian Canadian studies' more hegemonic 'sister' discipline—but with Asian Canadian studies, which has had its own history of contestation, both with regard to mainstream 'Can. Lit'. and Asian *American* studies. As Roy Miki has written of the first instance—the attempt to challenge the dominant field of Canadian literature: 'The lack of sustained theoretical disturbance in CanLit and English studies concerning the institutionalization of racialized texts perhaps bespeaks the capacity of liberal thought to cover over its own transgressionary practices' (1998: 161). Perhaps even more problematic, because it is more unexpected than this academic hegemony of CanLit, is the tendency of Asian American Studies merely to subsume Asian Canadianness (Ty 2000), a gesture that has been most pronounced in the inclusion of Sui Sin Far under the rubric of Asian *American* literature. In this context, to simply speak of an 'Asian diasporic studies' may run the risk of obfuscating the internal dynamics and heterogeneity of power within such a comparative framework.

A similar kind of intersection between fields—between a field which is only emerging and one which has already been established—surfaces in Wayde Compton's Black British Columbian anthology, *Bluesprint*.[1] In order to create a sense of a black presence in British Columbia, Compton emphasises the ways in which such an effort has seemed possible only through reference to the paradigm of African American studies. The dynamics of bringing a field into being that Compton addresses, I would argue, is similar to Khoo's own project. In either case, a presence hitherto unacknowledged by academic curricula or research is addressed by creating a new critical framework. This critical framework, in turn, can be brought into being only by referring to a framework that has already been established, Asian Canadian and African American studies, respectively. In both cases, there may be the danger of the new field being 'dwarfed' or dismissed in its specificity by the framework of reference. Compton (2001) describes it this way:

> In high school, I knew about Public Enemy and Bob Marley long before I'd heard a single word about Sylvia Stark or Mifflin Gibbs. But eventually the realization that my experience and the experience of my friends and family were not exactly represented by the images imported from afar began to take hold. I began to pay close attention to African-Canadian history ... (14)

At the same time, however, both Khoo and Compton implicitly argue that the emergence of their respective new fields might have been impossible without reference to a field that has already been 'canonised'. This essay seeks to glean from both Khoo's and Compton's arguments the 'abstract' parameters (if such abstraction is at all possible) of creating an academic field from scratch. Significantly, if Compton stresses the ambivalence of an African Canadian identification with African Americanness, an aligning of Asian German studies with an Asian Australian critical framework may not run the risk of being 'dwarfed' by a more established field, simply because both Australia and Germany, albeit to a different extent, seem to be on the periphery of debates about cultural dissemination.

In the German context, the attempt to create or even speak of an Asian German studies also involves sorting through the rubble of official debates, and to salvage from these debates the anecdotes, the off-handed remarks and gestures by which an Asian German presence is alluded to without being acknowledged. To call for an

Asian German studies, then, is also to try to establish an alternative *record* on which an Asian German presence could be registered. This essay is hence also concerned with ripple effects. What, then, are the ripple effects of foreignness on the German nation, and what is the relationship of ripple and record? As Compton has argued, it may be possible to speak of the presence of difference without the difference making the record. This seems solace because the record can often be arbitrary in what it does and does not keep. Using Kamau Braithwaite's image of 'tidalectics', Compton argues that the ripple, while often not distinctly visible, may nevertheless in time come to make a change:

> [T]*idalectics* describes a way of seeing history as a palimpsest, where generations overlap generations, and eras wash over eras like a tide on a stretch of beach. There is change, but the change arises out of slight misduplications of the pattern rather than from essential antagonisms. (2001: 17)

At the same time, the 'record' must be understood in both legal and cultural terms: citizenship is the ultimate acknowledgment of a hitherto 'foreign' presence by or in the records of a nation. It is for this reason that this essay is also concerned with the repercussions of both legal and cultural citizenship on the debate around ethnicity in Germany. If citizenship in the legal sense is already contested terrain, citizenship as cultural or academic acknowledgment is also continually denied in narratives of popular culture or literary canonisation. As Renato Rosaldo has proposed, it is crucial to inquire into the parameters of visibility in a given national context:

> Cultural citizenship operates in an uneven field of structural inequalities where the dominant claims of universal citizenship assume a propertied white male subject and usually blind themselves to their exclusions and marginalizations of people who differ in gender, race, sexuality, and age. (260)

This essay enquires into the intersections of various forms of citizenships in contemporary German cultural discourse. I suggest that different forms of citizenship are often in contradiction with each other: the lack of cultural recognition, for instance, may be based on the assumption that Asian German writers are not German writers to begin with, thus linking the political and the academic; at the same time, the denial of cultural recognition is often used to target ethnic communities that, for economic reasons, have already gained access to the German nation. In this sense, cultural citizenship would also include the acknowledgment of granting (literary) expressions of cultural difference the status of Germanness. Conversely, as I will try to demonstrate in the following, the expression of such difference in contemporary German academic and popular cultures is often held to index 'foreignness'.

The 'textual' examples which this essay focuses on—a TV commercial and an essay by an Asian German writer—are meant to convey the sense of the dire straits of ethnic representation in German (popular) culture, and the dire need for an Asian German studies through which these isolated 'incidents' of representation could be related, and talked back to. I argue that, without an adequate academic framework of analysis, these texts will remain anecdotes and will seem to have no representative meaning in which they could be seen as indicative of a wider state of cultural affairs. Asian German studies, then, would turn 'Asian' stereotypes in the German cultural imagination into symptoms of a society trying to come to grips with its own cultural heterogeneity. More basically, it would turn anecdotes into academic subject matter—a subject matter that would in turn have both political and historical repercussions. At the same time, because I am interested in the frameworks available for the reception of ethnic German cultural expression (or the absence of these frameworks), my focus will be not on Asian German literature proper (there are currently only a handful of writers who could be called Asian German authors, and they are considered 'Asian German' only in studies conducted outside of Germany), but on the comments by these writers on the reception of their work in Germany, and their own alien subjectivity in a country that has not yet developed a language for ethnicity to begin with. The linguistic impoverishment, then, may be that of the dominant culture, not the writers themselves. Yet this reversal of perspectives has not yet been institutionalised either culturally or academically. As Bulgarian German writer Trojanow (2000) comments, '[t]here is hardly a reading after which I am asked why I am so fluent in German. I haven't yet been able to think of a good answer' (11).[2]

While in the current academic debate in Germany Trojanow's remarks on the reception of his own work would seem anecdotal, their significance could well be expressed through Khoo's reference to Asian Australian and Asian Canadian writing:

> When Asian activists engage with discourses of how they and their creative works are represented, they work towards countering stereotypes and creating alternative, nuanced Asian-Canadian and Asian-Australian subjectivities. This necessary step of acknowledging the conditions of production and distribution for their work, and in other creative spheres, enables these groups to move towards fully exercising cultural citizenship. (3)

I want to explore this tension between Asian caricature in contemporary German popular culture and alternative concepts of ethnic German identity as they are expressed in Asian German writing. If popular culture perpetuates stereotypes and hence leads to a withholding of cultural citizenship from ethnic aliens, an alternative framework is still only in the making because even if the literature exists, there has not yet been an adequate framework for its critical reception. The balance between stereotype and counter-narrative, which is at the core of Khoo's study of Asian Australian writing, then, has not yet been achieved in the German context. To look at the field of Asian Australian studies is thus essential, I believe, in order to gauge the current location of ethnicity in Germany, as well as to assess the terrain still left to be covered.

In this context, my own situation has been somewhat paradoxical. Unlike a comparison between Asian Australian and Asian Canadian literature, the call for establishing an Asian German studies by aligning it with the field of Asian Australian studies is hampered by language. The question of audience remains unresolved. In order to leave a mark on the *record* of German cultural history, these lines would have to be written in German. Or would they? My argument rests on the assumption that 'language' may function on two registers here: on the linguistic level (making the record would be easier in German) and the level of argument, of content. In the absence of a conceptual acknowledgment of Asian German presences, the reference, for instance, to Asian Australian studies seems paramount. It may thus also be interesting to explore the relationship between message and detour. It has long seemed the case that engaging in an intercultural German studies is possible only from abroad. Both Deniz Göktürk (2000), who has been instrumental in addressing the Turkish German cultural production in Germany and the vexed parameters of its inclusion, and Arlene Teraoka (1990), whose pioneering article in Abdul JanMohammed and David Lloyd's *The Nature and Context of Minority Discourse* inaugurated explorations of ethnic German muteness, have long since relocated to the US. Ethnic German studies are hence called into being in English, and from within US academia. Göktürk's work in particular has addressed the institutional structure through which Turkish culture is allowed access to the German public consciousness. Crucially, she has characterised the attempt on the part of German national television to include films by Turkish directors into late night programs as an act characterised by a mixture of pity and a sense of duty on the part of the German dominant culture. This reading of the institutional avenues available, or rather, unavailable for the inclusion of Turkish as well as Turkish German culture may well be applied to the academic institutionalising of Turkish German minority studies. While Turkish German writers such as Emine Sevgi Özdamar and Renan Demirkan have increasingly become visible on the literary market, this visibility does not seem to have been translated into a transformation of German academia. Crucially, however, Göktürk continues to interfere in German discussions of ethnicity, as in her participation in a recent exhibit on the history of migration in Germany, fittingly entitled *Projekt Migration* (the *project*—rather than problem—of migration). The space of ethnic Germanness may hence be carved out precisely in the intersection between the national and the transnational.[3]

Germany, as well as German studies in Germany, have also been wary of incorporating frameworks from outside the German context. Mark Terkessidis has argued that,

> In fact, German literary philology has missed the phenomenon of ethnic cabaret and satire by oversleeping. Yet, this ignorance may allow for the possibility of adapting concepts which have been developed by Anglo-American cultural criticism to the German context in order to address these artistic forms—a debate which we can only hope will soon begin. (2000: 300)

But what are the reasons for this suspicion? There seem to be no ripple effects of cultural hyphenation on academic discourse, except in the mostly journalistic writings of hyphenated Germans themselves. There has been an almost clear-cut split between political and journalistic activism and academic work in the German context. This lack of dialogue may be due to the fact that such work is only emerging; it may be due to historical academic coincidence or, more disturbingly, to the fact that in 'xenology', German studies has already found a paradigm through which difference can be articulated. 'Xenology'—a curious theoretical framework rooted in the pedagogical notion of *Fremdverstehen,* of understanding, in a rather esoteric sense, the other—came to determine the reception of the 'other' German literature. One of the curiosities of this framework, which was invented by Alois Wierlacher in 1993, is that it exists only in Germany. Corinna Albrecht observes that '[a]mong the most remarkable achievements of intercultural German studies [*interkulturelle Germanistik*] is the inception of a transdisciplinary field of research for the study of foreignness, a field called xenology' (2003: 541). While xenology advocates multiculturalism and stresses the idea that each ascription of foreignness is itself culturally and historically conditioned, I believe that it is debatable because its perspective pivots on the *Fremdheitserfahrung* of the dominant culture, on the experience of foreignness this culture undergoes.

For ethnic German writers, this framework spells out an unwinnable situation. How can you be understood as a foreigner—xenology, quite literally, sets out to decipher that which is foreign—if your writing wants to demonstrate that the line between what is and what could be German needs to be denaturalised? There is a debatable gesture of acceptance here: granting presence, granting (cultural) citizenship. But who is the student here? To whom or rather, at whom is this pedagogy directed? How do you explain yourself so you can be deciphered, and who will read your explanation?

Ironically, becoming German, for ethnic German writers, thus becomes possible only from abroad. Trojanow's anecdote about his own identifying as German when he was in Bombay thus becomes a metaphor for the impossibility of including ethnic German writing into the canon of German literature. If Trojanow is German only to his Indian neighbour, but his Germanness in Germany is never unqualified, the idea that ethnic German literature is 'just' German literature may be conceivable only through a framework other than German studies:[4]

> I felt proud ... In this poor Indian neighborhood, I was the legitimate representative of Germanness. At home, the weekly paper was waiting for me. Its editorial debated the question who is allowed to be German and who is not, and I became aware that any inquiry about where I came from and with what I identified would never be easy to answer. The encounter in a chawl was only a momentary idyll. (2000: 9)

What is at stake is thus also the idea of 'claiming the nation', an idea that was originally at the forefront of creating, for instance, the field of Asian American studies. Trojanow's idea of 'Döner in Walhalla' is an attempt to juxtapose concepts which the German public and academic debates have deemed to be at variance with one another—the 'naturalness' of ethnicity in the German heartland: 'It is outrageous that after four decades of Germans living side by side with a few millions of Turks, only the word "Döner" has been granted access to the sesame of Germanic vocabulary' (2000: 15). If the 'mainstreaming' of Turkishness has taken four decades and has been confined to the palatability of Turkish food, my attempt to juxtapose an Asian presence with the concept of German national (self-) definition indeed seems sadly premature.

The *Reinheitsgebot* of (Cultural) Citizenship

In much the same vein, it may be interesting to consider whether a matter of German cultural and economic pride—the fact that German beer is still made according to a time-honoured traditional recipe, maintaining what in brewery lore is called the *Reinheitsgebot*, the law of the purity of beer—may not in fact have deeper, metaphorical and national repercussions. In August 2005, the Bavarian brewery Paulaner started airing a commercial that was set in a Munich beer garden. Three Indian men, all impeccably (and, in this setting, ridiculously) dressed in business suits, are trying to order beer. Their spokesman is holding a phrase book and announces to the waitress who, in her dirndl, is clearly a native here: 'I do not want to drink this coffee'. The waitress, exasperated and obviously used to the absurdities of inappropriate as well as inarticulate ethnic presences in her territory, shakes her head and returns with three glasses of beer. The Indian gives vent to his gratefulness: 'Have a good trip!' The waitress' ultimate response as she turns away—'S scho recht!' ('Never mind!')—signifies the shoulder-shrugging indifference of a Bavarian (and, in the logic of the commercial, German) public to physical manifestations of transnationalism in its midst. The waitress' shrug dismisses the ripple effects of Indianness on a German beer garden.

It is significant that the tourists' dislocation in a Bavarian beer garden, their spatial as well as cultural freakishness, should be heightened by their unlikely tourist gear. Yet, their business suits are inappropriate only within the visual politics of the commercial. Incidentally, Munich is the site, not only of Paulaner, but also of Siemens. Over the last five years, Siemens has hired a number of Indian IT professionals, a fact that has been much discussed both in political debates and in popular culture. The commercial hence seeks to contain an anxiety that is about much more than beer. The perceived economic displacement of the German workforce by Indian professionals is mapped onto a cultural sphere where mainstream Germanness is still in command. Ironically, no computer literacy is required in a beer garden. The idea that these Indian professionals are *tourists* is hence the wishful thinking of a culturally and economically uncertain German mainstream. Paulaner's commercial spells out the much lamented need for a German *Leitkultur* or core culture. It is by harking back to its most unadulterated cultural practices that the German nation can remain itself.

The commercial celebrates Bavarians as the least adulterated of German communities—just as the German *Reinheitsgebot* has held its own despite a changing and increasingly competitive market. This 'law of purity' holds that the only ingredients that may be used for brewing beer in Germany are water, malt, and hops; even under pressure by a global market, the German brewery trade has thus been preserved. What is much more disturbing, however, is the collapsing of the (possibly impending) adulteration of German beer into the adulteration (Asianisation) of the German population, which is implied by the commercial.

It is at this point that the Indians in business suits are rendered transient: it is in their (cultural and linguistic) inappropriateness that they become modern, more sophisticated versions of the guest worker who has been haunting the German public since the 1950s when foreign workers were first invited to help rebuild the post-war German economy. The commercial makes sure that there is no sense of Indianness as a permanent presence within the German nation. These three men are not part of the German workforce, they are mere visitors whose capital can help strengthen the economy of a nation which welcomes them economically even as it dismisses them culturally. Yet, even if they were considered part of the German workforce, their cultural and linguistic illiteracy would vouch for the fact that their presence in Germany is a transitory one. Legally, this was the set-up of the German green card (Holert 2005), which enabled IT-professionals to stay in the country for a period of up to five years. Yet, it is significant that the green card law has since been replaced by the *Zuwanderungsgesetz* (the new migration law of 2005), which allows for an unlimited stay for professionals in Germany. The commercial thus sets back the clock to the cultural logic of the green card law which, if controversial at the time of its implementation, in retrospect seems to be the lesser evil.

What if Paulaner were the equivalent of a green card? Read against the grain of its Germanism, the commercial acknowledges Indian professionals' willingness to engage in German cultural practices, and it cries out for a reversal of roles as much as of settings. In the computerised, transnational workplaces of Siemens in *Bangalore*, the Bavarian waitress could be out of place and a phrase book might not help her. Yet, such a reversal of sides would of course be highly problematic in class terms. What remains is the ripple effect of Indianness on the German brewery trade: a *Maß* (beer mug) of Paulaner in a brown hand as a potential granting of cultural citizenship; the reading of a 2005 beer commercial as indicative of a German anxiety that is both cultural and economic.

What is significant for my purposes here is that, from within the current German political or academic debate, it would seem impossible to read the commercial as anything other than a beer commercial. From the cultural disenfranchisement of the Indian 'tourists' (whose presence as even guest workers in Munich is not even contemplated) to the withholding of cultural citizenship, it seems a far cry indeed. It is a leap of faith, however, which can be undertaken only through Khoo's link, in the passage quoted at the beginning of this essay, between the denial of stereotype and the granting of cultural citizenship. In this very sense, it is indeed possible to read a 2005 German beer commercial through the alternative critical framework of Asian

Australian studies. If Khoo, in her establishing the very paradigm of Asian Australian writing, invokes the 'coalitional power' inherent in linking Asian Australian and Asian Canadian literature, my claim is that such a transnational coalition might also link Asian German presences to Asian Australian writing. If, from within the German context, Asian German presences cannot even be acknowledged as ethnic German presences (only as Asian tourists passing through Munich), they can be asserted as presences, written into the record of German national consciousness, through the framework of an Asian Australian studies, which Khoo establishes through a coalition of Asian Australia with Asian Canadian literature and criticism. This double echo (Khoo quoting the Candian writer and critic Larissa Lai to stress the salience of an Asian Australian presence, and myself trying to establish the legitimacy of Asian German subjectivity through Khoo's reference to both Australia and Canada), I believe, may serve to drive home the point that the Paulaner spot is much more than a beer commercial. Khoo points out that:

> In constructing a frame of political activism and knowledge of coalitional powers for Asian literary production in Australia and Canada, this book produces unique comparisons between Australian and Canadian racial minority writers and their communities ... These interventions into existing fields of national literature can transform writing and publishing conditions for Asian writers. Lai, and others, contend that 'asserting a presence' is a necessary step in validating cultural citizenship. (4)

If I now turn to the vexed politics of canonisation in contemporary German academia, where would the connection be between a beer commercial and a field of writing that has not yet been canonised? I suggest that the link between these two 'texts' (both of which have been relegated to a merely anecdotal status in the German debate) can be established, paradoxically, through Khoo's Asian *Australianist* intervention.

The Politics of Canonisation

The Paulaner beer commercial denies to the Indian professionals whose presence in Munich is by no means unpredictable the cultural citizenship of visual acknowledgment. What if cultural citizenship were conceived not only as the necessary step of granting cultural self-expression to those who are already citizens, but as the cultural acknowledgment of those who have not yet been naturalised? An Asian German studies, I believe, would enable us to address multiple forms of cultural disenfranchisement; and it is this disenfranchisement which would link a beer commercial to an Asian German literature that itself has been acknowledged neither as German nor as literature. Asian German authors such as Rajvinder Singh and Anant Kumar have been contesting the very image of themselves as alien to both Germany's everyday life and its academic and cultural imagination. Yet, it is significant that the latter critique is only implicit in their fictional and poetic writing;

it is never directly addressed. Asian German writers *are* the aliens in Paulaner's beer garden, and they are aware of the fact that the dominant German gaze deems them absurd.

This is a marginality that also surfaces in the publication framework of ethnic German literature which, in Germany, is known merely under the appellation of the 'other' German literature (Trojanow 2000). If 'ethnic' German authors set out to 'bend' the German language to make it their own, this bending has been conceived only as an attempt to alienate this language from the concerns of the dominant culture. The canon was said to be in danger of being submerged by ethnicity. As Trojanow puts it, '[u]neasiness about German literature being "swamped" by foreign literary texts manifested itself most saliently in the rejection, which lasted for decades, of neologisms [created by ethnic German writers]' (2000: 13). The rejection of this other German literature as German led to the fact that no critical paradigm was developed through which it could be read, except, of course, as sociological data through which guest workers chronicled their lives: 'Those who dared address more general topics, lost their right to be called authors. Their duty was considered to be the description of the problems which guest workers faced, and their account, given the sociological expectations it had to meet, had to be quasi-documentary' (2003: 13).

Interestingly, it is this documentary character of 'ethnic' fiction that Indian German author Anant Kumar (2004) satirises by 'recording' his own everyday life in Germany. Kumar writes down an anecdote which, through the very act of writing, becomes more than that. His writing thus puns on the 'anecdotal' status of his own hyphenated German existence as a mere footnote, at most, to the grand narrative of Germanness. The anecdote is thus symptomatic of the position of ethnicity in German contemporary culture that the essay into which the anecdote is embedded sets out to critique.

The anecdote runs thus: Kumar, who earns his living by going on endless reading tours, is sitting on a train from Passau to Kassel. The train which is to take the migrant German Indian writer back home to Kassel is called Joseph Haydn.[5] Kumar is caught in an Austrian-German border situation: Passau is a German town, albeit a German border town. So why should there be a passport control? For an unqualified citizenship holder, for a holder of unqualified citizenship, the absurdity of this incident would have made for a good anecdote to tell over dinner. Austrian police enforce the boundaries of the German nation on German soil on a train named after a famous Austrian composer, Joseph Haydn.

The explanation for this absurdity, of course, may be quite a practical one. The Austrian police walk down the aisles of the train, asking all passengers to identify themselves as the train crosses the border. Because Joseph Haydn is a long train, however, it has long left Austria and is now travelling through Germany. When Kumar, unsuspecting, gets on at Passau, the officers are still making their way through the train. Accidents cease to be accidental: if Joseph Haydn had been a small train (and, as a small train, would not have had a name), none of this would have happened.

Kumar is caught in a maze of authentication, producing document after document in an attempt to renaturalise himself. Not knowing he would hit a border control without even crossing a border, he has left his passport at home—the only document enabling him, as someone who is not a German citizen, to pass the border control, the one document authenticating his presence where all others fail:

> Contrary to my expectations, the Austrian police is checking IDs. My passport is sitting in a drawer in Sandershausen. Since I am in Germany, I stupidly believe that my other documents—student ID, insurance card, membership ID—will suffice. No, the Austrian police observes procedure and, for the time being, wants to take me to the police station. As a last resort, I show the civil servant the latest press reviews and my invitation to give a reading in Passau, and thereby succeed in escaping the claws of the state. (2004: 19)

I am interested in the anecdotal status of this story, which is also a story about citizenship or the lack of it. For, if Kumar had not managed to extricate himself from the situation and 'escape' the Austrian police in Germany, who would he have told the anecdote to? Would the Austrian police officer have been happy to hear that this could only be an anecdote because he had no authority to check people's IDs on German territory, even if they stood on this territory on a train called after a famous Austrian composer? Passports, the Indian American poet and critic Amitava Kumar (2002) has written, are also a kind of book. A book, he goes on to say, quoting Salman Rushdie, is also a kind of passport. Kumar's namesake, the Indian German writer Anant Kumar, can extricate himself from a border situation (without borders) only because, in the absence of a passport, he shows the police officer the authentication of his book. This authentication is doubly ironic: Kumar identifies himself through a document written by himself; and he identifies himself through a book that, given German academia's lack of definition or perhaps its lack of interest for ethnic German writing, has not made the record of German canonisation. Ironically, the Austrian police officer could hence be said to canonise Kumar's writing, and to canonise it as German. If the book is a kind of passport, the Austrian officer looking for a passport and being presented only with a book becomes a literary critic, and a *German* literary critic at that—an idea that would also make the fact that he can card innocent travellers on a train in Germany more plausible.

The fact that ethnic German literature has not yet been canonised is itself indicative of the reluctance, on the part of German academia, to debate the very definition of national belonging. On the level of cultural, legal, as well as academic acknowledgment, ethnic presences in Germany may still be confined to ripple effects. As Compton has emphasised, however, it is as ripple effects that they are nevertheless *on record*.

Conclusion

This essay has argued that the recording of an ethnic German presence may become possible only through alternative critical frameworks that have already been established—frameworks such as Asian diasporic studies, Asian American studies, Asian Candian studies, and Asian Australian studies. Of these theoretical paradigms, envisioning a coalitional link with Asian Australian studies seems especially intriguing given the fact that Asian Australian studies has been institutionalised only recently (see Lo 2006, in this issue). It is in this sense that I have tried to argue that it may be possible to resist stereotypes of 'Asian' characters on German television by watching TV through the alternative framework of Asian Australian Studies. The idea of linking Germany and Australia may hence not be as unlikely as it may at first seem. The downside of a more homogeneous European cultural politics as it is currently being proposed may also be the circulation of, for instance, a fear of Islam that surfaces in the German headscarf debate (Schoppelreich 2001; Campenhausen 2004) as much as in France's insistence on banning both Muslim headscarves and Sikh turbans in order to uphold the idea of itself as a secular state. In contexts *outside* Germany or Europe, however, the claim that banning a headscarf has nothing to do with preventing people from expressing their own cultural difference may seem debatable. It is in this sense that linking Asian German to Asian Australian presences may not be such an absurd idea, and it is a link that may benefit from a certain sense of contemporaneity, or rather, belatedness: to vastly different extents, both Australia and Germany seem to lag behind cultural debates that Canada and the US have been leading for decades. Even more importantly, however, the assumption of such belatedness itself needs to be contested, because it substitutes the possibility of a transnational dialogue with the idea that cultural progression needs to be modelled, above all, on US cultural politics.

At the same time, I believe that the possibilities inherent in Asian diasporic studies have not yet been adequately considered, especially since it has often been conceived as substituting a national with a global perspective. A more viable Asian diasporic perspective, I believe, would balance national with global perspectives, and might provide a valuable link between all the paradigms outlined above.

Finally, this essay seems to me a message in a bottle: Returning to the context I am writing in, to use an Asian Australian language to convey my own experience once again feels absurd, and being obsessed with writing about beer commercials seems a sorry fate indeed. If a diasporic perspective helps us maintain our sanity, the translation of this perspective into everyday life seems easier said than done. Yet, given the fact that globalisation encompasses not only economic goods but also the circulation of ideas, the option of sending out messages in bottles seems more feasible than ever. To believe that (Asian) ethnicity has already had its ripple effects on the nation, even if these effects have not (yet) been acknowledged as such, is solace indeed, and it may be solace in Melbourne as much as it is in Berlin.

Notes

[1] I am grateful to Roy Miki for pointing out to me both Wayde Compton's and Tseen Khoo's studies on the emergence of new, alternative critical paradigms.

[2] All translations from the German sources used in this essay are my own.
[3] The framework of German academia differs significantly from, for instance, the American and Canadian, because a broad grasp of the field is favoured over specialisation. However, even if the creation of an Asian German studies or a Turkish German studies might be feasible only as a sub-discipline within the department and field of German studies, the point is that the necessity of such a sub-discipline is not acknowledged by German academia. The fact that scholars such as Deniz Göktürk and Arlene Teraoka have been doing groundbreaking work, then, has not yet been addressed in, let alone translated into, institutional terms. Rather, minority studies have been confined to the marginal existence metaphorised in Trojanow's idea of an 'other German literature'.
[4] I am drawing here on the distinction between the discipline of *Germanistik* as it is currently established in German academia, and the field of German studies as it is engaged in overseas, an interdiscplinary field which would at the same time be called, from a 'mainland' perspective, *Auslandsgermanistik*.
[5] Idyllically, until recently, German fast trains used to have names that linked the origin of the train—its departure station—to the respective country's canonical culture. This custom was then discontinued because the trains could no longer be guaranteed to be on schedule; tardiness would hence be linked to harrowed figures such as Friedrich Schiller, a link that had to be prevented.

References

Albrecht, C. 'Fremdheitsforschung und Fremdheitslehre (Xenologie).' *Handbuch Interkulturelle Germanistik*. Eds. A. Wierlacher and A. Bogner. Stuttgart: Metzler, 2003. 541.

Campenhausen, A. F. von. 'The German Headscarf Debate.' *Brigham Young University Law Review* 2 (2004): 665–99.

Chiellino, C. 'Vorwort.' *Interkulturelle Literatur in Deutschland*. Ed. C. Chiellino. Stuttgart: Metzler, 2000. V–VIII.

Compton, W. (Ed.) *Bluesprint: Black British Columbian Literature and Orature*. Vancouver: Arsenal Pulp Press, 2001.

Dayal, S. 'Min(d)ing the Gap: South Asian Americans and Diaspora.' *A Part, Yet Apart: South Asians in Asian America*. Eds. L. D. Shankar and R. Srikanth. Philadelphia: Temple University Press, 1998. 235–65.

Desai, J. *Beyond Bollywood: The Cultural Politics of South Asian Diasporic Film*. New York: Routledge, 2004.

Göktürk, D. 'Migration und Kino—Subnationale Mitleidskultur oder transnationale Rollenspiele?.' *Interkulturelle Literatur in Deutschland*. Ed. C. Chiellino. Stuttgart: Metzler, 2000. 329–47.

Holert, T. 'Grüne Karte Qualifikation? Migrationssteuerung und Ökonomie des Wissens.' *Projekt Migration*. Köln: DuMont, 2005. 424–27.

Khoo, T. *Banana Bending: Asian-Australian and Asian-Canadian Literatures*. Hong Kong: McGill-Queens University Press and Hong Kong University Press, 2003.

Kumar, Amitava. *Bombay, London, New York*. New York: Routledge, 2002.

Kumar, Anant. *Die galoppierende Kuhherde: Essays und andere Prosa*. Schweinfurt: Wiesenburg, 2004.

Lo, J. 'Disciplining Asian Australian Studies: Projections and Introjections.' *Journal of Intercultural Studies* 27.1–2 (2006): 11–27.

Miki, R. *Broken Entries: Race, Subjectivity, Writing*. Vancouver: Mercury, 1998.

Schoppelreich, B. 'Konflikt um das Kopftuch auch in Krankenhäusern'. *Frankfurter Allgemeine Zeitung* 29, July (2001): 3.

Teraoka, A. A. '*Gastarbeiterliteratur*: The Other Speaks back.' *The Nature and Context of Minority Discourse*. Eds. A. JanMohamed and D. Lloyd. New York: Oxford University Press, 1990. 294–318.

Terkessidis, M. 'Kabarett und Satire deutsch-türkischer Autoren.' *Interkulturelle Literatur in Deutschland*. Ed. C. Chiellino. Stuttgart: Metzler, 2000. 294–301.

Trojanow, I. (Ed.) *Döner in Walhalla: Texte aus der anderen Deutschen Literatur*. Köln: Kiepenheuer and Witsch, 2000.

Ty, E. *Beyond Silence: Chinese Canadian Literature in English*, by Lien Chao (Review). *University of Toronto Quarterly* 70.1 (2000/2001). <http://www.utpjournals.com/product/utq/701/silence119.html> (accessed 28 January 2006).

Yano, H. 'Migrationsgeschichte.' *Interkulturelle Literatur in Deutschland*. Ed. C. Chiellino. Stuttgart: Metzler, 2000. 1–17.

Asian Australian Citizenship as a Frame of Enactment in the Parliamentary 'First Speech'

Jen Tsen Kwok

This essay stems from my interest in the formative space that both ethnic identity and Australian citizenship inhabits: a space that may be formally grounded by the policies of multiculturalism but ultimately is entangled in a confluence of more complicated social and cultural pressures. The problem is that, outside of material contexts, such a space is merely speculative. In reflecting upon the relationship between hybridity discourse and Chineseness, Allen Chun suggested that it is as important to understand why an identity is invoked as it is to understand from what identity is constituted. It is 'the need to articulate the various contexts wherein facets of identity are deemed to be relevant' (Chun 1996: 134). It is important, then, to consider how reliant identity performances are upon the material contexts that produce them. This essay represents a starting point for the analysis of the cultural junctures between 'Asian' and 'Australian' in relation to Australian political processes. Specifically, it attempts to qualitatively frame Asian Australian identity performances within the context of the parliamentary first speech. It is hoped that bringing the parliamentary first speech to the fore might encourage further consideration about how the politics of *intentional* hybridity (Lo 2000) are materially embodied and, perhaps, expand the ground rules in which politically-motivated cultural transformations are conceived.

'Chineseness' has been one recognisable ethnic subjectivity at the coalface of academia's engagement with identity politics. While there has been some analysis of how Chinese identity in economic and social situations is utilised (Christiansen 2003; Ong and Nonini 1997; Parker 1995), there has been a telling deficiency regarding the performance of Chineseness in relation to political and civic participation. Much of the academic literature that addresses diasporic Chinese political participation revolves around structural and institutional analyses—from Chinese community associations to formal political mechanisms (Anderson 1991; Freedman 2000; Kuah-Pearce and Hu-Dehart 2004; Lin 1998; Ng 1999; Skinner 1958)—without significantly identifying the political cultures and traditions in which these engagements reside. In particular, local characteristics of racialised citizenship and its effect upon political representation are inadequately addressed. This contrasts to a wealth of American critical race theory that problematises notions of citizenship within the multiracial state and the circumscribed participation of these citizens within the body politic (Lowe 1996; Omi and Winant 1986; Palumbo-Liu 1999).

In *Immigrant Acts*, Lisa Lowe draws from a wide textual palate to characterise Asian American citizenship. For Lowe, this approach delimits the control the state otherwise exercises over 'forms and sites of political contestation'. Lowe argues:

> Where the political terrain can neither resolve nor suppress inequality, it erupts in culture. Because culture is the contemporary repository of memory, of history, it is through culture, rather than government, that alternative forms of subjectivity, collectivity, and public life are imagined. (1996: 22)

Networks of political cooperation between Chinese Australian, let alone Asian Australian, groups may remain rudimentary, as the absence of nationwide peak representative bodies would indicate. Nonetheless, there is sufficient formal engagement in the political process by individuals of Asian Australian background to analyse notions of racialised citizenship. In Australia, there have been no fewer than twelve Asian Australian parliamentarians at state and federal levels. The purpose here is to explore the 'performance' of identity within local processes of racialisation, rather than focusing upon its manifest effects.

The parliamentary first speech represents a small component of a broad political terrain but it remains significant for numerous reasons, not the least being that its role in defining the political values of its speakers allows us to explore microsociological performances of ethnic identity. In employing terms such as 'performance', there is an obvious danger since its use is riddled by multivalent meanings across diverse disciplines, and these meanings are often constituted from highly theoretical and incompatible ontological frameworks. Shannon Jackson in *Professing Performance* alerts us to these difficulties when she observes that 'scholars continually find themselves rehearsing and revising various kinds of intellectual histories' (Jackson 2004: 4, 12). In light of these definitional nuances, performance is used in this essay in a sociological and social anthropological sense, originating once in dramaturgy (Goffman 1971: 9), but developed by social scientists such as Erving Goffman, Fredrik Barth and Richard Jenkins (Barth 1969; Goffman 1963, 1969, 1971; Jenkins 1996), to address the intentionality with which 'public selves' are presented to the world. It is a framing of performance that originates in recognising that identity is not only a catch-all for internalised notions of self through culture and memory, but has instrumental utility in particular social circumstances and contexts. The various uses of 'performance' and 'performative' in this essay remain within the spectrum of this approach, the emphasis being upon the explicit or semi-explicit utility of particular presentations—of or about self—to the external world.

Clearly, in present contexts, the promotion of collective or group identity is not an exclusive frame for political behaviour. It is helpful to forecast the parliamentary first speech as bound up in the exercise of political power. Performances of ethnic identity by Asian Australian parliamentarians must be appreciably tied to this. As Paulla Ebron argues in *Performing Africa*, it is imperative 'to see performance as more than a response to power; power *is* performative' (Ebron 2002: 5, emphasis in original). Ebron concludes:

> Elites and bureaucrats are also performers, and the full stage includes high players as well as low. To see the performative nature of power is not to trivialize power but to see how it works. Power is effective when people are enrolled in the rhetorics, the stances, and the subject positions of its projects. Through these performances, subjects take up the social statuses in the world. (2002: 5)

The first speech represents an ideal site for comprehending ethnic identity and discourses about citizenship as possible performative 'frames' for Asian Australian parliamentarians. It represents a site of discursive privilege, a site of interstitial contact for its subjects between the normative invisibility of the Asian Australian citizen and the acquisition of political and symbolic capital.

Mapping Asian Australian First Speeches

The first speech is not a phenomenon unique to Westminster systems. Within the Westminster system, however, it is limited to state and federal parliaments. There are two methodological impacts upon the data. This is convenient both because there does not appear to be a systematic way of categorising the ethnic background of

Australian legislative representatives across the three levels of government, and because the target sample is reduced from at least an unruly thirty-five to twelve parliamentarians. An initial qualifier is that the former Deputy Premier of the Northern Territory, Dr Richard Lim, did not deliver a first speech and so there are only ten speeches that need to be analysed.[1] It is also important to highlight that not all twelve are currently serving members: of the twelve, only eight are currently parliamentarians. Bill O'Chee, Bernice Pfitzner, Helen Sham-Ho and Tchen Tsebin have all left office. Nonetheless, all state and federal Asian Australian parliamentarians have served within the life of Australia's policies of multiculturalism (see Table 1).

In contrast to Asian Australian representation in local government, state and federal representation is a relatively recent phenomenon. While the first Victorian local councillor, David Wang, and Australia's first Chinese mayor, Harry Chan, can be traced back to the late 1960s, Australia's first state parliamentarian was Helen Shum-Ho, who was elected to the New South Wales (NSW) legislative council in 1988. Similarly, Australia's first federal parliamentarian was Bill O'Chee, who began his term for the National Party in the federal senate only in 1990.

We may also do a breakdown by country-of-origin (see Table 2). Eleven Asian Australian state and Federal parliamentarians listed here share Chinese heritage, and all but two are first generation Chinese Australian. The bias to parliamentarians of first generation Chinese background poses a series of interesting questions. For example, why is there an under-representation of other established Asian Australian communities such as Japanese or Vietnamese Australians, and what are the possible relationships between mainstream political support and transnational economic networks? Addressing these questions is important but beyond the scope of this essay. More relevantly, the shared Chinese heritage of the target sample reveals the national and cultural diversity of those ascribed ostensibly as 'Chinese'. This is not to say that similar cultural characteristics are merely coincidences. However, it is necessary to consider the specificity of cultural background as implicated in, and perhaps formative of, the political values of these parliamentarians. It might be reasonable to accept that a Chinese Australian from a recent Taiwanese background would have a greater familiarity with the democratic process than one from a recent Mainland Chinese background.

It is difficult to give a sufficient explanation within such limited space as to how these representatives find themselves in the breakdown between ideological perspectives. A sweeping generalisation would suggest that the current Australian political landscape is dominated by two parties, the Liberal Party and the Australian Labor Party (ALP), both generalisable as centrist, with the Liberal and National parties forming a conservative Coalition government at the national level, the ALP in contrast dominating state politics and employing broadly centre-left perspectives. The Country Liberal Party (CLP), which is not represented in the analysed speeches, has a unique Territory history, forming in 1974 as a convergence between the Country and Liberal parties but maintaining relations with both the current Liberal and National parties. The Unity Party developed as a response to the rising prominence of

Table 1 Past and Present Asian Australian Parliamentarians (Federal and State)

	Surname	First name	Party	State	Seat	House	Length of representation	First speech
Federal	Johnson	Michael	Liberal	QLD	Ryan	Assembly	From 01	13-Feb-02
	O'Chee	Bill	National	QLD		Senate	90 to 98	9-May-90
	Tchen	Tsebin	Liberal	VIC		Senate	1-Jul-99 to 04	11-Aug-99
	Wong	Penny	ALP	SA		Senate	From 1-Jul-02	21-Aug-02
State	Choi	Michael Wai-Man	ALP	QLD	Capalaba	Assembly	From 17-Feb-01	5-Apr-01
	Lim	Hong	ALP	VIC	Clayton	Assembly	From 96	15-May-96
	Lim	Richard Soon Huat	Country Liberal	NT	Greatorex	Assembly	From 4-Jun-94	
	Nguyen	Sang Minh	ALP	VIC	Melbourne West	Council	From 96	14-May-96
	Pfitzner	Bernice Swee-Lian	Liberal	SA		Council	23-Oct-90 to 11-Oct-97	6-Nov-90
	Sham-Ho	Helen Wai-Har	Liberal	NSW		Council	19-Mar-88 to 28-Feb-03	25-Aug-88
	Tsang	Henry Shui-Lung	ALP	NSW		Council	From 27-Mar-99	1-Jun-99
	Wong	Peter	Unity	NSW		Council	From 27-Mar-99	27-May-99

Table 2 Asian Australian Parliamentarians and Ethnic Background (Federal and State)

	Surname	First name	Party	Ancestry/Ethnicity	Country of Origin	Generation
Federal	Johnson	Michael	Liberal	British Chinese	Hong Kong	1
	O'Chee	Bill	National	Irish Chinese	Australia	4
	Tchen	Tsebin	Liberal	Chinese	Mainland China	1
	Wong	Penny	ALP	Chinese	Malaysia	1
State	Choi	Michael Wai-Man	ALP	Chinese	Hong Kong	1
	Lim	Hong	ALP	Chinese	Cambodia	1
	Lim	Richard Soon Huat	Country Liberal	Chinese	Malaysia	1
	Nguyen	Sang Minh	ALP	Vietnamese	Vietnam	1
	Pfitzner	Bernice Swee-Lian	Liberal	Chinese	Singapore	1
	Sham-Ho	Helen Wai-Har	Liberal	Chinese	Hong Kong	1
	Tsang	Henry Shui-Lung	ALP	Chinese	Mainland China via Hong Kong	1
	Wong	Peter	Unity	Chinese	Indonesia	1

Pauline Hanson's One Nation party in the 1998 Queensland state election (Healy 1999, 2001). At this election One Nation won 22.7 percent of the Queensland primary vote and eleven seats (Newman 1998), whittling away significant support from all three major parties and heralding the emergence of a new conservative voice in Australian politics that was unrepentantly anti-multicultural and anti-Indigenous. Unity in response assembled a host of political candidates, many from Asian Australian backgrounds, some of whom are still represented in Sydney's local councils.

While the political representation of Asian Australian populations remains poor, as does political representation across all ethnic minorities (Zappala 1998: 10), the means of access is significantly different from the US context in which non-compulsory voting, electoral colleges, etc., mould distinctive forms of political participation such as highly-politicised ethnic networks and organisations (Freedman 2000: 136–181). Comparisons with the US may be highly informative, but it is equally important to theorise the specificity of the Australian context. To posit the Unity Party as the focal point of Asian Australian political activity when there appears to be a meaningful engagement by Asian Australians in mainstream politics, for example, would be foolish.

The Parliamentary First Speech

The *NSW Legislative Assembly Practice Book* describes it as the 'inaugural speech'. In the Federal *House of Representatives Practice* it is called the 'first speech'. In both of these procedural manuals there is no prescription as to content. Both parliaments, however, draw attention to its significance by stating that these speeches are to be 'heard without interjection or interruption' (*NSW Legislative Assembly Practice and Procedure Book 2002*; *House of Representatives Practice 2005*). The Speaker must draw 'the attention of the House to the fact that a Member is making a first speech'. The parliamentary first speech effectively represents a site of discursive privilege. The privilege resides in a tension between the right of the speaker to speak off-topic and express one's political beliefs, and the increasingly flaunted convention that the first speech is meant to remain politically uncontroversial. Its affect is dependent upon tensions between the positionality of its speaker, the standpoints that person subsequently takes, and the audience to whom it is addressed. This is a dialogic approach to textuality and is influenced primarily by Mikhail Bakhtin, who was concerned with the transaction between text and context (Morson and Emerson 1990: 22–28; Shepherd 2001: 143–144).

In *Strategic Interaction,* Goffman coins the term *enforcement system* to describe the factors or 'conditions of adjustive action' that impinge upon the interactions each person makes in the world (Goffman 1969: 115, 119). It is clear that the first speech represents a site in which notions of self and identity are highly structured, at least, by the demands of public office and the forethought the first speech compels as a reflection of the speaker's political values. The first speech is regulated on one side by its public nature and thus may become dialogically-engaged with myths of the 'public good' and dominant Australian values. This is observable in the fact that parliamentary first speeches are published more widely than Hansard. They are republished on a number of parliamentary websites and, in some cases, legislators make photocopies of their first speech available in their electoral offices.

We can observe the possible consequence of speech tensions in Pauline Hanson's infamous inaugural address (Hanson 1996), an address that even now persists as a significant and controversial footprint on the cultural life of the Australian nation (Gibson et al. 2002). While there is significant debate about the role of the press in bringing Hanson to national prominence (Nolan 2001: 65–70), in the context of the speech we see not only its potential significance as a site of discursive privilege, but how hegemonies must enforce heightened subservience in specific sites and the problems enacted when these sites are not sufficiently managed. This heightened discursive privilege frames the context of what is spoken and what is spoken through it. The particular subjectivities expressed through these speeches are both products and expressions *of* political institutions. Political power conditions certain forms of subjectivity, demands certain sorts of allegiances, and intimately affects the scope of expression and self-construction.

The scope of these speeches is, to a great extent, regulated by emphases upon the interests of party politics. Political parties have broad ideological platforms through which society and the public good are conceived. The Australian 'history wars' are an ideal example of the relationship between history-telling and national identity, where the articulation of national identity has composed sets of symbols that have been recurrently manipulated in our public spheres (Davison 2000; MacIntyre and Clark 2003; Windschuttle 2003). In understanding the scope of Asian Australian self-construction, and perhaps how the conventions of racial discourse may be interrupted, we must consider these speeches as dependent upon both these frames and further sets of multivalent pressures masked by political institutionalisation. In particular, these pressures are complicated when we incorporate localised notions of racial difference and seek to comprehend how race problematises Australian citizenship.

Racialised Citizenship in Australia

In *Racial State*, David Goldberg advances a complex argument about how the modern nation-state is fundamentally implicated in the management and exclusion of people, and how categories for inclusion and exclusion are structured through an adaptive and open connotative capacity to signify race at different times and in different contexts (Goldberg 2002).[2] Such an argument is evident in Australia's own histories of migration and race relations, where batteries of legislation have formed social policies that have disenfranchised the citizenship aspirations and mediated the incorporation of numerous minority populations.[3] Goldberg's argument, however, propels Australian discourses on multiculturalism in new directions. Processes of racialisation continue to influence the citizenship aspirations of Asian Australians in spite of multicultural policy and the operation of anti-discriminatory legislation such as the Commonwealth *Racial Discrimination Act* (1975).[4] Criticism of Australian multiculturalism from both Left and Right sides of politics has focused upon multicultural 'orthodoxies', whether it be vitriolic attacks against the multicultural 'industry', or criticisms of multiculturalism's failure to guarantee more than simply the right to express one's culture.[5] Certainly, the dimensions of specific social policy hold some responsibility for problems in the way these policies operate on the ground. Nonetheless, it is significant to recognise the impetus towards containment and management that governmentality itself demands.

A greater problem is that Australian multicultural policy has failed to locate a place for political rights and responsibilities adequately, a principle that political theorists such as Bhiku Parekh consider the cornerstone for social stability in the modern multicultural nation-state (Parekh 2000: 341–2). As recently as the 1999 national policy document *Australian Multiculturalism for a New Century* (National Multi-cultural Advisory Council 1999), multiculturalism and citizenship were construed as separate, albeit 'symbiotic and complementary' (*National Multicultural Advisory Council* 1999: 6); one durable after-effect of this was the reification of 'Australian core values' (Kelly 2005). Most recently, the Federal Government has updated this document with *Multicultural Australia: United in Diversity*, a 12-page update that stamps Australian multiculturalism with the primacy of 'Australian Citizenship':

> These civic obligations reflect the unifying values of Australian Citizenship. Australian Citizenship involves reciprocal responsibilities and privileges and enables individuals to become fully contributing members of the Australian community. Citizenship is a strong unifying force in our diverse multicultural community. Our commitment to and defence of Australian values of equality, democracy and freedom unite us in our diverse origins, and enhance the ability of us all to participate fully in all spheres of Australian society. (*Multicultural Australia: United in Diversity* 2003: 6)

There is an observable shift in tone between these documents, beginning with an abandonment of a 'defensive' mode for multiculturalism. The statement that Australian citizenship should 'enhance the ability ... to participate fully in all spheres of Australian society' is encouraging, although the policy has not been complemented by public debates on citizenship or what the social contract of citizenship might substantively enshrine.[6] Citizenship in these documents is portrayed primarily as an acquiescence to pre-existing civic duties and institutions—what Castles would describe as 'passive' citizenship (Castles 2000)—rather than, say, the right to develop and contribute to Australian citizenship. Further, the translation from broad policy to institutional change has been muddied by a host of deportation and detention scandals that have engulfed government departments throughout 2005, from Cornelia Rau to 'Mr Z', from Vivian Alvarez to Ali Tastan and Robert Jovicic (Commonwealth Ombudsman 2005a, 2005b; King and Wallace 2006).[7] These scandals significantly destabilise the integrity of Australian citizenship as a unifying national principle.

As quoted at the start of this essay, Lisa Lowe suggests that the narrow regulation of citizenship discourse in politically-institutionalised settings results in an overflow into public spheres. In Australian public discourse, as Tseen Khoo observes, '[h]unger for the cosmopolitan face means that Australian civic acceptance is often conditional upon repeated and accepted versions of that difference' (Khoo 2003: 21). This is what Khoo describes as the struggle of the Chinese Australian citizen to place being 'visibly different' within being 'hegemonically invisible' (Khoo 2001: 105). In the repetition of popular culture in Australian public space, references to a national mythology defined through narratives of British tradition and hegemonic 'white' values over-mediate notions of national belonging. Asian Australian subjectivities are consistently 'disavowed'. This produces what Ghassan Hage describes as a different *mode* of existence for Asian Australians, a mode dependent upon discourses of enrichment (Hage 1998: 121). David Pearson explains this as a process of *ethnification*, a 'discursive and material process of state categorization of 'others' as being culturally and racially distinct, and the consequent practices and outcomes of such labelling' (Pearson 2002: 1002). For Pearson this process occurs as a result of the relatively recent liberalisation of formal migration policies in many British settler countries and may displace long-standing assumptions of a 'nominal subjectivity framed through British kinship' (1002).

In Australia, these processes are ontologically underpinned by what Toula Nicolacopoulos and George Vassilacopoulos (2004) describe as the 'onto-pathology of white Australian subjectivity'. Nicolacopoulos and Vassilacopoulos argue that 'white' Australia's engagement with Indigenous Australia frames the relationship between ethnic communities and mainstream Australian society. This onto-pathology conditions and positions ethnic Australians as the 'perpetual-foreigners-within', a positioning that balances a desire to recognise Australia as culturally-diverse with a fixation upon disciplining the discursive presence of minority populations. Its effect is that:

> in our public lives we are systematically discouraged from invoking what we might call richly-filled universal values. Outside our designated private spaces, we are called upon always to speak from our positions as *particular* individuals or collectives, as *particular* embodiments of this way or that way of being and doing. (Nicolacopoulos and Vassilacopoulos 2004: 34, emphasis in original)

The space between 'Asian' and 'Australian citizen' is both distinguished and recurrently policed. The Asian Australian citizen is to be seen, but not heard.

Performing Asian Australian Citizenship and the 'Grateful Migrant' Narrative

Consequently, the inaugural speeches of Asian Australian parliamentarians raise a host of fascinating questions: Is ethnicity utilised in these speeches? When is it utilised and in what contexts? How centrally is ethnicity constructed within the formation of political attitudes? How are these values situated between Asia and Australia? How is Australia imagined? How are Australian values portrayed? In addressing these questions, it was necessary to chart the major themes and issues that arose in the ten speeches (see Table 3).

A few preliminary conclusions can be made from this table. There were a number of terms so frequently repeated that one would presume their use in speeches of this sort. This includes: 'nation', 'community' and 'economy'. One exception would be terms covered by the umbrella of migration politics, or frequency of terms such as 'immigration', 'migrant' and 'immigrant'. All Asian Australian parliamentarians engaged with 'migration politics' (see Figure 1), and it is relevant to note that, on casual perusal, this does not occur in the first speeches of Anglo Australian parliamentarians.

Derivable from this dataset, one may also make a comparison of the frequency of times ethnicity or terms beginning with 'Asia' are repeated to the frequency with which 'Australia' and terms starting with 'Austral' are invoked. Of the most telling thematic patterns to emerge, it should be uncontroversial to suggest that ALP parliamentarians discuss their ethnicity at both a numerically and proportionally higher level than Coalition parliamentarians (that is, those from the Liberal and National Parties). It is fair to assume that the recurrent critique of multiculturalism in conservative circles would have some impact on the way ethnic identity is constructed and represented by Coalition parliamentarians. When Coalition members invoke their ethnicity, it seems they are often compelled to represent it as a component of a greater national whole. Michael Johnson states:

> My father is of British heritage and my mother from the southern Chinese province of Guangzhou. Therefore, being the first member of the House to have a part Chinese heritage is clearly a source of emotional pride. That said, however, like all Liberals in this House, I am first and foremost a proud and loyal Australian. (Johnson 2002)

One major exception to Coalition members' reluctant engagement with ethnicity is Helen Sham-Ho, who mentions her ethnicity more times than any other parliamentarian. In her speech, Sham-Ho recognises that she is often typecast as a representative of 'the aspirations of thousands of Australians who migrated to this country to seek a better way of life', yet she positions herself as Australian (Sham-Ho 1988). Sham-Ho invokes her ethnicity to circumscribe it within an identity which is 'first and foremost' as an 'ordinary Australian woman'.

This pattern may display to some extent the Coalition's ambivalent engagement with multiculturalism, reflected in declining Federal support for the multicultural sector over many years (Jakubowicz 2002: 109, 111). It may also reflect a myth about Australian history that is conditioned by Howard's insistence upon a heroic 'white' Australian story, marked only by the occasional 'blemish' (Howard 1999). Such an argument however is complicated by a lack of clear differentiation between the performative tropes employed in Coalition and ALP first speeches relating specifically

Table 3 Major Themes of Asian Australian Maiden Speeches, Coded By Repetition of Term

Themes and Codes	MC	MJ	HL	WO	BP	HSH	TT	HT	Pen W	Pet W	TOTAL
Immigration/immigrants/migrants	X	X	X	X	X	X	X	X	X	X	10
Nation/country	X	X	X	X	X	X	X	X	X	X	10
Economy/economics/economic	X	X	X	X	X	X		X	X	X	9
Community	X	X	X	X		X	X	X	X	X	9
Young people/youth/children	X	X	X	X	X			X	X	X	8
Environment/environmental	X		X	X	X			X	X	X	7
Marginality/marginality/disadvantage*	X		X		X	X			X	X	7
Rural	X	X		X			X		X	X	6
Citizenship/citizen	X	X	X				X	X	X		6
Unemployment/employment			X	X	X		X	X	X		6
Cultural diversity/diversity/diverse	X		X			X		X	X	X	6
Democracy/democratic		X				X	X	X		X	5
Education	X		X			X		X	X		5
Indigenous/Aboriginal/Aborigine	X				X	X		X	X		5
Opportunity (land of)	X					X		X	X	X	5
Racism/racial	X				X		X	X	X		5
Aspiration/aspirational		X						X	X	X	4
Asylum seekers/refugees					X			X	X	X	4
Compassion/compassionate	X						X	X	X		4
Ethnic communities			X				X	X	X		4
Globalisation/global		X		X				X		X	4
Prosperity/prosperous/prosper		X		X			X	X			4
Social cohesion/cohesion					X	X		X	X		4
White Australia	X					X			X	X	4
Pauline Hanson/One Nation	X						X		X		3

Abbreviations: Michael Choi (MC); Michael Johnson (MJ); Hong Lim (HL); Bill O'Chee (WO); Bernice Pfitzner (BP); Helen Sham-Ho (HSH); Tchen Tsebin (TT); Henry Tsang (HT); Penny Wong (Pen W); Peter Wong (Pet W).

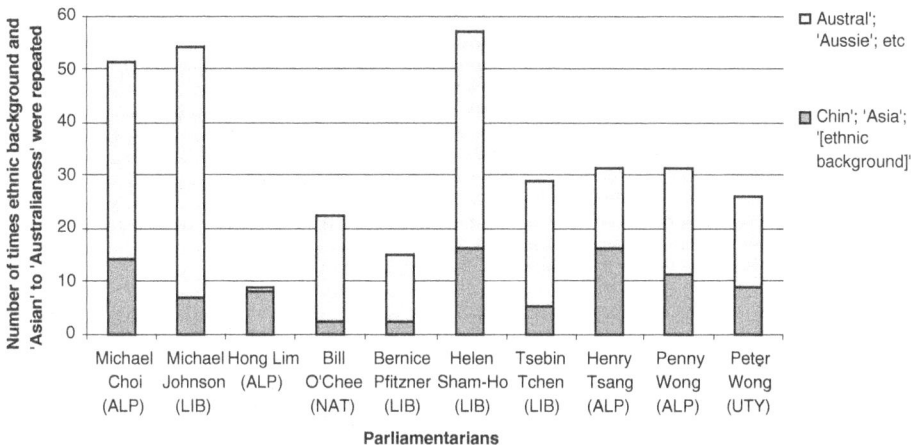

Figure 1 Repetition of ethnicity as a proportion of repetition of 'Australianess'

to ethnicity. On an initial reading, one might assume that ALP members engage with their ethnicity in more diverse ways. For example, the ALP Member for Capalaba, Michael Choi, on a number of occasions utilises Chinese values or the experience of the migrant Australian humorously: 'To my children Priscilla, Rachel and Claudia: thank you for your understanding and patience. All of you are indeed a godsend. I love you all, and remember to do your homework!' (Choi 2001). However Choi equally locates his enthusiastic and comical construction of the ethnic experience within strong and repeated assertions of pride and loyalty as an Australian.

Within the context of the parliamentary first speech each Asian Australian parliamentarian flags her or his ethnic identity, albeit sometimes briefly. The brevity of some discursive engagements, however, may tellingly suggest the speakers have a limited interest in the politics of identity. For example, one speech that minimally engages with identity politics is the one delivered by Hong Lim, ALP parliamentarian for the Victorian seat of Clayton, who pauses long enough only to recognise that he is the first Chinese Cambodian to sit in parliament (Lim 1996). While he makes no mention of Cambodia, Chineseness, or the values this background imparts upon him, he spends a significant proportion of the speech discussing the economic marginality of his mainly ethnic electorate and in recognising the ethnic community groups that supported his campaign. If the politics of identity were capable of providing momentum for political influence, it would be expected that a parliamentarian serving as a state member in a largely-impoverished ethnic electorate would have the most interest in carefully articulating ethnic identity, especially during a time when Hanson received increasing amounts of press attention. Lim's speech reflects less a lack of sensitivity to ethnic interests, as his extensive reference to ethnic community organisations would refute, and more about the limited discursive benefit in addressing his constituents through those performative tropes. It is telling to note that Lim also mentions 'Australia' the least of any other Asian Australian parliamentarian. Overwhelmingly, the political stage is broad enough to elicit through the first speech a range of narratives. There are refractions of the 'model minority' through the repetition of the term 'proud' and 'loyal' by Michael Choi, Michael Johnson and Bill O'Chee. Model minority discourse originates from the US where Asian Americans in the last thirty years have often been considered ideal migrants, as productive and successful 'Americans' (Chae 2004: 61–2). An example of the model minority trope in Australian contexts can be observed in the joint statement against Hanson made by the five standing Chinese parliamentarians in 1996:

> Asian-Australians have participated positively and fully in Australia making a valuable contribution to all aspects of society including the arts, education, medicine, law and business. We have brought with us strong family values, work ethics and have worked hard to integrate into the wider Australian community. (Sham-Ho 1996)

We also have the appeal to Australia's 'multicultural tapestry' in comments from Coalition members such as Bernice Pfitzner and Tchen Tsebin, and the sole Unity representative Peter Wong. Wong, in fact, frames his entry into NSW parliament in terms of his desire to 'promote and protect such a society—one that recognises physical, cultural and linguistic differences and perceives them as values that enrich rather than divide' (Wong 1999).

Upon further analysis what emerges from across the data are a number of less obvious phrases such as 'aspiration', 'aspirational' and 'land of opportunity'. These terms are invoked most often in the context of representatives (including most ALP representatives) providing some sort of anecdote about their migrant origins or observations of life in their 'homeland'. In framing his desire to enter politics, Henry Tsang, an ALP legislative councillor in NSW and former deputy mayor, discusses his Tiananmen Square experiences in 1984. His conclusion is:

> Yet balancing the anger and horror of what happened in Beijing was a powerful desire to protect and rejoice in our democracy. The event was a violent reminder that we must never take our democracy for granted, and never become complacent about our gift of freedom. (Tsang 1999)

Peter Wong, the NSW state representative for the Unity Party, talks about his experiences in Indonesia:

> The tragic and revolting violence that has beset Indonesia in recent times is not unique in that nation's history. When I was a child I witnessed the implementation of policy that was rooted in discrimination. The history of Indonesia, one of Australia's closest neighbours, provides many lessons for our country. We can never afford to falter when the danger of racism, hatred and fear arise. (Wong 1999)

Similar anecdotes are repeated by Michael Choi, with regard to the lack of education and health services in Hong Kong, and Penny Wong, in a reminiscence of her father's poverty in Malaysia. In contrast, both Michael Johnson and Tchen Tsebin repeat the word 'aspirational' to describe their family's attitudes here.

Researchers in Australian race-relations history would be familiar with some of the typologies that categorise various historically-marginalised Australian minority groups, from Indigenous to Irish Australians. The Chinese, and metonymically Asian Australians in general, are subject to transnational and persistent typologies. We can trace public remonstrances of the fear of the invading horde and the plodding coolie to more recent ideas of the Asian Australian as model minority citizen (Broinowski 1992; Cronin 1975, 1982; Ip and Murphy 2005; Khoo 2001: 98; Lee 1999; Markus 1979; Price 1974; Walker 1999). In the political arena, we observe in the performative disjuncture between Australian and Asian identity a slightly less obvious yet similarly recognisable narrative. At work here is a theme related to recognition of the Asian migrant's social debt.

The repetition of Australia as a land of opportunity signifies what I describe as the 'grateful migrant narrative'. In this narrative:

1. the world's ills are expelled or positioned outside the Australian nation, and
2. Australian civic and cultural traditions are reified, performatively internalised through use of terms such as 'aspiration', 'aspirational' and 'land of opportunity'.

The 'grateful migrant narrative' is generated as much out of dominant political culture as from the agency of Asian Australian parliamentarians. This term appears particularly useful to those Asian Australian parliamentarians who refuse to submit themselves as 'model minorities'. The statement of gratitude appears to be a sufficient grounding, addressed most likely at dominant Australian audiences, to 'remain in the conversation' (Ebron 2002: 29). The repetition of the grateful migrant narrative is important because it is unlike Hage's assertion that ethnic Australians are only discursively embraced as 'enriching cultures' (Hage 1998; see also Ang and Stratton 2001). There appears to be enough flexibility for the 'content value' of Asian Australian cultures to not be specifically addressed at these sites (or maybe it is presumed). Nevertheless, this grateful migrant narrative falls in with other critiques made by Hage in that ethnic communities are set, and thus set themselves, at the peripheries of a 'white' Australian centre. The political agency of ethnic collectivities is constructed in a way that is structurally ambivalent to the legitimacy of their cultural identity.

Asian Australian Citizenship in the Context of Racism

Helen Sham-Ho expresses her antipathy to racism in her 1988 first speech:

> Racism is a form of violence which I abhor. It has caused the deaths of millions and untold suffering. I am sure that all who came to Australia regarded this country as a sanctuary where racism would be left outside, and I am committed totally to this viewpoint. (Sham-Ho 1988)

Sham-Ho is significant because hers is the first inaugural speech made by either a Chinese or Asian Australian parliamentarian. She begins with a Chinese proverb: 'The journey of a thousand miles must start with the first step'. She then proceeds to provide a comprehensive historical account of White Australia and the antecedents of anti-Chinese racism. What is more interesting, however, is that she projects racism as outside the Australian national imaginary, inadvertently distancing 'the unwanted'—including both its perpetrators and recipients—outward into Asia. Within such a discrete passage, we can glimpse significant hegemonic devices at work. Karen Shimakawa would tender Sham-Ho's performance—in the Asian American context—as characterising national abjection, where the symbolic coherency of 'Americanness' necessitates that the nationally abject must be *both* perpetually embraced and rejected or, as Shimakawa states, 'made present and jettisoned' (Shimakawa 2002: 3). In her ethnic performance, Sham-Ho mirrors the hegemonic conception of Asia as *abject*, as effectively 'othered'.

Let us move to a crucible in recent Australian race relations history. Pauline Hanson gave her inaugural parliamentary speech in September 1996 (Hanson 1996). It was a speech that followed her rising prominence as a recently disendorsed Liberal candidate for the federal seat of Oxley. Soon afterwards, Sham-Ho tabled a joint statement against racism, signed by all five existing Chinese Australian parliamentarians, in the NSW Legislative Council (Sham Ho 1996; also Hickey 1996). The joint statement made an appeal through a number of 'performative tropes', such as the positive contributions of 'Asian Australians' and the decency and fairness of Australia's civic and political institutions. In effect, it reinforced the commitment of the five parliamentarians to Australia's policies of multiculturalism. Preceding this point, however, during a NSW parliamentary debate on 30 May 1996, Franca Arena, one of few Italian Australian parliamentarians, had spoken in parliament about the prevalence of racism in politics, and accused Sham-Ho of indifference (Arena 1996).

Arena's comments about parliamentary racism beg us to consider that some identities in certain discursive contexts might or must be strategically performed. In part, the joint statement is made on behalf of Chinese Australians; in part, it is a clumsy attempt at augmenting political and Coalition support against the popularity that Hanson increasingly commanded. It also represents a careful means of reminding political leaders about their ethical responsibilities to minority communities. The statement asserts:

> As acknowledged by our Prime Minister, the Hon. John Howard, Australia's cultural diversity is a rich resource and an asset to this country. All Australians regardless of their colour, race or religion should have the right to free speech *as well as* the equal right to a peaceful existence, free of racial taunts and vilification. (Sham-Ho 1996; emphasis added)

This statement is a public qualifier to Howard's assertions about welcoming 'the fact that people can now talk about certain things without living in fear of being branded as a bigot or as a racist' (Freedman 1996).

I want to draw attention now to Penny Wong's first speech in 2002, one where she problematises racism as a pervasive and recurring threat from within. Beginning with a personal anecdote of racial vilification, Wong does not then seek to cleanse dominant 'white' subjectivity by externalising the influence of race. Instead, she focuses upon its contemporaneous deployment as a tool for political power, directly engaging with Howard's various, flawed social policies. While Wong provides a limited example of how certain discursive 'trajectories' might be interrupted, simultaneously it is important to consider the political implications of Wong's use of antiracist rhetoric in attacking Coalition policy. Attacking Howard's social justice policies through the frame of race reflects, at once, discursive flexibility in the ALP's approach to national identity and history. Simultaneously, Wong's background as a 'racialised minority' provides her performative space to attack Howard through an association of these policies with prejudices manifest within mainstream Australia.

In utilising or ignoring tropes that are 'heard' by the national imagination, it appears impossible without more detailed contextual analysis to differentiate between what might or might not be strategic deployments made for the purposes of achieving particular political goals. Henry Tsang deploys the grateful migrant narrative to reinforce his commitment to Australia, while Peter Wong deploys it to encourage other Australians to wash their hands of Hanson. In this dataset, which is characterised by public, institutional and overwhelmingly instrumental forms of ethnic performance, we may expect that they are implicated in one another. However, the performance of these tropes does not occur just as an imitative repetition addressed toward the dominant culture or the political institutions that cultivated its speakers. Through these performative frames each Asian Australian parliamentarian asserts, either explicitly or implicitly, an interpretation of the political environment they enter and their place within it. In so doing they create a moral dimension to their 'performance' by obliging persons around them to value and treat them in a certain way (Goffman 1971: 24). The ethnic performance in these contexts is certainly conditioned by values that have already been internalised. However, it is also clear that through forms of 'mimicry' there are explicit incentives and rewards, and this includes beyond representations of collective cultural agency. In other words, signification of familiar and particular ethnic tropes within the first speech, and most likely other political environments, would underpin the visibility of one's political presence to certain normative audiences and, in some instances, might even enable the accumulation of social prestige and political influence. What is embedded in such a claim is the idea that the performance of ethnicity may have instrumental *and* situational utility.

Coercive Mimeticism and the Instrumentality of Ethnic Identity in the Asian Australian Parliamentary First Speech

It is relevant at this stage to briefly track back through some of the sociological and social anthropological traditions that are invoked in the theorisation of ethnic identity performance. One recent concept is described by Richard Jenkins as the 'internal-external dialectic of identification'. Jenkins defines this 'as an ongoing and in practice simultaneous synthesis of (internal) self-definition and the (external) definitions of oneself offered by others' (Jenkins 2004: 18). Within this internal-external dialectic, there are variously configured concepts of self. The most important of these is a dichotomy between self-image and public-image (Jenkins 1996). Such a distinction separates identifications we might internalise from the ones we present to the world. The self-image is experiential, while the public image is social and self-aware. The public-image is there for others and constructed instrumentally to make moral claims. It is significant to emphasise that, through this theoretical underpinning, there is a transparent necessity to recognise the *public image* that individuals 'present' to the world. Goffman explored this in great depth in *The Presentation of Self in Everyday Life* when he portrayed social interaction effectively as performance, constituted by a 'front', the part of an individual's performance that 'regularly functions in a general and fixed fashion to define the situation for those who observe the performance' (Goffman 1971: 32). This performance invokes, utilises and positions social norms as an essential characteristic of all social interaction. There is a fundamental necessity for this front to be acceptable within the scope of social expectations. It is through recognition, or what Goffman describes as 'dramatic realisation' (Goffman 1971: 40-44), that discursive exchange becomes possible.

Jenkins' and Goffman's assertions are fleshed out in the context of postcolonial and racialised subjectivities. In particular, contexts in which the 'public image' of individuals from minority or 'subaltern' populations are conscribed by robust and embedded 'nominal identities' (Jenkins 1996: 24) imposed by hegemonic, dominant culture. Rey Chow coins the term 'coercive mimeticism' in her book *The Ethnic Protestant and the Spirit of Capitalism*. Chow uses this term to describe:

> a process in which those who are marginal to mainstream culture are expected, by what Albert Memmi calls 'the mark of the plural' to resemble and replicate the very banal preconceptions that have been appended to them, a process in which they are expected to objectify themselves in accordance with the already seen, and thus, to authenticate the familiar imagining of them as ethnics. (Chow 2002: 107)

Ebron expands on this by suggesting that 'it is also possible that speakers are caught up in repetitive modes, that is, narrative conventions that encourage them to repeat stereotypes, which allow them to remain in the conversation' (Ebron 2002: 29). In analysing these speeches, the convergence of cultural and political capital upon ethnicity is apparent. What is of peculiar interest is the notion that use of these tropes and narratives may be instrumentally necessary to 'remain in the conversation'.[8]

Identity does involve a multivalent set of relationships between collectives that are effectively, as Ien Ang describes, 'open and indeterminate signifiers' (Ang 1994: 73). These collectives maintain relationships through discrete but perpetually reconstituting cultural markers. However, in recouping strategic essentialisms to given groups— for example, transnational subjectivity to the Chinese diaspora—we are simultaneously implicated in non-strategic essentialisms made *about* us as categories. Our relationships with particular groups—be they ethnic, gendered, etc.—are constituted from both our identifications with them and the way we are positioned within them, by members of that group and, more importantly, by entities outside of it. Often, these exist as stronger and more durable processes of cultural affixation. For example, David Parker brings attention to the 'racialized modes of visualization' that impact upon his interviewees' notions of selfhood (Parker 1995: 24; see also Omi and Winant 1986: 24). These 'nominal identities' are necessary to negotiate various roles, and thus become part of the identity performance necessary to interact socially in an external world that is often regulated by hegemonic norms circulating within dominant culture. It is relevant to observe, however, that such nominal identities may be discursively appropriated and are not always internalised. In the context of the first speech, enacting an identity performance through citizenship is conscribed by the desire to be recognised within that frame as a citizen and parliamentarian, and as an identity performance that serves other instrumental purposes.

A given performance's materiality insists we consider social norms as culturally and dialogically-situated. From within the context of Bakhtin's speech genre we find that coercive mimeticism may in some situations similarly enable the ethnic subject in that these 'utterances [may be] constructed through the sedimented and ideological expression of past interaction between a community of speakers', but 'have a particular meaning that is dislodged from a dialogical context to be transformed into "public property" to the extent that past accents can be appropriated by a new community of speakers and re-accented to gain new themes within a present social context' (Roberts 2004: 890). This occurs in what Ebron describes as a 'frame of enactment' (Ebron 2002:1). In situations where coercive mimeticism comes into play, in each recurrence of this social site a frame of enactment that allows moments for negotiating and constructing the self presents itself. This assertion about 'enacting' performative frames is not to trivialise the role of racial hegemonies in conditioning Asian Australian identity performances. It is, in fact, to assert that in the deployment of the identity performance Asian Australians are coopted, whether consciously or not, within the processes by which hegemonies are policed and perpetuated.

If we take Chun's advice and look at the 'contexts wherein facets of identity are deemed relevant' (Chun 1996: 134) it would appear the purpose of identity performance often lies beyond the formation of one's sense of self. These perspectives reflect with varying emphasis the complex engagements human beings make with the external world, and the abundant motivations by which we are conditioned. It is possible to utilise deeply-embedded cultural attachments for the purpose of financial or political gain. Kay Anderson, for example, illustrates this through Vancouver's Chinese community who:

> at strategic moments in their history consented to and even appropriated the identity and neighbourhood stereotypes that since the late nineteenth century had structured their subordination. This is particularly evident in recent years, when Canada's policy of multiculturalism has made 'Chineseness' a politically effective

counter-ideology. Chinatown merchants, in particular, have seen their own advantage in neighbourhood upgrading schemes that attempt to refurbish the district in the image of Western constructs of the East. (Anderson 1991: 27)[9]

Nonetheless, the exploitative use of cultural symbols does not in itself mean that there is an absence of behaviours and cultural traditions by which such a person or group might be entangled and attached. These are not incongruous motivations.

It is not possible to conclude in an analysis of this sort that Australian culture always compels coercively mimetic identity performances, but that was not the original intention. Rather, I argue that different contexts authorise and condition varying degrees and types of mimesis. In addition, Australian political cultures authorise and condition specific discursive boundaries, especially around Australian citizenship. Coercively mimetic identity performances have particular effect in certain contested sites, such as that of the parliamentary first speech. Identity performances and performative tropes in these and other discursive political contexts reflect sites where the perpetuation of ideological norms and cultural stereotypes are simultaneously tied to the trajectories of symbolic capital and political influence. Some of these trajectories are symbols of state power that encourage narrow, simplistic discourse, where citizenship is pressured into maintaining itself as both 'an instrument and object of interrelated and material symbolic closure' (Pearson 2002: 994) and where identity performances are compelled to be 'proper' (Goffman 1971: 45). My analysis suggests that Asian Australian parliamentarians, in general, have found symbolic capital in the performance of ethnic identity. When we acknowledge the trajectories of symbolic capital in sites of this sort, it is possible to conclude that a cautious deployment of agency does not necessarily occur through radically-divergent behaviours. We must look and think more critically about the boundaries by which certain sites are contained.

Notes

[1] Another important qualifer is that Sang Nguyen, the only Vietnamese Australian state parliamentarian, has been unintentionally excluded from this sample. In observation of this failing, however, Mr Nguyen's inclusion would not significantly improve the quality or complexity of the data represented here. His presence in Victorian state parliament, if anything, reinforces the under-representation of Vietnamese Australian communities in the centres of political influence.

[2] See also *Racist Culture* (Goldberg 1993) in which Goldberg explores the concept of racism and how the idea of race has been manipulated to exclude certain populations.

[3] Beyond the implications of the *Immigration Restriction Act* (1901) legislation such as the *Commonwealth War Precautions Regulations* (1916), *Aliens Registration Act* (1920) and the *National Security Act* (1939) have compelled the registration of 'alien' populations. Furthermore, the application of apparently unrelated legislation such as Queensland's *Licensing* and *Customs Duties Act* has previously classified and economically marginalised Chinese business owners (Queensland State Archives).

[4] David Brown characterises Australian multiculturalism as *corporatist*, in that the state finds it necessary 'to construct and institutionalise a static image of each community in which its

values, attributes, goals and leaders are stable and predefined' (Brown 2000: 143). To sustain this static image 'corporatism needs coopted leaders who can control their ethnic constituents, but who are not, in practice, responsive to the variations in the interests, situations and needs of those whom they claim to represent' (143).

[5] A recent convergence of these discourses is observable in the 'Killing Multiculturalism' (2004) episode of the forum-style current affairs TV program *Insight* that brought together a host of politically-divergent public commentators and generated vociferous debate. This episode occurred as a result of former ALP Opposition Leader Mark Latham's pre-election comments in which he sought to rearticulate the relevance of multiculturalism in Australia.

[6] Kim Rubenstein observes the lack of constitutional, judicial and legislative attention to the concept of Australian citizenship in *The High Court of Australia and the Legal Dimension of Citizenship* (Rubenstein 2000). As Rubenstein recognises in this article, much judicial attention revolves around defining who is included and excluded through the category of 'citizen'.

[7] Requests made by the Police Federation of Australia in October 2005 to indemnify police from civil actions for racial profiling indicate another disturbing trend in which racially-differentiated citizenship may soon be legislatively enshrined (AM Program 2005). One might also look at the continued paucity of the living standards of Indigenous Australians under Howard's policies of 'practical reconciliation' as other overt ways in which racial identity continues to disenfranchise specific minority populations.

[8] These considerations have also been inspired by Mary Louise Pratt's ideas around 'transculturation', which she suggests describes 'how subordinated or marginal groups select or invent from materials transmitted to them by a dominant or metropolitan culture' (Pratt 1992: 6).

[9] See also Flemming Christiansen in *Chinatown: Europe* who discusses 'the political economy of the ethnic boundary' and how this 'creates ingenious expressions of ethnic culture' (Christiansen 2003: 179).

References

'Killing Multiculturalism'. *Insight*. SBS. First aired 1 June 2004. Online transcript, <http://www.sbs.com.au/insight/mmarchive.php3?daysum=2004-06-01#> (accessed 28 January 2006).

'Police worried about legal action from anti-terrorism laws'. *ABC Radio AM Program*, 2005, 27 September, <http://www.abc.net.au/am/content/2005/s1469047.htm> (accessed 28 December 2005).

Anderson, K. *Vancouver's Chinatown: Racial Discourse in Canada, 1875–1980*. Montreal: McGill-Queen's University Press, 1991.

Ang, I. 'The Differential Politics of Chineseness.' *Southeast Asian Journal of Social Science* 22 (1994): 72–79.

Ang, I. and Stratton, J. 'Multiculturalism in Crisis: The New Politics of Race and National Identity in Australia.' *On Not Speaking Chinese: Living Between Asia and the West*. London: Routledge, 2001. 95–111.

Arena, F. *Raism*, 1996, 30 May <http://www.parliament.nsw.gov.au/prod/parlment/hansart.nsf/V3Key/LC19960530031> (accessed 15 October 2005).

Barth, F. 'Introduction.' *Ethnic Groups and Boundaries: The Social Organization of Cultural Difference*. Ed. F. Barth. London: George Allen and Unwin, 1969. 9–38.

Broinowski, A. *The Yellow Lady: Australian Impressions of Asia*. Melbourne: Oxford University Press, 1992.

Brown, D. *Contemporary Nationalism: Civic, Ethnocultural and Multicultural Politics*. London: Routledge, 2000.

Castles, S. 'The Future of Australian Citizenship in a Globalising World.' *Individual, Community, Nation: Fifty Years of Australian Citizenship*. Ed. K. Rubenstein. Melbourne: Australian Scholarly Publishing, 2000. 119–34.

Chae, H. S. 'Talking Back to the Asian Model Minority Discourse: Korean-Origin Youth Experiences in High School.' *Journal of Intercultural Studies* 25.1 (2004): 59–73.

Choi, M. W. *First Speech*, 2001, 15 April <http://www.parliament.qld.gov.au/hansard/view/legislativeAssembly/documents/memberBio/InauguralSpeech/Choi.pdf> (accessed 15 October 2005).

Chow, R. *The Protestant Ethnic and the Spirit of Capitalism*. New York: Columbia University Press, 2002.

Christiansen, F. *Chinatown, Europe: An Exploration of Overseas Chinese Identity in the 1990s*. London: RoutledgeCurzon, 2003.

Chun, A. 'Fuck Chineseness: On the Ambiguities of Ethnicity as Culture as Identity.' *Boundary* 23.2 (1996): 111–38.

Commonwealth Ombudsman *Complaint by Mr Z about his Immigration Detention*, 2005a <http://www.comb.gov.au/publications_information/Special_Reports/2005/abridged_immi_detention_may05.pdf> (accessed 27 December 2005).

———. *Inquiry into the Circumstances of the Vivian Alvarez Matter*, 2005b <http://www.comb.gov.au/publications_information/Special_Reports/2005/alvarez_report03.pdf> (accessed 27 December 2005).

Cronin, K. *Colonial Casualties: Chinese in Early Victoria*. Singapore: Melbourne University Press, 1982.

———. 'The Yellow Agony.' *Exclusion, Exploitation and Extermination: Race Relations in Colonial Queensland*. Eds. R. Evans, K. Saunders and K. Cronin. Sydney: Australia and New Zealand Book Company, 1975. 235–340.

Davison, G. *The Use and Abuse of Australian History*. Sydney: Allen and Unwin, 2000.

Ebron, P. A. *Performing Africa*. Princeton: Princeton University Press, 2002.

Freedman, A. L. *Political Participation and Ethnic Minorities: Chinese Overseas in Malaysia, Indonesia, and the United States*. New York: Routledge, 2000.

Freedman, B. 'Jewish Leaders Concerned by Howard speech.' *Australian Jewish News*, 1996, 27 September, <http://www.ajn.com.au/pages/archives/one-nation/one-nation-23.html> (accessed 23 August 2005).

Gibson, R., I. McAllister, and T. Swenson. 'The Politics of Race and Immigration in Australia: One Nation Voting in the 1998 Election.' *Race and Ethnic Studies* 25.5 (2002): 823–44.

Goffman, E. *Stigma: Notes on the Management of Spoiled Identity*. New York: Touchstone, 1963.

———. *Strategic Interaction*. Philadelphia: University of Pennsylvania Press, 1969.

———. *The Presentation of Self in Everyday Life*. New York, Doubleday Anchor Books, originally published in 1959, 1971.

Goldberg, D. T. *Racist culture*. Cambridge, Mass: Blackwell Publishers, 1993.

House of Representatives Practice, 5th Edition, 2005 <http://www.aph.gov.au/house/pubs/PRACTICE/chapter5.htm#fir> (accessed 15 October 2005).

Goldberg, D. T. *Racist State*. Oxford: Blackwell Publishers, 2002.

Hage, G. *White Nation: Fantasies of White Supremacy in a Multicultural Society*. Sydney: Pluto Press, 1998.

Hanson, P. *Maiden Speech*, 1996, 10 September <http://parlinfoweb.aph.gov.au/piweb/view_document.aspx?ID=41338&TABLE=HANSARDR> (accessed 15 October 2005).

Healy, E. 'The Unity Party and the Attempt to Mobilise Australian Electoral Support for Multiculturalism.' *People and Place* 7.3 (1999): 51–62.

———. 'The Unity Party and the Myth of the Ethnic Vote.' *People and Place* 9.4 (2001): 61–70.

Hickey, M. *8. Reconciliation and Multiculturalism: Seventh Assembly First Session 19/11/96 Parliamentary Record No. 28*, 1996, November 20 <http://notes.nt.gov.au/lant/hansard/

HANSARD7.NSF/0/d2a0628beb5a1a6569256464001579e6?OpenDocument > (accessed 15 October 2005).

Howard, J. W. *Motion of Reconciliation*, 1999, 26 August <http://www.pm.gov.au/news/speeches/1999/reconciliation2608.htm> (accessed 15 October 2005).

Ip, M., and N. Murphy. *Aliens at my Table: Asians in the Eyes of New Zealanders*. New Zealand: Penguin Books, 2005.

Jackson, S. *Professing Performance: Theatre in the Academy from Philology to Performativity*. Cambridge: Cambridge University Press, 2004.

Jakubowicz, A. 'White noise: Australia's Struggle with Multiculturalism.' *Working Through Whiteness: International Perspectives*. Ed. C. Levine-Rasky. Albany: State University of New York Press, 2002. 107–25.

Jenkins, R. *Social Identity*. London: Routledge, 1996.

——. *Social Identity*, Second edition. London: Routledge, 2004.

Johnson, M. *First Speech*, 2002, 13 February <http://www.aph.gov.au/house/members/first-speech.asp?id=AMX> (accessed 15 October 2005).

Kelly, P. 'Howard and his haters miss real migration story.' *The Australian*, 2005, 21 December, <http://www.theaustralian.news.com.au/common/story_page/0,5744,17625992%255E12250,00.html> (accessed 28 December 2005).

Khoo, T. *Banana Bending: Asian-Australian and Asian-Canadian Literatures*. Hong Kong: McGill-Queens University Press and Hong Kong University Press, 2003.

——. 'Re-Siting Australian Identity: Configuring the Chinese Citizen in Diana Giese's *Astronauts, Lost Souls and Dragons* and William Yang's *Sadness*.' *Bastard Moon: Essays on Chinese Australian Writing. Special Issue of Otherland Literary Journal (No. 7)*. Ed. W. Ommundsen. Melbourne: Otherland, 2001. 95–109.

King, D. and Wallace, R. 'Court rules 30-year resident wrongly deported.' *The Weekend Australian*, 2006, 7–8 January. 4.

Kuah-Pearce K. E. and Hu-Dehart, E. Eds. *Voluntary Associations in the Chinese Diaspora*. Hong Kong: Hong Kong University Press, 2004.

Lee, R. G. *Orientals: Asian Americans in Popular Culture*. Philadelphia: Temple University Press, 1999.

Lim, H. *First Speech (Address-in-reply)*, 1996, May 15. <http://tex.parliament.vic.gov.au/bin/texhtmlt?form=VicHansard.dumpall&db=hansard91&dodraft=0&house=ASSEMBLY&speech=26285&activity=Governor's+Speech&title=Address-in-reply&date1=15&date2=May&date3=1996&query=true%0a%09and+%28+data+contains+'SPEAKER'%0a%09or+data+contains+'LIM'+%29%0a%09and+%28+members+contains+'SPEAKER'%09or+members+contains+'LIM'+%29%0a%09and+%28+hdate.hdate_3+=+1996+%29%0a%09and+%28+hdate.hdate_2+contains+'May'+%29%0a%09and+%28+hdate.hdate_1+=+15+%29> (accessed 15 October 2005).

Lin, J. *Reconstructing Chinatown: Ethnic Enclave, Global Change*. Minneapolis: University of Minnesota Press, 1998.

Lo, J. 'Beyond Happy Hybridity: Performing Asian Australian Identities.' *Alter/Asian: Asian Australian Identities in Art, Media and Popular Culture*. Eds. I. Ang, S. Chalmers, L. Law and M. Thomas. Annandale, NSW: Pluto Press, 2000. 152–68.

Lowe, L. *Immigrant Acts*. London: Duke University Press, 1996.

Multicultural Australia: United in Diversity. Updating the 1999 New Agenda for Multicultural Australia: Strategic directions for 2003–2006, 2003 <http://www.immi.gov.au/multicultural/_inc/pdf_doc/united_diversity/united_diversity.pdf> (accessed 28 December 2005).

Macintyre, S., and A. Clark.. *The history wars*. Melboune: Melbourne University Press, 2003.

Markus, A. *Fear and Hatred: Purifying Australia and California 1850–1901*. Sydney: Hale and Iremonger, 1979.

Morson, G. S., and C. Emerson. *Mikhail Bakhtin: Creation of a Prosaics*. Stanford: Stanford University Press, 1990.
National Multicultural Advisory Council *Australian Multiculturalism for a New Century. Report*, 1999, April. <http://www.immi.gov.au/multicultural/_inc/publications/nmac/report.pdf> (accessed 28 December 2005).
Newman, G. *Queensland Election, 1998 (Research Note 49 1997–98)* <http://www.aph.gov.au/library/pubs/rn/1997-98/98rn49.htm> (accessed 28 December 2005).
Ng, W. C. *The Chinese in Vancouver, 1945–80*. Vancouver: UBC Press, 1999.
Nicolacopoulos, T., and G. Vassilacopoulos. 'Racism, Foreigner Communities and the Ontopathology of White Australian Subjectivity.' *Whitening Race*. Ed. A. Moreton-Robinson. Canberra: Aboriginal Studies Press, 2004. 32–47.
Nolan, D. 'Interpellating Audiences: The Public, the Media and Pauline Hanson.' *Southern Review: Communication, Politics and Culture* 34.1 (2001): 60–77.
NSW Legislative Assembly Practice and Procedure Book 2002. <http://www.parliament.nsw.gov.au/prod/la/precdent.nsf/0/F1A09C05D2919A08CA256AD4001B7A21> (accessed 15 October 2005).
O'Chee, W. G. *First Speech*, 1990, 9 May <http://parlinfoweb.aph.gov.au/piweb/view_document.aspx?ID=153754&TABLE=HANSARDS> (accessed 15 October 2005).
Omi, M., and H. Winant. *Racial Formation in the United States: From the 1960s to the 1980s*. New York: Routledge, 1986.
Ong, A. and Nonini, D. (Eds.) *Underground Empires: The Cultural Politics of Modern Chinese Transnationalism*. New York: Routledge.
Palumbo-Liu, D. *Asian/American: Historical Crossings of a Racial Frontier*. Stanford: Stanford University Press, 1999.
Parekh, B. *Rethinking Multiculturalism: Cultural Diversity and Political Theory*. London: Macmillan, 2000.
Parker, D. *Through Different Eyes: The Cultural Identities of Young Chinese People in Britain*. Aldershot: Avebury, 1995.
Pearson, D. 'Theorizing Citizenship in British Settler Societies.' *Ethnic and Racial Studies* 23.6 (2002): 989–1012.
Pfitzner, B. S. 'First Speech.' *South Australia Parliament, Legislative Council Debates*. Adelaide: Govt. Print, 1990. 1475–478.
Pratt, M. L. *Imperial Eyes: Travel Writing and Transculturation*. London: Routledge, 1992.
Price, C. A. *The Great White Walls are Built: Restrictive Immigration to North America and Australasia 1836–1888*. Canberra: Australian Institute of International Affairs, 1974.
Queensland State Archives (Files PRV6817, 6932, 6719, A73463, PRV7449-1-1).
Roberts, J. M. 'From Populist to Political Dialogue in the Public Sphere: A Bakhtinian approach to understanding a place for radical utterances in London 1684–1812.' *Cultural Studies* 18.6 (2004): 884–910.
Rubenstein, K. 'The High Court of Australia and the Legal Dimension of Citizenship.' *Individual, Community, Nation: Fifty Years of Australian Citizenship*. Ed. K. Rubenstein. Melbourne, Australian Scholarly Publishing, 2000. 21–32.
Sham-Ho, H. W. *Racism and Joint Statement from the five Members of Parliament of Chinese Descent*, 1996, 30 October <http://www.anzacatt.org.au/prod/parlment/hansart.nsf/V3Key/LC19961030051> (accessed 15 October 2005).
——. *Maiden Speech*, 1988, 25 August <http://www.parliament.nsw.gov.au/prod/parlment/members.nsf/1fb6ebed995667c2ca256ea100825164/bc83f47fefc3937b4a25672e0002e1d6/$FILE/Sham-Ho.PDF> (accessed 15 October 2005).
Shepherd, D. 'Bakhtin and the Reader.' *Bakhtin and Cultural Theory*. Eds. K. Hirschkop and D. Shepherd. Manchester: Manchester University Press, 2001. 136–154.

Shimakawa, K. *National Abjection: The Asian American Body Onstage*. Durham: Duke University Press, 2002.

Skinner, W. *Leadership and Power in the Chinese Community of Thailand*. Ithaca: Cornell University Press, 1958.

Tchen, T. *First Speech*, 1999, 11 August <http://parlinfoweb.aph.gov.au/piweb//view_document.aspx?TABLE=HANSARDS&ID=2106961> (accessed 28 January 2006).

Tsang, H. S. *First Speech*, 1999, 1 June <http://www.parliament.nsw.gov.au/prod/parlment/hansart.nsf/V3Key/LC19990601036> (accessed 15 October 2005).

Walker, D. *Anxious Nation Australia and the rise of Asia 1850–1939*. St Lucia: University of Queensland Press, 1999.

Windschuttle, K. *The Fabrication of Aboriginal History*. Syndey: Macleay Press, 2003.

Wong, P. *Motion of Condemnation*, 1999, 27 May <http://www.parliament.nsw.gov.au/prod/parlment/hansart.nsf/V3Key/LC19990527025> (accessed 15 October 15).

———. *First Speech*, 2002, 21 August http://www.aph.gov.au/Senate/senators/homepages/first_speech/sfs-aou.htm, (Retrieved October 15 2005).

Zappala, G. 'The Influence of the Ethnic Composition of Australian Federal Electorates on the Parliamentary Responsiveness of MPs to their Ethnic Sub-constituencies.' *Australian Journal of Political Science*, 33.2 (1998): 187. (Accessed from World Magazine Bank, 23 March 2004).

'Flexible Citizenship': Strategic Chinese Identities in Asian Australian Literature

Regina Lee

In her book *Flexible Citizenship: The Cultural Logics of Transnationality*, Aihwa Ong writes:

> For over a century, overseas Chinese have been the forerunners of today's multiply displaced subjects, who are always on the move both mentally and physically ... [and whose] very flexibility in geographical and social positioning is itself an effect of novel articulations between the regimes of the family, the state, and capital, the kinds of practical-technical adjustments that have implications for our understanding of the late modern subject. (1999: 2–3)

Similarly, Ouyang Yu's observation, that 'Chinese have been in Australia for the last 149 years ever since they arrived in 1848' (1998: 84), bears testimony to the enduring presence of the minority Chinese community alongside historical accounts of white settlement in Australia. Yet, in spite of the Chinese community's historical presence, 'Australian-Chinese literature is a latecomer to the scene' (Ouyang 1998: 84). It is the aim of this essay to investigate the extent to which articulations of cultural citizenship in the Chinese diaspora are enhanced as well as tempered by the flexibility and fluidity of diasporic subjectivities, with particular reference to Ouyang's *The Eastern Slope Chronicle* (2002; hereafter referred to as *ESC*). This novel represents an important development in the field of Asian Australian studies because of its timely illumination of concerns by new Chinese migrants, unveiling the conditions and the extent to which the new Chinese diaspora practice and assert their national and cultural citizenship. In addition, the notion of 'flexible citizenship' is an integral part of Asian Australian cultural identity formation, imbuing the negotiation of identity politics with an inherent fluidity that renders diasporic subjects to be extremely flexible and even unpredictable. Ong defines 'flexible citizenship' as

> the cultural logics of capital accumulation, travel, and displacement that induce subjects to respond fluidly and opportunistically to changing political-economic conditions. (1999: 6)

In this essay, an example of the 'Tiananmen Square generation' of migrants is examined in terms of hybrid national and cultural identities, focussing especially on the moments and motivations behind the shifts and slippages from one subject position to another.

In the construction of the Australian national self, the exclusion of non-white communities has performed a crucial role; as Wenche Ommundsen demonstrates, '"White Australia" would not have been possible without the spectre of a non-white future, a "yellow peril" whose main function, it would seem, was to define racial and cultural whiteness' (2005: 406). Largely owing to the model of bi-polar engagement between Australia and Asia, the inclusion of Asian Australian artists into the Australian literary canon has been highly problematic because it 'disrupts the notion of opposition between Australia and Asia by offering a more complex equation of difference' (Chiu 2000: 27). Melissa Chiu, former director of the Asia Australia Arts Centre in Sydney, has observed that 'the contribution of Asian Australian artists to this area [of cultural exchange] has been relatively limited' (2000: 27). However, with recent waves of Asian immigration and multicultural national agendas operating to erode the cultural and racial bias inherent in older models of national identity (Ommundsen 2005: 406), the concept of 'Asian Australian' has gained in popularity and usage to address a growing segment of the migrant population that identified increasingly with dual and hybrid national and cultural identities.

Ouyang's novel, as one of the more recent publications dealing with issues of hybrid diasporic subjectivity, identity politics and cross-cultural translations from the perspective of a mainland Chinese migrant in Australia,

> portrays the dilemmas facing the NESB (non-English-speaking background) migrant who has been educated to the highest level in the English language and

Australian literature only to find himself barred from academic work in his area because of his 'foreignness' and accented English. (Ommundsen 1998: 602)

Ouyang's protagonist, Dao Zhuang, serves as a thinly-veiled self-portrait, embodying the author's well-known agendas—critiquing the Australian literary establishment and institutions, the strength of the country's commitment to multiculturalism, the provision of spaces for racial minorities to engage in artistic and cultural practices— while writing about his experience as a Chinese migrant in Australia in the 1990s, 'viewing this would-be Asian country from the perspective of a dominant Asian culture' (Ommundsen 1998: 596). In her survey of Ouyang's work, Ommundsen describes him as 'The Angry Chinese Poet', 'howling his frustration, anger and infinite loneliness at an indifferent moon in a sleeping or dead suburb' (1998: 595), while challenging and disturbing his readers with the provocative nature of his writing.

Because Ouyang's personal history with Australia began only in 1991 (Ommundsen 1998), his writing deals mainly with contemporary experiences of Chinese migrants to Australia, especially during and after the June 1989 Tiananmen Square incidents. His perspective is therefore particularly illuminating for the insights it offers on yet another aspect of Chinese diasporic condition—that migratory phenomenon known as the 'Tiananmen Square generation' of migrants: 'students or "students" taking advantage of relaxed immigration regulations but without the language skills or financial backing necessary to smooth their passage into Australian society' (Ommundsen 1998: 599). This group of migrants has created a new and distinct profile among the existing communities of diasporas settled in Australia, and establishing within the Chinese community another sub-enclave that further differentiates Chinese experiences of migration. *ESC* focuses on the life of one such migrant (Dao) from China, with two other narrative voices alternately representing his alter egos: the first, Wu Liao, is a supposedly fictive character conjured by Dao, while the second, Warne, is Dao's roommate who has been issued a restraining order against approaching his ex-wife. Warne's situation appears the most unfortunate of the three characters not only because of the separation from his wife, whom he had sponsored to come to Australia 'to learn English and lead a better life' (*ESC* 370), but also because of the loss of employment and income owing to a work-related injury. From that perspective,

> [Warne] had now come to think most Australians in this country were bad, trying to hurt him and harm him, these including the insurance company, his solicitor, some of the specialists who gave him low points on the scale of evaluation, and only a handful were good, such as his interpreter who constantly rang him up to remind him of his medical appointments one day before they were due and his family doctor who was kind enough to regularly write him medical certificates. (*ESC* 29)

It is common for a migrant in this position to harbour such views because the trauma of physical and cultural dislocation is now exacerbated by the bureaucracy of the new country that has marginalised him and denied him access to socio-economic forms of support and other resources. This disheartening aspect of migration, explored in

Ouyang's novel, articulates an often underrepresented and unaccounted experience of diasporic Chinese in Australia. The two characters Wu and Warne supplement Dao's main narrative voice in providing a fuller picture of the migration process, creating a dualistic narrative structure between Dao and Wu. This dualism, Ommundsen (2005) suggests, is a 'mirroring' or 'doubling' that has become a recurrent motif of diasporic writing wherein the question of defining 'Chineseness' has become an object of obsessive interest and contestation over the last decade. At another level, the dual narrative mode also signals an identity crisis in the protagonist who, having migrated to Australia, is now confronted with cultural conflict of a different kind when he returns to his homeland as an Australian.

The Eastern Slope Chronicle is the title that Dao gives to his 'Australian novel in Chinese' (20), a project in which he is painstakingly engaged.[1] In writing this novel, Dao inevitably touches on the lives of people in his immediate circle, namely his wife, roommates in Australia and friends in China when he returns to his hometown. Dao's novel also serves as a means for him to record and disseminate his observations about the Australian way of life in his particular experiences. One particular observation that he shares with migrants is the feeling of tremendous isolation, that 'Australia was found to be a continent empty of memory, of history, of anything human' (*ESC* 21). Similarly, his wife had come to Australia under the impression, after reading Henry Lawson, that 'the bush in his stories represented the quintessential Australia'. However, upon arriving, she found instead 'miles and miles of monotonous, drab, boring suburbia which nearly drove her mad' (*ESC* 14). In addition to this sense of physical isolation, the experience of exclusion at more symbolic levels is also a common one that faces these Chinese migrants. As Dao writes,

> Like many who came before or around the time when I came, I regarded Australia as a land of opportunity. However, that opportunity seemed to exist only for Australians and people from other countries of the British Commonwealth and not the likes of me. Even though I had sworn my allegiance, Australia saw in me an un-Australian. (*ESC* 25)

Geo-physical isolation and exclusion notwithstanding, the greatest difficulty for these Chinese migrants appears to be the negotiation of 'Australianness', or the sense of an Australian identity, while overcoming the complexities of cross-cultural exchanges and differences. Here, the issue of what it means to be Chinese is briefly cast aside, or perhaps subsumed, in order to engage with questions about the constitution of Australian identity. The inclusion of 'Asian' in 'Australian' represents, in this case, an attempt to fully immerse the migrant narrative into the national imaginary and consciousness. This move, however, has repercussions when Dao finds himself fielding questions about his political and cultural citizenship during his time in China. In a letter that Dao receives from an associate in China, from the Shanghai Oriental University, the question is raised as to 'how cultural identity persists despite changes' (*ESC* 27). His correspondent, Professor Zhong, writes:

> A living example is that many Chinese, once they become citizens of other countries, still try to keep their own culture alive. They eat their own food, wear their own types of clothing, speak their own language, and go their own ways. Does the foreign citizenship do nothing at all to change them? Do they themselves not feel that in adopting a foreign citizenship they would be obliged to adopt the culture of the mainstream society of the country and become more like them than us? How many years does it normally take a foreign citizen to shed his cultural, if not racial, identity in this identity-changing process or does their identity remain unchanged for always? (*ESC* 27)

This passage addresses salient points that arise in any discussion of dual or hybrid identities, and is especially relevant to the study and development of 'Asian Australian' as a concept as well as in the form of visible and physical difference. The passage begins with a reference to the homeland-idealising practices and tendencies of new Chinese migrants in Western countries and draws the two cultures into diametrical opposition; in focussing on the process by which migrants become 'more like them than us', the two cultures are already predicated as being mutually exclusive and, moreover, that the embracing of one cultural identity will result in the 'shedding' or 'loss' of another. This perspective lends itself to the belief in the *quantifiable* aspects of cultural identity, surmising that the 'shoring up' of traits of one cultural identity will act as a defence against being influenced by another cultural identity. In other words, this passage highlights commonly held beliefs in the mutual exclusivity of different or opposing cultures, and the conviction that taking on foreign citizenship and adopting foreign cultural habits will lead to the erosion and eradication of one's 'original' cultural identity. This narrow, but pervasive, view of cultural difference sees the acquisition of a new cultural identity not as an adding on to, but as a replacement of, one's previous cultural identity and affiliations. Although Dao experiences the acquisition of his Australian citizenship as an 'adding on' to his Chinese identity, he is also constantly having to renegotiate the meaning/s of his new dual citizenship and identity within himself as well as communicating this process and its predicaments to people around him. Here, the concept of 'Asian Australian' is keenly felt *not* as empowerment for the diasporic subject but as a crisis of identity and source of bewilderment and contestation.

Throughout the novel, comparisons between and complaints about life in both China and Australia abound, mainly because of the promises—often unfulfilled—of opportunities and a better life that Australia represents to the diasporic Chinese imagination. The novel opens with its first chapter titled 'A New Beginning', which belies any propitiatory notions about Dao's life in Australia. Although this was perhaps meant to signify auspiciously the new life that was expected to accompany the granting of his Australian citizenship, the changes and upheavals that quickly follow set the tone for the cynical pragmatism and gloomy pessimism in the novel. As far as his wife was concerned, Dao's 'living conditions fell far short of her expectations' (*ESC* 14), because her status as a professional means that the experience of migrating to Australia is seen as a regressive move on the socio-economic ladder.

The 'better life' sought by many migrants often remains illusory because of language difficulties and/or the lack of other qualifications that hinder and impede assimilation into Australian society. The disgruntlement and frustrations of migrants, as depicted in the novel, stem from restrictions and curtailments of their social, cultural and economic mobility in a new and foreign space. The attempts by Dao's wife to integrate with white Australian society can be seen as representing the desire by migrants to assimilate quickly so as to exploit the advantages offered by their changed circumstances. In portraying Dao's wife in this harsh and unsentimental light, Ouyang not only reverses the stereotypical assumptions that are frequently attached to gender roles—such as perceptions that men dominate the migration process, with the women who tend to accompany them being in supporting roles—but also undermines several clichéd cultural 'norms' concerning male and female behaviour in the process and aftermath of migration. Confronted with change, Dao's insecurities begin to surface while his wife, on the other hand, revels in and even schemes to take advantage of her new-found and novel experiences brought on by migration.

After Dao's wife leaves him and takes out an intervention order against him, he begins to suspect that 'she would go for another man, preferably a white man with blue eyes with whom she could have a blue-eyed and perhaps black-haired baby' (12). In this, Dao realises that she would probably succeed because 'Australian men had a peculiar fondness for Asian women in general and Chinese women in particular' (*ESC* 17).

In spite of her educational qualifications and professional status, she nonetheless succumbs to the belief that

> Western men looked far nicer than the ordinary Chinese men on the street and they are far less chauvinistic and more humane as you could easily see in the imported films from Hollywood. (*ESC* 17)

The power of the Western media is, in this instance, too conveniently held responsible for shaping and affirming her (and many Asian women's) attitudes towards race and culture, culminating in the presumed preference for particular cultural types. In addition, the naïve and unquestioning readiness with which she places her faith in Western institutions and their products means that her engagement with Australia can only ever be a superficial one because of her preoccupation with image-based notions of 'reality' (when we consider her desire to believe in Hollywood films). This is particularly accurate when we consider that much of her dissatisfaction with Dao stemmed mainly from the physical and material aspects of their lives in Australia. In writing the character of Dao's wife, the author pointedly acknowledges and emphasises the perpetuation of Orientalist fantasies by both Asian and Western cultures, especially the stereotype of the submissive and exotic Asian woman vis-à-vis the more dominant white male. The concept of 'Asian Australian', when applied to Asian women, in this instance carries with it a certain cultural 'cachet' because of deeply ingrained Western attitudes and perceptions about Asian, especially Chinese, femininity. These attitudes, moreover, are frequently compounded by many Asian women too, who readily and willingly perform Orientalist notions of femininity because of the desire to be seen or partnered with a white Western male—an arrangement that is often seen as elevating the social status of the Asian woman. Dao's wife's own admission that 'Western men looked far nicer' (especially in Hollywood films) attests to this culpability, which also exposes her motives for wanting to assimilate quickly.

Among the groups of Chinese migrating to Australia in recent years, the Tiananmen Square generation of migrants also represents a distinct community who had applied for and obtained permanent residency or Australian citizenship but are now choosing to return to China.[2] As one such migrant himself, Dao acquires not only a new Australian citizenship status but also, along with it, a stronger sense of socio-economic and political security *relative* to his Chinese nationality and identity. Echoing the sentiments of many of his compatriots who have chosen to return to China, he believes himself to be fortunately well-positioned to exploit the benefits of his dual citizenship. While in Australia, he enjoys access to the 'very good system of social security' that paid 'unemployment benefits on a fortnightly basis that was worth more than a Chinese professor's monthly salary on the current international exchange rate' (*ESC* 45). At the same time, and more importantly for Dao, Australian citizenship meant that 'if things did not work out [in China], I could always pack up and go, safe in the knowledge that I now was an Australian, without the restrictions that a Chinese national would normally have' (*ESC* 72). In economic and socio-political terms, Dao's migration to Australia has certainly yielded the very benefits that migrants often seek in relocating to a new country.

However, Dao's rather smug sense of security and political freedom, when conceptualised as 'self-sufficiency', is also quickly and grimly underscored by his subsequent realisation that

> he could not possibly have the best of both worlds, that is, to have the kind of human activity available in China that makes you feel like a human being and to have the kind of freedom in Australia that helps you to do whatever you wish to do. On the contrary, he was now stuck helplessly with the worst of both worlds, the kind of quiet that Australia condemned the poor to and the lack of China. (*ESC* 100)

This desire for some form of security while not letting go of the comforts of a familiar environment explains, to a large extent, the return to China by many of Dao's friends who have obtained their permanent resident status and citizenship. The notion of 'flexible citizenship' in this instance carries with it very tangible economic and political benefits that seemingly enhance the hybrid subject positions of diasporic Chinese. Indeed, while being held up at the airport in China, Dao finds himself observing the commotion as 'an outsider' and crediting Australia with '[having] done much to improve [his] patience or impatience' (*ESC* 36). As a returning migrant, he admits to finding himself being 'more tolerant, perhaps because I was Australian?'

(*ESC* 36). This shift in his national-political affiliations represents a sudden and unexpected distancing from his Chinese cultural identity; now in China, Dao chooses to validate his foreign citizenship, when he had previously been lamenting 'the lack of China' and yearning for the comforts of his homeland. The ease with which Dao shifts his national and cultural affiliations thus undermines any sense of permanence or stability about his new identity as an Australian. Nonetheless, in spite of being marginalised in Australia, he manages to draw empowerment from the fluidity and transience of his doubtful positioning in Australian society. Dao's dual citizenship status therefore exemplifies that type of flexibility upon which Ong has commented. However, the mood of the novel speaks more about a pervasive sense of desolation stemming from having 'escaped' the idealised homeland than about the liberating effects of being a multiple-passport holder. While this can be largely attributed to the lack of opportunities for Dao to integrate socially and economically with his adoptive country, there is also another aspect of his now-flexible citizenship status that requires scrutiny.

A significant and especially engaging aspect of being a diasporic Chinese person in Australia, as highlighted in this novel, is the subject's identification with a *particular type of Chineseness*. Because of the difficulties and constraints that Dao has experienced in his migration, his perspectives on and relationships with both China and Australia have become increasingly ambivalent and complex. Towards China, his feelings

> were not unlike those of a former prisoner who, having broken free, vows never to return but nevertheless cannot resist the dreams of a long-forgotten past that keeps haunting him, dreams that are to become part of his Australian identity. (*ESC* 20)

While

> Australia, in its own quiet and unassertive ways, seems to have a shrinking effect on me so that by the end of ten years I found myself leaner, tighter-lipped, silenter [*sic*], moving closer to the edge of life. I wouldn't even wish to utter the name of China. (*ESC* 20)

In Australia, socio-economic circumstances seem to have conspired to make him feel trapped and helpless, without a job or drifting from one to another while living on social welfare payments. This exclusion from mainstream Australian society and its workforce represents, to him, a real impediment to his successful integration and assimilation with Australian culture and leads to deep cynicism about the freedoms that had attracted him to the country in the first place. In the words of his roommate Warne, 'The Australian government is as bad as the Chinese government. If they don't want you to stay in Australia, they will invent a perfect China and talk you into going back to it' (*ESC* 32).

With this statement, the mutual exclusion of 'Asian' and 'Australian' renders the concept of 'Asian Australian' null and void, while also serving as a reminder that 'Asian Australian' has yet to receive validation as a full-fledged entity in the political arena. When the categories of 'Asian' and 'Australian' are pitted against each other in mutual exclusion, there is hardly any middle ground or 'in-between' space for the dual citizenship holder to comfortably inhabit. Consequently, in spite of advancements in the field of diaspora studies and the popularisation of concepts such as 'hybridity' and 'flexible citizenship', the tendency still remains for identity and citizenship to be conceptualised in a polarised and fundamentally essentialised manner. This accounts largely for the choice that Dao feels compelled to make between his Chinese and Australian identities when he finds himself in China after having spent ten years in Australia. The flexibility of his dual citizenship status that Dao had earlier exploited gives way to a highly circumspect view of migration when he delivers his lecture on the topic of culture and multiculturalism to a group of students in China. Based on his personal experiences, and having learnt that the 'responsibilities and privileges' as an Australian citizen in no way guaranteed that he would 'get a job consistent with [his] qualifications' (*ESC* 48), his lecture provides a platform from which he gives vent to particular frustrations, as well as to illuminate his underlying and personal agendas. His talk, however, represents only one perspective about multicultural living in Australia and is necessarily tainted by his personal vendettas against the dominant cultural establishments and authorities that regulate in his life in Australia. From this skewed perspective, he can therefore only speak of the negative aspects of migration and Australian multiculturalism to his audience. However, the irony about the topics of his lecture—cultural identity and multiculturalism—is that he is still in the position of an 'outsider' to Australian society. He is also now in the position of an outsider to China because of his efforts to dissociate himself from Chinese society.

From the time Dao arrives in China, he begins to assume, very self-consciously, the role of the token Australian to his Chinese friends: 'Here I sat like a fool, aware of other eyes on me, which were probably observing how *the Australian* would behave in front of these oriental, I mean Chinese girls'. (*ESC* 81; emphasis added)

In China and in the presence of his Chinese friends, Dao's labelling of the girls as 'Oriental' is an especially affected gesture that signifies his increasing identification with the West and his adoption of a Westernised perspective. The seriousness with which he carries his new national identity gestures towards self-aggrandisement; yet this identity instantly comes under scrutiny when one of the girls in the dance hall questions its 'authenticity': 'How can it be that you are an Australian? [...] You look Chinese. You speak Chinese. And you look no different from your friends' (*ESC* 82). Dao realises the difficulty of explaining 'about the confusing meaning of identity and nationality', because he had not even worked that one out himself (*ESC* 82). Still, this has not prevented him from assuming an Australian *identity* vis-à-vis the locals, as an analysis of his encounters with the taxi driver and Chinese prostitute demonstrates.

The line between Dao's cultural (Chinese) and national (Australian) identities at times becomes highly distinct and yet, at other times, blurred, allowing him to lapse into positions of ambiguity according to the situation. When in Australia, Dao's references to 'Australians' were always made with the exclusion of himself, intending only to nominate 'Westerners'. Yet, once in China, he does not refrain from telling the prostitute that his movement was 'an Australian movement' (*ESC* 77), too readily assuming the position of a 'foreigner' (*ESC* 79), and moreover revelling in its novelty and pomposity: 'Am I not an Australian in Eastern Slope? Perhaps the first one ever?' (*ESC* 123). However, in the taxi ride from the airport, he chooses not to reveal his Australian identity, telling the taxi driver instead that he was from Wuhan, because [he was] 'remembering friends' advice against revealing [his] foreign identity, for financial reasons' (*ESC* 38). More specifically, it was because '[i]n this situation or any other situation, if a foreign national was mixed up with a bunch of Chinese guys, that foreigner was expected to pay for the show because he was *supposed to be richer*' (*ESC* 83; emphasis added).

Once again, the assumptions of diasporic migrants making a better life for themselves in the new country are emphasised here, as revealed in Dao's awareness of the expectations that Chinese mainlanders had towards their overseas counterparts. His careful avoidance of any mention of his Australian identity in some situations, coupled with the enthusiastic assertion of his foreignness in other situations, indicates on the one hand, the complex negotiation of his (cultural and national) allegiances to both China and Australia. On the other hand, however, the ease with which he slips between his Chinese and Australian identities unveils a highly *motivated* and *strategic* affiliation with a particular type of each identity, dependent upon the extent to which circumstances can be exploited for his personal benefit.

In her consideration of autobiography 'as a more or less deliberate rhetorical construction of a 'self' for public, not private purposes', Ien Ang writes that 'the displayed self is a strategically fabricated performance, one which stages a *useful* identity, an identity which can be put to work' (2001: 24).

The Eastern Slope Chronicle displays the many different types of identities available to the diasporic migrant—especially the multiple-passport holder—for strategic manipulation, stemming from various motivations and for different purposes and effects. The multiplicity of diasporic subject positions illustrated here points to an increasing array of the types of diasporic consciousnesses that transcend the homeland idealising and multicultural 'gaming' variety, or the superficial and exploitative engagement with the ethos of cultural pluralism in multicultural societies. In the process of migration and cross-cultural translation, migrants are inevitably subject to complex negotiations of identity and cultural politics, such that the range of diasporic conditions, subjectivities and consciousnesses has extended beyond any notion of a single diasporic type or normative diasporic condition.

Yet, in spite of the multiple and hybrid forms of diasporic conditions and consciousnesses, perspectives from mainstream Australian society still unveil a monolithic conception of Chinese culture and identity by the dominant host culture and its institutions. In Dao's novel, his 'fictional' character, Wu, comes to Australia 'ostensibly for the study of the history of that country but secretly he knew that there was nothing much there for him to study' (*ESC* 52). He is supervised in his MA thesis by Professor Sean Dredge, a historian who knew little about Chinese and what they thought. The only reason he accepted Wu was because he thought Wu was useful to him as he was researching for a book he was going to write on the recent Chinese experience in Australia, particularly after the June 4th, 1989. [...] In a climate where all things Asian were good, the Chinese were quite a commodity to the market. As a historian, and one with a business mind, Sean was quick to seize the opportunity while others were still debating whether the option was viable. He knew he had made a fine choice because the first time he saw Wu he realised that there was a lot to get out of him in terms of raw information. (*ESC* 60)

While the novel frames the relationship between Dredge and Wu in a satiric and revisionist manner, the above passage, in addition, touches upon a prominent aspect of Sino-Australian political and economic relations, and attests to the dominance and persistence of white Australian perspectives towards China and the Chinese. The professor's views and his exploitation of Wu are an extension, even manifestation, of the prevailing ideology and rhetoric that are centred upon an exploitative and superficial type of multiculturalism.

Additionally, because 'China favoured the only choice of Westernisation at the expense of its old cultural traditions' (*ESC* 137), the tendency for many Chinese was towards a valorisation of the West, which included Australia. However, Dao realises after moving to Australia, that, 'white people were not what they made out to be, powerful, always in the right, honest and straightforward' (*ESC* 42). This awareness is accompanied by the gradual discovery that, while migrants have come to a certain provisional understanding of Australia and its culture, mainstream Australian society has remained relatively insular against other parts of the world, most notably Asia, of which it claims to want to be a part. For instance, Wu comes to realise that

For all his profound knowledge of Western culture and history, the professor did not know this current popular saying in China that went, 'as poor as a professor and as stupid as a PhD student'. (*ESC* 91)

This observation highlights the ignorance about Chinese and other minority cultures by the predominantly white Australian society, adding to Wu's discovery that '[the] Australian's mind was very narrow compared with the extensive space of the country' (*ESC* 92). Wu's appeal to Dredge's business sense stems purely from the former's use-value, as a "commodity to the market", 'a man affable enough and malleable enough for [Dredge's] own use' (*ESC* 60). While the position and views of Professor Dredge may not be adequately representative of mainstream Australian society, they nonetheless represent an important and influential sector of the Australian public. The perspectives embodied by Professor Dredge are symptomatic of a white Australian attitude towards its Chinese migrants that is still underpinned by what Ghassan Hage calls the 'discourse of productive diversity' (2000: 128). In this scenario, 'multiculturalism constituted an economically exploitable resource in the form of hitherto untapped potential', so as 'to give Australia an "advantage" it was much in need of in a competitive international environment' (128). In other words, this is 'a much clearer discourse of exploitation rather than consumption' (128).

On Dao's part, as the ethnic migrant who has understood the multicultural rhetoric and above all the superficial treatment to issues of cultural diversity, the translation and footnoting work that he undertakes occasionally for Professor McLoughlin is viewed with a healthy dose of personal scepticism as well. As he explains,

> In our literary tradition in the past, it was common to write footnotes to poetry. For one poet, there would be hundreds of footnoters. This tradition had now slightly changed. We did not write footnotes for Chinese now. We wrote them for Westerners *to cater for their love of Chinoiserie*. I mean I wrote them for Australians. (*ESC* 114; emphasis added)

Amidst Dao's complex negotiations of his troubled perspectives and relations with China and Australia, he has nonetheless picked up on the multicultural 'game' and its terms of engagement. Drawing upon his knowledge of 'Chinoiserie' as well as his strategic position in a minority, he is empowered to a certain extent, and in a cynical fashion, to cater to and engage with the literary and academic worlds at a superficial level, thereby providing the enrichment to Australian multicultural society by producing 'a kind of ethnic surplus value' (Hage 2000: 128) for his Australian employer.

The similarities and/or parallels between the narratives of Dao, Wu Liao and Warne accentuate the difficulties involved in migrating from one country to another. In each of their accounts, the process is extremely disruptive because of their marginalised positions in the new country. Although they have now attained personal and political freedom—'freedom that was not available and could not be bought for any price in China' (*ESC* 37)—the truth of the situation was that 'it's like a hell when there are no friends, no relatives, no faces of your own race' (*ESC* 41). In addition, being unemployed and living on social security also meant that even though he was an Australian citizen, as Dao's sister tells him, 'your position is not *that* attractive to Chinese women these days' (*ESC* 103, emphasis in original). The expectations of greater socio-economic mobility that attach to the diasporic condition have not materialised at all for these men who now feel trapped, 'cast out of history', 'unwanted by either country and reduced to this dump' (*ESC* 137). Although their multiple-citizenship affords them some measure of flexibility in choosing to move between countries, their marginalised status has severely limited the extent to which they are able to exercise any choice in this matter. The experience of marginalisation in both countries, moreover, has also reinforced their experiences as disadvantaged diasporic subjects rather than as freely moving, active and fully empowered social and economic beings.

One of the concerns that this novel illuminates is the exclusion and/or erasure of diasporic lives and histories from the history of the nation. Cast out from the history of their homeland, diasporas similarly encounter resistances to their incorporation or successful integration into the national, social and cultural fabric of their new country. In Wu's writing, he believed that 'everyone was a historian' and that there should be 'as many [history] books as people', because

> some people, like history, will never write their own history all their life but then they don't cease to be history themselves. [...] I am often left with a regret how much is left out in our history that is written by their historians, who, it seems to me, exist for the sake of exclusion (*ESC* 167).

In a gesture that aims to challenge that exclusion from mainstream Australian and Chinese Australian history, Dao's writing and translating of his 'Australian novel in Chinese' is an attempt at redressing what he perceives to be a social and cultural injustice. Like Wu, whose 'strong point' was his 'ability to historicise his daily reality, meaning that he was able to turn his or other people's lives into a history in his head in the minutest details possible without ever committing his memories to paper' and who 'had lately come to despise history books that were supposed to be about the real history' (*ESC* 96), Dao's 'layperson' approach to 'history', as he sees it, is part of the novel's aim of dis/uncovering and communicating the histories that are contingent to, but marginalised by, mainstream accounts of historical events. Although limited and confined to local events and personal accounts, the history that he has chronicled—'a day-to-day account of my characters' life in Australia for the duration of a year' (*ESC* 20–21)—is seen in the novel as being no less valid or pertinent than other forms of historical documentation.

This novel illuminates the various types of subject positions and identities experienced by the diasporic individual, drawing upon commonly used tropes of alienation, isolation, cross-cultural translation, assimilation and identity politics that attach to or are often associated with the diasporic condition. However, it also goes beyond simplistic narrative modes by framing one character's narrative within another's account, and especially by the use of an unreliable narrator. *ESC* has aptly addressed several issues facing migrants, especially those for whom the material lures of diaspora have faded or not materialised in the first place. In fleshing out the less salubrious aspects of migration, the novel's characters present a negative, at times bleak, picture of the migration process. Using the multicultural rhetoric of Australian national discourse—which has pervaded the consciousness of many white Australians and influenced mainstream conceptions of cultural diversity in purely economic or value-production terms—the novel exposes the country's superficial engagement with other minority ethnic groups. The significance of Chinese perspectives on Australia provides a counterpoint, by reiterating and reinforcing images of Australia as 'blankness' (*ESC* 54), 'silence' (*ESC* 98) and 'solitude' (*ESC* 100), void of any human activity. In addition, the increasing affluence of Chinese nationals has also perhaps begun to stem or reverse the trend towards migration, so that the condition of being in diaspora has lost some of its perceived benefits and attractions, and migration is no longer driven by only material and/or economic motivations. Those remaining in the homeland also cannot be deemed as being any worse off. In other words, the position of the aspirational diasporic individual is gradually losing its appeal, even credibility, among those in the homeland and those in diaspora as well.

The diverse and highly differentiated positions of Chinese diasporic migrants present a complex process of negotiating cultural diversity, cross-cultural translations and identity politics. As China pushes ahead with its reforms, growing in economic and political stature on the international arena, the significance of Chinese identities and identifications cannot help but be invested, even constructed, with greater and more open-ended potential. Ang argues in a similar vein that,

> as 'China' and 'Chineseness' are increasingly becoming signs for global political and economic power in the early twenty-first century, there is no necessary political righteousness in Chinese diasporic identity, the long-standing Chinese tradition of feeling victimized and traumatized notwithstanding. Indeed, there could well be circumstances and predicaments in which it would be politically more pertinent to say *no* to a particularist Chinese identity, at least if our commitment is a universalist and cosmopolitan one, encompassing all people of the world, not just 'our own'. (2001: 12)

This novel, then, in shedding light on the vicissitudes of heterogeneous Chinese diasporic conditions, problematises many aspects of migration that are germane to cultures and communities the world over, so that its illuminations on the Chinese diaspora may also be read as an indicator of other diasporic groups' deliberations about identity and belonging, and the ways in which these desires manifest in their cultural production.

The Eastern Slope Chronicle tackles head-on the complexities of re-negotiating racial and cultural identity amidst changing environments, sentiments and perceptions, offering no satisfactory resolution to the dilemma of migrants 'trapped in between', but rather, a realistic—and sometimes brutally honest—analysis of contemporary identity politics in the Chinese diaspora.

Notes

[1] The Chinese title *Dongpo Jishi* refers on the one hand to a place in China while on the other hand possibly suggesting, by its use of 'eastern slope', the erstwhile practices of identifying physical and/or facial features characteristic of Chinese persons in denigrating ways.

[2] Ronald Skeldon's research on Chinese migration indicates that, in the surge of independent migration of professional or skilled migrants from China to the United States in 1993 and 1994, a large proportion—37,131 of the 57,775 immigrants admitted from China in 1993 and 31,913 of the 47,964 admitted in 1994—comprised students who were in the United States around the time of the massacre in Tiananmen Square. He writes:

> In the United States, the Students Protection Act of 1992 allowed thousands of students who had been living in the country continuously to adjust to permanent status. Canada and Australia made similar provision. (1996: 445-446)

In addition,

only about one third of the 220,000 students from China who have gone overseas since 1979 have returned, and the proportion returning from the United States is about one fifth. China, ideally, wanted all the students to return versed in the ways of foreign technology, so that they could contribute to economic development and nation building. (1996: 447)

With government initiatives firmly in place in China to encourage return or reverse migration of its overseas students and settlers, the rate of return migration is likely to increase among these groups.

References

Ang, I. *On Not Speaking Chinese: Living Between Asia and the West*. London: Routledge, 2001.
Chiu, M. 'The Transcultural Dilemma: Asian Australian Artists in the Asia Debate.' *Diaspora: Negotiating Asian-Australia*. Eds. H. Gilbert, T. Khoo and J. Lo. St. Lucia: University of Queensland Press, 2000. 27–34.
Hage, G. *White Nation: Fantasies of White Supremacy in a Multicultural Society*. London: Routledge, 2000.
Ommundsen, W. 'Not for the Faint-Hearted; Ouyang Yu: The Angry Chinese Poet.' *Meanjin* 57.3 (1998): 595–609.
———. 'Behind the Mirror: Searching for the Chinese-Australian Self.' *East by South: China in the Australasian Imagination*. Eds. C. Ferrall, P. Millar and K. Smith. Wellington: Victoria University Press, 2005. 405–421.
Ong, A. *Flexible Citizenship: The Cultural Logics of Transnationality*. Durham and London: Duke University Press, 1999.
Ouyang, Y. 'Is Literature Dead—A look at the problems facing Contemporary Australian-Chinese Writing.' *Westerly* 43.2 (1998): 84–89.
———. *The Eastern Slope Chronicle*. Blackheath, NSW: Brandl and Schlesinger, 2002.
Skeldon, R. 'Migration from China.' *Journal of International Affairs* 49.2 (1996): 434–56.

Afterword:
Other Genealogies of Asian Australian Studies: A Trans-Pacific Perspective

Evelyn Hu-DeHart

Separated by the vast expanse of the Pacific Ocean, Australia and the United States have histories with some prominent common features. Both white settler societies that enacted white supremacist postcolonial regimes and whose indigenous peoples suffered physical and cultural decimation, they are also countries of immigrants with recurring nativist manifestations. Though their numbers in neither country have ever been substantial, Asians provided critical labour for extractive and agricultural economies and helped open up commerce in frontier regions. They were then targeted for exclusion when they were deemed inherently inassimilable to whiteness, and later invited back into the national fold under the banner of multiculturalism. Australia and the US have both reinvented themselves in the modern era as cosmopolitan and democratic nations that celebrate differences, where racism is imagined as largely a thing of the past. Thus, Asians in both countries—now representing a diversity of national origins—are exalted as successful immigrants and model minorities, and their countries of origin are sought after as trading partners in this new age of globalisation. It is no surprise, then, that Asians in America and Asians in Australia have become objects of serious academic study. For more than thirty years, Asian American Studies has developed, flourished and gained legitimacy in the US academy. It is fully institutionalised in the form of programs and, most importantly, departments with degree-granting prerogatives and dedicated faculty of their own,[1] two academic journals published by prestigious university presses,[2] and an annual professional meeting that routinely draws participants in the mid-hundreds or higher when held in demographically dense locations such as Los Angeles. From their birth in the cauldron of the Civil Rights movement and early framing in cultural nationalist terms, Black Studies, Chicano Studies, American Indian Studies and Asian American Studies have all moved well beyond tendencies towards contributionist and identity politics perspectives to become critical race studies grounded in racial formation theories and intersectionalities of race, class, gender, and sexuality. More recently, they have become increasingly occupied with high theory and cultural critique, and taken serious turns towards incorporating diasporic, transnational, and globalisation frameworks.[3]

In the development of all these studies, historians played critical leadership roles in building the foundational knowledge grounded in US history around big themes such as slavery and racial segregation, internal colonialism, immigration, citizenship and exclusion, empire and territorial incorporation, and the ideology of white supremacy. In the case of Asian American studies, some scholars in the founding generation were trained in American history, but a notable number also emerged from area studies backgrounds.[4] Younger Asian Americanists are now often trained in American studies, or work in American studies environments, so that today, Asian American studies is closely allied with American studies, more so than it ever has been with Asian Studies, a powerful field that has never felt at ease with Asian American studies. Asian Australian studies has been slower to develop. According to Jacqueline Lo's essay in this issue, it did not take off until the late 1990s, and while the field has grown steadily, progress is limited. The first program is still in search of an institutional home with its own name on the door and a few permanent resident scholars fully dedicated to its well-being and maintenance. As a leader of the field that has self-consciously named itself such, Lo has mapped one genealogy of Asian Australian Studies in which her own scholarship and professional formation, as well as her 'diasporised and hybridised Malaysian-Chinese-Australian identity', have played a key role.

Indeed, I first became aware of this emerging field in 2000 when I acquired a copy of Helen Gilbert, Tseen Khoo, and Lo's edited volume entitled *Diaspora: Negotiating Asian-Australia*. Significantly, it was published that year as a joint special issue of the *Journal of Australian Studies* (No.65) and *Australian Cultural History* (No.19), which signaled the field's affiliation with, if not yet solid location within, Australian studies. The large number of brief contributions cover a wide range of new Asian Australian cultural formations and politics, a rich and impressive gathering that should disabuse any skeptic of doubts regarding Australia's reinvented identity as a vast multicultural space in the Asia-Pacific.

Not long after this, I also became acquainted with Ien Ang's provocative work that combines self-interrogation and critical analysis of Chineseness in the diaspora, with the provocative title *On Not Speaking Chinese: Living Between Asia and the West* (2001). A product of the increasingly complex migration patterns of the Chinese diaspora and, like Lo and Khoo, also a relatively new Asian migrant to Australia—in her case from Indonesia via the Netherlands—Ang became the voice of the 'postcolonial diasporic intellectual' caught between the Third World of her birth and the West of her education, work and residence. She struck a chord not only among many cosmopolitan Asian Australians, but also with current generations of Asian Americans and Asian Canadians across the Pacific who share a similar predicament of hybridity and in-betweenness.[5]

In June 2005, five years after my initial exploration of Asian Australian studies, I was a participant in the Locating Asian Australian Cultures symposium hosted by the National Centre for Australian Studies at Monash University in Melbourne. Convened by Khoo, editor of this volume based on papers from that symposium, the event marked another stage in the maturation of the field and suggests further fruitful collaboration with and integration into Australian studies.

If anyone on my side of the Pacific were to ask me about Asian Australian studies, I would recommend they begin with the Gilbert, Khoo and Lo anthology cited above, read Ien Ang on locating identity in the diaspora and within Australian multiculturalism, and continue with this new collection on Asian Australian cultures, paying particular attention to Lo's careful mapping of the development of the field. In this forthright analysis, Lo does note a certain limitation in the development of Asian Australian studies to date, in that 'the disciplinary approach is dominated by ... a cultural studies approach to cultural analysis' (). Perhaps because most of the practitioners of Asian Australian studies appear to be located in literary, performance, media and cultural studies programs in Australian universities and cultural institutions, and are, as Lo notes, primarily 'of Asian descent, tertiary educated ... comfortably middle class ... first and second generation migrants, in their twenties and thirties' () they have a strong presentist orientation. They appear less concerned with the past, more fascinated with contemporary cultural productions than with historical cultural formations. Nevertheless, it is indisputable that, along with her growing roster of collaborators, Khoo, as co-editor of *Diaspora: Negotiating Asian-Australia* and editor of this volume, provides the critically important thread of continuity and semblance of stability in a fragile field. In addition, she has clearly identified an academic movement that is also a political project, much as Asian American studies was, in that Asian Australian studies has to negotiate for space, resources and legitimacy in the Australian academy.

My recent acquaintance with this self-named and intentional Asian Australian studies has actually opened my eyes to another genealogy of Asian Australian studies that I have witnessed from far and near, one with different roots and shoots. This other, or perhaps proto, Asian Australian studies has been nurtured primarily by historians located in Australia or trained in Australian universities. Because of their orientation to the earliest significant group of Asian migrants to Australia, their attention has been turned almost exclusively on the Chinese workers of the nineteenth century Gold Rush era, followed by the settled Chinese communities after Federation when the Immigration Restriction Act of 1901 enacted the White Australia policies that severely curtailed Chinese immigration and access to citizenship.

These historians were trained in Chinese history, and branched out to trace the history of Chinese immigration to Australia and their subsequent experiences with settlement, community building, new identify formation and cultural change once in the diaspora. The inspiration for this strand of *de facto* Asian Australian studies, or at the least the variant of Chinese Australian studies, is historian Wang Gung-Wu. Wang traces his lifelong interest in the study of Chinese outside China—in places like Indonesia where he was born, Malaysia where he put down roots as a citizen, Australia where he studied and taught modern Chinese history, Hong Kong where he served as the first Chinese vice-chancellor and the last colonial vice-chancellor of the University of Hong Kong, and Singapore where he is currently sojourning. His research is especially concerned with the transformation he has witnessed in his own lifetime of many 'sojourners' like himself—*huaqiao* or Chinese residing abroad— assimilating and accepting their place as 'citizens of the new nation-states of Southeast Asia' (Wang 1999: 2–4).

While teaching at Australian National University (ANU) in Canberra in the 1960s and 1970s, after witnessing first-hand the formation of the Malaysian federation by 'joining together several former British colonies with large Chinese communities' (Wang 1999: 8), Wang wrote papers on topics such as Chinese Politics in Malaya. As his postcolonial subjectivity evolved, he began to advocate that the 'Chinese overseas be studied in the context of their respective national environments, and taken out of a dominant Chinese reference point' (Wang 1999: 1). Moreover, Wang argues, these Chinese communities must be subject to comparative study, both among themselves as well as with other migrant communities. He was also quick to recognise the interplay between how China viewed these overseas communities and the view these communities outside China had of themselves. Thus, given his unease with the concept 'diaspora' (which presupposes in its purest form an immutable Chinese culture and identity fixed by an inextricable pull to the homeland), Wang articulated an alternative approach to diaspora that emphasises variations in new community and identity formations in permanent resettlement elsewhere. Given the postcolonial moment that he experienced, his diaspora project was academic but also political, to ensure that the Chinese in former British colonies claimed their rightful place as equal citizens with former colonial masters, as well as native subjects who inherited political power with independence.

Wang was in good company during the 1960s and 1970s, as other scholars from across the globe joined him in this endeavor to conduct research on 'localised Chinese' in respective countries around the world. By the 1990s, the diaspora movement had spread worldwide, so much so that in 1991 he joined forces with Wang Ling-chi, a leader of the Asian American movement in the 1960s and then chair of Berkeley's large and distinguished Asian American Studies department, to form the International Society for the Study of Chinese Overseas (ISSCO). In recognition of his prodigious and original scholarship as well as his intellectual leadership, Wang has been rightfully acknowledged as the leading pioneer of Chinese diaspora studies. In 1991, he co-edited a two volume collection of mostly scholarly articles culled from over one hundred papers presented at the first ISSCO conference held in San

Francisco in 1991, by way of showcasing the importance of examining Chinese diasporic communities in global comparative context (Wang and Wang 1998).

Many decades before Ang, Wang Gung-Wu began asking similar questions about Chineseness in the diaspora. He observed that officials in China had 'always underestimated the resources the Chinese overseas have been able to muster to cultivate new kinds of Chineseness among themselves' (Wang 1999: 9). He understood that political changes in China (Japanese invasion during the 1930s; Communist triumph in the 1940s; isolation during the early Cold War) as well as in countries that hosted the Chinese diaspora (independence for former colonies in Southeast Asia; abandonment of white supremacist ideologies in the US and Australia) created new identity formations and cultural change in these dispersed Chinese communities, such that '[T]here is nothing essentialist about the Chinese identity they affirm, and their members negotiate interminably as to what they want' (Wang 1999: 14). Chinese Australians would appreciate his insight that 'a diaspora today would include many kinds of Chinese for whom there are specific terms, or who are accustomed to distinctive identities' (Wang 1999: 16).

There is no question that Wang Gung-Wu's physical presence in Australia and his approach to Chinese diaspora studies has helped stimulate the study of Chinese in Australia in the 1970s. In short succession, two seminal studies appeared: C. Y. Choi's *Chinese Migration and Settlement in Australia* (1975), and C. F. Yong's *The New Gold Mountain: The Chinese in Australia 1901–1921* (1977; derived from his 1966 ANU dissertation). After a lull in the 1980s, a robust burst of regional histories in the 1990s have added to the increasingly rich scholarship on the Chinese in Australia. They include: Cathy May's *Topsawyers: The Chinese in Cairns 1870–1920* (1984); Timothy Jones's *Chinese in the Northern Territory* (1990); Jan Ryan's *Ancestors: Chinese in Colonial Australia* (1995); Shirley Fitzgerald's *Red Tape, Gold Scissors: The Story of Sydney's Chinese* (1997); and Jane Lydon's *Many Inventions: The Chinese in the Rocks 1890–1930* (1999). Also important are edited volumes by Jan Ryan, *Chinese in Australia and New Zealand: A Multidisciplinary Approach* (1995); Paul Macgregor, *Histories of the Chinese in Australasia and the South Pacific* (1995); and Henry Chan et al., *The Overseas Chinese in Australasia: History, Settlement and Interactions* (2001). Because so much of this history is focused on Chinese mine workers, market gardeners, hawkers, laundrymen, artisans and petty shopkeepers—typical occupations of the early Chinese migrants—there is an implicit, if not always explicit, class dimension to the analyses. I do not suggest that all these studies derive from Wang's mentorship, because, indeed, the field is now plowed by many gifted hands and leadership is decentralised and dispersed. A growing list of academics and graduate students, public historians, local and community-based scholars, write books and articles, edit collections of essays, organise conferences and museum exhibits, chair historical societies and heritage projects. All of these individuals engage with the project of uncovering, recovering, telling and retelling the history of Chinese experiences and communities in Australia. Meanwhile, ISSCO serves as a vibrant link for some of these scholars to the enduring leadership of Wang Gung-Wu and the worldwide network of Chinese diaspora studies. ISSCO conferences have brought Chinese Australian scholarship to the attention of the rest of the world, creating spaces and forums for the cross-fertilisation of Chinese Australian studies with their international counterparts, including, notably, Asian American studies.

One of the critical links in this genealogical chain is John Fitzgerald, who studied modern Chinese history under Wang Gung-Wu at ANU and who has gone on to a distinguished academic career in the Asian Studies Program at La Trobe University (Melbourne) and at the Australian National University where he is now Director of the International Centre of Excellence in Asia-Pacific Studies. In 2000, he helped organise the Chinese Australian Federation conference, an international meeting held as part of the Chinese Heritage of Australian Federation Project to examine closely the Chinese communities in Australia and their contribution to the early founding and development of the modern nation of Australia. Building on the momentum generated by this conference, Fitzgerald invited ISSCO to co-sponsor a conference in July 2005 with the Asian Studies Association of Australia. This conference focused on Chinese Australians and the Chinese diaspora, meeting at the highly symbolic site of the goldfields of Bendigo. It drew hundreds of participants from around Australia, New Zealand, Philippines and the Pacific, China, Hong Kong, Taiwan and Southeast Asia, the US and Canada, and Europe.

From the 2000 conference, Sophie Couchman, Fitzgerald, and Macgregor co-edited a collection of sixteen research papers culled from the fifty or so presented at the conference; this volume was titled *After the Rush: Regulation, Participation, and Chinese Communities in Australia 1860–1940*. Almost all the contributors to *After the Rush* are emerging scholars and newcomers to this field of study, and all papers appear to be original research representing a range of topics. As might be expected, many are local studies with a community base, and touch upon Australian-specific issues such as the exclusion of Chinese players from Australian rules football. Others address questions of Chinese Christians; Chinese-white interracial sex, marriages, and families; constructions of 'Chinese-ness' and 'whiteness'; and Chinese strategies of passing for white. Gender roles are highlighted, and gender relations and intersections with race and class inform several papers.

Most striking about these essays is the attention each paper pays to the historical context of the Chinese experience, particularly as Australia moved towards Federation and its attendant White Australia Policy in 1901. Even more notable is the connection many of the authors make between the Chinese question and the construction of Australia's first forms of national identity, which was predicated on Chinese exclusion from both immigration and citizenship. As John Hirst remarks in the opening sentence of his essay, 'There appears to be a clear connection between the exclusion of the Chinese and the federation of the Australian colonies' (2004: 11). In noting that the term 'White Australia' was 'coined in the context of an immigration policy directed against Asians' (2004: 11), he concludes: 'The anti-Chinese agitation popularized the national ideal and gave it of course a much stronger racial content. White was not merely a symbol, it was the colour of the citizens' skins' (2004: 19).

Afterword: Other Genealogies of Asian Australian Studies

Similarly, Fitzgerald asserts that 'rabid anti-Chinese racism was one of the hallmarks of the nationalist' (2004: 61).

In short, identifying the Chinese as the racial Other in Australia's national history entails applying racial formation theories to the study of the Chinese in Australia (and to white Australia as well). In doing so, this privileges local and national concerns over the diasporic and transnational. By identifying the centrality of race to understanding the Chinese Australian experience, these essays begin to mark some separation, but not a rupture, between Asian Australian studies and Asian studies in Australia. At the same time, situating Asians within Australia's racial discourse signals closer integration into Australian studies. This is not accidental, as a number of contributors to *After the Rush* are not trained as China scholars, but in Australian politics and national history, that is, Australian studies, broadly speaking.

The obvious next step for Asian Australian studies is for these two strands, which have developed largely independently and oblivious of each other, to make contact and cross-fertilise. While not necessarily converging or combining, they can nevertheless support each others' continuing development, one emphasising history, the other, cultural critique; one based on empirical research, the other textual and theoretical. Together, they can make inroads into Australian studies while nurturing roots in Asian studies. As the historians expand their research scope in time past White Australia to multicultural Australia, they will encounter new waves of Chinese immigrants to Australia from diverse origins in the vast diaspora, as well as a wider range of ethnic Asian migrants to Australia since the 1960s, a fact that acts as the starting point for the emerging scholars of this volume on 'locating Asian Australian cultures'.

Where these two genealogies meet is a challenge for Asian Australian studies, but a recent book suggests an exciting possibility. I am grateful to Tseen Khoo for sending me a copy of *Lost in the Whitewash: Aboriginal-Asian Encounters in Australia, 1901–2001* (Edwards and Shen 2003). Covering the entire twentieth century and both the white supremacist (federation) and multicultural (reconciliation) eras of Australian history, this collection of essays delves into history and cultural critique, community constructions and identity formations, and where 'Asian' embodies Chinese, Japanese, Malay and other migrant groups from the Asia-Pacific. Here is a glimpse of yet another genealogy descending from Aboriginal and Torres Strait Islander studies that incorporates interactions with various Asian migrant groups through time and space. The goal of examining Asian-indigenous contact and interactions is nothing less than what Regina Ganter calls an ambitious 'reconfiguring of Australian history' (2003: 69). In her essay, 'Mixed Relations', Ganter makes a strong case:

> For over a decade I have conducted a wide-ranging investigation of the various forms of contact between Asians and Aborigines in the far north of Australia; from the Kimberly across to Torres Strait; from pre-British Macassan contact to more recent efforts of mixed descendants to reconnect with severed patrilineal connections—by embracing Islam, by organizing family reunions, or by traveling

to Indonesia, China, the Philippines or the Pacific. Here I offer a sketch of the implications of this work in the wider framework of Australian history. (2003: 69)

The genealogies of Asian Australian studies can be traced to Asian, Australian, Aboriginal, diasporic and cultural studies, which is to say that the project is local, national and transnational, because Asians in Australia cross and criss-cross all these geographic and social fields.

Notes

[1] The newest department of Asian American Studies is the University of California Los Angeles (UCLA). This department is also destined to become the largest and most significant, given the size of its faculty, its first endowed chair (in Japanese American studies), publication of an academic journal (see next note), affiliation with the longtime Asian American research center, and its location in Asian-dense southern California.

[2] The two journals are the first and long running *Amerasia Journal*, edited and published by UCLA Asian American Studies Centre since 1971, and the newer *Journal of Asian American Studies* (JAAS), established in 1998 as the official journal of the Association for Asian American Studies, published by Johns Hopkins UP. In addition, Asian American scholarship is published in a plethora of humanities and social science journals, as well as law, education, business and other professional studies journals.

[3] The most recent entry along this line is the latest issue of the *Journal of Asian American Studies* (October 2005), dedicated to Asian American studies and transnationalism. See also Hu-DeHart (1999) and Okamura (2003).

[4] Area studies has served as the training ground and launching pad for several well-known first and second generation leaders of Asian American studies, such as Yuji Ichioka, Franklin Odo, Sucheta Mazumdar, and Marlon Hom from Asian Studies; Gary Okihiro was trained as an Africanist, while Lane Hirabayashi and I came out of Latin American/Caribbean studies. Of this group, all but Hom and Hirabayashi are historians. Ron Takaki is also a historian, but his background is American history and African American history. Of course, many other disciplinary trained scholars were involved in building the studies, but my point here is that the historical foundation was laid early and solidly.

[5] Rey Chow and Aihwa Ong in the US are two other cosmopolitan, postcolonial diasporic intellectuals born in Asia, and educated in the West where they now work and live, and who have theorised extensively about diaspora and the diasporic predicament in their respective ways. Along with Ang, they have lit new fires in the imagination of Asian American and Asian Australian studies, are hugely influential as theorists and frequently cited in the new scholarship on Asian American and Asian Australian cultural studies, but have chosen to remain outside the formal academic structures of these fields. In mapping genealogies of Asian American and Asian Australian studies, however, it would be remiss to leave out their names and works, despite their open ambivalence about ethnic studies.

References

Ang, I. *On Not Speaking Chinese: Living Between Asia and the West*. London: Routledge, 2001.

Chan, H., Curthoys, A. and Chiang, N. (Eds.) *The Overseas Chinese in Australasia: History, Settlement and Interactions*. Canberra and Taipei: Centre for the Study of the Chinese Southern Diaspora, Australian National University, and the Interdisciplinary Study Group on Australian Studies, National Taiwan University, 2001.

Choi, C.Y. *Chinese Migration and Settlement in Australia*. Sydney: Sydney University Press, 1975.

Couchman, S., Fitzgerald, J. and MacGregor, P. (Eds.) *After the Rush: Regulation, Participation, and Chinese Community in Australia 1860–1940*. Melbourne: Otherland.

Edwards, P. and Shen, Y. (Eds.) *Lost in the Whitewash: Aboriginal-Asian Encounters in Australia, 1901–2001*. Canberra: Humanities Research Centre, 2004.

Fitzgerald, J. 'Advance Australia Fairly: Chinese Voices at Federation.' *After the Rush: Regulation, Participation, and Chinese Community in Australia 1860–1940*. Eds. S. Couchman, J. Fitzgerald and P. MacGregor. Melbourne: Otherland, 2004. 59–74.

Fitzgerald, S. *Red Tape, Gold Scissors: The Story of Sydney's Chinese*. Sydney: State Library of New South Wales Press, 1997.

Ganter, R. 'Mixed Relations: Towards Reconfiguring Australian History.' *Lost in the Whitewash: Aboriginal-Asian Encounters in Australia, 1901–2001*. Eds. P. Edwards and Y. Shen. Canberra: Humanities Research Centre, 2003. 69–83.

Gilbert, H., Khoo, T. and Lo, J. (Eds.) *Diaspora: Negotiating Asian-Australia*. Brisbane: University of Queensland Press, 2000.

Hirst, J. 'The Chinese and Federation.' *After the Rush: Regulation, Participation, and Chinese Community in Australia 1860–1940*. Eds. S. Couchman, J. Fitzgerald and P. MacGregor. Melbourne: Otherland, 2004. 11–20.

Hu-Dehart, E. (Ed.) *Across the Pacific: Asian Americans and Globalization*. Philadelphia: Temple University Press, 1999.

Jones, T.G. *Chinese in the Northern Territory*. Darwin: Northern Territory University Press, 1990.

Lo, J. 'Disciplining Asian Australian Studies: Projections and Introjections.' *Journal of Intercultural Studies* 27.1–2 (2006).

Lydon, J. *Many Inventions: The Chinese in the Rocks 1890–1930*. Clayton: Monash Publications in History, 1999.

MacGregor, P. *Histories of the Chinese in Australasia and the South Pacific*. Melbourne: Museum of Chinese Australian History, 1995.

May, C.R. *Topsawyers: The Chinese in Cairns 1870–1920*. Townsville: James Cook University, 1984.

Okamura, J.Y. 'Asian American Studies in the Age of Transnationalism: Diaspora, Race, Community.' *Amerasia Journal* 29.2 (2003): 171–193.

Ryan, J. *Ancestors: Chinese in Colonial Australia*. Fremantle: Fremantle Arts Centre Press, 1995.

—— (Ed.) *Chinese in Australia and New Zealand: A Multidisciplinary Approach*. New Delhi: Wiley Eastern, 1995.

Wang, G. 'A Single Chinese Diaspora? Some Historical Reflections.' *Imagining the Chinese Diaspora: Two Australian Perspectives*. Eds. G. Wang and A. Shun Wah. Canberra: Centre for the Study of the Chinese Southern Diaspora, 1999. 1–17.

Wang, L. and Wang, G. (Eds.) *The Chinese Diaspora: Selected Essays. Volumes 1 and 2*. Portland: International Specialised Book Services, 1998.

Yong, C.F. *The New Gold Mountain: The Chinese in Australia 1901–1921*. Richmond, SA: Raphael Arts, 1977.

Conclusion: Locating Asian Australian Cultures

Tseen Khoo

As the foregoing essays demonstrate, the breadth of engagement with cultural formations within Asian Australian studies is wide and complex. Far from presenting a definitive collection of Asian Australian scholarship, however, this volume hopes to generate further debate and inquiry about the notion of this relatively new field of research. What are the boundaries of Asian Australian studies, and where are the limits to be drawn for such interdisciplinary work? How does it enter into dialogue with Australian and Asian studies, as well as other diasporic Asian contexts? Considering the emerging field of Asian Australian studies is always already questioning its composition and positioning within external frames of reference such as Australian studies, Asian studies or, more specifically, diasporic Asian studies, there is no end-point such as the contentious comfort of 'claiming the nation' for this ongoing critical project. Infused in the field is an awareness of the limitations of a culturally nationalist approach.

If Asian Australian studies were to make institutional in-roads, how does this form of recognition affect notions of its 'validity' and purpose? This is an issue worth investigating, perhaps more fruitfully in a few years' time, when a larger core of Asian Australian critique is in circulation. Roy Miki, speaking of the Asian Canadian context, warns against the automatic assumption that a wider embrace of racialised material means noteworthy change to systemic, discriminatory perspectives. Specifically addressing the situation of Canadian literature and the Canadian academy, Miki states:

> The invisibility of racialization sets up a pattern of contradictions and constraints for the handful of graduate students and faculty of colour whose research and pedagogy involve the application of race theory to the study of literary texts. Since

> no courses exist for such work, they often have to incorporate it in existing courses, or to offer it as a unique event, in a special topics course. In the process, they often come to be identified as a zone of so-called 'issue-oriented' scholarship, its boundary becoming the social equivalent of ghettoization. (1998: 167)

He iterates the importance of identifying the continued prevalence of white perspectives and the common defusing effect of 'managing diversity' in public spheres. The advent of 'whiteness' studies in Australia—a majority of which currently focuses on Aboriginal/white issues—developed from preceding years of postcolonial and Australian studies research into the dynamics of racialisation (e.g. Lake 2003), as well as the 'whiteness' studies that became prominent in the US in the 1990s. Only a few years ago, in 2003, the Australian Critical Race and Whiteness Studies Association (ACRAWSA) was created, and the inaugural issue of the *ACRAWSA Journal* was published. Engagement with this new field of whiteness studies is a direction for Asian Australian studies that could open it up to the broader field of critical race theory, though I would argue that maintaining a companion focus on Asian diaspora theory is essential.

The profile of Asian Australian studies is growing but relatively low right now. As Lo has delineated, there are many reasons for this and I would venture to say that the unpredictability of academic positions accounts for a lot of the inconsistent momentum for the field. Accompanying the few options to work on Asian Australian studies in the academy, there is the pressure for scholars to do more than 'just' Asian Australian studies topics, which are viewed as too specialist or narrow. This type of opinion echoes Miki's comment about the lazy 'ghettoisation' of racialisation scholarship that takes place. As multicultural studies has never been only relevant for (or only about) the 'ethnics', Asian Australian studies is not only for, or about, Asians or Australians. The broader contexts into which this field contributes—such as multicultural critique, formations of race and nation, and the politics of identity—need to be recognised. With Miki's statements in mind, and particularly in light of Rey Chow's deliberations in *The Protestant Ethnic* about 'ethnic *ressentiment*' (181) and 'coercive mimeticism' (107), Asian Australian studies as a field and Asian Australians as 'objects' of study require a complex, layered approach informed by both localised politics and diasporic cultural theories.

This volume's posing of broader questions about the limits of the Asian Australian studies field by no means indicates that areas within the field are 'full'. In the extensive area of history, for example, much work remains to be done, particularly in the areas of regional, community and oral histories, transnational community connections, and Adam McKeown has called for 'a new synthetic history of the Chinese—or of Asians in general—in Australia' (2004: 1).

When compiling this collection of essays, I wanted to bring together a wide range of scholars and disciplines in this project of 'locating Asian Australian cultures' and, for the most part, this volume succeeds in showcasing a diverse and complementary collection of work. There are still many absences with regard to other cultural groups that are subsumed within the term 'Asian Australian', and there is undoubtedly a majority of Chinese Australian material. This reflects the general state of Asian Australian studies thus far (indeed, Chinese material also dominates Canadian and US contexts). That said, I want to mention briefly the contributions that were solicited but do not appear in the collection for various reasons. This is both to profile other activity that is ongoing in Asian Australian studies and to allay probable critique about the collection's composition (as such critique seems the norm for these kinds of volumes). Other essays that were solicited include: Romit Dasgupta's work on Safina Uberoi's film *My Mother India*, Nina Koutts' research on Australia's Chinatowns, Nira Rahman's project on Bengali Australians, Don Nakanishi's work on Asian Australian politicians, and Francis Maravillas' research on Asian Australian visual art. It is worthwhile to note again here that most of the research taking place in Asian Australian studies is by early career academics, mostly research postgraduates.

Building research in currently neglected or thinly addressed Asian Australian cultural and historical areas, with appropriate and developed engagement with the nuances of the Australian context, is a necessary and pressing aim. In his conclusion to *Asian/American*, David Palumbo-Liu argues that Asians and Asian Americans 'have been incorporated variously into America as their image has coincided with particular historical American interests; yet they have been reparticularized by race as well' (1999: 389). Ien Ang has written similarly about Australia's conditional relationship with Asia and Asian Australians (Ang 1996). The major difference in the Australian context is that the collection of cultural research and historical 'salvaging' is at an emergent phase. It is building capacity while engagement with diasporic debates expands and comparative projects proceed. The disparity between Asian Australia's archive and that of more established diasporic community contexts is large and undoubtedly affects the types of comparative research that can take place. Hence, contributions such as Banerjee's positing of an Asian German studies read through an Asian Australian framework are especially valuable because of their contestation of, and challenge to, the predominance of Asian American theorisations. That is not to say that these theories do not offer significant insight into the dynamics of racialisation, and much besides. My simple point—which echoes the more detailed arguments of Lo and Banerjee in this volume—is that Asian Australian, and other diasporic sites are not obliged to 'develop' along the same trajectory as has Asian American studies. In conversations with some American colleagues, the implicit assumption on their part has been that those working in Asian Australian studies desire the development of a similar institutional network to what is in place in the US. Asian Australian studies will probably never have the political and institutional prominence of Asian American studies for a range of reasons including population momentum and the lack of a sociopolitical crucible such as the Civil Rights era in its history. With the majority of its momentum devoted to building important archives of sociocultural history, contemporary cultural critique and engaging with international contexts, the strategic deployment of 'Asian Australian studies' in collections such as this one can draw these dispersed energies together for contingent political and profile reasons without having any formal infrastructure.

Considering Australia's current climate of employment and funding shrinkage in tertiary institutions, this flexible form of engagement may be a key mode of expansion and survival for Asian Australian studies.

References

Ang, I. 'The Curse of the Smile: Ambivalence and the 'Asian' Woman in Australian Multiculturalism.' *Feminist Review* 52 (1996): 36–49.

Chow, R. *The Protestant Ethnic and the Spirit of Capitalism*. New York: Columbia University Press, 2002.

Lake, M. 'On Being a White Man, Australia, c. 1901.' *Australian Cultural History*. Eds. H. Teo and R. White. Sydney: University of New South Wales Press, 2003. 98–112.

McKeown, A. 'Introduction: The Continuing Reformulation of Chinese Australians.' *After the Rush: Regulation, Participation, and Chinese Community in Australia 1860–1940*. Eds. S. Couchman, J. Fitzgerald and P. Macgregor. Melbourne: Otherland, 2004. 1–9.

Miki, R. *Broken Entries: Race, Subjectivity, Writing*. Toronto: Mercury Press, 1998.

Palumbo-Liu, D. *Asian/American: Historical Crossings of a Racial Frontier*. Stanford: Stanford University Press, 1999.

Index

Page numbers in **bold** represent figures. Page numbers in *italics* represent tables.

Aboriginal art 29–42
Aboriginal Australians 3, 24, 26, 201, 235
Aboriginal culture 31, 35
    appropriation by whites 40–42
African American studies 173
AIDS-related illness 89, 93, 94–96, 97
Albrecht, Corinna 177
Alter/Asian conference (Sydney, 1999) 17–18
Alter/Asians (2000) 20, 24
Alvarez, Vivian 195
American Asian studies 1, 7, 13, 22, 23, 24, 25, 188, 229–230
Anderson, Kay 205–206
Ang, Ien 16, 17, 20, 66, 67, 68, 70, 75, 78, 79, 118–120, 130, 131, 155, 201, 204, 230–231, 233, 241
Anggraeni, Dewi 125
appearance and racial assumptions 65–78
appropriation of Aboriginal art 40–42
Arena, Franca 202
Armentrout, Eve 109, 110, 111
Ashton, Paula 134, 137–143
Asia Australia Arts Centre, Sydney 20, 214
Asialink, Melbourne 20
Asian Australian citizenship 187–206
Asian–Australian Identities conference (Canberra, 1999) 13–14, 17–18, 19, 20
Asian Australian literature 117–131, 213–226
Asian Australian parliamentarians 190, *191*, *192*, **199**
Asian German studies 167–183
Asian studies 21, 22, 65
Association for the Study of Australian Literture (ASAL) conference (2001) 21
Australian Association for Asian Studies conference (2004) 21
Australian Bureau of Statistics 21
Australian citizenship 217
Australian Critical Race and Whiteness Studies Association (ACRAWSA) 240
Australian identities 151–164, 216
Australian Labour Party (ALP) 190, *191*, *192*, 197, 199, **199**

Australian Multiculturalism for a New Century (1999) 195
Australian National University (ANU) 19, 232, 234
Australian Research Council 19
Australian studies 21, 22
Ayres, Tony 66, 72, 84, 161

Baohuanghui 104
Barth, Fredrik 189
Barthes, Roland 89, 91–93
Bashevis Singer, Isaac 89, 91
Bataille, Georges 46, 60, 61
Beadnell 98
Behind the Moon (2005) 128–130, 151–164
Bell, V. 88, 96–97
Bennett, Tony 136, 138, 146
Benthien, Claudia 157
Bhabha, Homi 13, 140–141, 155
Blainey, Geoffrey 17
Blake, Sir Henry 107, 111
Bobis, Merlinda 20
Bowlby, Rachel 121
Boxer Rebellion 108
Braithwaite, Kamau 174
British Asian studies 24
Brookes, Sue 46, 55, 56, 57
Brown, David 206–207
Brown, Donna 38
Brown, Wendy 87, 88, 136
Burying Mother (1996) 11–12, 13, 25
Butler, Judith 87–88, 96–97

Cabravale Park War Memorial 133–149, **149**
Cai, S. 103
Camus, Albert: *L'Étranger* 121
Canadian Asian studies 3, 24, 172, 173, 180
Canton *see* Guangzhou
Castles, Stephen 5, 195
Castro, Brian 20, 120
Chai, Arlene 121, 125–127
Chakrabarty, Dipesh 41
Chan, Dean 86
Chan, Harry 190

Chan, Henry 5, 233
Chan, Jachinson 161
Chen Shaobai 108
Cheng, Anne Anlin 88
Chin, Daryl 74, 76
Chin, Ernie 73, 77
Chin Seet, Elizabeth 76
Chinese Australian identities 65–78, 85, 86, 87, 127, 188, 213–226
    responses to racialising processes 73–77, 188
Chinese diasporic art 29–42
Chinese Exclusion Act (Canada, 1923) 3
Chinese Independence Party of Australia 104
Chinese secret societies 101, 103–104
Chinese Studies Association of Australia (CSAA) conference (2005) 5
Chiu, Melissa 37–38, 214
Choi, C. Y. 233
Choi, Michael Wai-Man *191*, *192*, *198*, 199, **199**, 200
Choo, Christine 85, 86, 91
Chow, Rey 13, 139, 144–145, 204, 236, 240
Chow, V. Y. 102, 103–104, 112–114
Christiansen, Flemming 188, 207
Chua, Siew Keng 48
Chuh, K. 18
Chun, Allen 187–188, 205
cinematic representations of Asians 45–60
Civil Rights Movement (USA) 229
Clarke, Maree 38
Clifford, James 42
coercive mimeticism 203–206
Collette, Toni 55, 58
Collins, Felicity 53, 54, 55–56, 58
Compton, Wade 173, 182
Costello, Peter 3–4
Couchman, Sophie 5, 234
Country Liberal Party (CLP) 190, *191*, *192*, **199**
Cramer, Sue 41
critical multiculturalism 18
Croft, Brenda 35
cross-cultural representations of Aboriginality 33–40
Crowe, Russell 53, 54
cultural appropriation 40–42, 45
cultural citizenship 178–180
cultural stereotypes 50, 54, 55, 56
Cunningham, Alfred 110, 111
current state of Asian Australian studies 19–22
Curthoys, Ann 29–30, 41, 135, 143

D'Alpuget, Blanche 50
Damousi, Joy 156
Dasgupta, Romit 241
Davila, Juan 40

Davis, Therese 53, 58
Dayal, Samir 171
de Certeau, Michel 136
defacement, significance of 143
Derrida, Jacques 16, 93, 117, 119, 121, 128, 131
Desai, Jigna 169–170
Diaspora (2000) 20, 24
disciplinary background to Asian Australian studies 13–15
Do, Khoa 20
Do, Nhon 133–149, **149**
Downer, Alexander 47
Duarte, Bernardo 38
Dunn, Kevin 145–146
Düttman, Alexander García 136–137
Dyer, Richard 156, 157

Eastern Slope Chronicle, The (2002) 214–226
Ebron, Paulla 189, 201, 204
Edith Cowan University 19
Edwards, Penny 5, 20, 24, 37, 235
enforcements systems 193–194
ethnic German identities 171, 176, 181
ethnification 196

Fanon, Frank 85, 87, 161
filmic representations of Asians 45–60
Fitzgerald, John 6, 234, 235
Fitzgerald, Shirley 233
Fleming, Victor 152
flexible citizenship 213–226
Floating Life (1996) 60
Fong, Lyn 69, 72–73, 76–77
foreigner as outsider 121–122
Fourmile, Henrietta 40
Fraser, Nancy 136
Freebury, Jane 153
Freedman, A. L. 188, 193, 202
Freestone, Rendra 20
Freud, Sigmund 88, 95
Frost, Stephen 145
Furen Wenshe 104–105, 107, 114
future of Asian Australian studies 22–25

Gallerie Dauphin, Singapore 37
Gallipoli (1981) 134, 152–164
Ganter, Regina 5, 30, 235–236
Garnaut Report (1989) 145
Garma Festival 35
gay identities 154, 159–163
gay subculture 84, 94–96
Geia, Jacqui 38
German studies 167–183
Gibson, Mel 48, 134, 153
Gibson, R. 53, 194

Giese, Diana 4–5, 34, 35, 66, 73, 78, 79
Gilbert, Helen 15–16, 230, 231
Gilroy, Paul 125, 169
Goddess of 1967, The (2000) 55, 57
Goffman, Erving 189, 193, 203, 204, 206
Göktürk, Deniz 176
Goldberg, David 194–195, 206
Golden Dragon Museum, Bendigo, Melbourne 37
graffiti, significance of 134, 142, 143
green card (Germany) 179
Greenway, Bishop 103
Guangzhou uprisings (1895, 1903) 102, 104, 105–106, 108–111, 114
guest workers (Germany) 170
Gumana, Gawirrin 35
Gunew, Sneja 16, 17, 18
guohua 30–33, 42
Guomindang 113

Hage, Ghassan 4, 16, 196, 201, 223
Hall, Stuart 13, 36, 161
Hallett, Bryce 85
Hamilton, Paula 134, 137–143
Hankou uprising (1900) 109, 110, 114
Hanson, Pauline 17, 22, 46–47, 69, 193, 194, 199, 202, 203
Hao Yen-p'ing 106
Hawke, Bob 46
Hayes, Paul 85, 89
Heaven's Burning (1997) 46, 52–55, 58
Henderson, Ian 158–159
Henson, Bill 89
Hokari, Minoru 41
Hollywood images 218, 219
homosexuality 154, 159–160
Hong Kong, University of 232
Hong Qanfu 109, 110–111
Horne, Donald 141
hospitality, nature of 117–131
'hosti-pets' 118
Howard, John 3, 46, 47, 197, 202, 203
Huang Yongshang 104, 105
Hughes, Langston 97
Huizhou uprising (1900) 109, 110, 114
Hundred Days of Reform (1898) 106, 107
Hung Men 103, 110
Hunt, Linda 46, 48, 50

Immigration Museum 38
Immigration Restriction Act (1901) 3, 104, 130, 331
Indigenous *see* Aboriginal
Indonesia 48–50
Inglis, Ken 135, 144
Institute of Modern Art, Brisbane 40

intercommunal dialogue 23–24
International Society for the Study of Chinese Overseas (ISSCO) 232–233
Irish Australians 201

Jackson, Peter 158
Jackson, Shannon 189
Jacobs, Lyn 131
Jakubowicz, Andrew 17, 197
JanMohammed, Abdul 176
Japanese Australians 190
Japanese stereotypes 54, 55, 56
Japanese Story (2003) 46, 53, 55–59
Jayasuriya, L. 3, 4
Jenkins, Richard 189, 204
Jing Yuanshan 107, 110
Johnson, Michael *191*, *192*, *198*, 197, **199**, 200, 201
Johnson, Tim 33, 40, 41
Johnson, Vivien 40
Jones, N. 5
Jovicic, Robert 195
Julien, Isaac 97

Kang Guangren 106, 107
Kang Youwei 106, 110
Kant, Immanuel 119
Kapetopoulos, F. 31, 35
Keating, Paul 46, 60
Khan, Adib 20
Khoo, Olivia 129
Khoo, Tseen 2, 20, 26, 36, 66, 89, 161, 169ff., 196, 201, 230, 231, 235
King Jung Sao 103, 112, 113
Kondo, Dorinne 33
Koori Heritage Trust 38
Koutts, Nina 241
Kremmer, C. 142
Kumar, Anant 180–182
Kwok, Jen Tsen 39

La Trobe University 234
Labour Party *see* Australian Labour Party
Lahiff, Craig 46, 55
Lai, Larissa 180
Lake, Marilyn 156, 240
Langton, Marcia 35, 36
language questions 176
language studies 23–24
Last Time I Saw Mother, The (1995) 121, 125–127
Law, Clara 57, 60
Lawson, Henry 216
Lazaroo, Simone 120, 121–124, 131
Lee, Mark 153
Lee, Regina 2, 201

Lee Long, Robyn 71, 73–74
Leong, Greg 66, 84, 86
Leong, Hou 32–33
Li, David Leiwei 125
Li Hongzhang 108
Li Jitang 109, 110
Liang Qichao 104, 107, 109–111
Liberal Party (Australia) 190, *191*, *192*, 197, **199**, 202
Lim, Hong *191*, *192*, *198*, 199, **199**
Lim, Richard Soon Huat 190, *191*, *192*, *198*, **199**
Lim, Yean Leng 32–33
Ling, Chek 20
Lingard, Bob 40, 41–42
Lingis, Alfonso 93–94, 98
Literary Society for the Promotion of Benevolence *see* Furen Wenshe
literature of Asian Australians 117–131, 213–226
Little, Alicia 107
Little Fish (2005) 59–60
Liu, William 112, 113
Lloyd, David 176
Lo, Jacqueline 16, 183, 231
local interests 24–25
locating Asian Australian studies 15–18
Lohrey, Amanda 153
Loong Hung Pung 103, 112, 113
Lord of the Rings, The (2001–2003) 158–159
Lowe, Adam 75
Lowe, Lisa 16, 188, 196
Lowe, Pat 34
Lydon, Jane 233

McCalman, Ian 135, 136
MacCannell, Dean 137, 144
McFarlane, Brian 158
McFarlane, Kate 32–33
McGregor, Paul 233, 234
McKinnon, Kenneth 162
McKeown, Adam 240
Mahood, Marguerite 39
Maravilla, Francis 241
Marawilli, Djambawa 35
Markus, A. 4, 201
Marynowsky, Wade 20, 24
masculinity and 'mateship' 152, 154–164
May, Cathy 233
Mei, Lau Siew 20
melancholic community 94–98
Melbourne, University of 19
Memmi, Albert 204
Miki, Roy 172–173, 239–240
Miller, George 45
Miller, Mark 5

Min, Susette 88
mistaken identities 70–75
Monash University, Melbourne 19, 20, 21, 231
Moon, Michael 97
Morris, Meaghan 53, 135, 136, 141, 144–145
Morris, Robyn 2, 122
Morris-Suzuki, Tessa 13
Mosquera, Gerardo 37
'Mr Z' 195
Muecke, Stephen 39–40
Multicultural Australia: United in Diversity (2003) 195
multiculturalism, policy of 4, 16, 18, 193
multicultural studies 16
multiple mappings 18
Muñoz, José 95, 97

Nagata, Yuriko 5
Nakanishe, Don 241
Nancy, Jean-Luc 97
National Centre for Australian Studies 231
National Gallery of China 37
National Multicultural Advisory Council 195
National Party (Australia) 190, *191*, *192*, 197, **199**
Natural Foot Society 107, 111
naturalisation law reform (Germany, 2000) 168–169
nature of Asian Australian studies 18
Newman, John 143
Ng, Nicholas 20
Ngo, Phuong 136, 139–140, 142–143, 145
Nguyen, Sang Minh *191*, *192*, *198*, **199**, 206
Nguyen, T. 135
Nhon, Le Thanh 38
Nicholl, Fiona 67–68, 134, 144, 156
Nicolacopoulos, Toula 196
normality, desire for 160–163
Northern Territory University 31

O'Chee, Bill *191*, *192*, *198*, **199**, 200
Okamura, Jonathan Y. 25, 236
Oliver, Kelly 87
Omi, M. 188, 205
Ommundsen, Wenche 20, 214–215, 216
On, Robyn 68–69, 75
One Nation party 17, 22, 46–47, 193
Ong, Aihwa 213, 214, 236
Orientalism 12–13, 218, 219
Ou Qujia 109–110
Ouyang Yu 213–226
outsider as threat 121–122, 124, 155

Palumbo-Liu, David 120, 188, 241
Parekh, Bhuku 195
Parker, David 188, 205

parliamentary first speeches by Asian Australians 187–206, *191*, *192*, *198*, **199**
Pearson, David 196, 206
Peres da Costa, Suneeta 20
performance of identity 188
performing Asian Australian citizenship 196–201
Pfitzner, Bernice Swee-Lian 190, *191*, *192*, *198*, **199**, 200
Phelan, Peggy 73
Philippine society 126, 127
Pike, Jimmy 30–42
Plato 121
political participation of Asian Australians 187–206
politics of representation 23
Possum, Clifford 41
Protect the Emperor Society 104

Qinghua University Arts Centre, Taiwan 37
Queensland, University of 19–20, 21

race, concept of 15–16, 67
Racial Discrimination Act (1975) 195
racial stereotypes 50, 54, 55, 56, 74
racialised citizenship 194–196
racialising processes 67–75, 170, 188
racism 16, 17, 54, 70, 72, 118, 129, 130, 201–203, 235
Radhakrishnan, R. 23
Rahman, Nira 241
Ramsay, Guy 5, 30
Rattigan, Neil 158
Rau, Cornelia 195
Rayner, Jonathan 46, 53
reactive politics 22
Read, Peter 41
Reid, Thomas 110
Reinheitsgebot (Germany) 178–180
representative politics 23
Revive China Society *see* Xingzhonghui
Revolution and Independence Society of Australian Chinese 103, 112, 113
Rhoads, Edward 104, 108, 109, 110
Rong Hong *see* Yung Wing
Rosaldo, Renato 174
Rubenstein, Kim 207
Rushdie, Salman 182
Russell, Lynette 33–34
Ryan, Jan 4, 233

sacrifice of Asian characters in films 46, 50, 52, 58
Sadness (1992) 83–98, **84**, **90**, **94**, **95**
Sakai, Naoki 18
same-sex relationships 95
Sawer, M. 5

Scacchi, Greta 50
Schiffrin, H. 104, 105
See, James *see* Tse Tsan Tai
See, John *see* Tse Yet Chong
See, Thomas *see* Tse Tsi Shau
Seeto, Aaron 20
September 11 55
Sham-Ho, Helen Wai-Har 190, *191*, *192*, 197, *198*, **199**, 200, 201–202
Shen Yuanfang 5, 20, 24, 37, 86, 235
Shimakawa, Karen 18, 202
Shnukal, Anna 5
simplicity, aesthetics of 88–94
Singh, Rajvinder 180
Skeldon, Ronald 226–227
Sleeman, John 113
Smaill, Belinda 89
Sontag, Susan 89, 93
South China Morning Post 101, 111
Steele, William 20
Stephenson, Peta 4, 34–35, 37, 38–39
stereotypes, racial 50, 54, 55, 56, 74
Stevens, Wallace 124
strategic Chinese identities 213–226
Stratton, Jon 16, 17, 67, 68, 201
Students Protection Act (USA, 1992) 226
Sukarno 48
Sun Yat-sen 102, 103, 105–112
syncretic aesthetics 30–33

Tastan, Ali 195
Taussig, Michael 142, 143
Tavan, G. 3
Taylor, Charles 140–141
Tchen Tsebin 190, *191*, *192*, *198*, **199**, 200, 201
Teo, Hsu-Ming 20, 121, 128–130, 135, 151–164, 172
Teraoka, Arlene 176
Terkessidis, Mark 176
Thomas, Mandy 4, 78, 135, 141
Thorne, Mémé 11–12, 20
Through the Eyes of Two Cultures (1999) 30, 33, 37, 38
Thursday Island 30
Tienanmen Square 200, 215, 226
Tienanmen Square generation 214, 215
Tillers, Imants 33, 40
Tilson, Alison 55
Tjakamarra, Michael Nelson 40
tolerance, ambivalence of 118–119, 120
Torres Strait studies 5, 235
transnational perspectives 24–25
Trojanow, Ilija 171, 175, 177–178, 181
Tsang, Henry Shui-Lung *191*, *192*, *198*, **199**, 200, 203

Tse Tsan Tai 5–6, 101–114
Tse Tsi Shau 102, 110–111
Tse Yet Chong 102, 110–111, 112
Tucker, Shirley 122–123, 124
Tully, Peter 95–96
Turkish Germans 170
Turner, Graeme 15, 36
Turtle Beach (1992) 46, 50–52, 58, 61
Ty, E. 173

Uberoi, Safina 241
Unity Party (Australia) 190, *191*, *192*, 193, **199**, 200

Vassilacopoulos, George 196
Vietnam War (1962–1972) 133, 144
Vietnamese Australian War Memorial 133–149, **149**
Vietnamese Australians 135–139, 190
Vietnamese boat people 51, 129
Vietnamese stereotypes 74
visual arts 29–42

Wah, Annette Shun 72
Wallace, Stephen 46, 50, 51
Wang, Dorothy 122
Wang Gung-wu 232–234
Wang Ling-chi 232–233
Watanabe, Shin 38
Wei, Guan 20, 31
Weir, Peter 46, 48, 134, 152, 156, 162
Wenhui, K. 31
Westernisation of Chinese culture 223, 224
White, Richard 164
White Australia policies 3, 4, 46, 66, 120, 130, 231, 243
Wilton, Janis 20
Winant, H. 188, 205

Wizard of Oz, The (1939) 152–164
Wong, Penny *191*, *192*, *198*, **199**, 200–201, 203
Wong, Peter *191*, *192*, *198*, **199**, 200, 203
Wong, Sau-ling 2, 24–25
Wong, Wendy Siuyi 101
Wong Hoy, Ben 70
Wong Hoy, Vincent 70
Woods, Rowan 59–60, 61
World Waiting to Be Made, The (1994) 120, 121–124

xenology 177
Xian, Ah 20, 31
Xie Zuantai *see* Tse Tsan Tai
Xingzhonghui 104–111, 114

Yamanaka, Mami 38
Yan Wenliang 31
Yang, William 6, 20, 35, 66, 68, 72
    Sadness (1992) 83–98, **84**, **90**, **94**, **95**
Yang Quyun 103–108
Yano, H. 170
Year of Living Dangerously, The (1982) 46, 48–50, 56, 58
Yen, Anna 20
Yong, C. F. 233
Yong, W. S. 103
Yu, Henry 119
Yu, Sarah 30
Yuen, William Fang 84
Yung Wing 103, 107, 109, 111

Zappala, G. 5, 193
Zheng Shiliang 108, 109
Zhou Xiaoping 29–42
Zhu Dongren 31
Zuwanderungsgesetz (Germany, 2005) 179